About This Book

Why is this topic important?

While other books may be narrowly focused or represent unproven approaches, *The Value of Learning* presents a methodical approach that can be replicated throughout an organization, enabling comparisons of results from one program to another. The process described in this book is the most documented method in the world, and its implementation has been phenomenal, with over four thousand individuals participating in five-day certification programs designed for its implementation. While other books may delve into accountability in certain types of programs or data, this book shows a method that works across all types of programs, ranging from leadership development to basic skills training for new employees. With this approach, every program is evaluated at some level.

What can you achieve with this book?
A Guide to Learning Value

This book is a basic guide for anyone involved in implementing learning and development programs. Strategies that will assist in collecting data during and after program implementation are presented. This book addresses a results-based approach to program implementation, focusing on a variety of measures, categorized into seven data types:

1. Inputs and Indicators
2. Reaction and Planned Action
3. Learning and Confidence
4. Application and Implementation
5. Impact and Consequences
6. Return on Investment
7. Intangibles

The Value of Learning helps learning professionals identify, collect, analyze, and report all seven types of data in a consistent manner that ensures credible results.

Credibility Is Key

The Value of Learning focuses on building a credible process—one that generates a value that is believable, realistic, and accurate, particularly from the viewpoint of sponsors and stakeholders. More specifically, the methodology presented in this book approaches credibility head-on through the use of:

- Balanced categories of data
- A logical systematic process
- Guiding principles, a conservative set of standards
- A proven methodology based on thousands of applications and uses
- An emphasis on implementing the methodology within an organization so that the process is sustained
- A process accepted by sponsors, clients, and others who fund projects and programs

The book explores the challenges of collecting hard-to-measure data and placing monetary values on the hard-to-value. Building on a tremendous amount of experience, application, practice, and research, the book draws on the work of many individuals and organizations, particularly those who have been reaching the ultimate levels of accountability, the ROI. Developed in an easy-to-read format and fortified with examples and tips, this will be an indispensable guide for audiences who seek to understand more about bottom-line accountability.

How is this book organized?

The book follows the value chain of learning and development as the measures move through the learning and development cycle. The first two chapters set the stage for the entire process. Chapter One, Building a Comprehensive Evaluation Process, illustrates the challenges and opportunities for evaluating learning, outlining some of the progress made and challenges we face to bring more accountability to learning and development. This chapter also introduces the entire process explained in the book, detailing the types and levels of data, the systematic step-by-step method, and the standards and principles used throughout the book.

Chapter Two, Defining Needs and Objectives: Ensuring Business Alignment, describes the beginning point of any learning and development process. The focus of this chapter is identifying the need. Here, practical techniques and tips are provided to ensure that the program is aligned with the organization, particularly the business alignment link. It is at this stage that many programs go astray. Also this chapter shows how to develop objectives at different levels, moving beyond the traditional learning objectives to develop application, impact, and even ROI objectives.

Chapter Three, Measuring Inputs and Indicators, discusses the first of the data categories with a focus on inputs and indicators. Tracking the inputs to the process is a basic necessity, measuring data such as number of people, number of hours, and number of programs, as well as costs and efficiencies. This level of data is important, but does not show the value of the programs.

Chapter Four, Measuring Reaction and Planned Action, addresses the first level of results based on perceptions. This chapter shows how measurement at this fundamental level has been changed and altered recently to improve its value.

Next, Chapter Five, Measuring Learning and Confidence, focuses on measuring learning, the heart of any evaluation process for learning and development. It shows how learning measures are being addressed in a methodical and efficient way to ensure that participants leave programs having acquired the skills and knowledge necessary to take action in their organizations.

Chapter Six, Measuring Application and Implementation, measures the first level beyond the actual program. Essentially, data collected at this level answer a question: What are participants doing differently as a result of the program? This chapter presents ways in which this follow-up data can be captured and particular measures that must be monitored.

Chapter Seven, Measuring and Isolating the Impact of Programs, moves to impacts and consequences, which are key data that executives want to see. This chapter connects the learning program to the business, showing how the data are collected and how the impact of the program is isolated—showing how much of the impact data are actually from other factors.

Chapter Eight, Identifying Benefits and Costs, and Calculating ROI, shows how the ROI is developed and how the business impact measures are converted to monetary values. It also details how the costs of the program are tabulated so that a comparison can be made between the benefits and the costs of the program. For some, this is the ultimate level of evaluation.

Chapter Nine, Measuring the Hard to Measure and the Hard to Value: Intangible Benefits, addresses the important issue of intangibles. The intangible benefits are those measures that are purposely not converted to monetary values. They must be monitored properly, analyzed appropriately, and reported credibly.

Chapter Ten, Reporting Results, focuses on how to report data to a number of target audiences, illustrating some of the most efficient and effective ways to communicate data.

Finally, Chapter Eleven, Implementing and Sustaining a Comprehensive Evaluation System, provides detail on how to support and sustain this evaluation process. It addresses particular issues of how to overcome the resistance of the staff and get the management team more involved in the evaluation process.

About Pfeiffer

Pfeiffer serves the professional development and hands-on resource needs of training and human resource practitioners and gives them products to do their jobs better. We deliver proven ideas and solutions from experts in HR development and HR management, and we offer effective and customizable tools to improve workplace performance. From novice to seasoned professional, Pfeiffer is the source you can trust to make yourself and your organization more successful.

Essential Knowledge Pfeiffer produces insightful, practical, and comprehensive materials on topics that matter the most to training and HR professionals. Our Essential Knowledge resources translate the expertise of seasoned professionals into practical, how-to guidance on critical workplace issues and problems. These resources are supported by case studies, worksheets, and job aids and are frequently supplemented with CD-ROMs, Web sites, and other means of making the content easier to read, understand, and use.

Essential Tools Pfeiffer's Essential Tools resources save time and expense by offering proven, ready-to-use materials—including exercises, activities, games, instruments, and assessments—for use during a training or team-learning event. These resources are frequently offered in looseleaf or CD-ROM format to facilitate copying and customization of the material.

Pfeiffer also recognizes the remarkable power of new technologies in expanding the reach and effectiveness of training. While e-hype has often created whizbang solutions in search of a problem, we are dedicated to bringing convenience and enhancements to proven training solutions. All our e-tools comply with rigorous functionality standards. The most appropriate technology wrapped around essential content yields the perfect solution for today's on-the-go trainers and human resource professionals.

Pfeiffer
www.pfeiffer.com

Essential resources for training and HR professionals

This book is dedicated to our loving parents, who taught us more about value than we could ever appreciate:

Flo S. Pulliam
Benjamin F. Pulliam
Agnes B. Phillips
George W. Phillips

Pfeiffer™

Patricia Pulliam Phillips, Ph.D.
and Jack J. Phillips, Ph.D.

The Value of Learning

How Organizations Capture Value
and ROI and Translate Them into
Support, Improvement, and Funds

John Wiley & Sons, Inc.

Published by Pfeiffer
An Imprint of Wiley
989 Market Street, San Francisco, CA 94103-1741
www.pfeiffer.com

Wiley Bicentennial logo: Richard J. Pacifico

For additional copies/bulk purchases of this book in the U.S. please contact 800-274-4434.

Pfeiffer books and products are available through most bookstores. To contact Pfeiffer directly call our Customer Care Department within the U.S. at 800-274-4434, outside the U.S. at 317-572-3985, fax 317-572-4002, or visit www.pfeiffer.com.

Pfeiffer also publishes its books in a variety of electronic formats. Some content that appears in print may not be available in electronic books.

Library of Congress Cataloging-in-Publication Data

Phillips, Patricia Pulliam.
    The value of learning : how organizations capture value and ROI and translate them into support, improvement, and funds / Patricia Pulliam Phillips and Jack J. Phillips.
        p. cm.
    Includes bibliographical references and index.
    ISBN 978-0-7879-8532-5 (cloth)
    1. Employees—Training of—Evaluation. 2. Employees—Training of—Cost effectiveness.
3. Rate of return. I. Phillips, Jack J., 1945– II. Title.
    HF5549.5.T7P439 2007
    658.3'124—dc22   2007011227

Acquiring Editor: Matthew Davis   Production Editor: Michael Kay
Director of Development: Kathleen Dolan Davies   Editor: Rebecca Taff
Editorial Assistant: Julie Rodriguez   Manufacturing Supervisor: Becky Morgan

Printed in the United States of America
Printing   10 9 8 7 6 5 4 3 2 1

—ᴠᴠ— Contents

──⁓── List of Exhibits, Figures, and Tables

⤳ Preface

THE NEED

The learning and development (L&D) function has experienced a need for increased accountability, from several perspectives. For example, the L&D staff is concerned about the value from program initiatives, and so are the executives within their organizations. The value definitions from the L&D staff are much different from those of executives. The L&D staff may be comfortable with capturing input (for example, the number of hours), reaction (overall satisfaction), learning (knowledge and skills gained), and an occasional follow-up to measure application. However, executives value impact, the actual monetary contribution from L&D programs, and ROI. A range of "values" is needed to meet the needs of different stakeholders.

While this need to show value is important, other measures not converted to money are equally important, if not critical, to most programs. However, excluding the monetary contribution of the L&D function in a success profile is unacceptable in this age of the "show me" generation. Because many programs fail to live up to expectations, a systematic process is needed to uncover barriers and enablers to success and to drive program improvements. The challenge is in doing it—developing the measures of value for every program, including monetary value, when they are needed and presenting them in a way that stakeholders can use. *The Value of Learning* offers a guide that addresses this challenge.

ANOTHER BOOK ON EVALUATION?

At first glance, a logical question to ask is this: Is there a need for another book on evaluation? When the literature is examined, the initial answer would usually be no. Over forty books have been published on the evaluation of training—far too many for this field, at least in the view of some observers. A brief history of how we got to this point helps us to understand the current need.

Most of the interest in the evaluation of learning and development began when Don Kirkpatrick published the four steps of evaluation based on the evaluation of a human relations training program as part of his Ph.D. dissertation. Kirkpatrick used a logical sequence of steps of measuring reaction, learning, behavior, and results, as he called them when they were published as a four-article series by ASTD in 1959 and 1960. In these articles, Kirkpatrick presented, in theory, what should happen with learning and development. He did not show in detail how data are collected, analyzed, and reported. There was no system for the steps. It was not described as a model and there were no standards.

Kirkpatrick went on to work in other fields and devoted little of his work to evaluation. Because there were no systems, processes, or standards—not enough how-to information—practitioners were left to make the system work on their own. That's what we did in our work that began in the 1970s, with the initial application of our evaluation processes. Our first evaluation book, *Handbook of Training Evaluation Measurement Methods,* was first published in 1983 and was the first U.S. book on training evaluation.

In the 1970s, 1980s, and continuing into the 1990s, we built a system that has been tried and proven in all types of settings. Our team has worked full-time on evaluation for two decades. The original *Handbook* is now in its third edition and is a graduate text. This system includes how to make evaluation work, proper ways to collect data, techniques of data analysis, and various ways in which results are communicated to a variety of audiences. Along the way, a systematic process was developed with standards. This methodology is now being used by over three thousand organizations globally. This book presents the methodology in simple, straightforward terms that can help any learning professional make a difference with learning and development programs.

AUDIENCE

The primary audience for this book is learning and development managers and executives who are concerned about the value of projects and programs. Although these managers and executives are often committed to these programs, they need to see value in terms they can appreciate, understand, and communicate to others.

This book is also designed for learning professionals, analysts, and practitioners who are responsible for evaluating and influencing the success of L&D programs. It shows how the various types of data are collected, processed, analyzed, and reported.

Another audience includes consultants, researchers, and professors who are unraveling the learning value mystery, trying to understand more about the difficult and demanding challenges of developing measures and values for a variety of programs.

TARGET AREAS

The Value of Learning is designed for all types of L&D programs:

- Career development programs
- Coaching
- Computer training
- Executive education
- Language training
- Leadership development
- Literacy training
- Management development
- Mentoring
- Orientation/on-boarding
- Organization development
- Performance improvement
- Personal development
- Sales training
- Skills training
- Team building
- Technical training
- Workforce development

The approach described in this book can be applied to any program or initiative for which results are intended.

⟶〰⟶ Acknowledgments

No book is ever the work of the authors alone. Many individuals, groups, and organizations have participated in the development of this book. We owe particular thanks to the hundreds of clients we have had the pleasure to work with in the past two decades. They have helped shape, develop, mold, and refine this methodology. Their contributions are evident in this book.

We are particularly indebted to Pfeiffer for taking on this project. Matt Davis, acquisitions editor, was very patient with our delivery schedule. Matt and the entire Pfeiffer team have been very helpful, and we are impressed with their commitment to bringing innovative, cutting-edge processes to the learning and development field. This is our first book with Pfeiffer, but it is only the beginning of many other books with this great publisher.

From our ROI Institute, we give special thanks to Lori Ditoro, who accomplished the editing of this project under a very hectic schedule and with a demanding workload. Thanks, Lori, for delivering this quality manuscript on time. Also, the support of Katherine Horton, Crystal Langford, and Jaime Beard was very helpful on this project.

We would also like to thank our families. In spite of our "absence," you continue to cheer us on. We love you for that and much more!

From Patti:

As always, much love and thanks go to Jack. You invest in others much more than you get in return. Thank you for your inspiration and the fun you bring to my life.

From Jack:

I owe much of my success in this effort to my lovely wife, Patti, who is my partner, friend, and colleague. She is an excellent consultant, an outstanding facilitator, a tenacious researcher, and an outstanding writer. Her contribution is immeasurable in this book.

Building a Comprehensive Evaluation Process

easuring and evaluating learning has earned a place among the critical issues in the learning and development and performance improvement fields. For decades, this topic has been on conference agendas and discussed at professional meetings. Journals and newsletters regularly embrace the concept, dedicating increased print space to it. Professional organizations have been created to exchange information on measurement and evaluation, and more than twenty-five books provide significant coverage of the topic. Even top executives have an increased appetite for evaluation data.

Although interest in the topic has heightened and much progress has been made, it is still an issue that challenges even the most sophisticated and progressive learning and development departments. While some professionals argue that having a successful evaluation process is difficult, others are quietly and deliberately implementing effective evaluation systems. The latter group has gained tremendous support from the senior management team and has made much progress. Regardless of the position taken on the issue, the reasons for measurement and evaluation are intensifying. Almost all learning and performance improvement professionals share a concern that they must show the results of learning investments. Otherwise, funds may be reduced or the department may not be able to maintain or enhance its present status and influence within the organization.

The dilemma surrounding the evaluation of learning is a source of frustration with many senior executives—even within the field itself. Most executives realize that learning is a basic necessity when organizations experience significant growth or increased competition. They intuitively feel that providing learning opportunities is valuable, logically anticipating a payoff in important bottom-line measures, such as productivity improvements, quality enhancements, cost reductions, time savings, and improved customer service. Yet the frustration comes from the lack of evidence to show that programs really work. While results are assumed to exist and learning programs appear to be necessary, more evidence is needed, or executives may feel forced to adjust funding in the future. A comprehensive measurement and evaluation process represents the most promising, logical, and rational approach to show this accountability. This book shows how to measure the contributions of learning and development and performance improvement programs.

KEY QUESTIONS

When individuals pursue a comprehensive process, they often have anxiety, issues, and concerns. They have important questions that they want resolved. Exhibit 1.1 shows a list of the typical questions that in-

- How can I move up in the evaluation chain?
- How can I collect data efficiently?
- What data should be collected at each level?
- How can I design a practical evaluation strategy that has credibility with all stakeholders?
- What support do I need for evaluation?
- How can I integrate data in a management scorecard?
- How should evaluation data be used?
- How can I get the internal support to design and implement my evaluation strategy?
- How can I proceed if the evaluation reveals an unacceptable result?
- How can I develop practical and credible tests?
- How can I use the evaluation process to implement a result-based philosophy?
- How can I make cost-effective decisions at each evaluation level?
- How can I convince clients that my program is linked to business performance measures?

Exhibit 1.1. Typical Questions.

dividuals face, regardless of the type of organization or the organization's stage of growth and development. Each of these issues, as well as many others, is detailed in this book. Each question is covered with responses that can help resolve many measurement and evaluation system challenges.

Global Evaluation Trends

Measurement and evaluation have been changing and evolving—in both the private and public sectors—across organizations and cultures, not only in the United States, but across all developed countries. The following trends have been identified:

- Organizations are increasing their investments in measurement and evaluation with best practice groups spending 3 to 5 percent of the learning and development budget on measurement and evaluation.
- Organizations are moving up the value chain, away from measuring reaction and learning to measuring application, impact, and occasionally ROI.
- The increased focus on measurement and evaluation is largely driven by the needs of the clients and sponsors of learning projects, programs, initiatives, and solutions.
- Evaluation is an integral part of the design, development, delivery, and implementation of programs.
- A shift from a reactive approach to a proactive approach is occurring, with evaluation being addressed early in the cycle.
- Measurement and evaluation processes are systematic and methodical, often designed into the delivery process.
- Technology is significantly enhancing the measurement and evaluation process, enabling large amounts of data to be collected, processed, analyzed, and integrated across programs.
- Evaluation planning is becoming a critical part of the measurement and evaluation cycle.
- The implementation of comprehensive measurement and evaluation processes usually leads to increased emphasis on initial needs analyses.
- Organizations with comprehensive measurement and evaluation systems in place have enhanced their program budgets.

- Organizations without comprehensive measurement and evaluation systems have reduced or eliminated their program budgets.
- The use of ROI is emerging as an essential part of many measurement and evaluation systems. It is a fast-growing metric—70 to 80 percent of organizations have it on their wish lists.
- Many successful examples of comprehensive measurement and evaluation applications are available in all types of organizations and cultures.

These trends are creating a never-ending appetite for more information, resources, knowledge, and skills in the measurement and evaluation process.

Measurement and Evaluation Challenges

Although measurement and evaluation are increasing, why aren't organizations doing more? Even though the need is evident, establishing the process can be formidable. Twelve basic barriers to conducting meaningful evaluations exist. They are described in detail below:

1. TOO MANY THEORIES AND MODELS. Since Kirkpatrick published articles on the four levels of evaluation in the late 1950s, dozens of evaluation books have been written, primarily for the social sciences, education, and government organizations. Then add the twenty-five-plus models and theories for evaluation offered to practitioners to help them measure the contributions of learning and development, each claiming a unique approach and a promise of addressing evaluation woes. Choosing the model to follow can seem as daunting as establishing world peace.

2. MODELS ARE TOO COMPLEX. Evaluation can be a difficult issue. Because situations and organizations are different, implementing an evaluation process across multiple programs and organizations is sometimes quite complex. The challenge is to develop models that are theoretically sound, yet simple and usable.

3. LACK OF UNDERSTANDING OF EVALUATION. Learning this process hasn't been easy for practitioners. Some books on the topic have over

six hundred pages, making absorbing the information through reading alone impossible for practitioners. Not only is understanding the evaluation processes essential for the evaluator, but the entire learning and development staff must learn parts of the process and understand how they fit into their roles. To remedy this situation, the organization must focus on how expertise is developed and disseminated within the organization.

4. THE SEARCH FOR STATISTICAL PRECISION. The use of complicated statistical models is confusing and difficult to absorb for most practitioners. Statistical precision is needed when a high-stakes decision is being made and when plenty of time and resources are available. Otherwise, simple statistics are appropriate.

5. EVALUATION IS OFTEN CONSIDERED A POST-PROGRAM ACTIVITY. When evaluation is considered an add-on activity, it loses the power to deliver the needed results. The most appropriate way to use evaluation is to consider it early—prior to program development—at the time of conception. With this approach, an evaluation is conducted efficiently and the quality and quantity of data collected are enhanced.

6. FAILURE TO SEE THE LONG-TERM PAYOFF OF EVALUATION. Developing the long-term payoff of evaluation requires examining multiple rationales for pursuing evaluation. Evaluation can be used to:

- Determine success in accomplishing learning and performance improvement program objectives.
- Prioritize resources for learning and performance improvement programs.
- Enhance the accountability of learning and performance improvement programs.
- Identify the strengths and weaknesses of the learning and development process.
- Compare the costs to the benefits of programs.
- Decide who should participate in future programs.
- Test the clarity and validity of tests, cases, and exercises.
- Identify which program participants were most successful.
- Reinforce major points made to the participants.

- Improve the quality of learning and development.
- Assist in marketing future programs.
- Determine whether the program was an appropriate solution for the specific need.
- Establish a database that can assist management in decision making.

7. LACK OF SUPPORT FROM KEY STAKEHOLDERS. Important customers, those who need and use evaluation data, sometimes don't provide the support needed to ensure the process's success. Specific steps must be taken to win support and secure buy-in from key groups, including senior executives and the management team. Executives must see that evaluation produces valuable data to improve programs and validate results. When the stakeholders understand what is involved, they may offer more support.

8. EVALUATION HAS NOT DELIVERED THE DATA SENIOR MANAGERS WANT. Today, clients and sponsors ask for data beyond reaction and learning. They need data on the application of new skills on the job and the corresponding impact of this application on the business units. Sometimes, they want ROI data for major programs. They request data about the business impact of learning—both from short-term and long-term perspectives. Ultimately, these are the executives who fund learning and development. If the desired data are not available, future funding could be in jeopardy.

9. IMPROPER USE OF EVALUATION DATA. Improper use of evaluation data can lead to four major problems, which are described here:

1. Too many organizations do not use evaluation data at all. Data are collected, tabulated, catalogued, filed, and never used by any group, other than the individual who initially collected the data.
2. Data are not provided to the appropriate audiences. Analyzing the target audiences and determining the specific data needed for each group are important steps for communicating results.
3. Data are not used to drive improvement. If not part of the feedback cycle, evaluation falls short of its intended purpose.
4. Data are used for the wrong reasons—to take action against an individual or group or to withhold funds, rather than to im-

prove processes. Sometimes, the data are used in political ways to gain power or advantage over another person.

10. LACK OF CONSISTENCY. For evaluation to add value and be accepted by stakeholders, it must be consistent in its approach and methodology. Tools and templates have to be developed to support the method of choice to prevent perpetual reinvention of the wheel. Without this consistency, evaluation consumes too many resources and raises too many concerns about the quality and credibility of the process.

11. LACK OF STANDARDS. Closely parallel with consistency is the issue of standards. Standards are rules for making evaluation consistent, stable, and equitable. Without standards, little credibility in processes and stability of outcomes exists.

12. SUSTAINABILITY. A new model or approach often has a short life and, therefore, is not sustained. Evaluation must be integrated into the organization so that it becomes routine and lasting. To accomplish this, the evaluation process must gain the respect of key stakeholders at the outset. The evaluation process must be well documented, and stakeholders must accept their responsibilities to make it work. Without sustainability, evaluation will be on a roller-coaster ride, where data are collected only when programs are in trouble and less attention is provided when they are not.

Benefits of Measurement and Evaluation

Although the benefits of measurement and evaluation may appear obvious, several distinct and important payoffs can be realized.

RESPOND TO REQUESTS AND REQUIREMENTS. Today's executives and administrators need information about application and implementation in the workplace and their corresponding impacts on key business measures. In some cases, they ask for an ROI analysis. Developing a comprehensive measurement and evaluation system is the best way to meet these requests and requirements.

JUSTIFY BUDGETS. Some learning and performance functions use evaluation data to support a requested budget, while others use the data to prevent the budget from being slashed, or in drastic cases, eliminated entirely. Additional evaluation data can show where programs add value and where they do not. This approach can lead to protecting successful programs as well as pursuing new programs.

IMPROVE PROGRAM DESIGN. A comprehensive evaluation system should provide information to improve the overall design of a program, including the areas of learning design, content, delivery method, duration, timing, focus, and expectations. These processes may need adjustment to improve learning, especially during new program implementation.

IDENTIFY AND IMPROVE DYSFUNCTIONAL PROCESSES. Evaluation data can determine whether the up-front analysis was conducted properly, thereby aligning the program with the organizational needs. Additional evaluation data can help pinpoint inadequacies in implementation systems and identify ways to improve them.

ENHANCE LEARNING TRANSFER. Learning transfer is perhaps one of the biggest challenges that the learning and development field faces. Research shows that 60 to 90 percent of job-related skills and knowledge acquired in a program are not implemented on the job. A comprehensive evaluation system can identify specific barriers to implementing learning. Evaluation data can also highlight supportive work environments that enable learning transfer.

ELIMINATE UNNECESSARY OR INEFFECTIVE PROGRAMS. Program evaluation can provide rational, credible data to help support the decision to implement or discontinue a program. In reality, if the program cannot add value, it should be discontinued. *One caveat:* Eliminating programs should not be a principal motive or rationale for increasing evaluation efforts. Although it is a valid use of evaluation data, program elimination is often viewed negatively.

EXPAND OR IMPLEMENT SUCCESSFUL PROGRAMS. The flip side of eliminating programs is expanding their presence or application. Positive results may signal the possibility that a program's success in one division or region can be replicated in another area, if a similar need exists.

ENHANCE THE RESPECT AND CREDIBILITY OF THE STAFF. Collecting and using evaluation data—including application, impact, and ROI—builds respect for learning and respect for the learning and performance staff. Appropriate evaluation data can enhance the credibility of the learning and development and performance improvement functions when the data reveal the value added to the organization.

SATISFY CLIENT NEEDS. Satisfying clients is a critical objective for the learning and performance improvement function. If clients are not pleased with the data, they may decline the opportunity to use the staff in the future. If they are satisfied, they may use the program again and even recommend the program to others.

INCREASE SUPPORT FROM MANAGERS. Participants' immediate managers need convincing data about the success of learning. They often do not support learning processes because they see little value in taking employees away from the job to be involved in a program with little connection to their business units. Data showing how learning helps them achieve their objectives will influence their support.

STRENGTHEN RELATIONSHIPS WITH KEY EXECUTIVES. Senior executives must perceive the learning and development staff as business partners who should be invited to the table for important decisions and meetings. A comprehensive measurement and evaluation process can show the contribution of the function and help strengthen this relationship.

SET PRIORITIES FOR LEARNING AND DEVELOPMENT. A comprehensive measurement system can help determine which programs represent the highest priority. Evaluation data can show the payoff or potential payoff of important and expensive programs—the programs that support strategic objectives.

REINVENT LEARNING AND DEVELOPMENT AND PERFORMANCE IMPROVEMENT. Measurement and evaluation reveal the link between learning and the business and can drive increased alignment in the future. Connecting learning with business objectives requires a continuous focus on critical organizational needs and results that can and should be obtained from programs.

ALTER MANAGEMENT'S PERCEPTIONS OF LEARNING AND DEVELOPMENT. Middle-level managers often see learning as a necessary evil. A comprehensive evaluation process may influence these managers to view learning as a contributing process and an excellent investment. It can also help shift the perception of learning from a dispensable activity to an indispensable, value-adding process.

ACHIEVE A MONETARY PAYOFF. In some situations, an actual monetary value can be calculated for investing in measurement and evaluation. This is particularly true with implementation of ROI, and many organizations have even calculated "the ROI on the ROI process." They determine the payoff of investing in a comprehensive measurement and evaluation process—the ROI methodology. The payoff is developed by detailing specific economies, efficiencies, and direct cost savings generated by the evaluation process.

These key benefits, inherent with almost any type of evaluation process, make additional measurement and evaluation an attractive challenge of the learning and performance function.

The Myths of Measurement and Evaluation

Practitioners recognize that additional measurement and evaluation is needed. However, regardless of the motivation to pursue evaluation, they struggle with how to address the issue. They often ask, "Does it really provide the benefits to make it a routine, useful tool?" "Is it feasible within our resources?" "Do we have the capability of implementing a comprehensive evaluation process?" The answers to these questions often lead to debate and controversy. Controversy stems from misunderstandings about what the additional evaluation can and cannot do and how it can or should be implemented in organizations. The following is a list of myths, including the appropriate clarifications:

MEASUREMENT AND EVALUATION, INCLUDING ROI, IS TOO EXPENSIVE. When considering additional measurement and evaluation, cost is usually the first issue to surface. Many practitioners think that evaluation adds cost to an already lean budget that is regularly scrutinized. In reality, when the cost of evaluation is compared to the budget, a comprehensive measurement and evaluation system can be implemented for less than 5 percent of the total direct learning and development or performance improvement budget.

EVALUATION TAKES TOO MUCH TIME. Parallel with the concern about cost is the time involved in evaluation—time to design instruments, collect data, process the data, and communicate results to the groups that need them. Dozens of shortcuts are available to help reduce the total time required for evaluation.

SENIOR MANAGEMENT DOES NOT REQUIRE IT. Some learning and development staff think that if management does not ask for additional evaluation and measurement, the staff does not need to pursue it. Sometimes, senior executives fail to ask for results because they think that the data are not available. They may assume that results cannot be produced. Paradigms are shifting, not only within learning and performance improvement, but within senior management groups as well. Senior managers are beginning to request higher-level data that shows application, impact, and even ROI.

MEASUREMENT AND EVALUATION IS A PASSING FAD. While some practitioners regard the move to more evaluation, including ROI, as a passing fad, accountability is a concern now. Many organizations are asked to show the value of programs. Studies show this trend will continue.

EVALUATION ONLY GENERATES ONE OR TWO TYPES OF DATA. Although some evaluation processes generate a single type of data (reaction-level, for example), many evaluation models and processes generate a variety of data, offering a balanced approach based on both qualitative and quantitative data. The process in this book collects as many as seven different types of qualitative and quantitative data, within different timeframes, and from different sources.

EVALUATION CANNOT BE EASILY REPLICATED. With so many evaluation processes available, this issue becomes an understandable concern. In theory, any process worth implementing should be one that can be replicated from one study to another. Fortunately, many evaluation models offer a systematic process, with certain guiding principles or operating standards to increase the likelihood that two different evaluators will obtain the same results.

EVALUATION IS TOO SUBJECTIVE. Subjectivity of evaluation has become a concern, in part because of the studies conducted using estimates and perceptions that have been published and presented at conferences. The fact is that many studies are precise and are not based on estimates. Estimates usually represent the worst-case scenario or approach.

IMPACT EVALUATION IS NOT POSSIBLE FOR SOFT-SKILL PROGRAMS. This concern is often based on the assumption that only technical or hard skills can be evaluated, not soft skills. For example, practitioners might find measuring the success of leadership, team-building, and communication programs difficult. What they often misunderstand is that soft-skills learning and development programs can, and should, drive hard-data items, such as output, quality, cost, and time.

EVALUATION IS MORE APPROPRIATE FOR CERTAIN TYPES OF ORGANIZATIONS. Although evaluation is easier in certain types of programs, generally, it can be used in any setting. Comprehensive measurement systems are successfully implemented in health care, nonprofit, government, and educational areas, in addition to traditional service and manufacturing organizations. Another concern expressed by some is that only large organizations have a need for measurement and evaluation. Although this may appear to be the case (because large organizations have large budgets), evaluation can work in the smallest organizations and simply must be scaled down to fit the situation.

IT IS NOT ALWAYS POSSIBLE TO ISOLATE THE EFFECTS OF LEARNING. Several methods are available to isolate the effects of learning on impact data. The challenge is to select an appropriate isolation technique for the resources available and the accuracy needed in the particular situation.

A PROCESS FOR MEASURING ON-THE-JOB IMPROVEMENT SHOULD NOT BE USED. This myth is believed because the learning and development staff usually has no control over participants after they leave the program. Belief in it is fading, though, as organizations realize the importance of measuring the results of workplace learning solutions. Systems and processes can be implemented to influence application. Expectations can be created so that participants anticipate a follow-up and provide data.

A PARTICIPANT IS RARELY RESPONSIBLE FOR THE FAILURE OF PROGRAMS. Too often, participants are allowed to escape accountability for their learning experiences. It is too easy for participants to claim that the program was not supported by their managers, it did not fit the culture of the work group, or that the systems or processes were in conflict with the skills and processes presented in the program. Today, participants are held more accountable for the success of learning in the workplace.

EVALUATION IS ONLY THE EVALUATOR'S RESPONSIBILITY. Some organizations assign an individual or group the primary responsibility for evaluation. When that is the case, other stakeholders assume that they have no responsibility for evaluation. In today's climate, evaluation must be a shared responsibility. All stakeholders are involved in some aspect of analyzing, designing, developing, delivering, implementing, coordinating, or organizing a program.

SUCCESSFUL EVALUATION IMPLEMENTATION REQUIRES A DEGREE IN STATISTICS OR EVALUATION. Having a degree or possessing some special skill or knowledge is not a requirement. An eagerness to learn, a willingness to analyze data, and a desire to make improvements in the organization are the primary requirements. After meeting these requirements, most individuals can learn how to properly implement evaluation.

NEGATIVE DATA ARE ALWAYS BAD NEWS. Negative data provide a rich source of information for improvement. An effective evaluation system can pinpoint what went wrong so that changes can be made. Barriers to success as well as enablers of success can be identified. Such data will generate conclusions that show what must be changed to make the process more effective.

KEY STEPS AND ISSUES

Instead of examining a particular model or process, identifying some of the key issues, steps, and processes involved in measurement may be helpful. All these must be addressed in some way to have a comprehensive process.

Stakeholders

Many stakeholders are involved in comprehensive measurement and evaluation systems. A stakeholder is defined as any individual or group interested or involved in the program. Stakeholders may include the functional manager where the program is located, the participants, the organizer, the program leader, facilitators, and key clients, among others. Below are descriptions of these stakeholders, and they will be referred to routinely throughout the book.

SPONSOR/CLIENTS. The individual(s) who fund, initiate, request, or support a particular project or program. Sometimes referred to as the sponsor, it is the key group—usually at the senior management level—who cares about the program's success and is in a position to discontinue or expand the program.

PARTICIPANTS. These are the individuals who are directly involved in the program. The term "employee," "associate," "user," or "stakeholder" may represent these individuals. For most programs, the term "participant" appropriately reflects this group.

IMMEDIATE MANAGERS. These are individuals who are one level above the participant(s) involved in the program. For some programs, this is the team leader for other employees. Often they are middle managers, but most important, these people have supervisory authority over the participants in the program.

CEO/MANAGING DIRECTOR/AGENCY EXECUTIVE. This person is the top executive in an organization. The top executive could be a plant manager, division manager, regional executive, administrator, or agency head. The CEO is the top administrator or executive in the operating entity where the program is implemented.

THE ORGANIZATION. The organization is the entity within which the particular program or process is evaluated. Organizations may be companies (either privately held or publicly held); government organizations at the local, state, federal, and international levels; non-profits; or non-governmental organizations. They may also include educational institutions, associations, networks, and other loosely organized bodies of individuals.

PROGRAM MANAGER. The individual(s) responsible for the project, program, initiative, or process. This is the individual who manages the program and is interested in showing the value of the program before it is implemented, during its implementation, and after it is implemented.

PROGRAM TEAM. The individuals involved in the program, helping to analyze and implement it. These are individual team members who may be full- or part-time on this particular program. For larger-scale programs, these individuals are often assigned full-time, on a temporary basis, or, sometimes, on a permanent basis. For small programs, these may be part-time duties.

EVALUATOR. This individual evaluates the program. This person is responsible for measurement and evaluation, following all the processes outlined in this book. If this is a member of the program team, extreme measures must be taken to ensure this person remains objective. It may also be a person who is completely independent of the program. This individual performs these duties full- or part-time.

FINANCE AND ACCOUNTING STAFF. These individuals are concerned about the cost and impact of the program from a financial perspective. They provide valuable support. Their approval of processes, assumptions, and methodologies is important. Sometimes, they are involved in the program evaluation; at other times they review the results. During major programs, this could include the organization's finance director or chief financial officer.

ANALYSTS. These individuals collect the data to determine whether the program is needed. They are also involved in analyzing various parts of the program. Analysts are usually more important in the beginning, but may provide helpful data throughout the program.

BYSTANDERS. The bystanders are the individuals who observe, sometimes at a distance, the program. They are not actively involved as stakeholders, but are concerned about the outcomes, including the money. These bystanders are important because they can become cheerleaders or critics of the program.

Levels and Steps

Most of the existing models have been developed to enhance, modify, or improve what was initially published fifty years ago by Don Kirkpatrick. His basic premise of considering evaluation as steps of measuring reaction, learning, behavior, and results, brought a novel and useful approach to practitioners. Although a few of the models take different approaches, the most-used, essential framework is Kirkpatrick's steps, now labeled levels. In the 1980s, Phillips added a fifth level and modified Kirkpatrick's level descriptions. The reality is that the Kirkpatrick-Phillips-based evaluation probably accounts for 80 to 90 percent of the models in use today, globally.

It may be helpful to examine measurement and evaluation of learning as a value chain, where data are collected at different times (sometimes from different sources) to provide a process. Figure 1.1 shows this value chain—fundamental to much of the current work in evaluation.

This concept shows how value is developed and also provides data from different perspectives. Some stakeholders are interested in knowing about the inputs so that they can be managed and made more efficient; others are interested in reaction; still others are interested in learning. More recently, clients and sponsors have become more interested in actual behavior change (application) and the corresponding business impact, while a few stakeholders are concerned about the actual return on investment.

Chain of Impact

The collected data are arranged as a chain of impact, shown in Figure 1.2. The chain of impact described in this figure must to be evident if the particular learning program or performance improvement project is adding business value. All stakeholders must be closely involved in the program to understand this chain of impact. The sponsor must see this chain as the data are generated throughout the process. Participants must realize that they have a critical role and that their involvement and success are shown through the chain. The designers, developers, and facilitators have to understand that the chain of impact is critical. It can be broken, essentially at any stage, and the evaluation data will indicate whether it is broken and where it is broken. Was it broken because of adverse reaction, no learning, no application? Or was there no connection to a business measure? The information described in this book will clearly indicate whether the chain of impact is intact and where it can be strengthened. Also, it will show when it breaks and there is no value.

When the chain of impact is considered throughout the process of evaluation, some interesting characteristics begin to evolve, as shown in Figure 1.3. The evaluation data are collected throughout the chain.

Level	Measurement Focus	Typical Measures
0. Inputs and Indicators	Inputs into the program, including indicators representing scope, volumes, costs, and efficiencies	Types of topics, content Number of programs Number of people Hours of involvement Costs
1. Reaction and Planned Action	Reaction to the program, including plans to take action	Relevance Importance Usefulness Appropriateness Intent to use Motivational
2. Learning and Confidence	Learning how to use the content and materials, including the confidence to use what was learned	Skills Knowledge Capacity Competencies Confidences Contacts
3. Application and Implementation	Use of content and materials in the work environment, including progress with implementation	Extent of use Task completion Frequency of use Actions completed Success with use Barriers to use Enablers to use
4. Impact and Consequences	The consequences of the use of the content and materials expressed as business impact measures	Productivity Revenue Quality Time Efficiency Customer satisfaction Employee engagement
5. ROI	Comparison of monetary benefits from the program to program costs	Benefit/cost ratio (BCR) ROI (%) Payback period

Figure 1.1. The Types and Levels of Data.

Level 1	Participant has a positive reaction to the program, plans specific actions, and . . .
Level 2	Participant acquires knowledge, develops skills, changes attitudes/perceptions, and . . .
Level 3	Participant uses new knowledge, skills, and attitudes on the job and . . .
Level 4	Use of new knowledge, skills, and attitudes drives business performance and . . .
Level 5	Monetary value of business performance exceeds cost of program.

Figure 1.2. Seeking the Chain of Impact.

Chain of Impact	Value of Information	Focus	Power to Show Results	Frequency of Use	Difficulty of Assessment
Reaction	Lowest	Consumer	Lowest	Frequent	Easy
Learning					
Application					
Impact					
ROI	Highest	Client	Highest	Infrequent	Difficult

Consumers: The customers who are actively involved in the process.
Clients: The customers who fund, support, and approve the project.

Figure 1.3. Characteristics of Evaluation Levels.

The data are more valuable as the process moves from reaction to ROI, at least from the client's perspective. The lower levels of data, for example, reaction and learning, are mostly consumer-oriented data, taken directly from the consumer. Reaction data are a consumer satisfaction index. Learning data are often provided to the consumer to build confidence, but impact and ROI data are more client-focused. They are the type of data that clients want to see from their learning and performance improvement programs. However, while the power to show results increases as data move through the chain, evaluating the data becomes more expensive and more difficult. However, the reverse is true for usage. As expected, a high level of data collection activity occurs at Level 1, but a low level of activity occurs around Level 4 and Level 5. And some good reasons for this exist, as will be described later in the book.

ROI Process Model

Measurement and evaluation must be systematic, methodical, and routine. Figure 1.4 shows the ROI Process Model used in this book. It illustrates the different steps in the process, beginning with objectives and proceeding through until an impact study is generated. However, the evaluation can stop at any level along the process. The first level, as described earlier, is basically inputs to the process. The data collected during programs at Level 1 and Level 2 and on a post basis for Levels 3 and 4, and Level 5 are an ROI process level.

Objectives

In the learning and development and performance improvement fields, the primary focus has been on developing learning objectives. However, for many, if not most, programs, objectives need to be enhanced to include Level 3 and Level 4 objectives. One of the most important developments in measurement and evaluation is the creation of higher levels of program objectives. Program objectives correspond with the different levels on the value chain. Ideally, the levels of objectives should be in place at the highest level desired for evaluation. Essentially, the levels of objectives are:

- Input objectives (number of programs, participants, hours, etc.)— Level 0

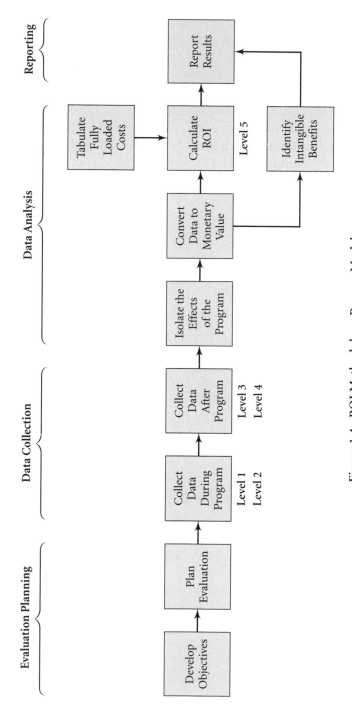

Figure 1.4. ROI Methodology Process Model.

- Reaction and satisfaction objectives—Level 1
- Learning objectives—Level 2
- Application objectives—Level 3
- Impact objectives—Level 4
- ROI objectives—Level 5

Exhibit 1.2 shows an example of the multiple levels of objectives taken from a coaching program.

LEVEL 1. REACTION OBJECTIVES

After participating in this coaching program, the executive will
- Perceive coaching to be relevant to the job
- Perceive coaching to be important to job success at the present time
- Perceive coaching to be value added in terms of time and funds invested
- Rate the coach as effective
- Recommend this program to other executives

LEVEL 2. LEARNING OBJECTIVES

After completing this coaching program, the executives should improve their understanding or skills for each of the following:
- Uncovering individual strengths and weaknesses
- Translating feedback into action plans
- Involving team members in programs and goals
- Communicating effectively
- Collaborating with colleagues
- Improving personal effectiveness
- Enhancing leadership skills

LEVEL 3. APPLICATION OBJECTIVES

Six months after completing this coaching program, executives should
- Complete the action plan
- Adjust the plan accordingly, as needed for changes in the environment
- Identify barriers and enablers
- Show improvements on the following items:
    Uncovering individual strengths and weaknesses
    Translating feedback into action plans

Exhibit 1.2. Examples of Objectives.

(Continued)

Involving team members in programs and goals

Communicating effectively

Collaborating with colleagues

Improving personal effectiveness

Enhancing leadership skills

LEVEL 4. IMPACT OBJECTIVES

After completing this coaching program, executives should improve at least three specific measures in the following areas:

- Sales growth
- Productivity/operational efficiency
- Direct cost reduction
- Retention of key staff members
- Customer satisfaction

LEVEL 5. ROI OBJECTIVE

- The ROI value should be 25 percent.

Exhibit 1.2. Examples of Objectives, Cont'd.

Before an evaluation is conducted, these objectives must be identified and developed. Ideally, they should be developed early when the program is designed. If they are not readily available, they'll have to be included to take the evaluation to the desired level.

Evaluation Planning

The time at which evaluation is considered has changed dramatically in recent years. The traditional instructional systems design model, called ADDIE (Analysis, Design, Development, Implementation, and Evaluation), has been replaced with a new model, as illustrated in Figure 1.5. Evaluation must be considered at the conception of the program and often throughout the process. If evaluation is not considered early, serious limitations occur in the quality and quantity of data that are collected for evaluation. ADDIE places evaluation at the end, and unfortunately, professional practitioners waited until after implementation to think about evaluation. That's too late.

Evaluation must be planned—overall and individually—for each program. When evaluation is conducted only at reaction levels, not

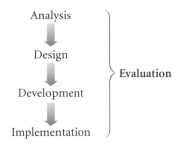

Figure 1.5. The New Design Model.

much planning is involved, but as evaluation moves up the value chain, increased attention and efforts need to be placed on planning. During the typical planning cycle, the purpose of evaluation must be reviewed for specific solutions and to determine where the evaluation will stop on the value chain. The feasibility of evaluating at different levels is explored, and two planning documents are developed when the evaluation migrates to application, impact, and ROI: the data collection plan and the data analysis plan. These documents are sometimes used in combination, but are often developed separately.

Data Collection

One important issue is the timing of data collection. In some cases, pre-program measurements are taken to compare with post-program measures, and in some cases, multiple measures are taken. In other situations, pre-program measures are not available and specific follow-ups are still taken after the program. The important issue is to determine the timing for the follow-up evaluation.

Another important issue is the data collection method used. Data are collected using the following methods:

- *Surveys* are administered to determine the extent to which participants are satisfied with the program, have learned the skills and knowledge, and have used different aspects of the program.

- *Questionnaires* are usually more detailed than surveys and can be used to uncover a wide variety of data. Participants provide responses to several types of open-ended and forced-response questions.

- *Tests* are conducted to measure changes in knowledge and skills. Tests come in a wide variety of formal (criterion-referenced tests, performance tests, simulations, and skill practices) and informal (facilitator assessment, self assessment, and team assessment) methods.

- *On-the-job observation* captures actual skill application and use. Observations are particularly useful in customer service training and are more effective when the observer is either invisible or transparent.

- *Interviews* are conducted with participants to determine the extent to which learning has been used on the job.

- *Focus groups* are conducted to determine the degree to which a group of participants has applied the training to job situations.

- *Action plans and program assignments* are developed by participants during the program and are implemented on the job after the program is completed. Follow-ups provide evidence of program success.

- *Performance contracts* are developed by the participant, the participant's supervisor, and the facilitator, who all agree on job performance outcomes.

- *Business performance monitoring* is useful when various performance records and operational data are examined for improvement.

Analysis

Evaluation requires analysis. Even if the evaluation stops at Level 1, analysis is required, usually involving simple averages and standard deviations. As organizations progress up the value chain, additional analyses are required. In some cases, not only are the averages and standard deviations used, but simple hypotheses testing and correlations may be required; however, these are very unusual situations. For the most part, analysis is simply tabulating, organizing, and integrating data and then presenting results in meaningful ways for the audience to understand and appreciate.

Isolation of the Effects of Learning and Development

An often-overlooked issue in some evaluations is the process of isolating the effects of learning on output data. This step is important because many factors will usually influence performance data after a learning program is conducted. Several techniques are available to determine the amount of output performance directly related to the program. These techniques will pinpoint the amount of improvement directly linked to the program, resulting in increased accuracy and credibility of the evaluation data. The following techniques have been used by organizations to tackle this important issue:

- *A control group* arrangement is used to isolate learning's impact. With this strategy, one group participates in a program, while another, similar group does not. The difference in the performance of the two groups is attributed to the program. When properly set up and implemented, the control group arrangement is the most effective way to isolate the effects of learning and development.

- *Trend lines and forecasting* are used to project the values of specific output variables as if the learning program had not been undertaken. The projection is compared to the actual data after the program is conducted, and the difference represents the estimate of the impact of learning.

- *Participants or managers* estimate the amount of improvement related to the learning and development program. With this approach, participants or managers are provided with the total amount of improvement that is actually related to the program.

- *Other experts,* such as customers, provide estimates of the impact of learning on the performance variable. Because the estimates are based on previous experience, these experts must be familiar with the type of program and the specific situation.

Conversion of Data to Monetary Values

To calculate the return on investment, business impact data collected in the evaluation are converted to monetary values and compared to program costs. This requires that a value be placed on each unit of data connected with the program. Several techniques are available to convert data to monetary values. In many cases, standard values are available as organizations have attempted to place value on measures they want to increase and develop costs for measures they want to avoid. When these are not available, the records (or a combination of records) may show the cost or value of the measure. Also, internal experts, external experts, or external databases can be sources of values. Sometimes, participants, supervisors, and other conveniently available staff members can provide the values.

This step is necessary for determining the monetary benefits from a learning program. The process is challenging, particularly with soft data, but can be methodically accomplished using one or more of the techniques described above.

The Cost of Programs

The cost of learning is usually developed from one of two perspectives:

1. For budgets, program approvals, and general information requests, costs are often reported systematically within the organization, and usually include only the direct costs. Executives and administrators are often interested in the direct costs. In some cases, these reports are changing to include other indirect costs.

2. When the actual ROI is calculated, the costs must be fully loaded to include all direct and indirect costs. In these situations, the cost components should include:

    • Needs assessment, design, and development, possibly pro-rated over the expected life of the program
    • All program materials provided to each participant
    • Instructor/facilitator, including preparation time as well as delivery time
    • Facilities for the learning program
    • Travel, lodging, and meal costs for the participants, if applicable
    • Salaries, plus employee benefits of the participants of the learning program
    • Administrative and overhead costs of the workplace learning and performance function, allocated in some convenient way
    • Evaluation, including planning, data collection, analysis, and reporting

The conservative approach is to include all these costs so that the total is fully loaded.

The Return on Investment Calculation

Dramatic changes have occurred in the need for data around learning and development programs. Many executives and managers have taken the approach, "Show me the money." Figure 1.6 shows how the "Show Me" request has evolved, leading up to an actual request for ROI. For some professionals, this is an issue that cannot be ignored because of the serious consequences. Executives and managers want this type of data, and it must be delivered. This requires at least a few major programs to be elevated to the ROI analysis level.

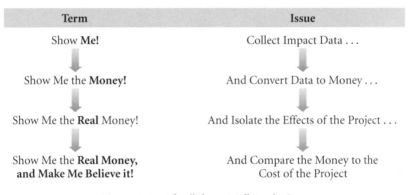

Term	Issue
Show **Me!**	Collect Impact Data . . .
Show Me the **Money!**	And Convert Data to Money . . .
Show Me the **Real** Money!	And Isolate the Effects of the Project . . .
Show Me the **Real Money, and Make Me Believe it!**	And Compare the Money to the Cost of the Project

Figure 1.6. The "Show Me" Evolution.

When the ROI is actually developed, it should be calculated systematically, using standard formulas. Two formulas are available. The benefit/cost ratio is the program benefits divided by the costs. In formula form, it is:

$$BCR = \frac{PROGRAM\ BENEFITS}{PROGRAM\ COSTS}$$

The return on investment calculation uses the net benefits divided by program costs. The net benefits are the program benefits minus the costs. In formula form, the ROI is:

$$ROI\ (\%) = \frac{NET\ PROGRAM\ BENEFITS}{PROGRAM\ COSTS} \times 100$$

This is the same basic formula used in evaluating other investments for which the ROI is traditionally reported as earnings divided by investment. An example of the benefit/cost ratio and ROI is illustrated below. A training program is delivered to fifty participants. Consider that, following the training program, the first-year program benefits (from Level 4 business impact data) are found to be $300,000 from the fifty participants, and the fully loaded costs to train these fifty participants is $200,000.

$$BCR = \$300,000/\$200,000 = 1.50:1$$

$$ROI = \$100,000/\$200,000 \times 100 = 50\%$$

The ROI calculation of net benefits ($300,000 minus $200,000) divided by total costs brings an ROI of 50 percent. This is what is earned after we get back the $200,000 spent for the program. The ROI calculation accounts for the program costs and shows the resulting net gain.

The BCR (benefit/cost ratio) calculation above uses the total benefits in the numerator. Therefore, the expressed BCR of 1.50:1 does not account for replacing the money expended. This is why, when using the same values, the BCR will always be 1 greater than the ROI. The BCR of 1.50:1 in the example means that, for every dollar spent, $1.50 is gained back. One dollar has to pay for the investment, so the net is $0.50 (as expressed in the ROI calculation).

Intangible Benefits

In addition to tangible benefits, most learning programs will influence intangible, non-monetary, benefits. Intangible benefits may include:

- Increased job satisfaction
- Increased organizational commitment
- Improved teamwork
- Improved customer service
- Reduced complaints
- Reduced conflicts

During analysis, hard data—such as output, quality, and time—are usually converted to monetary values. The conversion of soft data is attempted. However, if the process used for conversion is too subjective or inaccurate and the resulting values lose credibility during the process, then the data are listed as intangible benefits with an appropriate explanation given. For some programs, intangible benefits are extremely valuable, often carrying as much influence as hard data items.

Data Reporting

This critical step is often not given the proper attention and planning needed to ensure that it is successful. This step involves developing appropriate information as impact studies, executive summaries, one-page summaries, and other brief reports. The heart of the step includes the different techniques used to communicate to a wide variety of target audiences. In most situations, several audiences are interested in and need to know the information. Careful planning to match the communication method with the audience is essential to ensuring that the message is understood and appropriate actions are taken.

Operating Standards

To ensure consistency and replication of evaluation studies, operating standards should be developed and applied in the measurement and evaluation process. The results of an evaluation must stand alone and should not vary based on the individual who is conducting the study. The operating standards detail how each step and issue of the process should be addressed. The standards presented in this book are called the guiding principles. They are listed below:

1. When a higher-level evaluation is conducted, data must be collected at lower levels.
2. When an evaluation is planned for a higher level, the previous level of evaluation does not have to be comprehensive.
3. When collecting and analyzing data, use only the most credible sources.
4. When analyzing data, select the most conservative alternative for calculations.
5. At least one method must be used to isolate the effects of the solution/program.

6. If no improvement data are available for a population or from a specific source, it is assumed that little or no improvement has occurred.

7. Estimates of improvements should be adjusted for the potential error of the estimate.

8. Extreme data items and unsupported claims should not be used in ROI calculations.

9. Only the first year of benefits (annual) should be used in the ROI analysis of short-term solutions.

10. Costs of a solution, project, or program should be fully loaded for ROI analysis.

11. Intangible measures are defined as measures that are purposely not converted to monetary values.

12. The results from the ROI methodology must be communicated to all key stakeholders.

These specific standards not only serve as a way to consistently address each step, but also provide a much-needed conservative approach to the analysis. A conservative approach will build credibility with the target audience.

Implementation Issues

A variety of organizational issues and events will influence the successful implementation of measurement and evaluation. These issues must be addressed early to ensure that evaluation is successful. Specific topics or actions may include:

- A policy statement concerning results-based learning and development
- Procedures and guidelines for different elements and techniques of the evaluation process
- Meetings and formal sessions to develop staff skills with measurement and evaluations
- Strategies to improve management commitment and support for measurement and evaluation

- Mechanisms to provide technical support for questionnaire design, data analysis, and evaluation strategy
- Specific techniques to place more attention on results

Measurement and evaluation can fail or succeed based on these implementation issues.

FINAL THOUGHTS

More attention needs to be focused on measurement and evaluation; this is almost universally agreed on. The use of measurement and evaluation is expanding. The payoff is huge. The process is not very difficult. The approaches, strategies, and techniques are not overly complex and can be useful in a variety of settings. The combined and persistent efforts of practitioners and researchers will continue to refine the techniques and create successful applications. In the next chapter, the first step of the evaluation process, the needs analysis, will be explored.

CHAPTER TWO

Defining Needs and Objectives

Ensuring Business Alignment

———

This chapter presents the first step of a comprehensive ROI methodology: defining the initial needs and corresponding objectives for the program. If needs are not defined clearly and early in the process, an inadequate or incorrect solution may be the result, which will create inefficiencies and problems throughout the process. This chapter explores the five levels of needs assessments: (1) addressing payoff needs, (2) defining business needs, (3) analyzing performance needs, (4) determining learning needs, and (5) uncovering preference needs.

THE CHALLENGE
Business Alignment Issues

Based on the approximately two thousand evaluation studies that we have conducted or reviewed, the number one cause of program failure is undefined program needs. The second most common cause of failure is a misalignment between the program and the business. For example, in the learning and development field, research shows that

60 to 90 percent of learning is wasted. The principal culprit: lack of business alignment from the beginning. Alignment between the program and the business must be assured, particularly if the proposed program exceeds the specified cost threshold.

Begin with the End in Mind

Learning and development solutions must begin with a clear focus on the outcome. The end result must be specifically defined in terms of business needs and business measures so that the outcome—the actual improvement in the measures—and the resulting ROI are clear. This provides necessary focus on the problem through every step in the process. Beginning with the end in mind also involves pinpointing all the details to ensure that it is properly planned and executed.

Required Discipline

Proper analysis requires discipline and determination. A structured, systematic process that follows a set of standards is needed. A standardized approach adds credibility and allows for consistent application, allowing the study to be replicated, and it maintains process efficiency as different tools and templates are developed and used. The process calls for focus and thoroughness, leaving little room for major shortcuts.

While the process described in this book is comprehensive, not every program should be subjected to the type of analysis presented in this chapter. Some needs are obvious and require little analysis other than the analysis needed to develop the program or project. Additional analysis is often needed to ensure that the program is the right solution or perhaps to fine-tune it for future application. The amount of analysis required often depends on the stakes involved.

The Needs Analysis Dilemma

Whenever a needs analysis is proposed, many individuals respond with concern and, at times, with resistance. Some worry about "paralysis by analysis," fearing that requests and directives may place them in a cycle of additional analyses. This represents a dilemma for many organizations because, to ensure that programs are appropriate, analysis *must* occur. Unfortunately, analysis is often misplaced, misunderstood, and misrepresented, and individuals imagine the worst—complex problems, confusing models, and an endless array of data requiring complicated statistical techniques to ensure that all the bases are covered. In reality, analysis does not have to be so difficult. Simple techniques may uncover the cause of the problem or the need for a proposed program. Analysis is often not pursued for several reasons:

1. *The specific need appears to point to a particular solution.* When asked what they need on the job, individuals' responses may point to a legitimate solution, but in reality, the solution may be inadequate or inappropriate. For example, when employees are asked what they need to improve job performance in terms of productivity, they may identify specific tools or software. In reality, the solution may be as simple as learning to fully use existing tools. Implementing a solution based only on an individual request may be short-sighted and expensive. The credibility of the individual's description of the need and the potential bias or misinformation must be considered when accepting the need and identifying the solution.

2. *The solution appears to be obvious.* When examining a problem or potential opportunity, some solutions appear obvious. For example, if employee turnover is excessive, evaluators may quickly conclude that managers must be trained to resolve this issue. Although this solution appears obvious, further analysis may reveal that other issues—such as compensation or the job market—may be causing the problem.

3. *Everyone has an opinion about the problem's cause.* The requester of a particular program may think that his or her request is the best solution. Other executives may have different opinions. Choosing the solutions championed by the highest-ranking or most-senior executives is often tempting. After all, these are smart people. Unfortunately, they may not be the closest to the situations and, therefore, may not offer the best solutions.

4. *Analysis takes too much time.* Yes, analysis consumes time and resources. However, the result of *no* analysis can be more expensive. If a program is implemented that does not appropriately address the business needs, time and money may be wasted. The consequences of incorrect learning solutions implemented with

no analysis can be devastating. If planned properly and conducted professionally, an analysis can be completed within most organizations' budgets and time constraints. The secret is to focus on the right tools for the situation.

5. *Analysis appears confusing.* Determining a problem's causes may appear complex and puzzling. However, some analyses are simple and straightforward, achieving excellent results. The challenge is selecting the analysis that will yield the best solution, with minimum effort and the simplest technique.

With these misconceptions, the difficulty in using more analysis becomes apparent. This is a critical step that should not be omitted; otherwise, the process is flawed from the outset.

Before beginning the analysis, reviewing the model presented here as Figure 2.1, may be helpful. This chapter explores detailing the needs at the five levels described in the figure, beginning with payoff needs and progressing to preference needs. The objectives derived directly from these needs are defined, making a strong case for having multiple levels of objectives that correspond with specific needs. The right side of the model is essentially the ROI model presented in the previous chapter.

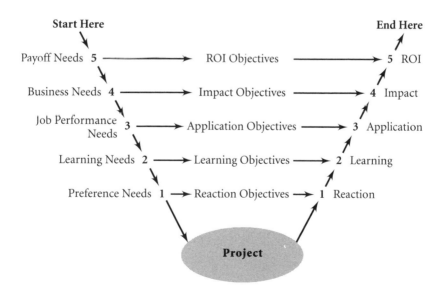

Figure 2.1. The ROI Methodology.

PAYOFF NEEDS

The initial step begins with a few crucial questions:

- Is this program worth doing?
- Does this address an issue worth pursuing?
- Is this an opportunity?
- Is it a feasible program?
- What is the likelihood of a positive ROI?

For proposed learning solutions that address significant problems or opportunities with potentially high rewards, the answers are obvious. The questions may take longer to answer for lower-profile programs or those for which the possible payoff is less apparent. In any case, these are legitimate questions, and the analysis can be simple or comprehensive. Figure 2.2 shows the potential payoff in monetary terms. A program's payoff will essentially be in either profit increases or in cost savings.

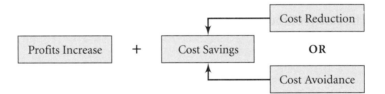

Figure 2.2. The Payoff Opportunity.

Profit increases are generated by programs that improve sales, increase market share, introduce new products, open new markets, enhance customer service, or increase customer loyalty. These should pay off with increases in sales revenue. Other revenue-generating measures include increasing memberships, increasing donations, obtaining grants, and generating tuition from new and returning students—all of which, after taking out the cost of doing business, leave a profitable benefit.

However, most programs will pay off with cost savings. Cost savings may be generated through cost reduction or cost avoidance. For example, learning and performance that improve quality, reduce cycle time, lower down time, decrease complaints, avoid employee turnover, and minimize delays are all examples of cost savings. When the goal is solving a problem, monetary value is often based on cost reduction.

Cost-avoidance programs are implemented to reduce risks, avoid problems, or prevent unwanted events. Some finance and accounting staff may view cost avoidance as an inappropriate measure for developing monetary benefits and calculating ROI. However, if the assumptions are correct, an avoided cost (for example, compliance fines) can be more rewarding than reducing an actual cost. Preventing a problem is more cost-effective than waiting for it to occur and then having to fix it.

Determining the potential payoff is the first step in the needs analysis process. This step is closely related to the next step, determining the business need, since the potential payoff is often based on a consideration of the business. Determining the payoff involves two factors: the potential monetary value derived from the business measure's improvement and the approximate cost of the program. Ascertaining these monetary values in detail usually yields a more credible forecast of what can be expected from the defined solution. However, this step may be omitted in situations in which the issue (business need) must be resolved regardless of the cost or if it is obviously a high-payoff activity.

The extent of the detail may also hinge on securing program funding. If the potential funding source does not see the value of the program compared to the potential costs, more detail may be needed to provide a convincing case for funding.

In summary, greater detail should be provided under the following circumstances:

- *When minimal support for the proposed program exists.* The payoff analysis can provide an estimated value of the improvement (or avoidance) and the potential contribution to business goals.
- *When the proposed program is anticipated to be very expensive.* Estimating the potential payoff is important before spending major resources on a program. Otherwise there is a danger of "throwing money at the solution."
- *When funding is needed for a program.* This is particularly true if the funding comes from external resources or when there is serious competition for internal funding sources.

- *When a key sponsor wants more analysis before the program moves forward.* Although he or she may support it enthusiastically, more analysis may solidify the sponsor's confidence in the proposed program and provide the needed information to secure final approval.

Knowledge of the potential payoff is not needed when most involved individuals agree that the payoff from the program will be high, or if the problem in question must be resolved regardless of the cost. For example, if the problem involves a safety concern, a regulatory compliance issue, or a competitive matter, then a detailed analysis is not needed.

Key Questions

To begin the analysis, several questions should be answered. Exhibit 2.1 presents some appropriate questions to ask about the proposed program. The answers may make the case for proceeding without analysis or indicate that additional analysis is needed. They may also show that the program is not needed. Understanding the implications of moving forward (or not) can reveal the legitimacy of the proposed program.

- Why is this an issue?
- What happens if we do nothing?
- Is this issue critical?
- Is this issue linked to strategy?
- Is it possible to correct it?
- Is it feasible to improve it?
- How much is it costing us?
- Can we find a solution?
- Are there multiple solutions?
- Who will support the program?
- Who will not support the program?
- How much will the solution(s) cost?
- How can we fund the program?
- Are there some important intangible benefits involved?
- Is there a potential payoff (positive ROI)?
- Is a forecast needed?

Exhibit 2.1. Key Questions to Ask About the Proposed Program.

The good news is that, for many potential programs, answers to these questions may be readily available. The need may have already been realized and the consequences might be validated. For example, many organizations with an employee retention problem for a critical talent group have calculated the cost of employee turnover—either developed from the existing data or secured from similar studies. With this cost in hand, the impact of the problem is known. The proposed program's cost can be compared to the problem's cost to get a sense of added value. The cost of the program can usually be estimated, if it is in a rough consideration at this point.

Obvious vs. Not So Obvious

The potential payoff is obvious for some programs but not so obvious for others. Exhibit 2.2 lists some opportunities with obvious payoffs. Each item is a serious problem that needs to be addressed by executives, administrators, or politicians. For these situations, moving to the business needs level would be safe. After the solution is developed at Level 3, a forecast may be appropriate.

- Excessive turnover of critical talent: 35 percent above benchmark data
- Very low market share in a market with few players
- Inadequate customer service: 3.89 on a 10-point customer satisfaction scale
- Safety record is among the worst in the industry
- This year's out-of-compliance fines total $1.2 million, up 82 percent from last year
- Excessive product returns: 30 percent higher than previous year
- Excessive absenteeism in call centers: 12.3 percent, compared to 5.4 percent industry average
- Sexual harassment complaints per 1,000 employees are the highest in the industry
- Grievances are up 38 percent from last year

Exhibit 2.2. Obvious Payoff Opportunities.

In other programs, the issues might be unclear and arise from political motives or biases. Exhibit 2.3 shows some opportunities for which the payoff may not be as obvious. The not-so-obvious opportunities need more detail. Some requests are common, as executives and administrators suggest a different process to change a dysfunctional process or to achieve vague or non-specific goals. The opportunities listed are common requests that can deliver value, but only if they are focused and clearly defined at the start. Some of the more open-ended and vague opportunities can pay off tremendously. In our work at the ROI Institute, we have seen most of these examples turn into valuable programs. Consequently, sometimes overlooking a vague request may be an injustice, because the program may be a valuable contribution if it is clearly defined, approved, and focused to secure the desired result.

- Improve leadership competencies for all managers
- Organize a business development conference
- Establish a project management office
- Provide job training for unemployed workers
- Develop highly effective employees
- Train all team leaders on crucial conversations
- Provide training on sexual harassment awareness for all associates
- Develop an "open-book" company
- Implement the same workout process that GE has used
- Become a technology leader
- Create a great place to work
- Implement a transformation program involving all employees
- Implement a career advancement program
- Create a wellness and fitness center
- Build capability for future growth
- Create an empowered workforce

Exhibit 2.3. Not-So-Obvious Payoff Opportunities.

The Reasons for New Programs

From the ROI perspective, the main reasons that programs fail are:

- They are not needed.
- They are not connected closely enough to a business issue to overcome the cost of the program.

A lack of initial business alignment brings into question the reasons for new program or project implementation. Exhibit 2.4 shows some of the main reasons new programs and projects are implemented.

Some of these appear to be legitimate reasons to move forward. If analysis supports a reason and it is credible, then it is probably needed. If a regulation requires it, then it must be implemented. The other reasons listed for a new program appear to be necessary, but they are necessary only if the program is implemented efficiently. For example, if a program supports new policies and practices; new equipment, procedures, or technology; or existing processes, it appears to be a legitimate request, but only if support for implementation exists.

1. An analysis was conducted to determine need.
2. A regulation requires it.
3. It appears to be a serious problem.
4. Management requests it.
5. It is a change that is needed.
6. Other organizations in industry have implemented it.
7. The topic is a trend.
8. It supports new policies and practices.
9. Staff members thought it was needed.
10. It supports new equipment, procedures, or technology.
11. It supports other processes such as Six Sigma, transformation, continuous process improvement, etc.
12. A best-selling book has been written about it.

Exhibit 2.4. **Reasons for Programs and Projects.**

Other reasons for a new program become suspect, and some are often misguided. For example, if other organizations have implemented a particular program or if it is based on a trend or touted in a best-selling book, it is suspect from the beginning. These are the types of programs that often do not add adequate value and create concerns about chasing a particular fad. Unfortunately, executives often pursue these programs in their never-ending desire to find the right solutions or to chase any new idea.

Determining Costs of the Problem

Problems are expensive and, once resolved, can have a tremendous impact. To determine the cost of the problem, the potential consequences of the problem must be examined and converted to monetary values.

Exhibit 2.5 shows a list of potential problems. Some can easily be converted to money, and some already are. Those that cannot be converted are left as intangibles. Inventory shortages often result in the direct cost of the inventory as well as the cost of carrying the inventory. Time can easily be translated into money by calculating the fully loaded cost of the individual's time spent on unproductive tasks. Calculating time for completing a program, task, or cycle involves measures that can be converted to money. Errors, mistakes, waste, delays, and bottlenecks can often be converted to money through their consequences. Productivity problems and inefficiencies, equipment damage, and equipment under use are other examples of easy conversions.

• Inventory shortages	• Incidents
• Time savings	• Excessive employee turnover
• Errors/mistakes	• Employee withdrawal
• Waste	• Accidents
• Delays	• Excessive staffing
• Bottlenecks	• Employee dissatisfaction
• Productivity problems	• Customer dissatisfaction
• Inefficiencies	• Excessive conflicts
• Excessive direct costs	• Tarnished image
• Equipment damage	• Lack of coordination
• Equipment underused	• Excessive stress
• Excessive program time	

Exhibit 2.5. Potentially Costly Problems.

When examining costs, considering *all* the costs and their implications is critical. For example, the full costs of accidents include not only the cost of lost workdays and medical expenses, but their effect on insurance premiums, the time required for investigations, damages to equipment, and the time of all employees who address the accident. The cost of a customer complaint includes the cost of the time in resolving the complaint, as well as the value of the item or service that is adjusted because of the complaint. The most important item is the cost of lost future business and goodwill from the complaining customer and potential customers who learn of the issue.

The Value of Opportunity

Just as the cost of a problem can be tabulated in most situations, the value of an opportunity can also be determined. Examples of opportunities include:

- Implementing a new process
- Installing new technology
- Upgrading the workforce for a more competitive environment

In these situations, a problem may not exist, but a tremendous opportunity to get ahead of the competition by taking immediate action may be available. Properly placing a value on this opportunity requires considering what may happen if the program is not pursued or taking into account the windfall that might be realized if the opportunity is seized. The monetary value is derived by following the different scenarios to convert specific business impact measures to money. The difficulty in this situation is ensuring a credible analysis. Forecasting the value of an opportunity takes into account many assumptions; whereas, calculating the value of a known outcome is often grounded in a more credible analysis.

To Forecast or Not to Forecast

Seeking and placing value on opportunity leads to an important decision: to forecast or not to forecast ROI. If the stakes are high and the support for the program is not in place, a detailed forecast may be the only way to gain needed support and funding for the program. When the forecast is pursued, the rigor of the analysis becomes an issue. In some cases, an informal forecast is provided, given certain assumptions about alternative outcome scenarios. In others, a detailed forecast is needed that involves collecting data from a variety of experts, using previous studies from another program or perhaps more sophisticated analysis.

Case Study, Part A

At this point, following a case study through the different levels of needs may be helpful. This section explores the analysis at Level 5, determining payoff needs. The following case study examines Southeast Corridor Bank (SCB), which operated branches in four states. (After expanding from a one-state operation to a multi-state network through a strategic acquisition campaign, SCB was acquired by Regions Bank, one of the nation's top ten banks.) Like many fast-growing organizations, SCB faced merger and integration problems, including excessive employee turnover. SCB's annual employee turnover was 57 percent, compared with an industry average of 26 percent. The first step in tackling the problem was answering these questions:

- Is this a problem worth solving?
- Is there a potential payoff to solving the problem?

To the senior vice president of human resources, the answers were clear. After reviewing several published studies about the cost of turnover, including one from a financial institution, he concluded that the cost of employee turnover ranged between 110 percent and 225 percent of annual pay. At the current rate, employee turnover was costing the bank more than $6 million per year. Lowering the rate to the industry average would save the bank at least $3 million annually. Although the structure and cost of the solution weren't known at this point, it became clear that this problem was worth solving. Unless the solution appeared to be very expensive, solving the problem would have a tremendous impact. This was all the analysis that was needed at this level. Level 4 will be discussed later.

BUSINESS NEEDS

Determining specific business needs is linked to the previous step in the needs analysis, developing the potential payoff. When determining the business needs, specific measures are pinpointed so that the business situation can be clearly assessed. The term "business" is used in governments, nonprofits, non-governmental organizations, and educational institutions, as well as in private-sector firms. Programs and projects in all types of organizations can show the money by improving productivity, quality, and efficiency, and by saving time and reducing costs.

Determining the Opportunity

A business need is represented by a business measure. Any process, item, or perception can be measured, and this measurement is critical to this level of analysis. If the program focuses on solving a problem, something clearly in the minds of program initiators, the measures are often obvious. If the program prevents a problem, the measures may also be obvious. If it takes advantage of a potential opportunity, the measures are usually still there. Otherwise, how will the opportunity be described? The important point is that measures are in the system, ready to be captured for this level of analysis. The challenge is to define the measures and to find them economically and swiftly.

Defining the Business Measure—Hard Data

To help focus on the desired measures, clarification between hard data and soft data is needed. Hard data are primary measures of improvement presented in rational, undisputed facts that are usually accumulated. They are the most desired type of data because they are easy to measure and quantify and are relatively easy to convert to monetary values. The ultimate criteria for measuring the effectiveness of an organization rests on hard data items—such as revenue, productivity, profitability, cost control, and quality assurance.

Hard data are objectively based and represent very common and credible measures of an organization's performance. Hard data can usually be grouped into four categories, as shown in Exhibit 2.6. These categories—output, quality, cost, and time—are typical performance measures in every organization, private-sector firm, government agency, non-governmental agency, nonprofit, and educational institution.

OUTPUT. The visible hard-data results from a particular program or project involve improvements in the output of the work unit, section, department, division, or entire organization. Every organization, regardless of type, must have basic measurements of output, whether they are the number of patients treated, students graduated, tons produced, packages shipped, or other production figures. Since these factors are monitored by organizations, changes can easily be measured by comparing before and after outputs. When programs are anticipated to drive an output measure, estimates of output changes can usually be made by those who are knowledgeable about the situation.

QUALITY. One of the most significant hard-data measure categories is quality. If quality is a major concern for the organization, processes are most likely in place to measure and monitor quality. Thanks in part to the rising popularity of quality-improvement processes (such as total-quality management, continuous quality improvement, and Six Sigma), tremendous success has been attained in pinpointing the correct

OUTPUT

Completion Rate

Units Produced

Tons Manufactured

Items Assembled

Money Collected

Items Sold

New Accounts Generated

Forms Processed

Loans Approved

Inventory Turnover

Patients Visited

Applications Processed

Students Graduated

Tasks Completed

Output Per Hour

Productivity

Work Backlog

Incentive Bonus

Shipments

COSTS

Shelter Costs

Treatment Costs

Budget Variances

Unit Costs

Cost by Account

Variable Costs

Fixed Costs

Overhead Cost

Operating Costs

Program Cost Savings

Accident Costs

Program Costs

Sales Expense

Participant Costs

TIME

Cycle Time

Equipment Downtime

Overtime

On-Time Shipments

Time to Program Completion

Processing Time

Supervisory Time

Time to Proficiency

Learning Time

Meeting Schedules

Repair Time

Efficiency

Work Stoppages

Order Response

Late Reporting

Lost Time Days

QUALITY

Failure Rates

Dropout Rates

Scrap

Waste

Rejects

Error Rates

Rework

Shortages

Product Defects

Deviation from Standard

Product Failures

Inventory Adjustments

Time Card Corrections

Incidents

Compliance Discrepancies

Agency Fines

Exhibit 2.6. Examples of Hard Data.

quality measures—and in many cases, with placing a monetary value on them. For programs or projects designed to improve quality, the results can be documented using the standard cost of quality as a value.

COST. Another important hard-data category is an improvement in cost. Many projects and programs are designed to lower, control, or eliminate the cost of a specific process or activity. Achieving these cost targets contributes immediately to the bottom line. Some organizations have an extreme focus on cost reduction. Consider Wal-Mart, whose tagline is "Always low prices. Always." The entire organization focuses on lowering costs on all processes and products and passing the savings along to customers. When direct cost savings are used, no efforts are necessary to convert data to monetary value. There can be as many cost items as there are accounts in a cost accounting system. In addition, costs can be combined in any number of ways to develop the costs needed for a particular program or project.

TIME. Time, which is becoming a critical measure in organizations, is also a hard-data category. Some organizations gauge their performance almost exclusively on time. For example, consider FedEx, whose tagline is "The World on Time." When asked what business FedEx is in, the company's top executives say, "We engineer time." For FedEx, time is so critical that it defines success or failure. Time savings may mean that a program is completed faster than originally planned, a product was introduced earlier, or the time to restore a network was reduced. These savings can translate into lower costs. In many organizations, it is an important measure, with projects and programs aimed directly at time savings.

Defining the Business Need—Soft Data

Hard data may lag behind changes and conditions in the human organization by many months. Therefore, supplementing hard data with soft data—such as attitude, motivation, and satisfaction—may be useful. Often more difficult to collect and analyze, soft data are used when hard data are not available or to supplement hard data. Soft data are also more difficult to convert to monetary values and are often subjective. They are less credible as a performance measurement and are often behavior oriented. Exhibit 2.7 shows common examples and types of soft data.

WORK HABITS
Tardiness
Visits to the Dispensary
Violations of Safety Rules
Communication Breakdowns
Excessive Breaks

WORK CLIMATE/SATISFACTION
Grievances
Discrimination Charges
Employee Complaints
Job Satisfaction
Organization Commitment
Employee Engagement
Employee Loyalty
Intent to Leave
Stress

INITIATIVE/INNOVATION
Creativity
Innovation
New Ideas
Suggestions
New Products and Services
Trademarks
Copyrights and Patents
Process Improvements
Partnerships
Alliances

CUSTOMER SERVICE
Customer Complaints
Customer Satisfaction
Customer Dissatisfaction
Customer Impressions
Customer Loyalty
Customer Retention
Customer Value
Lost Customers

EMPLOYEE DEVELOPMENT/ ADVANCEMENT
Promotions
Capability
Intellectual Capital
Programs Completed
Requests for Transfer
Performance Appraisal Ratings
Readiness
Networking

IMAGE
Brand Awareness
Reputation
Leadership
Social Responsibility
Environmental Friendliness
Social Consciousness
Diversity
External Awards

Exhibit 2.7. Examples of Soft Data.

WORK HABITS. Employee work habits are important to the success of work groups. Dysfunctional habits can lead to an unproductive and ineffective work group, while productive work habits can boost the group's output and morale. Some examples of work habits that may be difficult to measure or convert to monetary values were shown in Exhibit 2.7. The outcome of some work habits—including employee turnover, absenteeism, and accidents—are in the hard-data category because they are easy to convert to monetary values.

WORK CLIMATE/SATISFACTION. When employees are dissatisfied or the work climate is unfavorable, several measures can show the employees' discontent or dissatisfaction. Complaints and grievances are sometimes in the hard-data category because of their ease of conversion to money. However, most of the items are considered soft-data items. Job satisfaction, organizational commitment, and employee engagement show how attitudes shape the organization. Stress is often a by-product of a fast-paced work climate. These issues are becoming increasingly important.

CUSTOMER SERVICE. Because increased global competition fosters a greater need to serve and satisfy customers, more organizations are putting into place customer service measures that show the levels of customer satisfaction, loyalty, and retention. Few measures are as important as those linked to customers.

EMPLOYEE DEVELOPMENT/ADVANCEMENT. Employees are routinely developed, assigned new jobs, and promoted throughout organizations. Building capability, creating intellectual capital, enhancing readiness, and fostering networks are important processes. Many soft-data measures are available to indicate the consequences of those activities and processes.

INITIATIVE/INNOVATION. Creativity and innovation are critical processes within successful organizations. A variety of measures can be developed to show the creative spirit of employees and the related outcomes—such as ideas, suggestions, copyrights, patents, and products and services. While the collective creative spirit of employees may be a soft-data item, the outcomes of creativity and innovation may be placed in the hard-data category. Still, many executives consider innovation a soft-data item.

IMAGE. Perhaps some of the softest measures are in the image category. Executives are attempting to increase brand awareness, particularly with sales and marketing programs or projects. Reputation is another key area, as more organizations seek to improve their standing as a good employer, a good citizen, and a good steward of investors' money. Leadership is probably the most sought-after measure and is influenced by projects and programs designed to build leadership within the organization. Image, social responsibility, environmental friend-liness, and social consciousness are key outputs of a variety of pro-grams and projects aimed at making the organization well-rounded. Diversity is important for many organizations. Many programs are aimed at increasing diversity of ideas, products, people, and programs. Finally, external awards are the outcomes of many activities and pro-grams, often reflecting the external variation of an organization.

Using Tangible vs. Intangible—A Better Approach

The important issue with soft-data categories is the difficulty of con-verting them to monetary values. While some of the measures listed in Exhibit 2.7 could be converted to money, considering most of them soft-data items is more realistic and practical. It is important to remember that the definition of an intangible measure (based on the standards of the ROI methodology) is a measure that cannot be converted to money credibly or with minimum resources. If a soft-data measure can be con-verted to money, it becomes tangible. Data items that can be converted to money credibly using minimum resources are considered to be tangible and are reported as monetary values or placed in an ROI cal-culation. If a data item cannot be converted to money credibly with minimum resources, it is listed as an intangible measure; these are usu-ally referred to as the very soft categories. To avoid debates over what should be considered soft or hard data, the terms *tangible* and *intangible* will be used most often in this book. This is the best approach to pro-gram evaluation because the data classification is specific to the orga-nizational setting. Each organization determines whether a measure is tangible or intangible. For example, in most sales organizations, a mea-sure for customer satisfaction is easily available and costs little to ob-tain. Therefore, the measure is tangible because it can easily be converted to money. However, in other organizations where sales is not necessar-ily the focus, the measure is intangible.

Finding Sources of Impact Data

The sources of impact data, whether hard or soft, are plentiful. They come from routine reporting systems in the organization. In many sit-uations, these items have led to the need for the program or project. Exhibit 2.8 shows a sampling of the vast array of possible documents, systems, databases, and reports that can be used to select the specific measure or measures to monitor throughout the program.

Department records	Work unit reports
Human capital databases	Payroll records
Quality reports	Design documents
Manufacturing reports	Test data
Compliance reports	Marketing data
Sales records	Service records
Annual reports	Safety and health reports
Benchmarking data	Industry/trade association data
R&D status reports	Suggestion system data
Customer satisfaction data	Project management data
Cost data statements	Financial records
Scorecards	Dashboards
Productivity records	Employee engagement data

Exhibit 2.8. Sources of Data

Some program planners and program team members believe corporate data sources are scarce because the data are not readily available to them near their workplace or within easy reach through database systems. With a little determination and searching, the data can usually be identified. In our experience, more than 90 percent of the measures that matter to a specific program or project have already been developed and are readily available in databases or systems. Rarely do new data collection systems or processes have to be developed.

Identifying All the Measures

When searching for the proper measures to connect to the program and pinpoint business needs, considering all the possible measures that could be influenced is helpful. Sometimes, collateral measures move in harmony with the program. For example, efforts to improve safety may also improve productivity and increase job satisfaction. Thinking about the adverse impact on certain measures may also help. For example, when cycle times are reduced, quality may suffer; or when sales increase, customer satisfaction may deteriorate. Finally, program team members must prepare for unintended consequences and capture them as other data items that might be connected to or influenced by the program.

Exploring "What If. . . ?"

When settling on the precise business measures for the program, several "what if" scenarios can be examined. If the organization does nothing, understanding the potential consequences of inaction may be beneficial. In these cases, asking the following questions may help in understanding the consequences of inaction:

- Will the situation deteriorate?
- Will operational problems surface?
- Will budgets be affected?
- Will we lose influence or support?

Answers to these questions can help organizations settle on a precise set of measures with a hint of the extent to which the measures may change or improve.

At this level of analysis, understanding the process of typical work may be useful. Figure 2.3 shows a typical work cycle where there is input that leads to a process and then to an output (Langdon, 1995). Conditions are often imposed on the processes, and the outputs often cause unintended consequences. Finally, feedback on the processes and inputs is needed to make adjustments. When examining the full context of the work cycle, other measures could be identified that may influence the program. This is a way to see the complete processes and to pinpoint all the measures that may be connected to the project or program.

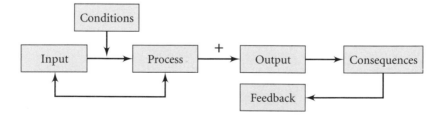

Figure 2.3. The Work Cycle.

Case Study, Part B

Let's return to the Southeast Corridor Bank (SCB), where employee turnover was excessive. After determining that the cost of turnover was high, the bank found that at least $3 million could be saved annually if turnover was lowered to the industry average. The specific measure in question was voluntary turnover: the number of employees leaving voluntarily divided by the average number of employees, expressed as a percent. Clearly defining the measure is important. Total turnover included voluntary and involuntary turnover. Using avoidable turnover can be useful, but SCB did not have the means to determine which involuntary turnovers could have been avoided. Still another possibility is turnovers classified as regrets and non-regrets. The difficulty with this measurement is that it is often a judgment call and may be based on a biased opinion. For example, if the manager of the departing employee labels the turnover as regrettable or non-regrettable, then a particular bias could enter the analysis.

Consequently, in the SCB case, voluntary turnover was used as the basis of the $3 million plus payoff. Still, with any measure that improves, other measures should also improve, depending on the specific solution. For example, staffing levels, job satisfaction, customer service, sales revenue, and other items may change. These are detailed more specifically when the solution is determined, which occurs in the next few steps.

JOB PERFORMANCE NEEDS

In the needs analysis, the next step is understanding what caused the business measure to miss its mark and not be where it should be. If the proposed program addresses a problem, this step focuses on the cause of the problem. If the program takes advantage of an opportunity, this step focuses on what is inhibiting the organization from taking advantage of that opportunity.

Analysis Techniques

This step may require using a variety of analytical techniques to uncover the causes of the problem or inhibitors to success. Exhibit 2.9 shows a brief listing of the many techniques used to uncover what can inhibit business measures. It is important to relate the issue to the organizational setting, to the behavior of the individuals involved, and to the functioning of various systems. These analytical techniques often use tools from problem solving, quality assurance, and performance improvement fields to search for these causes. Searching for multiple solutions is also important, since measures are often inhibited for several reasons. However, multiple solutions must be considered in terms of implementation—deciding whether they should be explored in total or tackled in priority order. The detailed approaches of all the techniques are contained in many references (Langdon, Whiteside, & McKenna, 1999). One such technique, nominal group technique, listed in Exhibit 2.9 is explored in the Southeast Corridor Bank Case Study, Part C.

• Statistical process control	• Diagnostic instruments
• Brainstorming	• Focus groups
• Problem analysis	• Probing interviews
• Cause-and-effect diagram	• Job satisfaction surveys
• Force-field analysis	• Engagement surveys
• Mind mapping	• Exit interviews
• Affinity diagrams	• Exit surveys
• Simulations	• Nominal group technique

Exhibit 2.9. Diagnostic Tools.

Taking a Sensible Approach

Considering the resources needed to examine records, research databases, and observe situations and individuals is important. Analysis takes time. The use of expert input, both internally and externally, can add to the cost and time of the evaluation. The needs at this level can vary considerably and may include:

• Ineffective behavior

• Dysfunctional work climate

• Inadequate systems

• Disconnected process flow

• Improper procedures

• Unsupportive culture

• Insufficient technology

• Unsupportive environment

These needs have to be uncovered using many of the methods listed in Exhibit 2.9. When needs vary and techniques are abundant, an opportunity exists for over-analysis and excessive costs. Consequently, a sensible approach must be taken.

Case Study, Part C

At the Southeast Corridor Bank (SCB), employee turnover was a serious problem, costing more than $6 million per year. The bank determined that it could save at least $3 million annually by reducing turnover, which would place it in line with the industry average. The specific measure is voluntary turnover. To uncover the actual need at Level 3, the cause of the problem had to be determined. Once the cause was known, a solution could be developed.

The nominal group technique was selected as the analysis method because it allowed unbiased input to be collected efficiently and accurately across the organization. A focus group was planned with twelve employees from each region, for a total of six groups representing all the regions. In addition, two focus groups were planned for the clerical staff in the corporate headquarters. This approach provided approximately a 10 percent sample and was considered to be a sufficient number to pinpoint the problem.

Focus group participants, who represented areas in which turnover was highest, described why their colleagues were leaving, not why they themselves would leave. Data were collected from individuals in a carefully structured format—during two-hour meetings at each location, using third-party facilitators—and were integrated and weighted so that the most important reasons were clearly identified. This process had the advantages of low cost and high reliability, as well as a low degree of bias. Only two days of external facilitator time were needed to collect and summarize the data for review.

The nominal group technique unfolded in ten steps:

1. The process steps were briefly described. A statement of confidentiality was presented. The importance of the participants' input was underscored so that they understood what they must do and the consequences for the bank.

2. Participants were asked to make a list of specific reasons why they felt their colleagues had left the bank and why others might leave. It was stressed that the question dealt with the actions or potential actions of employees other than themselves, although the bank realized that the participants' comments would probably reflect their own views (and that was what was actually needed).

3. In a round-robin format, each person revealed one reason for turnover, which was recorded on flip-chart paper. At this point, no attempt was made to integrate the issues, just to record the data on paper. The lists were placed on the walls so that, when this step was complete, as many as sixty items were listed and visible.

4. The next step was to consolidate and integrate the list. Some of the integration was easy because the items contained the same words and meanings. In other cases, ensuring that the meanings for the causes were the same before items were consolidated was important. When this process was complete, the list contained approximately thirty-five different reasons for turnover.

5. Participants were asked to review all the items, carefully select those they considered to be the top ten causes, and list them individually on index cards. Participants were asked not to concern themselves about which cause was number 1. (In this process, participants may become convinced that their original list was not complete or accurate or may identify other reasons for turnover.)

6. Participants ranked their top ten items by importance, with the first item as the most important.

7. In a round-robin format, each individual revealed his or her number 1 item, and 10 points were recorded on the flip-chart paper next to the item. Next, the number 2 reason was identified, and 9 points were recorded on the flip-chart paper next to the item. This process continued until all reasons had been revealed and points recorded.

8. The numbers next to each item were totaled. The item with the most points was the leading cause of turnover, and the one with the second-highest number of points was the second-most-important cause of turnover. This continued until the top fifteen causes had been captured based on the weighted average of causes of turnover from that group.

9. This process was completed for all six regional groups and the clerical staff groups. Trends began to emerge quickly from one group to the other.

10. The actual raw scores were then combined to integrate the results of the six regional focus groups and the clerical group.

The top fifteen scores were the top fifteen reasons for turnover across all the branches and clerical groups.

Here are the ten most important reasons given for turnover in the bank branches:

1. Lack of opportunity for advancement

2. Lack of opportunity to learn new skills and gain new product knowledge

3. Pay level not adequate

4. Not enough responsibility and empowerment

5. Lack of recognition and appreciation of work

6. Lack of teamwork in the branch

7. Lack of preparation for customer service problems

8. Unfair and unsupportive supervisor

9. Too much stress at peak times

10. Not enough flexibility in work schedules

While a similar list was developed for the clerical staff, the remainder of this case study will focus directly on the efforts to reduce turnover in the branch network. Branch turnover was the most critical issue, involving the highest turnover rates and the largest number of employees, and the focus group results provided a clear pattern of specific needs. Recognizing that not all the causes of turnover could be addressed immediately, the bank's management set out to work on the top five reasons while it considered a variety of options.

A skill-based pay system addressed the top five reasons for turnover. The program was designed to expand the scope of the jobs, with increases in pay for acquiring skills, and to provide a clear path for advancement and improvement. Jobs were redesigned from narrowly focused teller duties to an expanded job with a new title: the tellers all became banking representative I, II, or III. A branch employee would be considered a banking representative I if he or she could perform one or two simple tasks such as processing deposits and cashing checks.

As an employee at the banking representative I level took on additional responsibilities and performed different functions, he or she would be eligible for a promotion to banking representative II. If the representative could perform all the basic functions of the branch, including processing consumer loan applications, a promotion to banking representative III was appropriate. Training opportunities were available to help employees develop the needed job-related skills, and structured on-the-job training was provided through the branch managers, assistant managers, and supervisors. Self-study information was also available. The concept of performing multiple tasks was intended to broaden responsibilities and empower employees to perform a variety of tasks that would provide excellent customer service. Pay increases recognized skill acquisition, demonstrated accomplishment, and increased responsibility.

Although the skill-based system had some definite benefits from the employees' perspective, the bank also benefited. Not only was turnover expected to decline, but actual staffing levels were expected to be reduced in larger branches. In theory, if all employees in a branch could perform all the duties, fewer employees would be needed. Prior to this time, minimum staffing levels were required in certain critical jobs, and those employees were not always available for other duties.

In addition, the bank anticipated improved customer service. The new approach would prevent customers from having to wait in long lines for specialized services. For example, in the typical bank branch, long lines for special functions—such as opening a checking account, closing out a certificate of deposit, or taking a consumer loan application—were not unusual, but routine activities, such as paying bills and receiving deposits often required little or no waiting. With each employee performing all the tasks, shorter waiting lines would not only be feasible, but expected.

To support this new arrangement, the marketing department referred to the concept in its publicity about products and services. Included with checking account statements was a promotional piece labeled "In our branches there are no tellers." This document described the new process and stated that all the branch employees could perform all branch functions and consequently provide faster service.

LEARNING NEEDS

The job performance needs uncovered in the previous step often require a learning component to address them—such as when participants and team members must learn how to perform a task differently or learn how to use a process or a system. In some cases, learning is the principal solution, as in competency development, major technology changes, capability development, and system installations. In these situations, the learning becomes the actual solution. For other programs, learning is a minor solution and often involves simply understanding the process, procedure, or policy.

For example, when implementing a new ethics policy for an organization, the learning component requires understanding how the policy works and the participants' role in the policy. In short, a learning solution is not always needed, but all solutions have a learning component. A variety of approaches are available to measure specific learning needs. Often, multiple tasks and multiple jobs are involved in any program, and each should be addressed separately. Sometimes, the least-useful way to find out what skills and knowledge are needed is to ask the participants involved in implementing the program. They may not be sure of what is needed or may not know enough to provide adequate input.

Subject-Matter Experts

One of the most important approaches to determine learning needs is to ask the individuals who understand the process. They can best determine what skills and knowledge are necessary to address the job performance issues defined above. Then it may be appropriate to understand how much of the knowledge and skills already exist.

Job and Task Analysis

A job and task analysis is effective when a new job is created or when an existing job description changes significantly. As jobs are redesigned and the tasks must be identified, this technique offers a systematic way of detailing the job and task. Essentially, a job analysis collects and evaluates work-related information. A task analysis determines specific knowledge, skills, tools, and conditions necessary to perform a particular job. The primary objective of a job and task analysis is to gather information about the scope, responsibilities, and tasks related to a particular job or new responsibilities. In the context of developing learning needs, this information is useful because it helps in preparing job profiles and job descriptions. These descriptions, in turn, serve as a platform for linking job requirements to specific information or training needs.

Performing a job and task analysis not only helps the individuals who will use the program develop a clear picture of their responsibilities, but will also indicate what is expected of them. The amount of time needed to complete a job and task analysis can vary from a few days to several months, depending on the complexity of the program. It involves identifying high performers, preparing a job analysis questionnaire, and developing other materials as necessary to collect information. During the job analysis, job responsibilities are defined, tasks are detailed, and specific learning requirements are identified (Gupta, 1999).

Observations

Current practices and procedures in an organization may have to be observed to understand the situation as the program is implemented. This often indicates the level of capability as well as the correct procedures. Observing is an established and respected data collection method. Observations can be used to examine work flow and interpersonal interactions, including those between management and team members. Sometimes, the observer is unknown to those being observed (placed in the environment specifically to observe the current processes). At other times, the observer is someone previously in the work environment but now in a different role. Another possibility is that the observer is invisible to those being observed. Examples include retail mystery shoppers, electronic observation, or individuals who have joined a group temporarily but have been there long enough to be considered part of the team. The advantages of observation as a data collection tool are described in Chapter Six. Here, it is important to remember that observation can be a tool used to uncover what individuals need to know or do as a program is changed.

Demonstrations

In some situations, having employees demonstrate their abilities to perform a certain task, process, or procedure is important. The demonstration can be as simple as a skill practice or role play, or as complex as an extensive mechanical or electronic simulation. The issue is to use this as a way of determining whether employees know how to perform a particular process. From that, specific learning needs can evolve.

Tests

Testing as a needs assessment process is not used as frequently as other methods, but can be very useful. Employees are tested to find out what they know about a particular situation. This information helps guide learning issues. For example, in one hospital chain, management was concerned that employees were not aware of the company's policy on sexual harassment or what actions constitute sexual harassment. In the early stages of the program analysis, a group of supervisors and managers, the target audience for the program, were given a twenty-item test about their knowledge of the sexual harassment policy (ten items) and knowledge about sexual harassment actions (ten items). The test scores revealed where insufficient knowledge existed and formed the basis of a program to reduce the number sexual harassment complaints.

Management Assessment

When implementing programs in organizations in which there is an existing manager or team leader, input from the management team may be used to assess the current situation and the knowledge and skills required by the new situation. This input can be collected through surveys, interviews, or focus groups. It can be a rich source of information about what the users of the program, if it is implemented, will need to know to make it a success.

Where the learning component is minor, learning needs are simple. Determining the specific learning needs can be very time-consuming for major programs for which new procedures, technologies, and processes are developed. As in the previous step, it is important not to spend excessive time analyzing at this early stage in the process but to collect as much data as possible with minimum resources.

Case Study, Part D

Now, we return to Southeast Corridor Bank (SCB), where an employee turnover reduction program was proposed to save the bank at least $3 million annually. At the Level 2 needs assessment, learning needs fell into two categories. First, for each learning program designed to build the skills of employees to be promoted, both skill acquisition and knowledge increase needs were identified. These learning measurements were self-assessment, testing, demonstrations, and others, and were connected to each specific program.

The second learning need was the need for employees to understand how the new program worked. As the program was introduced in meetings with all employees, a simple measurement of learning was necessary to capture the employees' understanding of the following issues:

• Why the program is being pursued

• What employees must do to be successful in the program

• How promotion decisions are made

• The timing of various aspects of the program

These major learning needs were identified and were connected specifically with the solution being implemented.

PREFERENCE NEEDS

The final level of needs analysis is based on preferences, which drive the program requirements. Essentially, individuals prefer certain processes, schedules, or activities for the structure of the learning and performance improvement program or project. The preferences define how the particular program will be implemented. If the program is a solution to a problem, this step defines how the solution will be installed. If the program addresses an opportunity, this step outlines how the opportunity will be addressed, taking into consideration the preference needs of those involved in the program.

Key Issues

Exhibit 2.10 shows the typical preference needs. These represent statements that define the parameters of the program in terms of timing, budget, staffing, location, technology, and extent of disruption allowed. Although everyone involved will have certain needs or preferences for the program, implementation is based on the input of several stakeholders rather than that of one individual. For example, participants involved in the program (those who must make it work) may have a particular preference, but their preference could exceed resources, time, and budget requirements. The immediate manager's input may help minimize the amount of disruption and maximize resources. The funds that can be allocated are also a constraining resource. The urgency for program implementation may create a constraint in the preferences. Those who support or own the program often place preferences around the program in terms of timing, budget, and the use of technology. Because this is a Level 1 need, the program structure and solution will directly relate to the reaction objectives and to the initial reaction to the program.

We need for this evaluation to be:	Parameter
Initiated by March 1	Timing
Completed by September 1	Timing
Within 3 percent of estimated budget	Budget
Under $400,000 total funding	Budget
Implemented with one additional staff member in each region	Staffing
Using current associates only	Staffing
Piloted in three locations	Location
Implemented for marketing only	Location
Using blended learning	Technology
Integrated with existing online systems	Technology
Implemented without disruption of work	Disruption
Seamless with our customers	Disruption

Exhibit 2.10. Typical Preference Needs.

Impact Studies

When conducting evaluations at the impact and ROI levels, there can never be too much detail. Some evaluations go astray and fail to reach their full success because of misunderstandings and differences in expectations. Several key issues should be addressed before the evaluation begins. These issues are often outlined in the program proposal or planning documentation. Regardless of when or for what purpose it is developed, each area listed below should be described in some way. More important, the sponsor and the evaluator need to agree on these issues.

SCOPE. The scope of the evaluation program needs to be clearly defined. Exhibit 2.11 shows typical scoping issues that should be determined for the program. Perhaps the evaluation is limited to certain employee groups, a specific sector, a functional area of the business, a specific location, a unique type of system, or a precise time frame. Sometimes, constraints are placed on the type of data collected or on access to certain individuals, such as customers. Whatever the scope, it should be defined in this section.

• Audience for the program	• Access to stakeholders
• Location of target group	• Functional area for coverage
• Time frame for the program	• Product line for coverage
• Technology used	• Type of process/activity

Exhibit 2.11. Typical Program Scoping Issues.

TIMING. Timing is critical, as it shows when activities will occur. This is not only the timing of the delivery of the final program report, but the timing of particular evaluation steps and events—including when data are needed, analyzed, and reported and when presentations are made. Exhibit 2.12 lists typical timing issues.

• Start of program	• Specific data collection issues (pilot testing, executive interviews)
• Solutions developed	
• Data collection design complete	• Data analysis complete
• Evaluation design complete	• Preliminary results available
• Data collection begins	• Report developed
• Data collection complete	• Report presented to management

Exhibit 2.12. Typical Evaluation Timing Events.

PROGRAM DELIVERABLES. The sponsor needs to know what will be delivered when the evaluation program is completed in terms of reports, documents, presentations, summaries, or flowcharts. Whatever the specific deliverables, they are clearly defined at this step. Most programs have a final report but often go much further, delivering a variety of communication pieces.

STEPS, PHASES, OR STAGES. The specific steps, phases, or stages that will occur should be defined, showing key milestones. This provides the sponsor with a step-by-step understanding and tracking of the evaluation. With this in place, the sponsor, at any given time, can see not only where progress is made, but where the program will go next.

PROGRAM RESOURCES. This step defines the resources required for evaluation. It could include access to individuals, vendors, technology, equipment, facilities, competitors, or customers. All resources that may be needed should be listed, along with amounts and timing.

COST. The specific costs for the evaluation, tied to the different steps of the process, are included. Sometimes, evaluators are reluctant to provide detailed costs because doing so exposes the actual program cost and reveals some of the mystery of the process. A better approach is to be very open with the fees, showing the different steps and issues relative to the costs. In general, sponsors will appreciate this openness, which sets the stage for a trusting relationship with all stakeholders.

Case Study, Part E

Now we return to the Southeast Corridor Bank (SCB) program, where the focus was on employee turnover reduction, with a tremendous opportunity for a $3 million annual cost savings. The program involved a major solution, skill-based pay, which addressed the top five reasons why employees were leaving the bank. As the program was rolled out and as a solution was developed, the preference needs were defined. The preference needs involved several issues. The program was to be rolled out as soon as possible so that its effects could be translated into lower employee turnover. All the training programs must be in place and made available to employees. The amount of time employees must spend away from their jobs to attend training was an issue, and the managers had some control over when the resulting promotions would occur. This process did not need to drag out for too long; otherwise it would disappoint employees who were eager to be trained and promoted. At the same time, the staffing and workload issues had to be balanced so that the appropriate amount of time was devoted to training and skill building. More specifically, when the program was announced, the desired employee reaction was defined. Program leaders wanted employees to view the program as very challenging, motivational, rewarding, fair, and a good investment in their futures. These needs easily translated into the solution design as well as the reaction detailed objectives.

LEVELS OF OBJECTIVES FOR PROGRAMS

Learning and performance improvement programs are driven by objectives. In some situations, the program is aimed at implementing a solution to address a particular dilemma, problem, or opportunity. In other situations, the initial program is designed to develop a range of feasible solutions, or one desired solution prior to implementation. Regardless of the program or project, multiple levels of objectives are necessary. These levels of objectives, ranging from qualitative to quantitative, define precisely what will occur as a program is implemented. Exhibit 2.13 shows the different levels of objectives briefly discussed in Chapter One. These objectives are so critical that they need special attention in their development and use.

Levels of Objectives	Focus of Objectives
Level 1. Reaction and Planned Action	Defines a specific level of reaction to the project or program as it is revealed and communicated to stakeholders
Level 2. Learning and Confidence	Defines specific skills and knowledge needed to implement the project or program
Level 3. Application and Implementation	Defines key issues for successful use of skills and application and implementation of the program
Level 4. Business Impact and Consequences	Defines the specific business measures that will change or improve as a result of the program
Level 5. ROI	Defines the specific return on investment from the implementation of the program, comparing program costs to monetary benefits

Exhibit 2.13. Multiple Levels of Objectives.

Reaction and Planned Action

For any program to be successful, various stakeholders must react favorably—or at least not negatively—toward the program. Ideally, the stakeholders should be satisfied with the program and see its value. This creates a win-win relationship for all stakeholders. Exhibit 2.14 shows some of the typical areas for specific reaction objectives. This information must be obtained routinely during the program so that feedback can be used to make adjustments, keep the program on track, and perhaps even redesign certain parts.

• Usefulness of materials	• Motivational effect of content
• Relevance of content	• Perceived support for the program
• Importance to success	• Intent to use content
• Perceived value	• Amount of new information
• Program necessity	• Overall satisfaction with the program
• Program appropriateness	

Exhibit 2.14. Typical Areas for Reaction Objectives.

Developing reaction objectives should be straightforward and relatively easy. The objectives reflect immediate and long-term satisfaction and explore issues important to program success. They also form the basis for evaluating the chain of impact. In addition, they emphasize planned action, when feasible and useful. Exhibit 2.15 provides some key issues about developing reaction objectives.

THE BEST REACTION OBJECTIVES
- Identify issues that are important and measurable
- Are attitude-based, clearly worded, and specific
- Specify what the participant has changed in thinking about the program
- Underscore the linkage between attitude and the success of the program
- Represent a satisfaction index from key stakeholders
- Can predict program success

KEY QUESTIONS ARE
- How relevant is the program?
- How important is the program?

Exhibit 2.15. Developing Reaction Objectives.

- Are the facilitators effective?
- How appropriate is the program?
- Is this new information?
- Is the program rewarding?
- Will you implement the program?
- Will you use the concepts/advice?
- What would keep you from implementing objectives from the program?
- Would you recommend the program to others?

Exhibit 2.15. Developing Reaction Objectives, Cont'd.

Learning Objectives

Every program or project involves at least one learning objective and usually more. With major skill-building programs, the learning component is incredibly important. In other situations, such as the implementation of a new policy, the learning component is minor but necessary. To ensure that the various stakeholders learn what they need to know to make the program successful, learning objectives are developed. Exhibit 2.16 shows some typical learning objectives.

Learning objectives are critical to measuring learning because they communicate the expected outcomes of learning and define the

After completing the learning session, participants will be able to:

- Identify the six features of the new ethics policy
- Demonstrate the use of each software routine in the standard time
- Use problem-solving skills when faced with a problem
- Know whether they are eligible for the early retirement program
- Score 75 or better on the new-product quiz
- Demonstrate success with all five customer interaction skills
- Explain the value of diversity in a work group
- Document and submit suggestions and ideas for award consideration
- Score at least 9 out of 10 on a sexual harassment policy quiz
- Identify five new technology trends explained at the conference
- Name the six pillars of the division's new strategy
- Successfully complete the leadership simulation

Exhibit 2.16. Typical Learning Objectives.

desired competence or performance necessary for program success. Learning objectives provide a focus for participants, indicating what they must learn and do—sometimes with precision. Developing learning objectives is straightforward. The key issues are presented in Exhibit 2.17.

Learning objectives are critical to measuring learning because they:
- Communicate expected outcomes from learning
- Describe competent performance that should be the result of learning
- Provide a basis for evaluating learning
- Focus on learning for participants

The best learning objectives:
- Describe behaviors that are observable and measurable
- Are outcome-based, clearly worded, and specific
- Specify what the participant must do as a result of the program
- Have three components:
    Performance—what the participant will be able to do during the program
    Condition—circumstances under which the participant will perform the task
    Criteria—degree or level of proficiency that is necessary to perform the job

Three types of learning objectives are:
- Awareness—familiarity with terms, concepts, and processes
- Knowledge—general understanding of concepts and processes
- Performance—ability to demonstrate a skill, at least at a basic level

Exhibit 2.17. Developing Learning Objectives.

Application and Implementation Objectives

As the program is implemented, the application and implementation objectives clearly define what is expected and often to what level of performance. Application levels are similar to learning objectives but reflect actual use on the job. They also involve specific milestones, indicating when part or all of the process is implemented. Exhibit 2.18 shows typical application objectives.

When the program is implemented . . .

- At least 99.1 percent of software users will be following the correct sequences after three weeks of use

- Within one year, 10 percent of employees will submit documented suggestions for saving costs

- The average 360-degree leadership assessment score will improve from 3.4 to 4.1 on a 5-point scale

- 95 percent of high-potential employees will complete individual development plans within two years

- Employees will routinely use problem-solving skills

- Sexual harassment activity will cease within three months after the zero-tolerance policy is implemented

- 80 percent of employees will use one or more of the three cost-containment features of the health-care plan

- 50 percent of conference attendees follow up with at least one contact from the conference

- Pharmaceutical sales reps have communicated adverse effects of a specific prescription drug to all physicians in their territories

- Managers will initiate three workout projects

- Sales and customer service representatives use all five interaction skills with at least half the customers

Exhibit 2.18. Typical Application Objectives.

Application objectives are critical because they describe the expected outcomes in the intermediate area—between the learning of new tasks and procedures and the impact that the learning will deliver. Application and implementation objectives describe how things should be or the state of the workplace after the program is implemented. They provide a basis for the evaluation of on-the-job changes and performance. They emphasize what has occurred on the job as a result of the program.

Exhibit 2.19 shows the key issues involved in developing application objectives. Application objectives have almost always been included to some degree in programs or projects, but have not always been as specific as they could be or need to be. To be effective, they must clearly define the expected environment in the workplace following the successful program implementation.

THE BEST APPLICATION OBJECTIVES

- Identify behaviors, tasks, and actions that are observable and measurable
- Are outcome-based, clearly worded, and specific
- Specify what the participant will change, or has changed, as a result of the program
- May have three components:

  Performance—what the participant has changed or accomplished at a specified follow-up time

  Condition—circumstances under which the participant performed the task, procedures, or action

  Criteria—degree or level of proficiency under which the task or job was performed

KEY QUESTIONS ARE

- What new or improved *knowledge* was applied to the job?
- What new or improved *skill* was applied to the job?
- What is the *frequency of skill* application?
- What new *tasks* will be performed?
- What new *steps* will be implemented?
- What new *action items* will be implemented?
- What new *procedures* will be implemented or changed?
- What new *guidelines* will be implemented or changed?
- What new *processes* will be implemented or changed?

Exhibit 2.19. Developing Application Objectives.

Business Impact Objectives

Learning and development and performance improvement programs should drive one or more business impact measures. Impact objectives represent key business measures that should be improved as the application and implementation objectives are achieved. Exhibit 2.20 shows typical business impact objectives. Business impact objectives are critical to measuring business performance because they define the ultimate expected outcomes of the program. They describe business-unit performance that should be connected to the program. Above all, impact objectives emphasize achieving bottom-line results that key client groups expect and demand. Exhibit 2.21 shows key steps in developing impact objectives.

After completion of this program, the following conditions should be met:

- Grievances should be reduced from three per month to no more than two per month at the Golden Eagle tire plant.
- The average number of new accounts opened at Great Western Bank should increase from 300 to 350 per month.
- Tardiness at the Newbury foundry should decrease by 20 percent within the next calendar year.
- There should be an across-the-board reduction in overtime for front-of-house managers at Tasty Time restaurants in the third quarter of this year.
- Employee complaints should be reduced from an average of three per month to an average of one per month at Guarantee Insurance headquarters.
- The average number of product defects should decrease from 214 per month to 153 per month at all Amalgamated Rubber extruding plants in the Midwest region
- The company-wide job satisfaction index should rise by 2 percentage points during the next calendar year.
- Sales expenses for all titles at Proof Publishing Company should decrease by 10 percent in the fourth quarter.
- There should be a 10 percent increase in Pharmaceuticals Inc. brand awareness among physicians during the next two years.

Exhibit 2.20. Typical Business Impact Objectives.

The best impact objectives:

- Must contain measures that are linked to the skills and knowledge gained as a result of the program
- Describe measures that are easily collected
- Are results-based, clearly worded, and specific
- Specify what the participant has accomplished in the business unit as a result of the program

Four types of impact objectives involving hard data are:

- Output-focused
- Quality-focused
- Cost-focused
- Time-focused

Three common types of impact objectives involving soft data are:

- Customer-service focused
- Work-climate focused
- Job-satisfaction focused

Exhibit 2.21. Developing Business Impact Objectives.

ROI Objectives

The fifth level of objectives for programs is the acceptable return on investment (ROI), the monetary impact. These objectives define the expected payoff from the program and compare the input resources (the cost of the program) to the value of the ultimate outcome (the monetary benefits). An ROI objective is typically expressed as an acceptable return on investment percentage that compares the annual monetary benefits minus the cost, divided by the actual cost, and is multiplied by one hundred. A 0 percent ROI indicates a break-even program. A 50 percent ROI indicates that the cost of the program is recaptured and an additional 50 percent "earnings" (fifty cents for every dollar invested) is achieved.

For some programs, the ROI objective is larger than what might be expected from the ROI of other expenditures—such as the purchase of a new company, a new building, or major equipment. However, the two are related, and the calculation is the same for both. For many organizations, the ROI objective for a learning or performance improvement program is set slightly higher than the ROI expected from other "routine investments" because of the relative newness of applying the ROI concept to these types of programs. For example, if the expected ROI from the purchase of a new company is 20 percent, the ROI from a new team leader development program might be in the 25 percent range. The important point is that the ROI objective should be established up-front and in coordination with the sponsor.

The Importance of Specific Objectives

Developing specific objectives at different levels for projects and programs provides important benefits. First, they provide direction to the participants directly involved in making the program work—to help keep them on track. Objectives define exactly what is expected at different timeframes and show the ultimate outcomes of the program. Objectives provide guidance for the facilitators so that they understand the ultimate goal and impact of the program. They also provide information and motivation for the program designers and developers as they see the implementation and impact outcomes. In most programs, multiple stakeholders are involved and will influence the results. Specific objectives provide goals and motivation for the stakeholders so that they see the gains that should be achieved. Objectives provide important information to help the key sponsor groups clearly understand how the landscape will look when the program is successful. Finally, from an evaluation perspective, objectives provide a basis for measuring the success of the program.

FINAL THOUGHTS

This chapter outlines the beginning of the ROI methodology. It shows how learning and performance improvement programs can be structured from the outset, with detailed needs identified, ultimately leading to program objectives at five levels. This kind of detail ensures that the program is aligned with business needs and is results-focused throughout the process. Without this analysis, the program runs the risk of not delivering the value that it should, or failing to align with one or more business objectives. These steps are tedious but essential for success. They are systematic and structured. When followed in a disciplined and determined way, they can make a program highly successful. The chapter began by defining payoff needs and addressing the question, "Is the proposed program worthwhile?" Next, specific business needs were identified, followed by the identification of job performance needs. Job performance needs, in their simplest sense, say, "Here is what must change for this business measure to improve." They define what should be accomplished to make that happen. Then the learning and preference needs were identified to round out the five levels of needs. Next, the objectives were detailed, with guidance on developing objectives and typical objectives given for each level. The output of this chapter is objectives, which provide a focus for designers, developers, and facilitators, as well as participants and users who must make the program successful.

References

Gupta, K. (1999). *A practical guide to needs assessment.* San Francisco, CA: Jossey-Bass.

Langdon, D. (1995). *The new language of work.* Amherst, MA: HRD Press.

Langdon, D., Whiteside, K., & McKenna, M. (Eds.). (1999). *Intervention resource guide: 50 performance improvement tools.* San Francisco, CA: Pfeiffer.

CHAPTER THREE

Measuring Inputs and Indicators

The initial category of data presented in this book, briefly described in Chapter One, is presented in this chapter. Inputs and Indicators are the first step in capturing data about learning and development and performance improvement programs. For some, this is the principal type of data collected for learning and development. For example, the annual industry reports published by *Training* magazine and the American Society for Training and Development (ASTD) are dominated by this type of data. The ASTD annual report, for example, devotes about 90 percent of the document to this level of data. Critics of these data emphasize that this is only the input, and they accuse the learning and development community of trying to substitute input data for output. While knowing what's committed to the process is more important, knowing the output measures is equally important. Regardless of the position, the input is a set of measures that is needed.

This chapter highlights some of the more common measures, including tracking people, hours, jobs, areas, topics, programs, requests, and training delivery. It also explores the importance of tracking the costs in a variety of ways and presenting how the learning and development and performance improvement functions have been managed. The chapter ends with key concerns and issues about this type of data.

MEASURING INPUT AND INDICTORS

While there is some debate over the importance of this level of data, few would say that it is not needed. Inputs and indicators are an important first step in the analysis and provide data that show insight, commitment, and support for the learning and development function.

Defines the Input

The set of measures included in this category represents the beginning of the process. It shows what is put into the process in terms of energy, effort, cost, and time. In the early days of formal learning and development and performance improvement evaluation, this category of data was the only data presented. Unfortunately, it is still the dominant method used by some, although it is changing.

Reflects Commitment

For some organizations, the amount of input reflects commitment and support for learning and development. This is particularly helpful for industries and organizations in which the commitment is quite low. Often, the executives in these organizations boast about the amount of commitment to learning, indicating the statistics such as the total number of people trained, the number of hours, the cost as a percent of employee compensation, and other impressive measures to show the amount of resources allocated to this effort. A few organizations prefer not to measure the consequences of learning, but to invest heavily, hoping that the money will be spent wisely and used appropriately to deliver the desired results.

Facilitates Benchmarking

This level of data represents the most common benchmarking data— it's easy to count. In several organizations, these data must be counted because they are part of the budgeting and cost control processes. Consequently, these data dominate benchmarking. As the opening paragraph described, even some of the best benchmarking sources, such as ASTD and *Training* magazine, devote much of their coverage to this level of data. When these data are collected from those organizations that represent best practices, then the benchmark becomes more meaningful.

Two important benchmarking studies that should be consulted are available in the United States. The first is available from the ASTD. ASTD presents benchmarking data from its benchmarking survey of about three hundred organizations. These are voluntary participants in the survey. This is probably closest to the U.S. norm. ASTD also collects data from their benchmarking forum, which includes some twenty-five or thirty organizations. These are individuals who are very serious about measurement and provide ample data throughout the annual membership process. Also, ASTD includes data from their BEST award winners. The BEST programs are their rewards system, and winners are selected through a rigorous, blind review process. Usually, twenty-five or thirty are in the sample. These data are collected annually and contain dozens of data sets, some of which are described in this chapter.

The second benchmarking report is published by *Training* magazine. The 2005 annual report represented the twenty-fourth publication of this industry report. The participants for this study included organizations listed in Dunn & Bradstreet's database of U.S. organizations. The 2005 report contained 1,488 participants, and this report is regarded by some as the most effective benchmarking data. Some of the measures included in the annual report are reflected in this chapter.

Explains Coverage

An important consideration for organizations is to make sure that the correct individuals receive the proper learning and development and that performance improvement programs are engaged in the proper areas. Tracking inputs and indicators shows where learning and development and performance improvement are being applied and used by job function, by area, by topic, and a variety of other areas. This helps management to understand what is being achieved and to identify gaps or necessary adjustments.

Highlights Efficiencies

An important consideration is the way that the investment in learning and development is used and managed. A variety of efficiencies can be captured to indicate the extent to which processes are streamlined, deadlines and cycle times are being met, and the organization is operating on a lean basis, with a constant focus on improving efficiencies and effectiveness throughout the organization. The learning and development function must do its part to show that it is being properly managed. Also, many of the efficiencies focus on the length of time taken to accomplish certain tasks. This responsiveness to clients is often an important measure of customer service.

Provides Cost Data

Many influences have increased attention on the accurate monitoring of learning and development costs. Every organization should know how much money is spent on development. Although comparisons are difficult to make because of differing bases for cost calculations, many organizations calculate this expenditure and make comparisons. Some organizations calculate training and development (T&D) costs as a percentage of payroll and set targets for increased investment. In the United States, the average is about 2 percent, whereas in Europe, Asia, and Latin America, the average is higher.

An effective system of cost monitoring allows an organization to calculate the magnitude of its total expenditures. Collecting this information also helps top management answer two important questions:

1. How much do we spend on learning and development compared with other organizations?
2. How much should we spend on learning and development?

The learning and development staff must know the relative cost effectiveness of programs and their components. Monitoring costs by program allows the staff to evaluate the relative contribution of a program and to determine how those costs change. If a program's cost rises, reevaluating the program's impact and overall success might be appropriate. Comparing specific components of costs with those of other programs or organizations may also be useful. For example, the cost per participant for one program could be compared with the cost per participant for a similar program. Huge differences may indicate a problem. Also, costs associated with design, development, or delivery could be compared with those of other programs within the organization and used to develop cost standards.

Accurate costs are necessary to predict future costs. Historical costs for a program provide the basis for predicting future costs of similar programs or budgeting for programs. Sophisticated cost models make estimating and predicting costs with reasonable accuracy possible.

When a return on investment or benefit/cost analysis is needed for a specific program, costs must be developed. One of the most important reasons for collecting costs is to obtain data for use in a benefit/cost comparison. In this comparison, cost data are as important as the program's economic benefits.

To improve the efficiency of the learning and development function, controlling costs is essential. Competitive pressures place increased attention on efficiencies. Most learning and development departments have monthly budgets with cost projections listed by various accounts and, in some cases, by program. Cost monitoring is a valuable tool for identifying problem areas and taking corrective action. In the practical and classical management sense, the accumulation of cost data is a necessity.

Capturing costs is challenging because the figures must be accurate, reliable, and realistic. Although most organizations develop costs with much more ease than they develop the economic value of benefits, the true cost of learning and development is often an elusive figure, even in some of the best organizations. While the total direct budget is usually an easily developed number, determining the specific costs of a program, including the indirect costs related to it, is more difficult. To develop a realistic ROI, costs must be accurate and credible. Otherwise, the painstaking difficulty and attention to the benefits will be wasted because of inadequate or inaccurate costs.

TRACKING PARTICIPANTS

The most obvious place to start with input is by tracking the people involved. Several measures may be important to show the impact that learning and development has throughout the organization. The first measure, total number trained, is the actual number of participants in a formal, organized, learning and development function or activity. This can also be expressed as a percent of total employees. Ideally, all employees, or at least the vast majority, would be involved in some type of learning activity. The sheer number of people can also be divided into different categories. For example, showing participants of learning and development by age presents interesting data. Mike Johnson advocates reporting activities and efforts in this area along six categories.

- Twinkies (still at college and under 20);
- Point 'n Clickers (20 to 25);
- Generation X (25 to 35);
- Middle-Aged and Manic (35 to 45);
- Growing Old Frantically (45 to 55);
- Grey Tops (55 and over).

While this may be a bit overboard for some, it underscores the importance of presenting data by key groups in the organization. Some of these groups represent important challenges for the learning and development community. The Point 'n Clickers and the Generation X will need different types of learning approaches than the older generations. Some will prefer classroom activity, while others will prefer online learning (Johnson, 2002).

Another way to count people is to divide them by gender. Some organizations want to ensure that upward mobility exists for all employees, particularly females. The glass ceiling is still alive and well in many organizations, and to prepare females for opportunities will require not only appropriate learning and development programs but an appropriate number of female participants.

Extending beyond gender and providing the numbers of participants in learning and development by diversity categories (race, national origin) are important considerations. Programs must be in place to ensure that minorities are involved and are provided opportunities to further their careers.

Still other indicators, such as participants divided by specific tenure, could be helpful. In this case, the most important issue is to ensure that those with the least tenure receive the most development, and this is contrary to the situation in some organizations. For example, Caltex, a very large petroleum organization based in Asia, had a particular problem based on some cultural issues. When new training opportunities became available, the most-senior people would attend, and sometimes the funding may run out before the least-senior people attended. The reverse situation should occur, with the least-senior people receiving the training. Carefully monitoring the data over a period of time enabled the learning and development team to make adjustments, even though many of the most-senior employees wanted to attend.

TRACKING HOURS

Tracking participants is important, and tracking the time they spend participating is one of the most common measures for benchmarking learning and development. Some organizations may track the total hours participating to create an impressive figure of the amount of time that participants spend in learning and development programs. A more appropriate measure would be the hours spent per person, targeting a particular amount of learning and development for a particular job or job group. Consequently, breaking the number of hours down into job or job groups and even functional areas is more meaningful. Still others track the number of hours involved by various diversity groups, including age, gender, and race. Some organizations make a commitment for an average number of hours per person. While this is an admirable goal, it may create more activity than actual change.

One organization, a large automotive company based in the United States, developed a policy that each employee would have a minimum of 120 hours of learning each year. This policy was implemented to support learning and development and send a message to the management team that learning was important. Also, executives envisioned that employees would need to learn multiple skills to operate in a new environment, which was part of this organization's new approach. However, the experiment backfired, for the most part. To enforce the policy, the top executives required that the target be met. Otherwise, the executive and management bonus would be diminished drastically. It would only take a few individuals not meeting the target for executive bonuses to erode substantially. Therefore, the executives had a desire to ensure that the target was met. Unfortunately, a visit to the corporate learning center in December, at the end of the calendar year, showed tremendous activity, far beyond what was normally experienced in any other month, and many individuals were there, and proclaimed so, only to get credit for the course. They were not necessarily interested in learning the content. This is an example of a good intention gone astray, and is a problem with any commitment to a target number of hours. On a positive note, average hours per person by specific job groups and categories, benchmarked with best-practice organizations, can provide information for adjustments and changes to ensure that the proper amount of focus is on the learning and development process.

TRACKING COVERAGE BY JOBS AND FUNCTIONAL AREAS

Perhaps the most important way to track people and hours is to track the actual coverage by jobs and job groups and even functional areas. With the current focus on talent management, some organizations track the critical talent coverage. This involves tracking the numbers and hours of individuals who are in the critical talent categories, and critical talent can vary with the organization. For some, such as pharmaceuticals, it's the R&D staff. For others, such as Amazon.com, the critical talent may be in the IT department. For still others it may be in the front-line sales team, such as the couriers for the FedEx Corporation. In any case, showing the amount of training to this critical group shows the commitment and coverage.

Another way to illustrate the coverage is by a particular function and involves showing the breakdown of coverage by people and hours—according to the different functions of the organization—beginning with research and development through sales, marketing, and customer support. This helps to see which part of the organization receives the most of the learning and development investment, particularly if gaps need to be addressed. Another way to express coverage is by specific job levels. For example, Table 3.1 shows some industry data taken from *Training* magazine's 2005 report. This shows the training by four general groups: executives, managers, professional, and non-exempt employees. Further detail can be provided on an individual basis to show where the training goes and who gets it.

Many organizations are concerned about particular job groups, for example, first-level supervisors. As an individual job category, perhaps this important group in an organization should receive the most

Job Category	Percent of Budget Spent on . . .
Executives	14%
Managers (Exempt)	25%
Professionals (Exempt)	29%
Non-Exempt	36%

Table 3.1. Industry Data by Job Category.
Adapted from *Training* magazine's 2005 industry report.

training and development. When they receive training and use it on the job, it has a multiplicative effect. As they work with their teams, they drive team performance. Based on our studies in ROI, no other job group produces as high a return on investment as supervisory management and leadership development tied directly to the first-level supervisors, team leaders, and managers.

Coverage can also be focused on specific strategic objectives. Often, the learning and development function is aligned with the particular strategic objectives. When this is the case, certain programs are designed to support them. The total hours and people can be presented by a particular strategic objective. This shows current alignment with an important strategy. It can be revealing. When particular strategic objectives have little or no coverage, it is cause for immediate action to perhaps to devote some resources directly to it.

Finally, another way to show coverage by people and hours is to focus on particular operational problems. For example, one organization was experiencing serious customer service problems and, consequently, several learning and development programs were aimed at improving customer service, reporting the number of people trained and the number of hours involved. The customer service function was very pleasing to the senior executives because they saw appropriate coverage in that critical area.

TRACKING TOPICS AND PROGRAMS

Sometimes, showing how the content of learning and development is divided into different categories can be helpful. Tracking the percent of the budget, for example, can be insightful. For example, Figure 3.1 shows the breakdown of the percent of content devoted to a particular area in ASTD's benchmarking forum data. These are the more than two hundred organizations considered to be best-practice organizations. For these organizations, over 50 percent of the content is industry-specific, IT systems, and business practices. This underscores the dramatic shift in the learning content as more organizations are focusing on technology and job- and industry-specific activities.

Some organizations find it helpful to organize all of human resource development into three categories and track the coverage in those categories. Table 3.2 shows the three categories and some basic characteristics of those categories. Training is regarded as very job-

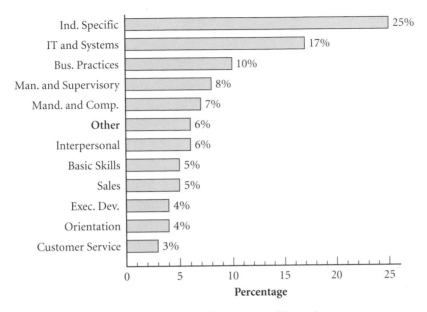

Figure 3.1. Average Percentage of Learning.

specific, with a low risk for poor return on investment. Education is preparation for the next job and has more risk and takes more time to receive a payback. Development is gradually changing mindsets and attitudes and takes much longer for payback and has a much higher risk. This relationship presents a dilemma for many learning and development professionals. Executives who are comfortable taking very low risks will invest heavily in training and only give sporadic coverage to education and development. However, an organization interested

	Focus	Costs Per Employee	Time for Payback	Risk for Payback
Training	Job-related skills	Low	Short	Low
Education	Preparation for the next job	Moderate	Medium	Moderate
Development	Cultural change and continuous learning	High	Long	High

Table 3.2. HRD Issues.

in growth, development, and change will invest significant amounts in both education and development. However, categorizing each program in these three areas and presenting them to the management team can show how this changes over a period of time and may drive some actions or adjustments.

TRACKING REQUESTS

An often overlooked tracking issue is the percent of the programs that are requested and why they were requested. As discussed in Chapter Two, many learning and development programs are implemented for the wrong reasons—or at least questionable reasons. Coding each program based on where and how it originated can provide some insightful information about why a specific learning and development program was implemented. Exhibit 3.1 shows the tracking of reasons for learning and development programs at one large financial services firm. What is revealing in this example is that over 50 percent of the programs are being implemented for questionable reasons. These are reasons 4, 5, 6, 8, and 11. By tracking this information over time, the L&D staff and executives can see this critical issue and how it is changing or should change in the future.

1. An analysis was conducted to determine need.	12%
2. A regulation requires it.	8%
3. It appears to be a serious problem	5%
4. Management requests it.	23%
5. Other organizations in industry have implemented it.	11%
6. The topic is a trend.	13%
7. It supports new policies and practices.	6%
8. Staff members thought it was needed.	2%
9. It supports new equipment, procedures, or technology.	10%
10. It supports other processes such as Six Sigma, transformation, continuous process improvement, etc.	6%
11. A best-selling book has been written about it.	4%

Exhibit 3.1. Sources of L&D Requests.

TRACKING DELIVERY

One of the most interesting and mysterious processes is the extent to which e-learning and a variety of online learning are being used. Although significant progress is being made in transforming from traditional, instructor-led processes to more technology-based delivery, progress has been slower than most experts forecasted. For an organization attempting to make dramatic shifts in delivery, this becomes an important area to monitor. Figure 3.2 shows how learning methods have evolved over time, as reported by the benchmarking service from ASTD. The benchmarking service involves three hundred organizations, and as the figure reveals, there is an upward trend in delivery by learning technology each year. This is consistent with other data provided in *Training* magazine studies or other industry reports.

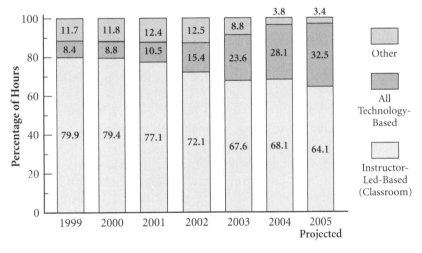

Figure 3.2. Average Percentage of Learning Hours
Provided Via Different Methods.
Source: ASTD, 2005.

Technology is broken down into different categories. Figure 3.3 shows the average percent of learning hours provided by various technology-based delivery methods. Other organizations are making these adjustments because of the cost and the tremendous cost savings that can be achieved through a variety of online learning methods. However,

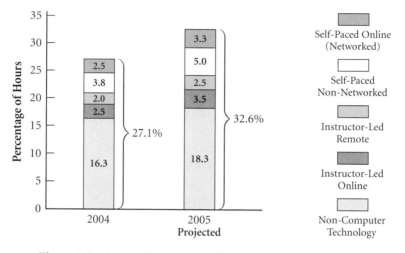

Figure 3.3. Average Percentage of Learning Hours Provided
Via Technology-Based Delivery Methods.
Source: ASTD, 2005.

this is only achieved if the learning is as effective as traditional methods. Other levels of data described later in this book will show how
the success of different methods is evolving, reassuring some executives that the cost savings generated through online learning is a true
cost savings for the organization.

Because of this concern, there is some disillusionment with e-learning, as it may not be providing the advantages that it should be. A
more appropriate approach may be the use of blended learning, which
combines classroom learning with online learning solutions and other
methods. This is a critical area that almost every organization will
need to monitor, reporting the delivery mechanism by program,
hours, and individuals. This kind of data can be revealing and helpful
for making changes as well as for measuring progress.

TRACKING COSTS

The cost of providing learning and development is increasing—creating more pressure to know how and why money is spent. The total
cost of training is required, which means that the cost profile goes beyond the direct costs and includes all indirect costs as well. Fully

loaded cost information is used to manage resources, develop standards, measure efficiencies, and examine alternative delivery methods.

Tabulating program costs is an essential step in developing the ROI calculation, and these costs are used as the denominator in the ROI formula. It is just as important to focus on costs as it is on benefits. In practice, however, costs are often more easily captured than benefits.

Pressure to Disclose All Costs

Today, increased pressure to report all training costs exists, or what is referred to as fully loaded costs. This takes the cost profile beyond the direct costs and includes the time that participants train, including their benefits and other overhead. For years, management has realized that many indirect costs of learning and development are accumulated. Now, they want these costs included. Perhaps this concept is best illustrated in a situation that recently developed in state government. The management controls of a large state agency were being audited by the state. A portion of the audit focused on training costs. The following comments were taken from the auditor's report.

Costs tracked at the program level focused on direct or "hard" costs and largely ignored the cost of time spent participating in or supporting the training. The costs of participant time to prepare for and attend training were not tracked. For one series of programs, including such costs raised the total training cost dramatically. The agency stated that the total two-year cost for the specific program was about $600,000. This figure includes only direct costs and, as such, is substantially below the costs of the time spent by staff in preparing for and attending the program. When accounting for pre-work and attendance, the figure would rise to $1.39 million. If the statewide average of 45.5 percent for fringe benefits was considered, the total indirect cost of staff time to prepare for and attend the program would escalate to $2 million. Finally, if the agency's direct costs of $600,000 were added to the $2 million total indirect cost just noted, the total would become over $2.6 million. Among other factors that would drive actual total costs higher were:

- Cost of travel, meals, and lodging for training participants
- Allocated salaries and fringes of staff providing administrative and logistic support

- Opportunity costs of productivity lost by staff in doing pre-work and attending training

Failure to consider all indirect or "soft" costs would expose the agency to non-compliance with the Fair Labor Standards Act (FLSA), particularly as training spread through rank-and-file staff. Since FLSA requires that such staff be directly compensated for overtime, it was no longer appropriate for the agency to ask employees to complete training pre-work on their own time. Continuing to handle such overtime work this way could also encourage false overtime reporting, skewed overtime data, and/or increased uncompensated overtime.

Numerous barriers exist that could hamper agency efforts in determining how much their training costs.

- Cost systems tended to hide administrative, support, internal, and other indirect or "soft" costs.
- Costs generally were monitored at the division level rather than at the level of individual programs or activities.
- Cost information required by activity-based cost systems was not being generated.

As this case vividly demonstrates, the cost of training is much more than direct expenditures, and learning and development departments are expected to report fully loaded costs in their reports.

The Danger of Costs Without Benefits

Communicating the costs of training without presenting the benefits is dangerous. Unfortunately, many organizations have done this for years. Costs are presented to management in all types of ingenious ways, such as the cost of the program, cost per employee, and cost per development hour. While these cost reports may be helpful for efficiency comparisons, they may be trouble if presented without the benefits. When most executives review learning and development costs, the logical questions is: What benefit was received from the program? This is a typical management reaction, particularly when costs are perceived to be high. Because of this, some organizations have developed a policy of not communicating learning and development cost data for a specific program unless the benefits can be captured and presented with the costs. Even if the benefits data are subjective and intangible, they are included with the cost data.

Sources of Costs

The sources of training and performance improvement costs must be considered. The three major categories of sources are illustrated in Table 3.3. The L&D staff expenses usually represent the greatest percent of the costs and are sometimes transferred directly to the client or program sponsor. The second major cost category is the participant expenses, both direct and indirect. These costs are not identified in many training and performance improvement programs, but, nevertheless, reflect a significant amount. The third cost source is the payments made to external organizations. These include payments directly to hotels and conference centers, equipment suppliers, and services used for the program. As Table 3.3 shows, some of these cost categories are often understated. The finance and accounting records should be able to track and reflect the costs from these three different sources. The process presented in this chapter helps track these costs, as well.

Source of Costs	Cost Reporting Issues
1. L&D staff expenses	A. Costs are usually accurate.
	B. Variable expenses may be underestimated.
2. Participant expenses (direct and indirect)	A. Direct expenses are usually not fully loaded.
	B. Indirect expenses are rarely included in the costs.
3. External expenses (equipment and services)	A. Sometimes understated
	B. May lack accountability

Table 3.3. Sources of Costs.

Learning Program Steps and Costs

Another important way to think about learning and performance improvement costs is in following how the program unfolds. Figure 3.4 shows the typical training and development cycle, beginning with the initial analysis and assessment and progressing to the evaluation and reporting of the results. These steps represent the typical flow of work during a program. As a performance problem is addressed, a solution is developed or acquired and implemented within the organization. Implementation is often grouped with delivery. The entire process is reported to the client or sponsor and evaluation is undertaken to show the program's success. Costs are also incurred for supporting the process—administrative support and overhead costs. To fully understand costs, the program should be analyzed in these different categories, as described later in this chapter.

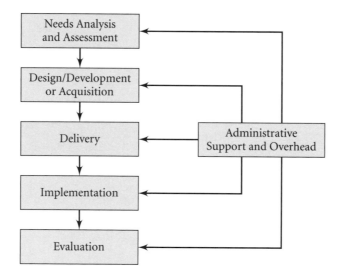

Figure 3.4. Training Functions and Cost Categories.

Prorated Versus Direct Costs

Usually, all costs related to a program are captured and charged to that program. However, three categories—needs assessment, design and development, and acquisition—are significant costs that should be prorated over the shelf life of the program. A conservative shelf life estimation should be very short. Some organizations will consider one year of operation for the program; others may consider two or three years. If a dispute arises about the specific time period to be used to prorate, the shorter period should be used. If possible, the finance and accounting staff should be consulted.

Employee Benefits Factor

When presenting salaries for participants and L&D staff, the benefits factor should be included. This number is usually well-known in the organization and is used in other cost applications. It represents the cost of all employee benefits expressed as a percent of base salary. In some organizations, this value is as high as 50 to 60 percent. In others, it may be as low as 25 to 30 percent. The average in the United States is approximately 38 percent (*Nation's Business,* 2006).

Major Cost Categories

The specific costs to be included in the program costs must be defined. Input from the finance and accounting staff and the L&D staff and management approval may be needed. Table 3.4 shows the recommended cost categories for a fully loaded, conservative approach to estimating costs. Each category is described below.

- Needs assessment and analysis
- Design and development costs
- Acquisition costs (in lieu of development costs, many organizations purchase programs)
- Delivery/implementation costs (five categories)

    Salaries of facilitators and coordinators

    Program materials and fees

    Travel, lodging, and meals

    Facilities (for external and in-house)

    Participants' salaries and benefits
- Evaluation
- Overhead

Cost Item	Prorated	Expensed
Needs Assessment and Analysis	✓	
Design and Development	✓	
Acquisition	✓	
Delivery/Implementation		✓
Salaries/Benefits—Facilitators		✓
Salaries/Benefits—Coordination		✓
Program Materials and Fees		✓
Travel/Lodging/Meals		✓
Facilities		✓
Participants Salaries/Benefits		✓
Contact Time		✓
Travel Time		✓
Preparation Time		✓
Evaluation		✓
Overhead/Training and Development	✓	

Table 3.4. Program Cost Categories.

Cost Reporting

Actual costs are reported in several ways. The two most common ways are the cost per employee and the cost of training as a percent of payroll. Figure 3.5 shows the cost per employee from the ASTD Benchmarking Forum—as this number suggests, the costs range from $1,300 to $1,500. The Benchmarking Forum data seem to be more of the best practice. Data taken from the benchmarking survey shows $1,000 projected for 2005. The average data are consistent with data reported by the Saratoga Institute, which is now part of PricewaterhouseCooper. Figure 3.6 shows data from the ASTD benchmarking survey. As the figure shows, the expenditure has been going down slightly from a high of 3.37 to a projected 2.26 for 2005. Since these are the best-practice organizations, the actual number from all organizations is probably lower—closer to 2 percent.

Costs can also be reported as a percent of profit or as a percent of revenue. However, the most common way is to report the investment

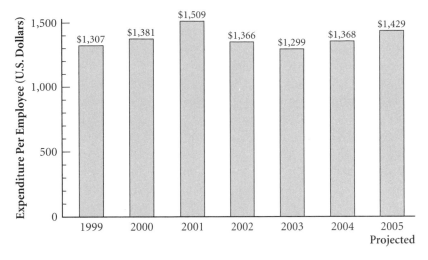

Figure 3.5. Average Expenditure Per Employee (U.S. Dollars).
Source: ASTD, *State of the Industry Report*, 2005.

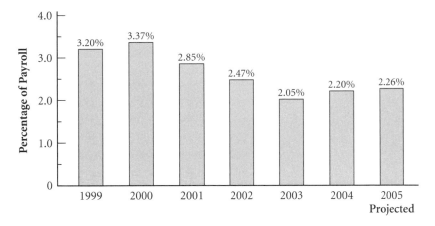

Figure 3.6. Average Expenditure as a
Percentage of Payroll (Without Benefits and Taxes).
Source: ASTD, *State of the Industry Report*, 2005.

as a percent of payroll. This makes sense because organizations use learning to develop their employees, whose salaries are represented in the total payroll number. However, this can also be misleading—sometimes underdeveloped nations will have a higher expenditure in percent of payroll because of the low cost of payroll. The costs reported in both *Training* magazine and the ASTD report contain direct costs only. All costs must be included, and this presents significant challenges for the learning and development function. The difficulty is that some of these costs—if not the majority of them—are in other functions. For example, the salaries, adjusted for benefits, of participants for the time that they attend training would be absorbed by the department, division, or area in which they work. Thus, these costs are not under the control of the learning and development function.

TRACKING EFFICIENCIES

Efficiency is an extremely important issue for learning and development organizations, particularly the larger ones. Efficiency is measured in different ways and from different viewpoints. One of the first measures is the efficiency of using the learning and development staff. Sometimes, a measure presented is the number of participants per learning and development staff member. From an efficiency standpoint, this number should be as high as possible. Another way to report efficiency is analyzing the learning hours received and provided per learning and development staff member. The learning hours provided reflect how much learning content was taught by each learning and development staff member. The average learning hours received per L&D staff member is a measure of consumption per staff member.

Another efficiency measure is the average cost per learning hour received (Figure 3.7). This can also be compared to the average cost per learning hour provided. These two values can be combined to show the average reuse ratio, which is the ratio of learning hours received to learning hours provided.

Other efficiency measures can focus on the time to accomplish certain tasks—the average time to conduct a needs assessment, the average time to design an hour of instructional classroom content, the average time to design an hour of e-learning or online content. Additional time measures can include the time an individual takes to

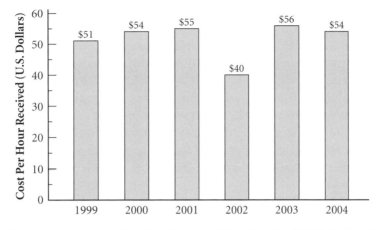

Figure 3.7. Average Cost Per Learning Hour Received (U.S. Dollars).

complete a program—particularly helpful with e-learning. Also, the time from a request to the launch of a new program can be helpful if there are many data points and many different programs. In short, efficiencies are extremely important and can be analyzed from a variety of angles. They show the learning and development staff and other interested individuals how well the process is organized and managed.

TRACKING OUTSOURCING

More organizations are outsourcing part of, and in some cases almost all, the learning and development functions. As the organization moves in this direction, if that is the goal, tracking the extent to which outsourcing is developed is helpful. One particular measure in the development area represents the percent of training programs developed by external contractors compared to those developed by the internal staff. This can be divided into both technology-based learning and traditional training. Another area is the outsourcing of delivery, showing the percent of programs delivered by external services compared to the percent delivered by internal sources. This can also be divided into traditional and technology-based.

In the 2005 industry report from *Training* magazine, the percentage of training developed by external contractors was 44 percent, whereas the percent of delivery by external contractors was at 36 percent for traditional training and 27 percent for technology-based training. This is similar to studies by ASTD that suggest about 40 percent of both development and delivery is being outsourced. Outsourcing can also occur in other areas. Learning technology infrastructure, learning administration, learning operations, and the entire learning function are all possibilities. Measuring progress is essential to determine whether internal or external development and delivery is more effective or cost-effective. This varies significantly with the philosophy of the organization and the particular success achieved in the outsourcing part of the process.

TRACKING FOR THE SCORECARD

Data collected for each program represents micro data. In essence, data can be collected for each program for the seven types of measures included in this book. However, the challenge is to select programs for the higher levels of analysis, that is, deciding when to stop the evaluation because only a few evaluations will go to the ROI level. With this approach, each program then is measured at the micro level. Another issue is to show the combined contribution of all programs. For very large learning and development organizations, there may be 500 to 1,000 or even more programs, and management needs some scorecard information that shows the total contribution across all programs. The approach is to take parts of the micro data and include them in an overall scorecard, a macro-viewpoint. Only a few data sets at each level would be captured to include in the macro scorecard. In this chapter and in the next five, specific data sets will be suggested for all macro data. Table 3.5 shows micro level data suggested for Level 0 in the large macro scorecard. For the most part, these data mirror what is recommended by ASTD but represent some of the essential input and indicator data. Although many other measures could be presented, as explained in this chapter, these are some of the critical ones. Of course, this decision would depend on the desires of the management team and the particular need to emphasize certain parts of the process.

Chapter Ten, Results Reporting, will show how this overall macro-level scorecard concept works. However, each chapter will have a recommendation that will then be included in the overall scorecard.

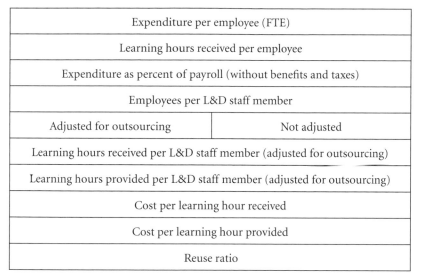

Expenditure per employee (FTE)	
Learning hours received per employee	
Expenditure as percent of payroll (without benefits and taxes)	
Employees per L&D staff member	
Adjusted for outsourcing	Not adjusted
Learning hours received per L&D staff member (adjusted for outsourcing)	
Learning hours provided per L&D staff member (adjusted for outsourcing)	
Cost per learning hour received	
Cost per learning hour provided	
Reuse ratio	

Table 3.5. Essential Indicators for Macro-Level Scorecard.

DEFINING KEY ISSUES

It is fitting to end this chapter with several key issues that have been addressed or discussed in a brief fashion. These are important points to be made about this level of data, which is often considered controversial. It is the largest data set, but considered the least valuable for many reasons.

Input Is Not Results

The L&D staff and others must be reminded that input data do not represent results. They only show what goes into the process and in no way reflect any of the outcomes described in the subsequent levels. However, value is here and it must be emphasized as these data are reported.

Reports to Executives Should Be Minimized

Executives care little about this level of data. In a broad sense, they certainly are curious about certain measures that represent volumes and efficiencies, but for the most part, they want to see data that represent application, impact, and ROI. Consequently, evaluators should pick the few data sets that would attract management attention, or emphasize some of the areas under consideration or need attention. Above all, data at this level should be minimized in the report in terms of the space and time used to present them.

These Data Represent Operational Concerns

The most important value for this level of data is the operational management perspective. This represents costs, inputs, efficiencies, and other data that are necessary to use, organize, and manage the process. It is ideal for the operations of the L&D staff and must be used in a way to drive maximum effectiveness and efficiency.

The Data Must Be Automated

Because of the sheer volume of this data, it must be automated as it is captured, integrated, and reported. Fortunately, many learning management systems and learning content management systems provide mechanisms for capturing most of the data sets described in this chapter. Because these data sets represent the greatest amount of data but represent the least value to executives, they must be captured in the most efficient way; thus, automation is critical.

FINAL THOUGHTS

This chapter is the first of seven chapters describing the different levels of data. At Level 0, inputs and indicators describe what goes into the process. Abundant amounts of information are available to be captured, analyzed, and reported to various stakeholders. These include capturing data about people; the number of hours; coverage of jobs and functions; tracking programs, topics, and issues; and tracking learning and development by request.

In addition, tracking costs and efficiencies are important for a variety of uses and applications. They help the learning and development staff manage their resources carefully, consistently, and efficiently. They also allow for comparisons between different elements and cost categories. In many situations, costs will be fully loaded to include both direct and indirect. However, from a practical standpoint, including certain cost items may be optional based on the organization's guidelines and philosophy.

Capturing data about outsourcing and building a scorecard to show the overall contributions of learning and development rounded out this chapter. When the data are collected, organized, and integrated, they provide information to make adjustments and changes and a way to manage the process efficiently and effectively.

References

Johnson, M. *Talent magnet: Getting talented people to work for you.* (2002). Englewood Cliffs, NJ: Prentice Hall.

Sugrue, B., & Rivera, R.J. (2005). *State of the industry: ASTD's annual review of trends in workplace learning and performance.* Alexandria, VA: ASTD.

2005 industry report. (2005, December). *Training,* p. 14.

CHAPTER FOUR

Measuring Reaction and Planned Action

T he next four chapters present techniques to measure the first four types of results data described earlier. This chapter focuses on measuring reaction and planned action. Chapter Five covers measuring learning and confidence; Chapter Six covers measuring application and implementation; and Chapter Seven covers measuring business impact and consequences, including the hard to measure.

Data collection at all four levels is necessary because of the chain of impact that must exist for a program to be successful. Participants in the program should experience a positive (or at least not adverse) reaction to the program and its potential application. During the program, participants acquire new information, skills, or knowledge needed to implement the program. This leads to changes in behavior, actions, and tasks that should bring about a positive implementation. Successful implementation should drive changes in one or more business impact measures. The only way to know if the chain of impact has occurred is to collect data along all levels.

Collecting reaction and planned action data at the beginning of the program is the first operational phase of the ROI methodology. The chain of impact can be broken at the first level if participants have an adverse reaction to the program. Participant feedback can be powerful data to use when making adjustments and measuring success. Many methods may be used to capture reaction and planned action data—at the beginning and during the program. This chapter outlines the most common approaches for collecting data and explores ways to use the information for maximum value.

WHY MEASURE REACTION AND PLANNED ACTION?

It would be difficult to imagine a learning program being conducted without collecting feedback from those involved in it. Collecting this type of data involves several key issues and audiences, making collecting reaction and planned action one of the most important data collection steps in the process. Participant feedback is critical to understanding how well the program is perceived. Because of its importance, this level of evaluation is recommended for every program.

Customer Service

With the constant focus on customer service, measuring customer satisfaction with each program is important. Without continuous improvement from customers and favorable reactions, programs will not succeed. Consider the different key customers involved in learning and performance improvement programs. The individuals who have a direct role in the program, the participants, are very important customers. They are key stakeholders who must change processes, procedures, or make other job adjustments. In addition, they must learn new skills, tasks, and behaviors to make the program successful. Participant feedback is critical to making adjustments and changes in the program as it is implemented.

The next key customer group is the facilitators, the individuals who play an important role in making the program successful. They facilitate the different learning processes and influence the participants. Facilitators are very important, and feedback from them will be helpful as the program is implemented.

The third group of key customers is the individuals on the sidelines and not directly involved, but they have an interest in the program.

Sometimes called the supporters, they are concerned about the program and are usually supporting or assisting it in some way. Their perception of the program's success or potential success is important feedback because this group will be in a position to influence the program's continuation and development.

The fourth group of key customers is perhaps the most important. It is made up of the sponsors who fund or approve the program. This individual, or group of individuals, requested the program, supports the program, approves budgets, allocates resources, and ultimately lives with the program's success or failure. This important individual or group must be completely satisfied with the program—with his or her level of satisfaction being determined early, often, and at the end of the program.

In short, customer satisfaction is critical to the program's success and must be collected and used in a variety of ways.

Early Feedback Is Essential

Sometimes, a new program ends up being the wrong solution for the specified problem. Early feedback is necessary so that adjustments can be made. Doing this helps avoid misunderstandings, miscommunications, and, more importantly, misappropriations.

For example, in one program aimed at reducing sexual harassment complaints at a large hospital chain, early feedback was taken at the introduction of the program. Feedback was provided on the appropriateness of the particular solution. The organizers were concerned about whether the actual cause of excessive sexual harassment complaints had been precisely pinpointed and the solution was appropriate and the right one. Early feedback involving the first group of participants in meetings, activities, and learning sessions confirmed the organizer's suspicions. Many individuals lacked the knowledge of what constitutes inappropriate and illegal behavior under federal and local laws, and second, many lacked the knowledge of the organization's current policy on sexual harassment. With the early confirmation, the organizers were pleased that the program stayed on track, and the ultimate payoff was a significant ROI value as the number of sexual harassment complaints reduced 36 percent in one year, and employee turnover associated with this activity reduced 18 percent in the same year.

Making Adjustments and Changes

The concept of continuous process improvement suggests that a program must be adjusted and refined throughout its duration. There must be an important link between obtaining feedback, making changes, and reporting changes to the groups who provide the information. This survey-feedback-action loop is critical for any program.

For example, a large government agency attempted to implement a new human performance improvement initiative to change the approach the agency took toward addressing developmental needs for its front-line staff. The process was expected to eliminate redundancies within the training and education directorate, as well as reduce costs to the client organizations.

After fifteen of the key performance consultants attended fifteen days of class and attempted to implement action plans, a comprehensive measurement of reaction and planned action was taken from the participant groups, their supervisors, and a sample of the clients. The participants responded negatively. This was anticipated due to periodic feedback during the fifteen days of classes. Participants did not understand the need for a change in approach and indicated that clients typically asked for what they wanted with little room for persuasion otherwise. Supervisors perceived the concept as viable but questioned the practicality. The few clients responding provided only minimal data useful to program improvement. Upon consideration of the initial feedback, the program was revised, as was the process to introduce it to participants, supervisors, and clients.

Predictive Capability

A recent application of reaction data is using it to predict the future success of a program using analytical techniques. This involves asking the participants of a program to estimate the application and, in some cases, the subsequent value of that application. The reaction data become a forecast. Figure 4.1 shows the relationship between data points when reactive feedback correlates with application data. Countless studies have been conducted to validate this correlation with certain reaction measures.

In this analysis, the reaction measures are taken as the program is conducted, and the success of the implementation is later judged using

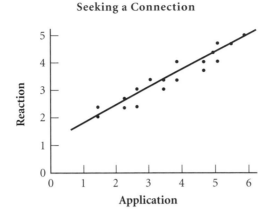

Seeking a Connection

Figure 4.1. Correlations Between Reaction and Application.

the same scales (for example, a 1 to 5 rating). When positive, significant correlations are developed, reaction measures can have predictive capability. Some measures shown to have predictive capabilities are:

1. The program is relevant to my job.
2. This program is necessary for my job.
3. The program is important to my success.
4. The program contains new information.
5. I intend to use the skills and knowledge.
6. I would recommend this program to others in similar jobs.

Although other measures have predictive capabilities, these consistently develop strong, positive correlations and consequently become more powerful feedback than typical measures of overall satisfaction.

For Some, This Is the Most Important Data

Because feedback data are important to a program's success, they should be collected for every program. They have become some of the most important data collected. Unfortunately, for some programs, success is only measured by reaction data. For example, in one financial services firm in Israel, the traditional method of measuring the ethics program in place was to rely entirely on feedback data from employees, asking whether the ethics policy is appropriate, fair, and necessary. Positive results were obviously critical to the acceptance of the policy. However, as subsequent policy changes were made, the firm became more interested in other measures including:

- The extent to which employees actually understand the policy (learning)
- The extent to which employees were following the policy in their jobs and work lives (application)
- The impact of the policy in reducing ethical violations and infractions (impact)

While reaction data are and should be an important measure, they should be included with other measures in the value chain. As this book clearly shows, feedback data are only one of the seven types of data.

Comparing Data with Other Programs

Some organizations collect reaction and planned action data using standard questions, and the data are then compared with data from other programs so that norms and standards can be developed. This is particularly helpful in the early stages of a new program. Overall satisfaction data are collected and compared. Some firms even base part of the learning team's success on the level of client satisfaction, making reaction and satisfaction data important to the success of every program.

Creating a Macro Scorecard

As briefly described in a previous chapter, one of the important reasons for collecting data at each level is to create a scorecard. This scorecard shows the contribution of learning and development and performance improvement across all programs. While individual evaluation measures collect a micro scorecard of performance, a macro scorecard shows performance throughout the system. An important and necessary part of the scorecard is the reaction data. Unfortunately, all the reaction data collected should not be included in the macro scorecard but only small parts of it, as will be described later.

SOURCES OF DATA

When considering possible data sources to provide feedback on the success of a program, the categories are easily defined. Several categories of stakeholders can be found in all programs; long, complex programs may have over a dozen groups.

Participants

The most widely used data source for reaction is the participants, those directly involved in learning and applying the skills and knowledge acquired in the program. Sometimes, they are asked to explain the potential impact of those actions. Participants are a rich source of data for almost every issue or part of the program. They are credible, since they are the individuals who must achieve the performance results and often have the most knowledge of the processes and other influencing factors. The challenge is to find an effective, efficient, and consistent way to capture participant data.

Participants' Managers

Another important source of data is those individuals who directly supervise or lead participants. This group will often have a vested interest in evaluation, since they have a stake in the process because their employees are directly involved. Also, in many situations, they observe the participants as they attempt to apply the information, knowledge, and skills acquired in the program. Consequently, they can report on successes as well as difficulties and problems associated with it. Although manager input is usually best for reaction and learning data, it can also be useful for other levels of evaluation data.

Internal Customers

The individuals who serve as internal customers of the program are another source of data for a few types of programs. In these situations, internal customers provide reactions to perceived changes linked to the program. This source of data is appropriate when programs directly affect these customers. They report on how the program has (or will) influence their work or the service they receive. Because of the subjective nature of this process and the lack of opportunity to fully evaluate the application of skills of the participants, this source of data may be limited.

Facilitators

In some situations, the facilitator may provide input on the success of the program. The input from this source may be based on observations during the program. Data from this source have limited use because facilitators may have a vested interest in the outcome of evaluation, so their input may lack objectivity.

Sponsors/Senior Managers

One of the most useful data sources is the sponsor or client group, usually a senior management team. Whether an individual or a group, the sponsor's perception is critical to program success. Sponsors can provide input on all types of issues and are usually available and willing to offer feedback. Collecting data from this source is preferred if they can provide reaction.

AREAS OF FEEDBACK
Content vs. Non-Content

An important consideration in capturing reaction is to obtain data about the content of the program. Too often, feedback data reflect acsthetic issues that may not reflect the substance of the program at hand. Take, for example, an attempt to show the value of a sales and marketing program that focused on client development. The audience was relationship managers, those individuals who have direct contact with the customer. This particular program was designed to discuss product development and a variety of marketing and business development strategies. Exhibit 4.1 shows the comparison of content versus non-content issues that can be explored on a reaction questionnaire. The traditional way to evaluate these activities is to focus on non-content issues. As the exhibit shows, the column to the left represents areas important to activity surrounding the session, but few measures reflect results achieved from the program. The column on the right shows a tremendous focus on content, with only minor input on issues such as the facilities and service provided. This is not to imply that the quality of the service, the atmosphere of the event, and the quality of the speakers are not important. It is assumed that these is-sues will be taken care of and addressed appropriately. A more impor-tant set of data would be the tracking of detailed information about the perceived value of the program, the importance of the content, and the planned use of material or a forecast of the impact—indicators that successful results did and will occur. This example underscores the tremendous shift occurring in the meetings and events industry, which is moving from measuring entertainment to measuring reaction, learn-ing, and sometimes, the application, impact, and ROI.

Focus on Non-Content Issues	Focus on Content Issues
• Demographics	• Facilities
• Location	• Service
• Transportation	• Relevance of materials
• Registration	• Importance of content to job success
• Logistics	• Timing of program
• Hotel service	• Appropriate use of time
• Media	• Amount of new information
• Food	• Quality of facilitators
• Breaks and refreshments	• Perceived value of program
• Cocktail reception	• Contacts made
• Facilitator	• Planned use of material
• Materials/topics	• Forecast of impact
• Overall satisfaction	• Overall satisfaction

Exhibit 4.1. Comparison of Content vs. Non-Content.

The Deceptive Feedback Cycle

There is a danger of placing too much reliance on Level 1 feedback, particularly to use it for facilitator evaluation. The learning and de-velopment field has a history of playing games with Level 1 data. The objective is for the participants to enjoy the program, and the facili-tator is the centerpiece of that enjoyment. As shown in Figure 4.2, if the participants enjoy the program, the facilitator ratings are often high (Dixon, 1990). Consequently, in many organizations facilitators are primarily rewarded on those ratings. When this is the case, they naturally focus their behavior on enjoyment, making this totally an enjoyable experience. Certainly, nothing is wrong with enjoying the program. A certain level of enjoyment and satisfaction is an absolute must. However, if the focus is entirely on enjoyment and losing sight of the content, then we run the risk of focusing on the entertainment issue of what we do. As some of our professional colleagues say, "We quickly migrate to the business of entertaining instead of the business of learning." To avoid this, several actions can be taken:

- Facilitators' ratings should not be so focused on evaluating their effectiveness. They should also be evaluated on Level 2, learning; Level 3, application; and occasionally Level 4 and maybe even Level 5. This keeps a balanced perspective and prevents an over-reliance on reaction data.
- The evaluations should focus on content-related issues, as described in this section. The facilitator ratings are only a small part of the experience. This moves away from a predominance of feedback focused on the facilitator.
- The value of Level 1 data has to be constantly put into perspective. From the point of view of the client and sponsor, it is not very valuable, and many sponsors consider it essentially worthless. For other stakeholders—the designer, developer, facilitator, and participants, for example—it is very important, but for the individual funding the program, reaction data have very little value.

Figure 4.2. The Deceptive Feedback Cycle.

Key Areas for Feedback

Many topics are critical targets for feedback because so many issues and processes are involved in a typical program. Feedback is needed for almost every major issue, step, or process to make sure outcomes are successful. Table 4.1 shows the typical, major areas of feedback for most programs. The list shows the key success factors in a program, beginning with the objectives and moving through a variety of content-related issues.

Reaction Data

Type of Data	Reason for Collecting	Data Components
Participant demographics	Job match Audience served versus needs assessment Trends in attendance Future planning Diversity	Job Department/division Education Experience Length of service Reason for participation
Logistics and service	Facility change Facility complaint Customer satisfaction Critical to solution effectiveness	Location Room Comfort Communication Access to food and refreshments
Readiness	Right participant Proper timing Ready to learn	Appropriate experience Prerequisites Motivation to learn Opportunity to use the program Timing of program
Objectives	Proper objectives Progress	Clarity of objectives Appropriateness of objectives Success with objectives
Learning materials	Adjustments Design Stimulate interest	Usefulness of materials Appearance of materials Amount of new information
Facilitator	Performance data Complaints Contractors New facilitator New material	Facilitator experience Knowledge and expertise Communication success Responsiveness to participants Involvement of participants Pacing of program

Table 4.1. Detailed Reaction Data.

Reaction Data

Type of Data	Reason for Collecting	Data Components
Media/delivery	New media Comparison of types of media Effectiveness of media	Delivery Media effectiveness Timeliness Applicability to content
Value of content	Alignment with business Future planning Adjustments Design	Alignment with business need Why learning solution was selected Relevance of content to job Importance of content to job success Input into business strategies Customer satisfaction
Practice and labs	Effectiveness Transferability to job	Applicability to content Similarity to job
Value of problem	Marketing Pricing Commitment Support	Good investment in me Good investment of my time Fair price for program Overall satisfaction
Planned use	Follow-up Adjust Transfer learning Support	Planned actions Intent to use Recommend to others Barriers to implementation Enablers of implementation Willingness to provide data
Future needs	Planning	Additional needs Other programs
Marketing and registration	Source of enrollment Decision-making process Pricing Ease of registration	Source of enrollment Decision-making process Pricing Registration process
Open comments	Opportunity to identify unknown issues	Other comments

Table 4.1. Detailed Reaction Data, Cont'd.

Source: Adapted from *Rapid Evaluation,* Susan Barksdale and Teri Lund. Alexandria, VA: ASTD, 2001. Used with permission.

A few important areas are discussed in this section.

PROGRAM CONTENT. Program content includes the principles, steps, facts, ideas, and situations presented in the program. The content is critical and participant input is necessary.

AMOUNT OF NEW INFORMATION. In too many situations, programs simply rehash old material. Sorting out what is considered new information and what is old information can be helpful.

PROGRAM MATERIALS. The handouts, workbooks, job aids, books, and other materials should be evaluated regarding their applicability, usefulness, and relevance to the program. This is helpful in deciding whether adjustments should be made or whether materials should be added or deleted from the program.

ASSIGNMENTS AND EXERCISES. Often, assignments are provided to participants—some before the program, some during the program, and others after the program. An assessment of the effectiveness of these assignments and how they relate to program objectives is important.

PRESENTATION AND DELIVERY. Because many different ways are available for program delivery, participants should be encouraged to provide insight into the appropriateness and effectiveness of the particular delivery method. Whether the delivery is by case studies, coaching, discussions, lectures, exercises, or role plays, understanding the effectiveness of the process from the perspective of the consumer is important.

THE FACILITIES AND LEARNING ENVIRONMENT. Sometimes, the environment is not conducive to learning, and feedback can identify issues that may need attention. These types of data include the actual learning space, the comfort level in the learning environment, and several other environmental issues, such as temperature, lighting, and noise. *A word of caution:* If nothing can be done about the learning environment, then data should not be collected about it.

FACILITATOR EVALUATION. Perhaps one of the most common uses of Level 1 data is the evaluation of the facilitator. If properly implemented, helpful feedback data can be provided so that adjustments can be made to increase effectiveness. The issues usually involve preparation, presentation, level of involvement, and pacing of the process. Some cautions need to be taken since facilitator evaluations can sometimes be biased—either positively or negatively—and other evidence may be necessary to provide an overall assessment of facilitator performance.

PROGRAM RELEVANCE. Participants want to learn skills and knowledge that is relevant to their work. Consequently, exploring the relevance of the material to the participants' current work or future responsibilities is helpful. These types of data focus on a critical issue, helping ensure that the skills and knowledge will be used on the job. If they are relevant, more than likely they will be used.

PROGRAM IMPORTANCE. Participants need to see that the content is important to their job success. This provides a little of "What's in it for me?"

INTENT TO USE MATERIAL. Asking participants about their intentions to use the material can be helpful. The extent of planned use can be captured, along with the expected frequency of use and the anticipated level of effectiveness when using the skills and knowledge. Intent to use usually correlates to actual use and is important for enhancing the transfer of learning to the job.

PLANNED IMPROVEMENTS. Sometimes, gathering specific, detailed information about how participants will use what they have learned on the job is helpful. This input is often provided on a supplementary form and contains a sequence of questions about the intended use and the consequence of use. Supplementary questions are not appropriate for every program, but they could be helpful in many settings when the participants are in professional, supervisory, managerial, or technical positions. When completed, the responses provide an opportunity to show the anticipated value of the program.

OVERALL EVALUATION. Almost all organizations capture an overall satisfaction rating, which reflects the participants' overall satisfaction with the program. While this may have very little value in terms of understanding the real issues and the program's relationship to future success, comparing one program to another and with programs over time may be helpful. Because the data can be easily misinterpreted and misused, the other areas may provide a better understanding of needed adjustments or improvements.

TIMING OF DATA COLLECTION

The timing of data collection revolves around particular events connected with the program. Any particular topic, event, or activity is an appropriate time to collect data, beginning with pre-program data collection and progressing to end-of-program collection.

Early, Detailed Feedback

As discussed previously, the detailed feedback gathered during the early stages of implementation—particularly during a pilot program—is critical. For the most part, this feedback validates the decision to go forward with the program and ensures that alignment exists. Noting problems in this early feedback means that adjustments can be made early on in the program. In practice, however, this early feedback is often not taken with a comprehensive approach, waiting until significant parts of the program have been implemented, when feedback may be more meaningful. However, early feedback can help spot errors and save tremendous amounts of time when adjustments are made.

Pre-Assessments

Sometimes, collecting pre-assessment data is helpful to attending and participating in a particular program. Although this may not be common, it is certainly a way to solicit attitudes toward particular topics or issues that will be discussed during the program. The classic definition of reaction data is reacting to a program that is being presented to a participant. A pre-assessment is a way to gauge the current attitudes toward the issues that are discussed during the program, so it can be helpful. Also, pre-assessments may also involve learning assessments that can be used to understand the degree to which the participants currently understand a particular issue. Therefore, pre-assessments may contain both Level 1 and Level 2 questions.

Collecting at Periodic Intervals

Sometimes, collecting data during programs that occur over multiple days is important. For example, if a program lasts five days, then waiting until the end of the fifth day to collect feedback data may be inappropriate. By then, participants may not be able to judge some of the issues, events, and processes that occurred earlier in the week. Consequently, data may need to be collected during the program. Several approaches may be taken to do this. First, capturing daily feedback may be appropriate. Under this scenario, at the end of each day, feedback is taken about the material covered that day, including the pacing, flow, degree of involvement, and other important issues surrounding the program.

Another approach is to collect data immediately after each module, giving the participants the opportunity to judge several key issues about that particular module while it is fresh in their minds. Still another approach is to evaluate different events separately. For example, if a plant tour is connected to the program, the tour may need to be evaluated separately. Perhaps participants attend a separate networking event in the evening and are given an opportunity to provide quick feedback at the beginning of the next day. Even with daily or event-based feedback, capturing the end-of-program data is still important to reflect the entire program experience.

For Long Programs with Multiple Parts

Some programs have multiple parts spread over a long time period. In these cases, each individual part should be evaluated for reaction data. For example, in a program to show the impact of a master's degree program inside a government agency, reaction data were collected at several different times (Phillips, Phillips, & Stone, 2002). During the introduction of the program, reaction data were collected from the participants following a meeting. At the end of each program course, reaction data were collected concerning that particular course. At the end of each semester, reaction data were collected regarding the progress on the program. The important issue here is that multiple data collection points will be needed for these kinds of programs.

DATA COLLECTION WITH QUESTIONNAIRES AND SURVEYS

Many data collection methods are available to collect reaction data. The questionnaire or survey is the most common data collection method for measuring reaction. Questionnaires and surveys come in all sizes, ranging from short reaction forms to detailed, multi-paged instruments. They can be used to obtain subjective data about participants' reactions as well as to document data for future use in an ROI analysis. With their versatility and popularity, properly designing questionnaires and surveys is important.

Several basic types of questions are available. Depending on the purpose of the evaluation, the questionnaire or survey may contain any or all of the types of questions shown in Exhibit 4.2. The key is to select the question or statement that is most appropriate for the information needed. A dichotomous question (yes/no) and the numerical scale (1 to 5) are typical reaction measurement types. Essentially, the individual indicates the extent of agreement with a particular statement and gives an opinion of a varying degree on a particular issue. Still, open-ended questions can sometimes be used, particularly when asking for specific problem areas. Checklists, multiple-choice questions, and ranking scales are more appropriate to measure learning and application described in later chapters.

Surveys are a type of questionnaire but focus on participants' attitudes. Surveys have many applications for measuring reaction and satisfaction in programs designed to improve work, policies, procedures, the organization, or even the team. Measuring satisfaction and reaction is a complex task in which attitudes are crucial. Measuring an attitude precisely is impossible, since information gathered may not represent a participant's true feelings. Also, the behavior, beliefs, and feelings of an individual will not always correlate. Over time, attitudes tend to change, and several factors can affect an individual's attitude. Recognizing these shortcomings, obtaining a reasonable assessment of an individual's attitude about a program is possible.

Questionnaire/Survey Design

Survey and questionnaire design is a simple and logical process. An improperly designed or poorly worded questionnaire or survey will not collect the desired data. Poorly designed questionnaires/surveys are confusing, frustrating, and potentially embarrassing. The following steps will help ensure that a valid, reliable, and effective instrument is developed:

1. *Determine the information needed.* The first step of any instrument design is to itemize the topics, issues, and success factors. Questions are developed later. Developing this information in outline form is helpful in grouping related questions.

1. Open-Ended Questions:

   What problems will you encounter when attempting to use knowledge and skills in this program?

2. Checklist:

   For the following list, check all the business measures that may be influenced by the application of this program.

☐ Responsibility	☐ Cost Control
☐ Productivity	☐ Response Time
☐ Quality	☐ Customer Satisfaction
☐ Efficiency	☐ Job Satisfaction

3. Dichotomous Question (Yes/No Responses):

   As a result of this program, I have a better understanding of my job as a customer service representative.

   Yes ☐   No ☐

4. Numerical Scale:

Strongly Disagree	1	2	3	4	5	Strongly Agree
A. This program is relevant to my job.	☐	☐	☐	☐	☐	
B. This program is important to my job success.	☐	☐	☐	☐	☐	

5. Multiple-Choice Questions:

   Which of the following describes the pacing of this program?

   a. Too fast

   b. Too slow

   c. Just right

6. Ranking Scales:

   The following list contains five important factors that will influence the success of this program. Place a 1 by the item that is most influential, a 2 by the item that is second most influential, and so on. The item ranked 5 will be the least influential item on the list.

Proper Tools	_____	Technology	_____
My Team's Culture	_____	Management Support	_____
Communications	_____	Technical Support	_____

Exhibit 4.2. Sample Questionnaire.

2. *Select the type(s) of questions/statements.* Determine whether open-ended questions, checklists, dichotomous questions, multiple-choice questions, or a ranking scale is most appropriate for the purpose of the questions. Take into consideration the planned data analysis and variety of data to be collected.

3. *Develop the questions.* The next step is to develop the questions based on the types of questions planned and the information needed. The questions should be simple and straightforward enough to avoid confusion or lead the participant to a desired response. Terms or expressions unfamiliar to the participant should be avoided.

4. *Keep survey statements as simple as possible.* Participants need to understand the meaning of a statement or question. There should be little room for differing interpretations.

5. *Test the questions.* After the questions are developed, they should be tested for understanding. Ideally, the questions should be tested on a small sample of participants in the program. If this is not feasible, the questions should be tested on employees at approximately the same job level as the participants. Collect as much input and critique as possible, and revise the questions as necessary.

6. *Ensure that participant responses are anonymous.* Participants must feel free to respond openly to statements or questions. The confidentiality of their responses is of the utmost importance. If data are collected that can identify a respondent, then a neutral third party should collect and process the data.

7. *Design for easy tabulation.* In an attitude survey, a yes/no or varying degrees of agreement and disagreement are the usual responses.

8. *Prepare a data summary.* A data summary sheet should be developed so that data can be tabulated quickly for summary and interpretation. This step will help ensure that the data can be analyzed quickly and presented in a meaningful way.

9. *Develop the completed questionnaire or survey statement.* The questions should be finalized in a professional questionnaire with proper instructions. After completing these steps, the questionnaire is ready to be administered.

10. *Communicate the purpose of the survey.* Participants tend to cooperate in an activity when they understand its purpose. When a survey is administered, participants should be given an explanation of its purpose and told what will be done with the information that they provide. Also, they should be encouraged to give correct and proper statements or answers.

11. *Identify comparisons.* Reactions by themselves are meaningless. They need to be compared to objectives or expectations, to data before or after the program, or compared to another group or program. Data may be compared to all employees, a division, a department, or previous programs. For standard surveys, information may be available for similar programs. In any case, specific comparisons should be planned before administering the survey.

Uniform responses make tabulation and comparisons easier. On a scale of strongly agree to strongly disagree, numbers are usually assigned to reflect the responses. For example, a 1 may represent strongly disagree and a 5 strongly agree. If only 15 percent rated a 4 or 5 on a pre-program survey followed by a post-program response of 85 percent for a 4 or 5, a significant change in attitude is indicated. Some argue that a 5-point scale merely permits the respondent to select the midpoint and not to be forced to make a choice. If this is a concern, an even-numbered scale should be used. The key is to ensure that respondents can discern the difference between the numbers in the scale and can, as objectively as possible, respond to the question.

Some organizations use existing surveys designed by organizations with the sole purpose of taking similar measures. This approach can save time in development and pilot testing. Most of the reputable companies producing and marketing surveys have designed them to be reliable and valid for their intended purposes. Also, outside surveys allow for results comparisons with other organizations within the same industry or in similar industries. For example, Knowledge Advisors (www.knowledgeadvisors.com) offer subscribers the opportunity to measure reaction data using a standard questionnaire. By administering this particular questionnaire, an organization can compare its results to over a million other data points generated by other organizations using the system.

Intensities

Because different programs need different types of questions and questionnaires, thinking of three levels of reaction feedback instruments can be helpful. The first is low intensity and usually represents five to eight questions, simply worded, showing simple feedback. These are for programs that are short in duration, ranging from thirty minutes to four hours, where a need to obtain quick feedback exists. Using a scale that is suitable for automated analysis and avoiding written comments is essential for efficient scoring.

The second intensity is a moderate intensity and would cover most of the Level 1 feedback. This involves ten to twenty questions and covers many of the issues described in Table 4.1. The questions are designed for easy tabulation—either using the 5-point Likert Scale, true/false questions, or multiple-choice questions. Few open-ended questions are included.

The third category is the high intensity and is used to gather detailed feedback. This is designed for pilot programs, where quality, in-depth feedback is needed. Sometimes, a detailed questionnaire of up to forty or fifty questions may be necessary. In-depth interviews or focus groups could also be used. The purpose is to get high-quality, high-content feedback, taking one hour or less. Because of its expense, this type of questionnaire is reserved for situations in which this kind of feedback is critical to the program. Key introductions or the initial offerings to the first group of a pilot program would be a typical application of this type of data collection (Barksdale & Lund, 2001).

Questionnaire/Survey Response Rates

For most reaction evaluations, questionnaires and surveys will be used. When an evaluation is planned, exploring a wide range of issues and details is tempting. However, asking for too much detail in the reaction questionnaire can negatively impact the response rate. The challenge, therefore, is to approach questionnaire and survey design and administration for maximum response rate. The following actions can be taken to ensure a successful response rate. Although the term questionnaire is used, the following also apply to surveys:

• Early in the process, let participants know that they will need to complete a questionnaire.

- Indicate how the data will be used and perhaps how it has been used in the past.
- Design for a quick response, usually not to exceed ten to twenty minutes.
- Make responding to the questionnaire easy, using forced-choice questions.
- Communicate the estimated amount of time required to complete the questionnaire.
- Ask participants if they would like to see a copy of the summary.
- Make it look professional.
- Collect the data anonymously.

Sample Surveys

The design of the reaction surveys can vary considerably, as this chapter has shown. To show some appropriate questions for Level 1 reaction evaluation, we have a sample of a low-intensity and a moderate-intensity reaction sheet. Exhibit 4.3 shows the low-intensity feedback and focuses on six issues that are important for almost any type of program. Again, this is for use in short programs and would have to be tailored to specific programs, but for the most part would cover the issues across all content areas.

Instructions: Circle the appropriate response to each statement and add any comments you have about the program below.

	Strongly Disagree		Agree		Strongly Agree
The content was relevant to my job.	1	2	3	4	5
The facilitator was effective.	1	2	3	4	5
The materials were effective.	1	2	3	4	5
This was a good investment of my time.	1	2	3	4	5
I would recommend this to others.	1	2	3	4	5
Overall, I was satisfied with this program.	1	2	3	4	5

Exhibit 4.3. Low-Intensity Reaction Sheet.

Exhibit 4.4 shows a moderate-intensity reaction survey and would be the dominant form of most programs. It would be appropriate for one-day workshops all the way to one- or two-week workshops. The more detailed the workshop, the more this survey might need to be adjusted.

Instructions: Please circle the appropriate response to each statement, and add comments in the appropriate places.

Logistics and Service	Strongly Disagree				Strongly Agree
1. The learning environment was appropriate.	1	2	3	4	5
2. The food and refreshments were satisfactory.	1	2	3	4	5
3. The registration and enrollment process was satisfactory.	1	2	3	4	5

Objectives and Readiness

4. This program met the objectives.	1	2	3	4	5
5. I will have an opportunity to use the program.	1	2	3	4	5

Facilitator

6. The facilitator was knowledgeable.	1	2	3	4	5
7. The facilitator was responsive to participants.	1	2	3	4	5

Value of Delivery

8. Method of delivery was satisfactory.	1	2	3	4	5

Value of Content

9. The content was relevant to my job.	1	2	3	4	5
10. The content was important to my job success.	1	2	3	4	5

Value of Program

11. This was a good investment in me.	1	2	3	4	5
12. This was a good investment of my time.	1	2	3	4	5

Planned Use

13. I intend to use the material.	1	2	3	4	5
14. I can minimize the barriers to application.	1	2	3	4	5
15. I will recommend this program to others.	1	2	3	4	5

Exhibit 4.4. Moderate-Intensity Reaction Survey.

Comments

_____

_____

_____

Exhibit 4.4. Moderate-Intensity Reaction Survey, Cont'd.

DATA COLLECTION WITH INTERVIEWS AND FOCUS GROUPS

Another helpful data collection method is the interview, although it is not used as frequently as questionnaires to capture reaction data. Interviews may be conducted by the facilitator, the evaluator, or a third party. Also, the focus group is particularly helpful when in-depth feedback is used. A focus group involves a small group discussion of the participants facilitated by a person with experience with focus group process. The interviews and focus groups should be used only when a need to have in-depth feedback concerning the reaction to the program is present, and are only appropriate when this feedback is of significant consequence. This would normally occur when a program is on a pilot basis and a decision needs to be made to make serious adjustments or even implement the process. Also, they are useful when the programs are extensive and involved and adjustments need to be made quickly to make changes.

IMPROVING REACTION EVALUATION

There is no doubt that the value and use of Level 1 reaction evaluation is in question. There is much debate on its usefulness, even to the point at which there is some question about whether it should be collected at all (Boehle, 2006). The fact is that it is needed to complete the learning value chain and it does provide very valuable information, as we have shown in this chapter.

In addition to the questionnaire design principles, several helpful guidelines can improve the effectiveness of reaction data.

Keep Responses Anonymous

Anonymous feedback is highly recommended. It allows the participants to be open with their comments, which can be helpful and constructive. Otherwise, the input can be biased and perhaps stifled because of concerns about the direct reaction from the facilitator.

Have a Neutral Person Collect the Forms

In addition to anonymous responses, having a neutral person collect the feedback questionnaires may be helpful. In some organizations, the program coordinator or sponsor will conduct the evaluation at the end, independent of the facilitator. This action increases the objectivity of the input and decreases the likelihood of the instructor/facilitator reacting unfavorably to criticism contained in the feedback.

Provide a Copy in Advance

For lengthy evaluation forms covering programs that span several days, distributing the feedback questionnaire early in the program is helpful. This way, participants can familiarize themselves with the questions and statements. Participants can also address specific topics as they are covered and use more time to think through particular issues. They should be cautioned, however, not to reach a final conclusion on general issues until the end of the program.

Explain the Purpose of the Feedback and How It Will Be Used

Although this is sometimes understood, repeating where the information goes and how it is used within the organization is always a good idea. Some mystery still surrounds the use of feedback data. Restating the process in terms of the flow of data and the use of data can clarify this issue. Providing an example of how the data has been used to improve the program is also effective.

Explore an Ongoing Evaluation

For lengthy programs, an end-of-the-program evaluation may leave participants unable to remember what was covered at what time. As described earlier, an ongoing evaluation can be used to improve this situation. One approach is for the evaluation forms to be distributed at the beginning of the program, and participants are instructed when and how to supply the information. After each topic is presented, participants are asked to evaluate it and the facilitator. The participants can easily recall the information, and the feedback is more useful to program evaluators. Another approach is to use a daily feedback form to collect input on program pacing, degree of involvement, unclear items, etc. Exhibit 4.5 shows a recommended daily feedback form.

1. What issues presented today remain confusing and/or unclear?

   _____

   _____

   _____

2. The most useful topics presented today were

   _____

   _____

   _____

3. It would help me if you would

   _____

   _____

   _____

4. The pacing of the program is

   Just right

   Too slow

   Too fast

5. The participants' degree of involvement is

   Not enough

   Too much

   Just right

6. Three very important items that you should cover tomorrow are

   1. _____

   2. _____

   3. _____

7. Comments

   _____

   _____

   _____

   _____

   _____

Exhibit 4.5. Sample Daily Feedback Form.

Consider Quantifying Course Ratings

Some organizations attempt to solicit feedback in terms of numerical ratings. Although subjective, overall ratings can be used to monitor performance and make comparisons. For example, an overall rating is collected by the American Management Association in their public seminars. AMA monitors these overall ratings to compare them with similar programs and to track changes in ratings over time. With a large number of programs repeated several times, these ratings can be useful for comparisons. In some cases, targets or norms are established to compare ratings. When using a norm scale, a rating that is usually considered good may prove to be quite low when compared to the norm of the factor being rated. Another caution is needed since these ratings are subjective. Comparing numerical values may create an impression that the data are objective. This point should be underscored in evaluation communications.

Collect Information Related to Improvement

Although obtaining realistic input on a feedback form related to profits, cost reductions, or savings is difficult, it is worth the effort. The results may be surprising. Just a simple question may cause participants to concentrate on impacting monetary values. A possible statement might be:

> Please estimate the monetary values that will be realized (increased productivity, improved methods, reduced costs, etc.) as a result of this program, over a period of one year. Please explain the basis of your estimate.
>
> _____
>
> _____
>
> Express as a percent the confidence you place on your estimate. (0 = no confidence, 100 = certainty): _____

Additional detail on this concept will be provided in a later chapter on forecasting.

Allow Ample time for Completing the Form

A time crunch can cause problems when participants are asked to complete a feedback survey at the end of a program, particularly if they are in a hurry to leave. Consequently, participants may not provide complete information and may be cut short in an effort to finish and leave. A possible alternative is to allow ample time for evaluation as a scheduled session before the end of the program. This evaluation session could be followed by a wrap-up of the program and the last speaker. A thirty-minute session will provide much opportunity to enhance the quality and quantity of information.

Delayed Evaluation

An increasingly common approach is to delay the feedback evaluation until a later point. This avoids the pressure to provide part of the feedback to a facilitator and reduces the influence of the excitement that participants feel at the end of a program. After participants have returned to work and are on the job, their evaluations may be more objective. However, a downside may be that the response rate might not be as high. To overcome this, some of the techniques described in this chapter can help create the desire to send more information. Also, the methods to improve response rates described in later chapters may be helpful as well. Realistically, a 100 percent response rate is not necessary. A 70 percent response rate on a post-program collection may be appropriate.

A risk with delaying Level 1 data collection is that, if too much time passes, the data may not be as useful in making immediate change to the program content, design, or facilitation.

Ask for Honest Feedback

Too often, the facilitators do not explain how valuable the participants' feedback is. The facilitators must explain that they need honest feedback and that this feedback is used to make things better. Participants should know that the information they provide is used to determine when something should be improved or changed. Their feedback will be used for adjustments and fine-tuning of the program. When they are asked to be open, honest, and candid with their feedback, this may make a difference in their response rates.

USING DATA

Unfortunately, reaction and perceived value data are often collected and immediately disregarded. Too often, facilitators use the information to feed their egos and then let it quietly disappear into their files, forgetting the original purpose behind its collection. For successful evaluation, the information collected must be used to make adjustments or validate early program success; otherwise, the exercise is a waste of time. A few of the common uses for collecting reaction and satisfaction data are summarized below.

MONITOR CUSTOMER SATISFACTION. Because this input is the principal measure taken from participants, it provides an indication of their reaction to, and satisfaction with, the program. Therefore, facilitators, developers, and sponsors will know the participants' level of satisfaction. Data should be reported to these key stakeholders.

IDENTIFY STRENGTHS AND WEAKNESSES. Feedback is extremely helpful in identifying weaknesses as well as strengths of a program. Participant feedback on weaknesses often leads to adjustments and changes. Identifying strengths helps in future designs so that the strengths can be replicated. This may be the most important use of reaction data.

EVALUATE FACILITATORS. A common use of reaction data is to evaluate the facilitator. If properly constructed and collected, helpful feedback data can be provided to facilitators so that adjustments can be made to increase their effectiveness. Some caution needs to be taken, though, since participant evaluations can sometimes be biased. Other evidence is needed for an overall assessment of team performance.

DETERMINE PARTICIPANT NEEDS. An often overlooked reason to collect feedback is to determine additional needs or future needs of participants. Often a particular program sparks interest or perhaps has shortcomings. Participation in the program may provide participants with the knowledge and experience to indicate additional needs or future needs for continuing their development. This feedback can drive other programs or help enhance current programs and may be some of the most legitimate analysis of participant needs.

EVALUATE PLANNED IMPROVEMENTS. Feedback data from a questionnaire can provide a profile of planned actions and improvements. This can be compared with on-the-job actions resulting from the program. This initial input provides a rich source of data in terms of what participants may be changing or implementing because of their reactions to the program.

DEVELOP NORMS AND STANDARDS. Because reaction evaluation data can be automated and are collected in nearly all programs, developing norms and standards throughout the organization becomes easy. Target ratings can be set for expectations; particular results are then compared to those norms and standards.

LINK WITH FOLLOW-UP DATA. In many cases, planned actions are often inhibited in some way through on-the-job barriers. When a follow-up evaluation is planned, linking reaction data with follow-up data may be helpful to see whether planned improvements became reality. This validates the predictive relationship between reaction and application data.

MARKET FUTURE PROGRAMS. For some organizations, feedback data provide help for marketing future programs. Quotes and reactions provide information that may be convincing to potential sponsors. Marketing brochures for programs often contain quotes and summaries of feedback data.

Building the Macro-Level Scorecard

As described in Chapter Three, a macro-level scorecard, showing the combined contribution of all learning and development programs, is recommended. This involves collecting data at each level to be included in the overall scorecard. Because up to thirty or forty items can be selected, the challenge is to select only those measures that have value to the senior management team. Therefore, the following measures are recommended:

- How relevant is this to my job at the present time?
- How important is this to me and my job success?
- How much of the information is new information?
- I intend to use the materials from this program.
- This is a good investment in me.

SHORTCUT WAYS TO MEASURE REACTION AND PLANNED ACTION

At this point, the question is where to find the time and resources to collect reaction and perceived value data. While reaction data must always be collected, some shortcuts can be taken. A few essential items must be collected for very short, low-profile, inexpensive programs. Unfortunately, omitting this level is not an option because of the critical importance. Three particular actions can be helpful.

USE A SIMPLE QUESTIONNAIRE. A detailed, comprehensive, questionnaire isn't necessary for every program. The three intensity levels discussed earlier should be considered. A simple ten- to fifteen-item questionnaire using multiple choice or true/false questions or even a scale rating will be sufficient for most programs. Although interviews, focus groups, surveys, and questionnaires are all presented as options, the questionnaire can suffice for most situations.

COLLECT DATA EARLY AND REACT QUICKLY. Taking an early pulse is critical. Find out whether the program is being accepted and if there are any concerns about it. This step is critical, and action must be taken quickly. This ensures that the process remains on track and enjoys the success as planned.

AUTOMATE. Because Level 1 data are collected for each program, a tremendous amount of data is involved. Therefore, automation must be used to collect, analyze, report, and integrate data. Whether using spreadsheets or online data collection tools, factoring in automation is important to make this job as easy and pain-free as possible.

FOCUS ATTENTION ON PARTICIPANTS. As key stakeholders, participants are critical to the process. They can make or break any project or program, and their feedback is important. A general rule is to always listen to this group and react to their concerns, issues, and recommendations. Sometimes, the feedback will need filtering because of potential biases.

FINAL THOUGHTS

This was the first of four chapters on data collection, and it represents one of the seven measures of data reported in the ROI methodology. Measuring reaction and perceived value is included for every program and is an important part of the success. Although data are collected for many reasons, two important ones stand out. The first is making adjustments and changes throughout the program as problems or barriers are discovered. The second is capturing the participants' level of satisfaction with the program and having it included as one of the seven key types of data. Data can be collected in several ways, including questionnaires, surveys, interviews, and focus groups. By far, the questionnaire is the most common, and sometimes a simple, one-page reaction questionnaire is appropriate. Whatever method is used, the important point is to collect data, react quickly, make adjustments, and summarize the data for reporting and for use in an ROI impact study.

References

Barksdale, S., & Lund, T. (2001). *Rapid evaluation.* Alexandria, VA: ASTD.

Boehle, S. (2005, August). Are you too nice to train? *Training,* p. 16.

Dixon, M.N. (1990). *Evaluation: A tool for improving HRD quality.* San Francisco, CA: Pfeiffer.

Phillips, J.J., & Stone, R. (2002). *How to measure training results.* New York: McGraw-Hill.

CHAPTER FIVE

Measuring Learning
and Confidence

M easuring learning is a classic measure in program evaluation. Understanding how much learning has occurred is often critical, particularly in programs involved in significant skill building. The extent to which the participants learn new tasks and new processes may be one of the biggest determinants of the program's success. This chapter focuses on simple techniques for measuring learning. Many have been used for years in learning and development programs. Typical techniques are formal tests and skill practices. Others are less formal in structure and can be used when time and costs must be minimized.

WHY MEASURE LEARNING
AND CONFIDENCE?

Several key issues illustrate why learning is an important measure. While individually each can justify the need to measure learning, collectively, they provide motivation for taking a more rigorous approach for measuring the amount of skills, knowledge, or change that is achieved during a program.

The Importance of Intellectual Capital

Intellectual capital has become an important issue as organizations have progressed from agricultural to industrial to knowledge-based. Intellectual capital is what the organization knows and can be grouped in a variety of ways. Figure 5.1 shows one grouping of intellectual capital (Miller, 1999). This figure suggests that intellectual capital consists of a combination of human capital, renewable capital, structural capital, and relationship capital. Some learning and performance improvement programs are implemented to increase one or more of these major elements of intellectual capital. For some organizations, the intellectual capital translates into success, with the stock market often rewarding organizations for creating intellectual capital. For example, up to 80 percent of the market value in some firms is attributed to intellectual capital. Because of its importance, measuring learning becomes a major ingredient for success in programs when they are aimed at improving intellectual capital. When expertise, experience, and new knowledge arc essential, learning must be measured.

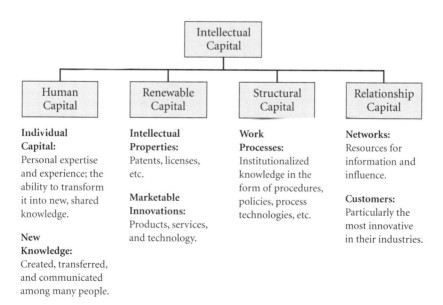

Figure 5.1. Categories of Intellectual Capital.

The Learning Organization

In the last two decades, organizations have experienced rapid transformation in competitive global markets and economic changes. Organizations must learn new ways to serve customers and use innovations and technology as they attempt to be efficient, restructure, reorganize, and execute globally. To meet this change in strategy, the concept of a learning organization has developed. This requires organizations to use learning proactively in an integrated way and to support and enhance growth for individuals, teams, and entire organizations. Peter Senge popularized the learning organization phenomena (Senge, 1990). A learning organization must capture, share, and use knowledge so that its members can work together to change the way the organization responds to challenges. Managers must question old social constructs and create new ways of thinking.

Learning must take place in and be supportive of teams and larger groups in which individuals can together create new knowledge. The process must be continuous because a learning organization is a never-ending journey (Watkins, 1996).

With the focus on creating learning organizations—where countless activities and processes are in place to promote, encourage, and support continuous learning—measurement becomes important. If an organization has become a learning organization, how do we know? How is it measured? Is learning actually measured on a large scale? These issues turn attention to the measurement of learning, and as programs and projects are initiated, learning is an essential factor.

The Learning Transfer Problem

A significant problem has plagued many programs: a lack of transfer to routine work activities of what is learned by participants. Participants may be involved in several learning activities. For most programs, learning is not transferred to the work environment as desired. Transferring this knowledge to the job is essential for success. To check for transfer, the learning must be measured early to see how much progress is being made.

The Compliance Issue

Organizations are facing an increasing number of regulations with which they must comply. These regulations involve all aspects of business, and governing bodies consider them necessary to protect customers, investors, and the environment.

Sometimes, programs are implemented to ensure that the organization is in compliance with regulations. For example, one large banking organization had to implement a major program to ensure that all employees were familiar with money laundering regulations. This program was precipitated by the bank's repeated failure to comply with the regulations. Thus, the problem appeared to be a lack of knowledge. As part of the settlement, along with fines, every employee underwent training on the regulations. Measuring learning became the most critical measure to ensure compliance. Employees must have a certain amount of knowledge about the regulation to be in compliance.

Sometimes, specific skills are needed. Consequently, knowledge, skills, and understanding are measured to ensure compliance. While some compliance issues focus on application, ensuring that employees perform in a particular way begins with measuring learning.

The Use and Development of Competencies

The use of competencies and competency models has dramatically increased in recent years. In a struggle to have a competitive advantage, many organizations have focused on people as the key to success. Competency models are used to ensure that employees are doing the right things. They clarify and articulate what is required for effective performance. The competency model describes a particular combination of knowledge, skills, and characteristics needed to perform a role consistent with the strategic direction of the organization. Competencies are used as a tool for recruiting, selecting, training, reviewing performance, and even removing individuals in an organization (Lucia, 1999). In some definitions, the concept of a competency includes innate and acquired abilities. Definitions include behavior, skills, and knowledge as well as aptitude and personal characteristics.

With this increased focus on competencies, the issue of measuring learning surfaces. Behaviors are learned or knowledge is acquired directly from learning and development programs. While some programs are implemented to develop new competencies, in almost every major program, existing competencies must be enhanced. Consequently, competencies and the focus on competencies are creating a greater concern for measuring learning.

The Role of Learning in Programs

When new equipment, processes, and technology are implemented, the human factor is critical to program success. Whether there is restructuring or the addition of new systems, employees must learn how to work in the new environment; this requires the development of new knowledge and skills. The days when simple tasks and procedures were built into work or automated within processes are gone. Instead, complex environments, complex processes, and complicated tools must be used in an intelligent way to reap the desired benefits for the organization. Employees must learn in different ways, not just in a formal classroom environment, but through technology-based learning and on-the-job learning. Also, team leaders and managers often serve as coaches or mentors in programs. In a few cases, learning coaches or on-the-job trainers are used in conjunction with a program to ensure that learning is transferred to the job and is implemented as planned. With this focus on learning, measurement of learning is critical.

The Chain of Impact

At times, participants don't fully understand what they must learn to make a program successful. The chain of impact, described in Chapter One, can be broken at any part of the chain. One place for the break is at Level 2, learning and confidence. Employees just don't know what to do or how to do it properly. When the application and implementation do not go smoothly, the first problem to examine is what went wrong: Where was the chain broken? What areas need to be adjusted? What needs to be altered? When learning is measured, evaluators can determine whether a lack of learning is the cause of the breakdown. In most cases, they may be able to eliminate the learning deficiency if one is the problem. Learning measurement is needed to understand why employees are, or are not, performing the way they should be.

Certification

The learning and development field has gone crazy about certification. Employees are becoming certified in a variety of processes, ranging from Microsoft™ products to Six Sigma implementation. With this focus on certification comes increased emphasis on measuring learning. Almost every, if not all, certification programs require an individual to demonstrate that he or she knows something or knows how to do something. It places more emphasis on measurement, much more than typical learning and development programs.

Consequences of an Unprepared Workforce

Perhaps the most important reason for the focus on measuring learning is to ensure that the workforce is prepared. There are many stories, some of them sad and disappointing, detailing how employees are not capable of doing what they need to do to perform their jobs and deliver excellent customer service. This has caused many management teams to ensure that the workforce is prepared. The only way to make sure that employees have the knowledge and skills to perform their jobs successfully is to measure it with some credible, valid, reliable process. The case study presented later in this chapter underscores the quest or desire for the management team to ensure that employees have the basic knowledge they need to successfully work with customers.

THE CHALLENGES AND BENEFITS OF MEASURING LEARNING

Measuring learning is not without its major challenges, which may inhibit a comprehensive approach to measurement. Besides being an essential part of the comprehensive evaluation system, this measure has many other benefits that may make a program successful.

The Challenges

Measuring learning is sometimes equated with testing, and there is a fear of testing. Few people enjoy taking tests. Even if it is a simple test, individuals or participants in a program may have a fear of not knowing or a fear of failing the test. Others resent being tested. The challenge is to make testing (or learning measurement) less threatening, and rarely, if ever, have testing scores affect a job situation.

Another important challenge of testing is that it questions the professional autonomy of many individuals. Occasionally, programs will involve engineers, scientists, accountants, physicians, lawyers, and many other professional employee groups. These individuals often feel that, because they are professional and have satisfied their professional credential requirements, they have all the knowledge and expertise needed for whatever problems arise in their professional roles. Even in a formal learning program, additional testing may seem to question their professional competence and thus, may be resisted. They want to be exempt from any testing or activity resembling a test. The challenge is to keep the testing processes at a low profile, show the importance of learning measurement to the program, and keep scoring and results confidential.

Other challenges for testing are ethical and legal considerations. When test scores affect participants and their job status, a test must be formally checked for validity and reliability. Although not common for most programs, test validity and reliability become concerns when certain skills or knowledge is important for program participants. The challenge is to take a reasonable approach, allocating resources to check for validity or reliability when necessary.

A related challenge is testing with diverse groups. Test results may differ significantly across diverse groups, sometimes creating an adverse impact with a particular group, and this group may be protected by federal or local laws. Even if they are not protected, ensuring that testing does not have a disparate impact is important. This issue is critical if the outcome of testing has an effect on job status.

A final challenge for measuring learning is the resources needed to do it. Budgets are often tight, and spending excessive amounts of resources on testing may not be desired or necessary. Therefore, there is always a tradeoff of additional resources versus the accuracy desired by some individuals. The important point is to control resource expenditures when possible. This often leads to some of the informal processes described later.

The Benefits

To a certain extent, the benefits of measuring learning mirror the reasons to measure learning described earlier. However, putting the benefits into focus with a particular program is helpful. First, a measurement at this level checks the progress with the objectives. As described in other parts of this book, objectives are critical to programs, and they should be set at each level. Learning measures provide the basis for success with the learning objectives, as they measure the extent of knowledge and skill acquisition in the program. This is necessary for most programs, and for some, this is a critical element, particularly knowledge-based programs, new technology applications, and programs involving building competencies. Without this level of measurement, no assessment of improvement in either skill or knowledge will be obtained.

Measuring at this level also provides feedback to the individuals delivering the knowledge, skills, or information. In many cases, a facilitator teaches these skills and knowledge, and measuring learning provides immediate feedback to him or her so that adjustments can be made. If participants are not learning, the problem may be with delivery. A learning measure identifies strengths and weaknesses of the learning and may signal that the design and delivery are not working well. Thus, measuring learning may pinpoint mismatches in several aspects of programs that could lead to changes or improvements.

Another important benefit is that, in many cases, learning measures enhance participant performance. Checking the knowledge and skills acquired often encourages participants to improve on certain areas. When they excel, this feedback motivates them to enhance performance further. In short, learning feedback builds the confidence and the desire to make things much better.

Finally, measuring learning helps complete accountability in learning systems. Because L&D programs are aimed at making organizations better—whether a learning organization is being built, competencies are being improved, or systems and processes are being enhanced—learning is an important part of the program. Learning measurement brings the appropriate accountability to learning systems.

Case Study

Perhaps the importance of measuring learning can best be illustrated by considering a program where learning was one of the most important, if not the most important, process to measure. A large pharmaceutical firm (in the top ten globally) was concerned about the interaction between a sales rep and a physician. Because the interaction is often limited to three to five minutes, having instant recall of a variety of information is essential for the pharmaceutical sales rep. In many cases, the physician doesn't even want to meet with the sales rep but is willing to meet when samples or other incentives are provided. Understandably, physicians are quite busy, and their time needs to be allocated to their patients. However, the frustration for the pharmaceutical industry is that they want their message to be relayed directly to the physician.

For each of the seven drugs marketed by the firm, the sales rep must have instant recall of the following information:

- The chemical composition of the drug
- The latest research trials that show the effectiveness of the drug

• The symptoms and side effects of each drug

• The marketing strategy of that particular drug

While this is a vast amount of information, it is understandable that it should be instantly available so that time is not wasted looking it up. Because of this, the firm launched a major program to build capability. The principal focus was to develop knowledge in the four areas listed for each of the seven drugs. Although the five levels of evaluation were appropriate in this program, the most important measure was learning and confidence, Level 2.

To measure learning, a comprehensive test for each of the seven drugs would be administered in six-month intervals. Taking about an hour, each test would address the information outlined above and would be administered under carefully controlled conditions. Failing to pass the test would mean that the individual had one more try, again under consistent and controlled conditions. If the test were failed again, the challenge was to find another job for the sales rep, away from interactions with physicians. If a different job was not available, then the person would be terminated. With these consequences, ensuring that the test was checked for validity and reliability was critical.

Measuring at Level 2 was essential because the knowledge of the skills must exist to ensure that the reps could answer any questions about the drugs before they approach busy physicians. At Level 3, assessment must be made to ensure that the reps apply this knowledge and give the physicians the information they need within a timeframe acceptable to physicians. Assessing application and implementation will be discussed in Chapter Six.

MEASUREMENT ISSUES

Several issues affect the nature and scope of measurement at the learning level. These involve objectives, measures, and timing.

Objectives

As mentioned earlier, the starting point in any measurement system is the objectives. As with other levels of measurement, the measurement of learning builds on the learning objectives. Learning and development professionals have excellent skills in generating detailed learning objectives following the process described in Chapter Two. The first step in the learning value chain is to ensure that objectives are in place. When they are in place, they are the basis for measuring learning.

Typically, the objectives are broad and only indicate specific major skills or knowledge areas that should be achieved as the program is implemented. These are sometimes called key learning objectives. As shown in Figure 5.2, these objectives break down into subcomponents. Each key objective may have sub-objectives that provide more detail. If necessary these sub-objectives are broken into supporting objectives and, even further, sub-supporting objectives. This is necessary when many tasks, procedures, and new skills must be learned to make the programs successful. For short programs for which the focus on learning is light, this level of detail might not be needed. Identifying the major objectives and indicating what must be accomplished to meet those objectives are often sufficient.

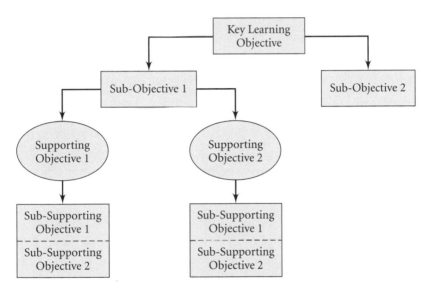

Figure 5.2. A Breakdown of Objectives.

Typical Measures

Learning measures focus on knowledge, skills, and attitudes as well as confidence to apply or implement the program or process as desired. Sometimes, these are expanded to different categories. Exhibit 5.1 shows the typical measures collected at this level. Obviously, the more detailed the skills, the greater the number of objectives. Programs can vary, ranging from one or two simple skills to large massive programs that may involve literally hundreds of skills.

• Skills	• Attitudes
• Knowledge	• Capability
• Awareness	• Capacity
• Understanding	• Readiness
• Information	• Confidence
• Perceptions	• Contacts

Exhibit 5.1. Typical Learning Measurement Categories.

Knowledge often includes the assimilation of facts, figures, and concepts. Instead of knowledge, the terms awareness, understanding, or information may be specific categories. Sometimes, perceptions or attitudes may change based on what a participant has learned. For example, in a diversity program, the participants' attitudes toward having a diverse work group are often changed with the implementation of the program. Sometimes, the desire is to develop a reservoir of knowledge and skills and tap into it when developing capability, capacity, or readiness. When individuals are capable, they are often described as being job-ready.

When participants use skills for the first time, an appropriate measure might be the confidence that the participants have to use those skills in their job settings. This becomes critical in job situations in which skills must be performed accurately and within a certain standard. Sometimes, networking is part of a program and developing contacts that may be valuable later is important. This may be within, or external to, an organization. For example, a leadership development program may include participants from different functional parts of the organization and an expected outcome, from a learning perspective, is to know who to contact at particular times in the future.

Timing

The timing of learning measurement can vary. In some situations, a pre-measure is taken, creating a pre-test to determine the extent to which participants understand or know the specific objectives in the program. A pre-test can be important to assess the current skills and knowledge so that learning additional skills and knowledge can be planned efficiently. This may prevent participants from repeating the learning of information that they already know, thereby reducing program costs by limiting participants to those who lack the knowledge. When the pre-test shows that knowledge is lacking, a post-test can show whether knowledge has been acquired. The post-test can be administered during learning or after learning is completed. The pre- and post-testing should be conducted under the same or similar conditions using content, questions, or test items that are identical or very similar.

Assuming that no pre-test is taken, measuring learning can occur at different times. In most formal programs, the measure of learning is taken at the end of those sessions. For long-term programs, as skills and knowledge grow, routine testing may be needed to measure both the acquisition of additional skills and knowledge and the retention of the previously acquired skills and knowledge. The timing of measurement is balanced with the need for knowing the level of skills and knowledge acquired; this is offset by the cost of obtaining, analyzing, and responding to the data. Ideally, when to measure learning is determined during the development of the data collection plan, described in several places throughout this book. The plan includes a column for the timing of measurements according to the level of evaluation. When agreed to in advance, the resources can be allocated and expectations can be generated.

Cognitive Levels of Bloom's Taxonomy

Bloom and other psychologists created a system for describing, in detail, different levels of cognitive functioning so that the precision of testing cognitive performance could be improved. The result of this extensive effort was a classification system that breaks cognitive processes into six types: knowledge, comprehension, application, analysis, synthesis, and evaluation. The scheme is called "taxonomy" because each level is subsumed by the next, higher level. Since its creation, the taxonomy has been widely used to classify the cognitive level of learning objectives and test items.

- *Knowledge* level is the lowest level of the taxonomy and simply indicates the ability to remember content in exactly the same form in which it was presented.
- *Comprehension* level consists of one of the following types:

  Learners restate material in their own words.

  Learners translate information from one form to another.

Learners apply designated rules.

Learners recognize previously unseen examples of concepts.

- The *application* level requires learners to decide what rules are pertinent to a given problem and then to apply the rules to solve the problem.

- At the *analysis* level, learners are required to break complex situations into their component parts and figure out how the parts relate to and influence one another.

- Objectives at the *synthesis* level require the creation of totally original material: original products, designs, equipment, etc.

- The *evaluation* level is the highest level of Bloom's taxonomy. This level requires learners to judge the appropriateness or value of some object, plan, design, etc. for some purpose. (Shrock & Coscarelli, 2000)

These levels often create some confusion in regard to Kirkpatrick's levels of evaluation and the different levels presented in this book. However, Bloom's levels apply to learning measures only. And, while they can be confusing, they are meant to focus on knowledge and skill acquisition.

DATA COLLECTION METHODS

One of the most important considerations with regard to measuring learning is the specific way in which data are collected. For some programs, collecting data at Level 2 involves what most consider testing, whether testing is objective or subjective.

Most types of tests used in programs can be classified in three ways. The first is based on *the method used* for administering the test. The most common media for tests are written or keyboard tests; performance tests, using simulated tools or the actual equipment; and computer-based tests, using computers and video displays. Knowledge and skills tests are usually written, because performance tests are more costly to develop, administer, and score. Computer-based and web-based tests are gaining popularity. In these tests, a computer monitor or video screen presents the questions or situations, and participants respond by typing on a keyboard or touching the screen. Interactive videos add a strong element of realism because the test-taker can react to images, often video clips, that reproduce real job situations.

The second way to classify tests is by *purpose and content*. In this context, tests can be divided into *aptitude* tests or *achievement* tests. Aptitude tests measure basic skills or acquired capacity to learn a job. An achievement test assesses a person's knowledge or competence in a particular subject.

The third way to classify tests is by *test design*. Some common types of tests are objective tests, criterion-referenced tests, essay tests, oral examinations, and performance tests. *Objective* tests have answers that are specific and precise, based on the objectives of a program. While objective tests are useful, attitudes, feelings, creativity, problem-solving processes, and other intangible skills and abilities cannot be measured accurately with objective tests. A useful form of objective test is the *criterion-referenced* test. Success with these tests is based on a specific score or criterion. *Performance* tests measure the success of demonstrable learning, meaning participants demonstrate their abilities to perform or execute knowledge and skills. *Oral examinations* and *essay tests* have limited use in program evaluations; they are probably more useful in academic settings. Criterion-referenced tests and performance tests are used more for program evaluations.

Exhibit 5.2 presents the types of data collection for measuring learning, integrating the three categories above. Sometimes, classification is difficult because of the overlap in methodologies. However, these are well-known approaches. Each major category is discussed next.

• Questionnaires/Surveys	• Case Studies
• Objective Tests	• Role Playing/Skill Practice
• Criterion-Referenced Tests	• Assessment Center Method
• Performance Tests	• Exercises/Activities
• Technology and Task Simulations	• Informal Assessments

Exhibit 5.2. The Many Ways to Measure Learning.

Questionnaires/Surveys

As with Level 1 data, Level 2 (learning) data are often collected using questionnaires and surveys. These tools are inexpensive, simple to administer, and easy to automate. Pre- and post-learning scales are often developed to assess knowledge level before and after a program. Skill inventories are used to gauge knowledge progression and are administered via a survey instrument. Rating scales are commonly used as previously described. The typical scale is a 5-point scale, although 4-point, 7-point, and 10-point scales are also used. These guidelines should be used when developing questionnaires and surveys (Shrock & Coscarelli, 2000):

- Each statement should focus on a single issue or specific topic.
- Use short statements to present less opportunity for measurement error.
- Ensure that statements are understandable to all respondents.
- Avoid over-sophisticated, complex vocabulary.
- Provide enough choices.
- Label the choices.
- Ensure that there is a difference between choices.
- Balance the scale properly.

Objective Tests

As pointed out earlier, objective tests require precise responses. Answers to questions are either right or wrong. Multiple-choice is the most common objective test, where the participants are asked to choose from a series of alternative answers. This type test has the advantage of easy scoring and is relatively unbiased. Two-way or true-false questions are often used. They are simple to develop and leave little room for interpretation, by either the respondent or the scorer.

Matching exercises, where participants match items on a choice basis, are also useful. They are easy to write and can be scored quickly. Fill-in-the-blank items are open-ended and easy to write, but more difficult to score. Short-answer questions can be easy to develop, but are also challenging to score. They often ask for responses or provide a place for a few sentences. Essay questions are less likely to be used because they are difficult to score and rely on a high degree of subjectivity by the scorer instead of the participant's actual knowledge.

Collectively, the two-way, multiple-choice, matching, fill-in-the-blank, and short-answer tests are primarily used as objective tests to measure learning. Exhibit 5.3 shows the basic guidelines for developing the different types of tests (Shrock & Coscarelli, 2000). Test development is a fairly simple and straightforward process and is covered adequately in many other resources (Phillips & Phillips, 2007).

TRUE/FALSE TESTS

- ☐ Use true/false items in situations in which there are only two likely alternative answers.
- ☐ Include only one major idea in each item.
- ☐ Make sure that the statement can be judged reasonably true or false.
- ☐ Keep statements as short and as simple as possible.
- ☐ Avoid negatives, especially double negatives.
- ☐ Randomly distribute both true and false statements.
- ☐ Avoid "always" and "never" in the statements.

MULTIPLE-CHOICE

Guidelines for Writing the Stem

- ☐ Write the stem using simple and clear language.
- ☐ Place as much wording as possible in the stem, rather than in the alternative answers.
- ☐ If possible, state the stem in a positive form.
- ☐ Highlight negative words if they are essential.

Guidelines for Writing the Distracters

- ☐ Provide four or five alternative answers, including the correct response.
- ☐ Make certain you can defend the intended correct answer as clearly the best alternative.
- ☐ Make all alternatives grammatically consistent with the stem of the item.
- ☐ Vary randomly the position of the correct answer.
- ☐ Vary the relative length of the correct answer.
- ☐ Avoid "all," "always," and "never."
- ☐ Use familiar looking or verbatim statements that are incorrect answers to the question.
- ☐ Use true statements that do not answer the question.
- ☐ Anticipate the options that will appeal to the unprepared test-taker.
- ☐ Avoid the use of "All of the above."
- ☐ Use "None of the above" with caution.
- ☐ Avoid alternatives of the type "both a and b are correct."
- ☐ If there is a logical order to options, use it in listing them; for example, if the options are numbers, list them in ascending or descending order.

MATCHING

- ☐ Include only homogeneous, closely related content in the lists to be matched.
- ☐ Keep the lists of responses short—five to fifteen entries.
- ☐ Arrange the response list in some logical order—chronologically or alphabetically.

Exhibit 5.3. Guidelines for Developing Tests.

(Continued)

☐ Clearly indicate in the directions the basis on which entries are to be matched.

☐ Indicate in the directions how often a response can be used; responses should be used more than once to reduce cueing due to the process of elimination.

☐ Use a larger number of responses than entries to be matched to reduce process-of-elimination cueing.

FILL-IN-THE-BLANKS

☐ State the item so that only a single, brief answer is likely.

☐ Use direct questions as much as possible, rather than incomplete statements, as a format.

☐ If you must use incomplete statements, place the blank at the end of the statement, if possible.

☐ Provide adequate space for the test-taker to write the correct answer.

☐ Keep all blank lines of equal length to avoid cues to the correct answers.

☐ For numerical answers, indicate the degree of precision required ("to the nearest tenth") and the units in which the answer is to be recorded ("in pounds").

SHORT-ANSWER

☐ State the question as clearly and succinctly as possible.

☐ Be sure that the question can be answered in only a few sentences.

☐ Provide guidance regarding the length of response anticipated (for example, fewer than seventy-five words).

☐ Provide adequate space for the test-taker to write the response.

ESSAY

☐ State the question as clearly and succinctly as possible; present a well-focused task to the test-taker.

☐ Provide guidance regarding the length of response anticipated ("in three to five pages...")

☐ Provide estimates of the approximate time to be devoted to each essay question.

☐ Provide adequate space for the test-taker to write the response.

☐ Indicate whether spelling, punctuation, grammar, and organization will be considered in scoring the response.

Exhibit 5.3. Guidelines for Developing Tests, Cont'd.

Criterion-Referenced Tests

The criterion-referenced test (CRT) is an objective test with a predetermined cutoff score. The CRT is a measure against carefully written objectives for the learning components of a program. In using a CRT, the interest lies in whether participants meet the desired minimum standards, not how participants rank among others. The primary concern is to measure, report, and analyze participant performance as it relates to the learning objectives.

Table 5.1 examines a reporting format based on criterion-referenced testing and helps explain how a CRT is applied to an evaluation effort. In the example, four participants have completed a learning component with three measurable objectives that correspond to each of the modules. Actual test scores are reported, and the minimum standard is shown. For example, on the first objective, Participant 4 received a pass rating for a test that has no numerical value but is simply rated pass or fail. The same participant met objective 2 with a score of 14 (10 was listed as the minimum passing score). The participant scored 88 on objective 3 but failed it because the standard was 90. Overall, Participant 4 satisfactorily completed the learning component. The column on the far right shows that the minimum passing standard for the program is at least two of the three objectives. Participant 4 met two objectives, the required minimum.

Criterion-referenced testing is a popular measurement tool in programs in which much learning is involved. The approach is helpful when a group of employees need to learn new systems, competencies, or technology. The process is frequently computer-based, making testing more convenient. It has the advantage of being objective-based, precise, and relatively easy to administer, but it requires clearly defined objectives that can easily be measured.

Performance Tests

Performance testing allows the participants to exhibit a skill (and occasionally knowledge or attitudes) that have been learned in a program. The skill can be manual, verbal, or analytical, or a combination of the three. Performance testing is used frequently in task-related programs for which the participants are allowed to demonstrate what they have learned and show how they would use the skill on the job. In other situations, performance testing may involve skill practices or role playing (for example, participants are asked to demonstrate discussion or problem-solving skills that they have acquired).

To illustrate the possibilities of performance testing, consider two examples. Computer systems engineers were participating in a system reengineering program. As part of the program, participants were given the assignment to design and test a basic system. A facilitator observed participants as they checked out the system, then carefully

	Objective 1	Objective 2			Objective 3			Total Objectives Passed	Minimum Standard	Overall Score
	P/F	Raw Score	Std	P/F	Raw Score	Std	P/F			
Participant 1	P	4	10	F	87	90	F	1	2 of 3	Fail
Participant 2	F	12	10	P	110	90	P	2	2 of 3	Pass
Participant 3	P	10	19	P	100	90	P	3	2 of 3	Pass
Participant 4	P	14	10	P	88	90	F	2	2 of 3	Pass
Total 4	3 Pass			3 Pass			2 Pass	8 Pass		3 Pass
	1 Fail			1 Fail			2 Fail	4 Fail		1 Fail

Table 5.1. Sample Reporting Format for CRT Test Data.

built the same design and compared her results with those of the participants. These comparisons and the performance of the designs provided an evaluation of the program and represented an adequate reflection of the skills learned in the program.

In the second example, as part of a reorganization program, team members learned new products and sales strategies. Part of the evaluation required team members to practice skills in an actual situation involving a sales presentation. Participants were asked to conduct the skills practice on another member of the group using a real situation and applying the principles and steps learned in the L&D program. The skill practice was observed by the team member, and a written critique was provided at the end of the practice. These critiques provided part of the evaluation of the reorganization program.

For a performance test to be effective, the following steps are recommended in the design and administration of the test:

- The test should be a representative sample of the work/tasks related to the program. The test should allow the participant to demonstrate as many of the skills taught in the program as possible. This increases the validity of the test and makes it more meaningful to the participant.

- Every phase of the test should be planned—the timing, the participant's preparation, the collection of necessary materials and tools, and the evaluation of the results.

- Thorough and consistent instructions are necessary. As with other tests, variations in the instructions can influence the outcome of a performance test. All participants should be given the same instructions—clear, concise, and to the point. Charts, diagrams, blueprints, and other supporting information should be provided if they are normally provided in the work setting. If appropriate and feasible, the knowledge or skills should be demonstrated against the testing criteria by the program leader or facilitator so that participants observe how the skill is practiced.

- Procedures should be developed for objective evaluation, and acceptable standards must be developed for a performance test. Standards are sometimes difficult to develop because varying degrees of speed, skill, and quality are associated with individual outcomes. Predetermined standards must be developed so that participants know in advance what has to be accomplished to be considered satisfactory and acceptable for test completion.

With these general guidelines, performance tests can be effective tools for evaluation. Although more costly than written tests, performance tests are essential in situations in which a high degree of similarity is required between work and test conditions.

Technology and Task Simulations

Another technique for measuring learning is simulations. This method involves the construction and application of a procedure or task that simulates or models the work involved in the program. The simulation is designed to represent, as closely as possible, the actual job situation. Participants try out their performance in the simulated activity and are evaluated based on how well they accomplish the task. Simulations offer several advantages. They permit a job or part of a job to be reproduced in a manner almost identical to the real setting. Through careful planning and design, the simulation can have all the central characteristics of the real situation. Even complex jobs, such as that of a manager, can be simulated adequately.

Although initial development can be expensive, simulations can be cost-effective in the long run, particularly in large programs or in situations in which a program may be repeated. Another advantage of using simulations is safety. The safety component of many jobs requires participants to be trained in simulated conditions. For example, emergency medical technicians risk injury and even death if they do not learn emergency medical techniques prior to encountering a real-life situation.

Although several simulation techniques are used to evaluate learning during a program, two of the most common techniques are *technology* and *task*. A technology simulation uses a combination of electronics and mechanical devices to simulate real-life situations. They are used in conjunction with programs to develop operational and diagnostic skills. Expensive examples of these types include simulated "patients" or a simulator for a nuclear power plant operator. Other less-expensive types of simulators have been developed to simulate equipment operation.

The following is an example of a task simulation. In an aircraft company, technicians are trained on the safe removal, handling, and installation of a radioactive source used in a nucleonic oil-quantity indicator gauge. These technicians attend a thorough training program on all the procedures necessary for this important assignment. To become certified to perform this task, technicians are observed in a simulation, where they perform all the necessary steps on a checklist. After they have demonstrated that they possess the skills necessary for the safe performance of this assignment, they are certified. This task simulation serves as the Level 2 evaluation.

Case Studies

A perhaps less-effective but still-popular technique of measuring learning is the use of a case study. A case study is as much a teaching tool as it is an evaluation method. A case study represents a detailed description of a problem and usually contains a list of several questions posed to the participant. The participant is asked to analyze the case and determine the best course of action. The problem should reflect conditions in the real world and in the content of the program.

The most common categories of case studies include:

- *Exercise case studies* provide an opportunity for participants to practice the application of specific procedures.

- *Situational case studies* give participants the opportunity to analyze information and make decisions surrounding their particular situations.

- *Complex case studies* are extensions of situational case studies, where the participant is required to process a large amount of data and information, some of which may be irrelevant.

- *Decision case studies* require the participant to go a step further than the previous categories and present plans for solving a particular problem.

- *Critical-incident case studies* provide the participant with a certain amount of information and withhold other information until it is requested by the participant.

- *Action-maze case studies* present a large case in a series of smaller units, and the participant is required to predict at each stage what will happen next.

The difficulty in a case study lies in objectively evaluating the participant's performance. Frequently, many possible courses of action are available, some equally as effective as others. This makes obtaining an objective, measurable performance rating for the analysis and interpretation of the case difficult.

Role Playing/Skill Practice

Role plays, sometimes referred to as skill practice, require participants to practice a newly learned skill as they are observed by other individuals. Participants are given their assigned roles with specific instructions, which sometimes include an ultimate course of action. The participant then practices the skill with other individuals to accomplish the desired objectives. This exercise is intended to simulate the real-world setting to the greatest extent possible. Difficulty sometimes arises when participants make the practice unrealistic by not reacting the way individuals would in an actual situation. To help overcome this obstacle, trained role players (non-participants trained for the role) may be used in all roles except that of the participant. This can possibly provide a more objective evaluation.

The success of this technique also lies in the judgment of those observing the role play. The skill of effective observation is as critical as the skill of the person playing the role. Also, the success of this method depends on the participant's willingness to participate in and adjust to the planned role. If participant resistance is extremely high, the performance in the skill practice may not reflect actual job performance. Nevertheless, these skill practices can be useful in helping participants practice discussion skills.

Assessment Center Method

Another method for measuring learning is a formal procedure called the assessment center method. Feedback is provided to participants by a group of trained observers called assessors. For years, the assessment center approach has been an effective tool for employee selection. It now shows great promise as a tool for evaluating the effectiveness of a major learning module in a program.

Assessment centers are not actually centers, locations, or buildings. The term refers to a procedure for evaluating the performance of individuals. In a typical assessment center, the individuals being assessed participate in a variety of exercises during which they demonstrate a particular skill, knowledge, or ability, usually called job dimensions.

These dimensions are important to on-the-job success for those involved in the program. Participants may take anywhere from four hours to three days to complete the exercises. The assessors then combine the ratings of each exercise for each dimension, removing subjectivity, to reach a final rating for each participant.

In the assessment center process, a rating or "assessment" of the participants is given prior to program implementation. After the program is implemented, the participants are assessed again to see whether their performance within the job dimensions has improved.

Although the popularity of this method is growing, it still may not be feasible for many programs. The use of an assessment center is quite involved and time-consuming for the participants and the assessors. The assessors must be carefully trained to be objective and reliable. However, for programs that represent large expenditures aimed at developing highly trained individuals, the assessment center approach may be the most promising way to measure the impact of the program. This is particularly true for an organization in which the assessment center process is already used for selection purposes.

Exercises/Activities

Many learning and development programs involve activities, exercises, or problems that must be explored, developed, or solved during the program. Some of these are constructed in terms of involvement exercises, while others require individual problem-solving skills. When these tools are integrated into the learning activity, several specific ways to measure learning are available:

- The results of the exercise can be submitted for review and for possible scoring by a member of the program team. This score becomes part of the overall measure of learning.
- The results can be discussed in a group, with a comparison of the various approaches and solutions, and the group can reach an assessment of how much each individual has learned. This may not be practical in many settings, but can work in a few narrowly focused applications.
- The solutions to the exercises can be shared with the group, and the participant can provide a self-assessment indicating the degree to which the skills and/or knowledge have been obtained

from the exercise. This also serves as reinforcement because participants quickly see the correct solution.

- The program leader or facilitator can review the individual progress of each participant to determine his or her relative success. This is appropriate for small groups, but can be very cumbersome and time-consuming with larger groups.

Informal Assessments

For most programs, an informal check of learning is sufficient to provide some assurance that participants have acquired the skills and knowledge or that needed changes in attitudes have occurred. This approach is appropriate when other levels of evaluation are pursued. For example, if a Level 3 application and implementation evaluation is planned, conducting a comprehensive Level 2 evaluation might not be as critical. An informal assessment of learning is usually sufficient. After all, if resources are scarce, a comprehensive evaluation at all levels becomes quite expensive. This is an alternative approach to measuring learning when inexpensive, low-key measurements are needed.

A commonly used informal assessment is participant self-assessment. Participants are provided an opportunity to assess their acquisition of skills and knowledge. A few guidelines can ensure that the process is effective:

- The self-assessment should be made anonymously so that participants feel free to express realistic and accurate assessments of what they have learned.

- The purpose of the self-assessment should be explained, along with the plans for using the data, such as program adjustments and changes.

- If no improvement has been made or the self-assessment is unsatisfactory, some explanation as to what that means and what the implications will be should be discussed. This will help ensure that accurate and credible information are provided.

In some situations, the facilitator may provide an assessment of learning. Although this approach is subjective, it may be appropriate when facilitators work closely with participants over a substantial time period. One of the most effective ways to accomplish this is to provide a checklist of the specific skills that should be acquired. Facilitators can then check off the assessment of the skills individually. Also, if a particular body of knowledge needs to be acquired, a checklist of the categories should be developed for assuring that the individual has a good understanding of those items.

Informal assessment has advantages. It is inexpensive, quick, and often user-friendly. In many cases, it is not invasive, rarely interrupting the work flow, because it often takes minimal time and can fit into most program time schedules. Informal assessments can be easily scored, interpreted, and used to make changes or improvements. However, with advantages come disadvantages. This type of assessment is more subjective than formal assessments and, therefore, is less reliable and valid. A potential low return rate may develop because participants do not take the exercise as seriously as formal processes. And because it is informal, the conditions in which the data are collected may vary, resulting in potential bias.

ADMINISTRATIVE ISSUES

Several administrative issues must be addressed when measuring learning. Each is briefly discussed in this section and should be part of the overall plan for administering learning measurement.

Reliability and Validity

When test design is considered, two important issues are *validity* and *reliability*. Validity is the extent to which an instrument measures what it is designed to measure. Reliability is the extent to which an instrument is stable or consistent over time. In essence, any instrument used to collect data should be both valid (measures what it should measure) and reliable (consistent over time). A reliable instrument means that if the same data were collected at different times and nothing intervened to cause a change in knowledge, then the response should be the same. Significant deviations mean that the instrument is unreliable. Table 5.2 shows the relationship between reliability and validity. In the ideal scenario, the instrument has to be both reliable and valid. It is not possible to have a valid instrument if it is not reliable.

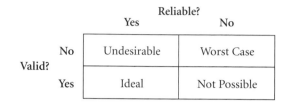

Table 5.2. Relationship Between Validity and Reliability.

The concept of validity and reliability and how to check for an adequate threshold of both are beyond the scope of this book. Other references are available to give more detail (Schrock & Coscarelli, 2002). However, a sensible approach when developing instruments is important. The use of subject-matter experts in the design, development, and use of the instruments is often enough to ensure that the instrument is valid. This is called content validity. Other methods for checking validity become more analytical than most managers and executives want to explore. In terms of reliability, having an appropriate number of questions on a survey and ensuring that no questions are vague and ambiguous can help improve reliability. Exhibit 5.4 provides a few tips for improving validity and reliability.

FOR IMPROVING VALIDITY
- Have test items reviewed by content "experts."
- Check for even and consistent representation of course objectives.
- Check with participants for face validity.
- Include an appropriate number of items.
- Reduce potential response bias.
- Administer objectively.

FOR IMPROVING RELIABILITY
- Provide clear and consistent instructions for test.
- Ensure sufficient time for responses.
- Ensure the same amount of time for responses.
- Ensure consistency in all steps and procedures.

Exhibit 5.4. Tips for Improving Validity and Reliability.

These two issues become more important when a human resource action (job status change) is taken as a result of a person's passing or failing a test. For example, if an individual is promoted, denied assignment, provided an increase in pay, or is placed in a career ladder because of passing the test or failing the test, the instrument must be defensible. In other words, if a challenge is raised, the reliability and validity must be defendable, up to and including a defense in the courts. In the vast majority of L&D programs, this will not be the case. Rarely do test failures result in job status changes.

Consistency

Tests, exercises, or assessments for measuring learning must be administered consistently from one group to another. This includes issues such as the time required to respond, the actual learning conditions in which the participants complete the process, the resources available to them, and the assistance from other members of the group. These issues can easily be addressed in the instructions.

Monitoring

When formal testing is used, participants should be monitored as they complete the test or other measurement processes. This ensures that each individual works independently and also that someone is available to provide assistance or answer questions as needed. This may not be an issue in all situations, but should be addressed in the overall plan.

Pilot Testing

Testing an instrument with a small group to ensure validity and reliability is advisable. A pilot test provides an opportunity to clarify confusion that might exist about the instructions, questions, or statements. When a pilot test is pursued, it should be timed to determine how long individuals take to complete it. Also, the individuals who take the pilot should provide input in terms of other ways to ask the questions and the flow of information and provide any other suggestions for improvement.

Readability

As with reaction questionnaires, readability is important. The reading level must be matched with the target audience. This could be a simple step in the process where the readability level can be checked with Microsoft Word® or other software.

Scoring

Scoring instructions have to be developed for the measurement process so that the evaluator will be objective and provide consistent scores. Ideally, the potential bias from this person should be completely removed through proper scoring instructions and other information needed to provide an objective evaluation.

Reporting

In some situations, the participants are provided with the results immediately, particularly with self-scoring tests or with group-based scoring. In other situations, the actual results may not be known until later. In these situations, a method for providing scoring data should be built into the evaluation plan unless it has been predetermined that participants will not know the scores. The worst-case scenario is promising test scores and delivering them late or not delivering them at all.

Confronting Test Failures

Test failures may not be an issue, particularly if the data are collected informally through a self-assessment process. However, when more rigorous and formal methods are used and individuals do not demonstrate the required competencies to pass the test, some consideration must be made for confronting these failures. An important issue is to ensure that the test and the testing procedures are defensible. As described earlier, a test must be both reliable and valid, and the cutoff score must also be defensible. Written guidelines should be developed to address this issue, and participants should know these in advance. The outcomes and consequences should be discussed with the individuals. A retest is allowed if appropriate; however, all individuals must be treated consistently.

USING LEARNING DATA

Data must be used to add value and improve processes. Although several uses of learning data are appropriate, those described in this section are most common.

ENSURING THAT LEARNING HAS BEEN ACQUIRED. Sometimes, knowing the extent and scope of learning is essential. Measuring learning, even informally, will provide input on this issue. It shows whether the learning component of the chain of input is successful.

PROVIDING INDIVIDUAL FEEDBACK TO BUILD CONFIDENCE. Learning data, when provided directly to participants, provide reinforcement for correct answers and enhance confidence. This reinforces the learning process and provides much-needed feedback to participants involved in learning and development programs.

IMPROVING THE PROGRAM. Perhaps the most important use of learning data is to improve the program. This is process improvement for designers, developers, facilitators, and L&D team leaders. Consistently low responses in certain learning measures may indicate that inadequate facilitation has been provided on that topic. Consistently low scores with all participants may indicate that the objectives and scope of coverage are misdirected or too ambitious.

EVALUATING FACILITATORS. Just as reaction and planned action data can be used to evaluate program leaders and facilitators, learning measures provide additional evidence of success. The facilitator has the responsibility of ensuring that participants have learned the new skills and knowledge needed for program success. Learning measures are a reflection of the degree to which the skills and knowledge have been acquired and internalized for application.

BUILDING A DATABASE. In major programs that are repeated, building a database of competency improvement, skills acquisition, or required knowledge may be helpful. These data sets may represent beneficial data to indicate how one program compares to another. Over time, they can also be used to set expectations and judge success.

FINAL THOUGHTS

This chapter briefly discussed some of the key issues involved in measuring learning—an important ingredient in the success of L&D programs. Even if it is accomplished informally, learning must be assessed to determine how well the participants in a program learn new skills, techniques, processes, tools, and procedures. Should any implementation problems arise later, knowing what went wrong would be difficult without measuring learning. Also, learning measurements provide an opportunity to make adjustments quickly so that changes can be made to enhance learning and ensure that proper program implementation occurs. Sometimes, a formal, objective process to accurately assess learning is needed. Several approaches were presented. However, the approach does not have to be formal, except for major programs. A less-formal, less-structured approach—even a self-assessment activity—is usually appropriate for most situations.

References

Lucia, A.D., & Lepsinger, R. (1999). *The art and science of competency models: Pinpointing critical success factors in organizations.* San Francisco, CA: Pfeiffer.

Miller, W. (1999, January). Building the ultimate resource: Today's competitive edge comes from intellectual capital. *Management Review,* pp. 42–45.

Phillips, P.J., & Phillips, P.P. (2007). *Handbook of training evaluation and measurement methods* (4th ed.). Woburn, MA: Butterworth Heinemann.

Senge, P. (1990). *The fifth discipline: The art and practice of the learning organization.* New York: Random House.

Schrock, S., & Coscarelli, W. (2000). *Criterion-referenced test development* (2nd ed.). Silver Spring, MD: ISPI.

Watkins, K.E., & Marsick, V.J. (Eds.). (1996). *Creating the learning organization.* Alexandria, VA: American Society for Training and Development.

Measuring Application and Implementation

M any learning and development programs fail because of breakdowns in application. Participants just don't use what they learned when they should, or at the expected level of effectiveness. Measuring application and implementation is critical to the understanding of program implementation. Without successful implementation, changes in business impact will not occur—and benefits will not be gained from the program.

A variety of methods—such as questionnaires, observation, action planning, and performance contracting—are available to measure program application and implementation. Along with describing the techniques to evaluate implementation, this chapter addresses the challenges and benefits faced with collecting data at this level and how to make data collection successful.

WHY MEASURE APPLICATION AND IMPLEMENTATION?

Measuring application and implementation is necessary. For some programs, it is the most critical data set because it provides an understanding of how successful implementation is, along with the barriers and enablers that influence this success.

The Value of Information

As briefly discussed in Chapter One, the value of information increases as progress is made through the chain of impact—from reaction (Level 1) to ROI (Level 5). Thus, information concerning application and implementation (Level 3) is more valuable to clients than reaction and learning data. This does not discount the importance of these first two levels, but emphasizes the importance of moving up the chain of impact. Measuring the program's implementation often provides critical data about not only the success of the program, but the factors that can contribute to greater success in future programs.

A Key Transition Time

The two previous measures, reaction (Level 1) and learning (Level 2), occur during the program, where more attention and focus are placed on the participants' direct involvement in the program. Measuring application and implementation occurs later and captures the participants' use of knowledge and skills on the job. Essentially, measures at this level reflect the degree of initial post-program success. This is a key transition period, making measuring application and implementation at this time critical.

The Key Focus of Many Programs

Because many programs focus directly on the need to use new skills or apply knowledge, the sponsor often speaks in these terms and has concerns about these measures of success. Major programs designed to empower employees, create self-directed teams, or build a loyal customer base will concentrate on the application of learned skills.

The Chain of Impact

The levels of data reflect the chain of impact that should occur from reaction to learning to application to impact and to ROI. For a program to add business value, the chain of impact must exist and not be broken. Unfortunately, measurement at Level 3 is often the weakest link as research shows that 60 to 80 percent of the knowledge acquired in a learning program is never applied. Individuals' failure to do what is expected is the most common reason for a break in the chain, leaving little or no corresponding impact data, and because of this, no positive ROI. This breakdown most often occurs because participants encounter barriers, inhibitors, or obstacles that may deter their implementation of the program. Although the reaction may be favorable and participants learn what they must, barriers prevent their application of the skills and knowledge to their jobs. Measurement at this level is vital to the validation of the chain of impact.

Barriers and Enablers

Often, when a program is unsuccessful, the first question asked is, "What happened?" When a program fails to add value, the first question should be, "What can we do to improve the program?"

In either scenario, identifying barriers to success, problems encountered during implementation, and obstacles to the actual application of the process is important. At this level of evaluation, these problems must always be examined. In many cases, the participants provide important recommendations for making improvements.

When a program is successful, the obvious question is, "How can we repeat this, or even improve on it, in the future?" The answer to this question is also found at this level of evaluation as enablers are identified. Identifying the factors that directly contribute to program success is always necessary. Those same items can be used to replicate the process to produce new or improved results in the future. When participants identify those issues, they provide an important prescription for success.

Reward Those Who Are Most Effective

Measuring application and implementation allows the sponsor and the L&D leader to reward those who do the best job of applying the skills and knowledge. Measures taken at this level identify clear evidence of success and achievement, providing an excellent basis for performance reviews or special recognition. Rewards often have a reinforcing value and help keep participants on track and communicate a strong message for future participants. Care must be taken, however: If Level 3 data are used for performance reviews, then Level 3 data collected from participants via self-administered questionnaire may be perceived as biased.

Case Study

The importance of measuring at this level can be highlighted by a brief example. Allied Irish Bank (AIB) based in Dublin, Ireland, engaged in a program to improve the leadership competencies and capabilities of their management team. Although AIB executives were interested in the impact of this leadership development, including monetary value, the most important data set was the change in leadership competencies. To conduct the study, all the managers received a 360-degree assessment, capturing data from the manager's immediate manager, colleagues, direct reports, and internal customers, as well as a self-assessment.

These multiple perspectives provided a current assessment of behavior based on observation collected through a survey. With this pre-assessment, the program was initiated and involved different techniques and processes to improve or enhance leadership competencies. An important part was for the leader to see his or her behavior assessed by others. Because of this input, these leaders wanted to improve these competencies. Follow-up assessments were taken at different time intervals to determine whether the competencies changed to the level desired by the senior management team. In the end, the behavior was improved.

CHALLENGES OF MEASURING APPLICATION AND IMPLEMENTATION

Collecting application and implementation data brings into focus some key challenges that must be addressed. These challenges may inhibit an otherwise successful evaluation.

Linking Application with Learning

Application data should be linked closely with the learning data discussed in Chapter Five. Essentially, program evaluators must know what has been accomplished, and this information is based on what the participants learned to do. During a program, participants learn information and develop skills to perform tasks on the job. Level 3 data measure the extent to which participants applied what they learned on their jobs. Sometimes, the objectives measured at Level 3 are the same as those measured at Level 2, but in the context of the job situation.

Designing Data Collection into Programs

Application data are collected after program completion, and because of the time difference, securing the appropriate quality and quantity of data is difficult. Consequently, designing data collection into the program from the beginning is one of the most effective ways to secure data. Data-collection tools, positioned as application tools, provide a rich source of data. These tools are built in as part of the implementation. For example, many software applications contain overlay software that shows a user performance profile. Essentially, the software tracks the user invisibly, capturing the steps, the pace, the time, and the difficulties encountered while using the software.

In another example, action plans are designed into a leadership development program and positioned as an application tool that also shows the impact of applying the leadership skills. When the process is completed, a credible data set is captured, only because data collection was built into the process from the beginning.

Building collection in from the beginning can also help in improving response rates. This is covered in detail later in this chapter.

Applying Serious Effort to Level 3 Evaluation

Because many programs are planned to include impact data, monetary values, and actual ROI, less emphasis may be placed on measuring application and implementation. For example, sales executives may look for sales increases when sales training is implemented, placing less emphasis on what the sales representatives did after the training.

Even when impact is desired, Level 3 evaluation is important. Consider, for example, the impact of the infamous GE workout processes. In those processes, GE management implemented a revolutionary method for removing bureaucracy and attacking organizational problems. While the goal was added value—ultimately shareholder value—to GE, the workout programs focused attention at this level of analysis—changing processes, changing procedures, changing tasks, and removing barriers. The focus was on what they were doing differently. While the ultimate monetary payoff existed, much of the effort focused on implementation and application.

Including Level 3 in the Needs Assessment

During the needs assessment, described in Chapter Two, the question is asked, "What is being done, or not being done, on the job that's inhibiting the business measure?" When this question is answered adequately, a connection is made between the solution and the business measure. When this is addressed, the activities or behaviors that need to change are identified, and they serve as the basis of the data collection.

Too many initial analyses focus on either impact measures, which define the business measures that need to be improved, or learning, which uncovers what people do not know. More focus is needed at Level 3, which involves the tasks, processes, procedures, and behaviors that need to be in place or change for successful implementation.

Developing ROI with Application Data

In certain situations, developing the monetary value and ROI directly from Level 3 data is desired. This can be accomplished in programs through which competencies are improved and are linked to the individuals' salaries. This method will be described in more detail later in this chapter.

KEY ISSUES

When measuring application and implementation of programs, several key issues must be addressed. Largely, they are similar to those encountered when measuring reaction and learning. A few may differ slightly because of the later collection timeframe.

Methods

When collecting Level 3 data, a variety of methods are available, as shown in Exhibit 6.1. These involve traditional methods of surveys and questionnaires, but also include rich methods for qualitative data collection, such as observation, interviews, and focus groups. This exhibit also contains powerful methods of action planning, where individuals plan their parts of the implementation; performance contracting, where participants agree to perform a certain way; and follow-up sessions that are designed exclusively for data collection.

METHOD	
• Follow-up surveys	• Action planning
• Follow-up questionnaires	• Performance contracting
• Observation	• Program follow-up sessions
• Interviews	• Performance records monitoring
• Focus groups	

Exhibit 6.1. Data Collection Methods.

Sometimes, program leaders must monitor participants' records to see how well they are performing or using a particular process. These methods are described in more detail later and are the principal focus of this chapter.

Objectives

As with the other levels, data collection begins with objectives that are set for the program's application and implementation. Without clear objectives, collecting data is difficult. Objectives define expected activity. Chapter Two lists the basic principles for developing these objectives, but they are underscored here because of their importance at this level.

Topics to Explore

The topics addressed at this level parallel many of those identified in Chapters Four and Five. However, because of the timeframe, additional opportunities to measure success arise. Therefore, many of the areas detailed in Chapters Four and Five can be mapped into this level. For example, questions about the intent to apply what is learned in the program are logical issues to measure at this time—when the application and implementation occur.

This level focuses on activity or action, not the consequences (which is Level 4, Impact), and the number of activities to measure can be mind-boggling. Table 6.1 shows some coverage areas for application. These examples can vary. However, these action items are included in most programs.

Action	Explanation	Example
Increase	Increase a particular activity or action.	Increase the frequency of the use of a particular skill.
Decrease	Decrease a particular activity or action.	Decrease the number of times a particular process has to be checked.
Eliminate	Stop or remove a particular task or activity.	Eliminate the formal follow-up meeting and replace it with a virtual meeting.

Table 6.1. Examples of Coverage Areas for Application.

(Continued)

Action	Explanation	Example
Maintain	Keep the same level of activity for a particular process.	Continue to monitor the process with the same schedule as previously used.
Create	Design, build, or implement a new procedure, process, or activity.	Create a procedure for resolving the differences between two divisions.
Use	Use a particular process, procedure, or activity.	Use the new skill in situations for which it was designed to be used.
Perform	Conduct or do a particular task, process, or procedure.	Perform a post-audit review at the end of each activity.
Participate	Become involved in various activities, projects, or programs.	Each associate should submit a suggestion for reducing costs.
Enroll	Sign up for a particular process, program, or project.	Each associate should enroll in the career advancement program.
Respond	React to groups, individuals, or systems.	Each participant in the program should respond to customer inquiries within fifteen minutes.
Network	Facilitate relationships with others who are involved or have been affected by the program.	Each program participant should continue networking with contacts on at least a quarterly basis.

Table 6.1. Examples of Coverage Areas for Application, Cont'd.

Sources

The sources of data include others identified in other chapters. Essentially, all key stakeholders are candidates as sources of data; key among them are participants, team leaders, and in some cases, organizational records or system.

Timing

The timing of data collection can vary. Since this is a follow-up after the program, the issue is to determine the best time for a post-program evaluation. The challenge is to analyze the nature and scope of the application and implementation and determine the earliest time that a trend or pattern will evolve. This occurs when the application of skills becomes routine and the implementation is progressing significantly. When to collect data is a judgment call. Collecting data as early as possible is important so that potential adjustments can still be made. At the same time, evaluations must allow for behavior changes so that the implementation can be observed and measured. In programs spanning a considerable length of time for implementation, measures may be taken at three- to six-month intervals. This provides successive input on progress and clearly shows the extent of improvement, using effective measures at well-timed intervals.

Convenience and constraints also influence the timing of data collection. Perhaps the participants are conveniently meeting in a follow-up session or at a special event. These would be excellent opportunities to collect data. Sometimes, constraints are placed on data collection. Sponsors or other executives are anxious to have the data, to make decisions about the program, which moves data collection to an earlier-than-ideal time.

Responsibilities

Measuring application and implementation involves the responsibility and work of others. Because these measures occur after the program, an important question may surface in terms of who is responsible for this follow-up. Many possibilities exist, from learning and development staff to the client staff, as well as the possibility of external, independent consultants. This matter should be addressed in the planning stage so no misunderstandings about the distribution of responsibilities occur. More importantly, those who are responsible must understand the nature and scope of their roles and what is needed to collect the data.

Perhaps the most critical issue involving data collection at this level is process improvement. This is the level at which barriers and enablers are captured. The barriers define areas that need to change, improve, or even be removed so that the program can be changed in the future if needed. Enablers provide rich information about activities that must be reinforced. They also give great insights as to how programs can be more successful in the future. The critical concept is that the data must be used routinely after the program is conducted to ensure that it adds the business value needed. If the data are not used, the program will be at a serious disadvantage, if not a complete failure. Additional information on the use of data will be covered later.

THE USE OF QUESTIONNAIRES

Questionnaires have become a mainstream data collection tool for application and implementation measures because of their flexibility, low cost, and ease of administration. The factors involved in questionnaire design discussed in Chapter Four apply equally to questionnaire development for measuring application and implementation. This section will be limited to the specific content of follow-up questionnaires.

One of the most difficult tasks is to determine specific factors that need to be addressed on a follow-up questionnaire. Although the content items can be the same as those used in reaction and learning questionnaires, the following are necessary for capturing application, implementation, and impact information (Level 3 and 4 data). Exhibit 6.2 presents a questionnaire used in a follow-up evaluation of a program to create a sales culture. The evaluation was designed to capture the ROI, with the primary method of data collection being the follow-up questionnaire.

Are you currently in a sales capacity at a branch?   Yes ☐   No ☐

1. Listed below are the objectives of the sales culture program. After reflecting on this program, please indicate the degree of success in meeting the objectives. Use the following scale:

   1 = No success at all

   2 = Limited success

   3 = Moderate success

   4 = Generally successful

   5 = Very successful

As a result of this program, branch employees will:	1	2	3	4	5
a. Use the tools and techniques to determine customer needs and concerns.	☐	☐	☐	☐	☐
b. Match needs with specific programs and services.	☐	☐	☐	☐	☐
c. Use the tools and techniques to convince customers to buy/use Progressive Bank products and services.	☐	☐	☐	☐	☐
d. Build a productive, long-term relationship with customers.	☐	☐	☐	☐	☐
e. Increase sales of each product line offered in the branch.	☐	☐	☐	☐	☐

Exhibit 6.2. Sales Culture at Progressive Bank's Follow-Up Questionnaire.

2. Did you develop and implement an on-the-job action plan for this program?
   Yes ☐   No ☐

   If yes, please describe the nature and outcome of the plan. If not, explain why.

   _____

   _____

   _____

   _____

   _____

3. Please rate the relevance to your job of each of the following components of the program using the following scale:

   1 = No relevance

   2 = Limited relevance

   3 = Moderate relevance

   4 = General relevance

   5 = Very relevant in every way

	1	2	3	4	5
Job Aids	☐	☐	☐	☐	☐
Group Learning Activities	☐	☐	☐	☐	☐
Incentive Opportunities	☐	☐	☐	☐	☐
Networking Opportunities w/Other Branches	☐	☐	☐	☐	☐
Reading Material/Videos	☐	☐	☐	☐	☐
Coaching Sessions	☐	☐	☐	☐	☐
Software/System Changes	☐	☐	☐	☐	☐
Database Enhancements	☐	☐	☐	☐	☐

4. Have you used the job aids provided during the program?   Yes ☐   No ☐
   Please explain. _____

   _____

   _____

   _____

   _____

   _____

**Exhibit 6.2. Sales Culture at Progressive Bank's
Follow-Up Questionnaire, Cont'd.**

(Continued)

5. Please indicate the change in the application of knowledge and skills as a result of your participation in the sales culture program. Use the following scale:

1 = No change

2 = Limited change

3 = Moderate change

4 = Much change

5 = Very much change

	1	2	3	4	5	No Opportunity to Use Skill
a. Probing for customer needs.	☐	☐	☐	☐	☐	☐
b. Helping the customer solve problems.	☐	☐	☐	☐	☐	☐
c. Understanding the features and benefits of all products and services.	☐	☐	☐	☐	☐	☐
d. Comparing products and services to those of competitors.	☐	☐	☐	☐	☐	☐
e. Selecting appropriate products and services.	☐	☐	☐	☐	☐	☐
f. Using persuasive selling techniques.	☐	☐	☐	☐	☐	☐
g. Using follow-up techniques to stay in touch with the customer.	☐	☐	☐	☐	☐	☐
h. Using new software routines for data access and transactions.	☐	☐	☐	☐	☐	☐

6. What has changed about your work (actions, tasks, activities) as a result of this program?

_____

_____

_____

_____

Exhibit 6.2. Sales Culture at Progressive Bank's Follow-Up Questionnaire, Cont'd.

7. Please identify any specific accomplishments/improvements that can be linked to this program.

_____

_____

_____

_____

8. Please define the specific measure in question. Use a unit of value such as one sale, one new account, one reject.

_____

_____

_____

_____

9. Provide the actual change in the unit measure since the program began. This would take the pre-program baseline data and subtract it from the current level to indicate a delta, a change.

_____

_____

_____

_____

10. Indicate the actual unit value for the specific measure in question. If it is a measure that is desired to improve, indicate the value add, such as one additional sale. If it is a value that needs to be minimized, such as one reject, indicate the money saved when the reject is avoided. Although this can be very difficult, please follow the instructions of how this value may be obtained.

_____

_____

_____

_____

11. Provide the basis for the above unit value. If it is a standard value, please indicate that it is a standard value; if it is an expert input, indicate that it is an expert input; if it is based on an estimate, indicate how the estimate was derived.

_____

_____

_____

_____

Exhibit 6.2. Sales Culture at Progressive Bank's Follow-Up Questionnaire, Cont'd.

(Continued)

12. Provide the total impact of the change. This involves taking the unit value times the change in the value for one year. This takes into account the frequency. If it is a monthly data item, then it would be times 12. If it is a weekly value, it would be times 52.

_____

_____

_____

_____

13. List other factors that could have influenced this improvement. Be very thoughtful and specific in listing the other influences.

_____

_____

_____

_____

14. Indicate the percent of improvement directly related to this program using a scale of 0 to 100. Zero percent is no improvement connected to the program. One hundred percent is all the improvement is connected to the program.

_____

_____

_____

_____

15. What level of confidence do you place in the above estimations? (0% = No Confidence, 100% = Certainty) _____%

Please explain. _____

_____

_____

_____

16. Do you think the sales culture program represented a good investment for Progressive Bank?   Yes ☐   No ☐

Please explain. _____

_____

_____

_____

Exhibit 6.2. Sales Culture at Progressive Bank's Follow-Up Questionnaire, Cont'd.

17. Indicate the extent to which you think this program has influenced each of these measures in your branch. Use the following scale:

    1 = No influence

    2 = Limited influence

    3 = Moderate influence

    4 = Much influence

    5 = Very much influence

	1	2	3	4	5
a. Productivity	☐	☐	☐	☐	☐
b. Sales	☐	☐	☐	☐	☐
c. Customer Response Time	☐	☐	☐	☐	☐
d. Cross-Sales Ratio	☐	☐	☐	☐	☐
e. Cost Control	☐	☐	☐	☐	☐
f. Employee Satisfaction	☐	☐	☐	☐	☐
g. Customer Satisfaction	☐	☐	☐	☐	☐
h. Quality	☐	☐	☐	☐	☐
i. Other _____	☐	☐	☐	☐	☐

18. Please rate the success of the immediate program team and the quality of the team's leadership. Use the following scale:

    1 = No success

    2 = Limited success

    3 = Moderately successful

    4 = Generally successful

    5 = Very successful

Team Characteristic	1	2	3	4	5	Leadership Issue	1	2	3	4	5
Capability	☐	☐	☐	☐	☐	Leadership Style	☐	☐	☐	☐	☐
Motivation	☐	☐	☐	☐	☐	Organization	☐	☐	☐	☐	☐
Cooperation	☐	☐	☐	☐	☐	Communication	☐	☐	☐	☐	☐
Communication	☐	☐	☐	☐	☐	Team Support	☐	☐	☐	☐	☐
						Team Training	☐	☐	☐	☐	☐

Exhibit 6.2. Sales Culture at Progressive Bank's Follow-Up Questionnaire, Cont'd.

(Continued)

19. What barriers, if any, have you encountered that prevented this program from being successful. Please explain, if possible.

_____

_____

_____

_____

_____

20. What has helped this program be successful? Please explain.

_____

_____

_____

_____

_____

21. Which of the following statements best describes the level of management support?
    - ☐ There was no management support.
    - ☐ There was limited management support.
    - ☐ There was a moderate amount of management support.
    - ☐ There was much management support.
    - ☐ There was very much management support.

22. Could other program solutions have been effective in meeting the business need(s)?   Yes ☐   No ☐

    Please explain. _____

    _____

    _____

    _____

23. What specific suggestions do you have for improving this program?

_____

_____

_____

_____

_____

Exhibit 6.2. Sales Culture at Progressive Bank's Follow-Up Questionnaire, Cont'd.

24. Other comments about this program:

_____

_____

_____

_____

_____

Exhibit 6.2. Sales Culture at Progressive Bank's
Follow-Up Questionnaire, Cont'd.

A discussion about Progressive Bank is used here to illustrate many of the elements of follow-up questionnaires. Following a carefully planned growth pattern through acquiring smaller banks, Progressive Bank initiated a program to develop a strong sales culture. The program involved four solutions, all geared toward developing the sales culture. Through a competency-based learning program, all branch associates were taught how to aggressively pursue new customers and cross-sell to existing customers in a variety of product lines. The customer relationship management (CRM) software and customer database were upgraded to provide faster access and enhanced routines to assist in the selling process. The incentive compensation system was also redesigned to enhance payments for new customers and to increase the sales of all branch products. Finally, a management coaching and reinforcement system was implemented to ensure that ambitious sales goals were met. All branch employees were involved in the program.

An evaluation was planned during program design. Each branch in the network had a scorecard that tracked performance through several measures, such as new accounts, total deposits, and growth by specific products. Six months after implementation, all product lines were monitored. All branch employees provided input on the questionnaire shown in Exhibit 6.1. Most of the data from the questionnaire covered application and implementation, while some involved impact measures. This type of feedback helped program leaders know which parts of the program were most effective and useful.

Let's now discuss some of the key questions on the questionnaire.

Progress with Objectives

Sometimes, assessing progress made with the objectives of the program in a follow-up evaluation, as illustrated by the first question in

Exhibit 6.2, is helpful. While some of the objectives were assessed during the program (reaction and learning), the Level 3 and 4 objectives must be revisited on a post-implementation basis as the objectives identify the specific behaviors that should occur during implementation.

Relevance/Importance of the Program

The relevance or importance of a program is often assessed during the program, as Level 1 data. However, analyzing the relevance or importance after implementation can be helpful. Question 3 attempts to verify that the perceived relevance still exists after implementation.

Knowledge/Skill Use

Perhaps one of the most important questions on the follow-up questionnaire focuses on the application of skills and knowledge. As shown in Question 5 in Exhibit 6.2, specific skills and knowledge areas are listed, with the question focusing on the amount of change since the program's implementation. This is the recommended approach when no pre-program data exist. If pre-data have been collected, comparing post-assessments with pre-assessments using the same question is more appropriate. Sometimes, determining the most frequently used skills that are directly linked to the program is helpful. For many skills, participants need to experience frequent use quickly after skill acquisition so that the skills become internalized and routine. When this is the case, the questionnaire should include a list of skills, asking participants to indicate their frequency of use.

Changes with Work/Action Items

A participant's work usually changes in some way because of his or her participation in a program. Capturing what specific elements change can be important data. As Question 6 in Exhibit 6.2 illustrates, the participant explores how the program application changed his or her work and may include a list of actions, steps, or activities that changed.

Improvements/Accomplishments

Question 7 begins a series of eight impact questions that are appropriate for most follow-up questionnaires where impact (Level 4) and ROI analyses (Level 5) are planned. More credible ways to capture these types of data exist and are described in Chapter Seven. The first question seeks specific accomplishments and improvements that are directly linked to the program. This question focuses on specific, measurable consequences that can be easily identified by the participants, represented by one or more business measures. These consequences are based on the application data and the changes with work data above. It answers the question, "So what?" Examples that indicate the nature and range of responses requested may be used, but may also limit the responses.

Define the Measure

Because some measures can be vague, a precise definition may be necessary. This not only clarifies the measure that changes but also helps improve the credibility of the study by indicating the specific improvement. Also, the participant is kept honest, detailing the specific changes and leaving the possibility that the data could be audited if desired or necessary. In Question 8, the unit is needed. Some examples are one absence, one call escalation, one additional sale, and one minute of downtime.

Provide the Change

Participants are asked to provide the actual change in the measure since the program was implemented. Since the unit measure is known and clearly defined, this is essentially the change representing how much has improved in the given time period. For example, if the measure were customer complaints, this change would indicate the actual number of customer complaints that have been reduced during implementation.

Monetary Value

Perhaps the most difficult question, Question 10 in the exhibit, asks participants to provide monetary values for the unit of measure identified in Question 8. Because these are business impact data, standard monetary values may already exist. If not, participants are asked to contact an expert or estimate the actual monetary value.

An important part of this issue is the basis for the monetary value, where participants must specify the steps taken to locate or develop the value and the assumptions made if it is an estimate. It is very important for the basis to be completed with enough detail to understand the process. Question 11 provides the basis.

Total Impact

Given the unit of measure, the unit of impact, and the frequency of change, calculating the total annual improvement is possible. For most programs, one year of data is needed to calculate the total annual improvement. For long-term programs, this amount might be prorated over several years.

List of Other Factors

In Question 13, participants indicate any other factors that might have caused the change or improvement during implementation. The participants should give serious thought to other influences, and they are almost always evident. For this question to be properly addressed, the credibility of participants, or other individuals answering the questionnaire, is important. They should be the most credible sources for this data item.

Improvements Linked with the Program

Question 14 in the exhibit isolates the effects of the program from the other factors listed. Participants indicate the percentage of total improvement that is directly related to the program. As an alternative, the various factors and solutions that have influenced the results may be listed. Participants are asked to allocate a percentage to each solution.

To adjust for the uncertainty of this estimate, participants are asked to give a level of confidence. This confidence factor is expressed as a percentage with a range of 0 to 100 percent, as shown in Question 15. This input adjusts the participants' estimates to account for their uncertainty and serves as an error adjustment. This conservative approach adds credibility to the estimates.

Perceived Value

The participants' perception of the value of the program is useful information. As illustrated in Question 16 in Exhibit 6.2, participants are asked whether they believe that the program was a good investment for the organization or sponsor. An option for this question is to present the actual cost of the program so that participants can respond more accurately. Also, the question can be divided into two parts: one reflecting the investment of money by the organization and the other an investment in the participants' time. The perceived value is an indicator that the program is successful.

Links with Output Measures

Sometimes, determining the degree to which a program has influenced certain impact measures is helpful. As shown in Question 17, participants are asked to indicate the degree to which they think certain measures have been influenced by the program. However, when this issue is uncertain, business performance measures known to have been influenced in similar programs are listed.

Success of the Program Team

Sometimes, soliciting input about the working relationship between the program team and the participants is beneficial. Multiple-solution programs rely on the quality of the program leadership team. Question 18 asks participants to indicate the degree to which the program team is successful and asks about the quality of their leadership. This information is helpful in making adjustments in future programs.

Barriers and Enablers

Barriers can influence the successful application of a program. Question 19 identifies these barriers. As an alternative, the perceived barriers could be listed and participants could be asked to check those that apply. Still another variation is to list the barriers with a range of responses, indicating the extent to which the barrier inhibited results.

Just as important as barriers are the enablers—those issues, events, or situations that supported the program's success. The same options are available with this question as with the question on barriers.

Management Support

Management support is often critical to the success of a program. At least one question should be included on the degree of management support. Sometimes, this question is structured so that various descriptions of management support are detailed, and participants check the one that applies to their situation. Question 21 in Exhibit 6.2 is an example.

Appropriateness of Program and Suggestions for Improvement

The implementation of a program is often only one of many potential solutions to a business performance issue. If the initial analysis and needs assessment is faulty or if alternative approaches to meeting the desired business need are possible, other solutions may achieve the same or greater results. The participant is asked to identify alternate solutions that could have been effective in obtaining the same or similar results. Question 22 represents this type of question. The evaluator can use this information to help improve processes and understand the use of alternative approaches.

Participants are asked to provide suggestions for improving any part of a program and to give any other comments about the program. These types of open-ended questions provide an opportunity to give additional intangible benefits, present concerns, or suggest issues that will need to be addressed in the future.

Checklist

Developing a checklist of the content issues to include on a follow-up questionnaire may be useful. Exhibit 6.3 shows a checklist of the key issues presented in the example discussed here and reflects much of the follow-up data that is often needed to measure application and implementation, and in this case, actual business impact.

Improving Response Rates

For most evaluations, questionnaires and surveys will be used. When a follow-up evaluation is planned, a wide range of issues and details will be collected in the follow-up questionnaire. However, asking for too much detail can negatively impact the response rate. The challenge, therefore, is to approach questionnaire and survey design and administration for maximum response rate. The following actions can be taken to ensure a successful response rate. Although the term "questionnaire" is used, the following list also applies to surveys:

☐ Progress with objectives

☐ Action plan implementation

☐ Relevance/importance

☐ Perception of value

☐ Use of materials

☐ Knowledge/skill enhancement

☐ Skills used

☐ Changes with work/actions

☐ Improvement/accomplishments

☐ Define measure

☐ Provide the change

☐ Unit value

☐ Basis

☐ Total impact

☐ List other factors

☐ Improvement linked with program

☐ Confidence estimate

Optional unless business impact and ROI analysis are pursued

☐ Linkage with output measures

☐ Other benefits

☐ Barriers

☐ Enablers

☐ Management support

☐ Other solutions

☐ Recommendations for other audiences/participants

☐ Suggestions for improvement

☐ Other comments

Exhibit 6.3. Questionnaire Content Checklist.

- *Provide advance communication.* If appropriate and feasible, participants and other stakeholders should receive advance communications about the plans for the questionnaire. This minimizes some of the resistance to the process, provides an opportunity to explain in more detail the circumstances surrounding the evaluation, and positions the evaluation as an integral part of the program—not an add-on activity. Communicate the purpose. Participants and other stakeholders should understand the reason for the questionnaire.

- *Identify who will see the data.* Respondents need to know who will see the data and the results of the questionnaire. If the questionnaire is anonymous, it should clearly be communicated to participants that anonymity will be ensured. If senior executives will see the combined results of the study, the respondents should know.

- *Describe the data integration process.* If the questionnaire is only one of the data collection methods used, the respondents should understand how the questionnaire results will be combined with other data. They should know how the data are weighted and how they will be integrated into the final reporting.

- *Design for simplicity.* Sometimes, a simple questionnaire does not provide the full scope of data necessary for a comprehensive analysis. The simplified approach should be followed when questions are developed and the total scope of the questionnaire is finalized. Every effort should be made to keep it as brief as possible.

- *Make responding easy.* Whenever possible, the response should be easy. If appropriate, a self-addressed stamped envelope should be included. Perhaps e-mail could be used for responses, if appropriate and available. Providing a drop box near respondents' workstations will make questionnaire return simple.

- *Use local management support.* Management involvement at the local level is critical for response-rate success. Managers can distribute the questionnaires themselves, make reference to the questionnaire in meetings, follow up to see whether employees have completed their questionnaires, and generally show support for completing the questionnaire.

- *Let the participants know that they are part of the sample.* For large programs, a sampling process may be used. When that is the case, respondents should know that they are part of a carefully selected sample and that their input will be used to make decisions regarding a much larger target audience. This action often appeals to a sense of responsibility for participants to provide usable, accurate data for the questionnaire.

- *Consider the use of incentives.* A variety of incentives to complete questionnaires can be offered, and they usually can be grouped into three categories.

  - First, an incentive is provided in exchange for the completed questionnaire. For example, if respondents return the questionnaire personally or through the mail, they will receive a small gift, such as an iPod Shuffle or a jump drive. If identity is an issue, a neutral third party can collect the questionnaires and advise the evaluator of the names of respondents.

  - A second category of incentive includes those to make participants feel guilty about not responding. Examples of "make you feel guilty incentives" include money clipped to the questionnaire or a pen enclosed in the envelope. Respondents are asked to "take the money, buy a cup of coffee or tea, and fill out the questionnaire."

  - A third category of incentives is designed to obtain a quick response. This approach is based on the assumption that a quick response will ensure a greater response rate. If an individual puts off completing the questionnaire, the odds of completing it diminish considerably. The initial group of respondents may receive a more expensive gift or they may be part of a drawing for an incentive.

- *Have an executive sign the introductory letter.* Respondents are always interested in who sent the letter with the questionnaire. For maximum effectiveness, a senior executive who is responsible for the area in which the participants are employed should sign the letter. The employees may be more willing to respond to a senior executive when compared to situations in which a member of the program team signs the letter.

- *Use follow-up reminders.* A follow-up reminder should be sent a week after the questionnaire is received and another sent two weeks later. Depending on the questionnaire and the situation, these times can be adjusted. In some situations, a third follow-up is recommended. Sometimes, the follow-up is sent in a different medium. For example, a questionnaire may be sent through regular mail, whereas the first follow-up reminder is from the immediate manager, and a second follow-up is sent via e-mail.

- *Send a copy of the results to the participants.* Even if it is an abbreviated report, respondents should see the results of the questionnaire. More importantly, participants should understand that they will receive copies of the impact study (at least in a summary form) when they are asked to provide the data. Following through on the promise will influence response rates for future evaluations.

- *Estimate the necessary time to complete the questionnaire.* Respondents often have a concern about the time necessary to complete the questionnaire. A very lengthy questionnaire may quickly turn off the respondents and cause it to be discarded. Sometimes, lengthy questionnaires can be completed quickly because many of them have forced-choice questions or statements that make responding easier. However, the number of pages may frighten the respondent. Therefore, indicating the estimated length of time needed to complete the questionnaire—in the letter or noted in the communications—is helpful. A word of caution is necessary, though: the amount of time must be realistic. Purposely underestimating it can do more harm than good.

- *Show the timing of the planned steps.* Sometimes, the respondents want to know more detail regarding when they can see the results or when the results will be presented to particular groups. A timeline should be presented, showing when different phases of the process—such as when to respond, when the data will be analyzed, when the data will be presented to different groups, and when the results will be returned to the respondents in a summary report. The timetable must be followed to maintain the confidence and trust of the individuals.

- *Make it look professional.* While it should not be a concern in most organizations, unfortunately, there are too many cases in which a questionnaire is not developed properly, does not appear professional, or is not easy to follow and understand. The respondents must gain respect for the process and for the organization.

- *Introduce the questionnaire during the program.* Sometimes, it is helpful to explain to the respondents and other key stakeholders that they will be required or asked to provide certain types of data. When this is feasible, questionnaires should be reviewed question by question so that the respondents understand the purpose, the issues, and how to respond.

- *Collect data anonymously or confidentially.* Respondents are more likely to provide frank and candid feedback if their names are not on the questionnaires, particularly when the program is going astray or is off-target. Every effort should be made to protect the anonymous input, and explanations should be provided as to how the data are analyzed, minimizing the demographic makeup of respondents so that the individuals cannot be identified in the analysis. Confidentiality means that data sources are protected along with their linkage to data.

Collectively, these items help boost response rates of follow-up questionnaires. Using all these strategies can result in a 60 to 80 percent response rate, even with lengthy questionnaires that might take thirty minutes to complete.

For a specific strategy, some individuals will respond (while others will not), bringing in a few more percentage points of return rate, perhaps 3 to 8 percent. Some techniques are more powerful. For example, reviewing a questionnaire in advance of sending it at a later time frame will often secure about 15 to 20 percent when the participants have a chance to understand the reason for the questionnaire, the questions, the data needed, and what will be done with the data. As each technique is used, the desired response rate can be achieved, often in the range of 60 to 90 percent. This requires determination, focus, and discipline. Too often, program team leaders don't put the effort into collecting data and have a miserable response rate. In reality, this is about changing culture, since the evaluator or program team leader is essentially having a dialogue with the participants or users of the program solution. When this dialogue is productive, trusting, and helpful, a tremendous amount of data can be collected.

DATA COLLECTION WITH INTERVIEWS

Another helpful data collection method is the interview, although it is not used as frequently as questionnaires. Interviews may be conducted by the facilitator, the evaluator, or a third party. Interviews can secure data difficult to obtain through written responses. Also, interviews can uncover success stories that can be useful in communicating the success of the program. Respondents may be reluctant to describe their results in a questionnaire but will volunteer the information to a skillful interviewer who uses probing techniques. The interview is versatile and appropriate for application and implementation data. A major disadvantage of the interview is that it consumes time, which increases the cost of data collection. It also requires preparing interviewers to ensure that the process is consistent.

Types of Interviews

There are two basic types of interviews: *structured* and *unstructured*. A structured interview is similar to a questionnaire. Specific questions are asked with little room to deviate from desired responses. The advantages of the structured interviews over questionnaires are that the interview process can ensure that the questionnaire is completed and that the interviewer understands the responses supplied by the interviewee. The unstructured interview permits probing for additional information. This type of interview uses a few general questions that may lead to more detailed information as data are uncovered. The interviewer must be skilled in the probing process, using probing questions such as:

- Can you provide that in more detail?
- Can you give me an example of what you are saying?
- Can you explain the difficulty that you say you encountered?
- Can you describe the concern in more detail?

Interview Guidelines

The design steps for interviews are similar to those for questionnaires. A brief summary of key issues with interviews is provided here:

- *Develop questions to be asked.* Once a decision has been made about the type of interview, specific questions have to be developed. Questions should be brief, precise, and designed for easy response.

- *Test the interview protocol.* The interview should be tested on a small number of participants, if possible during the early stages of the program. The responses should be analyzed and the interview revised, if necessary.

- *Prepare the interviewers.* The interviewer must have appropriate skills—including active listening, the ability to form probing questions, and the ability to collect and summarize information into a meaningful form.

- *Provide clear instructions.* The interviewer should understand the purpose of the interview and know what will be done with the information. Expectations, conditions, and rules of the interview should be thoroughly discussed. For example, the participant should know whether statements will be kept confidential.

- *Administer interviews with a plan in mind.* As with other evaluation instruments, interviews have to be conducted according to a predetermined plan. The timing of the interview, the person conducting the interview, and the location of the interview are relevant when developing an interview plan. For many stakeholders, interviewing only a sample may be necessary to save time and reduce evaluation costs.

DATA COLLECTION WITH FOCUS GROUPS

Focus groups are particularly helpful when in-depth feedback is needed. The focus group, designed to solicit qualitative judgments on a topic or issue, involves a small group discussion conducted by an experienced facilitator. Group members are all required to provide input, as individual input builds on group input.

When compared to questionnaires, surveys, or interviews, the focus group approach has several advantages. The basic premise of using focus groups is that when quality judgments are subjective, several individual judgments are better than one. The group process, whereby participants often motivate one another, is an effective method for generating and clarifying ideas and hypotheses. It is inexpensive, flexible, and can be planned and conducted quickly.

Applications for Focus Group Evaluation

The focus group is particularly helpful when qualitative information is needed about the success of a program. For example, the focus group can be used in the following situations:

- To evaluate reactions to specific procedures, tasks, schedules, or other components of the program
- To assess the overall effectiveness of the program as perceived by the stakeholders immediately following a program
- To assess the impact of the program

Essentially, focus groups are helpful when evaluation information is needed but cannot be collected adequately with simple, quantitative methods.

Guidelines

While the rules on how to use focus groups for evaluation vary, the following guidelines should be helpful:

- *Ensure that management and the client embrace focus groups.* Because focus groups may be new to your stakeholder group, the process may need clarification. Managers need to understand focus groups and their advantages, raising their confidence in the information obtained from group sessions.
- *Plan topics, questions, and protocol carefully.* As with any evaluation instrument, planning is critical. The specific topics, questions, and issues to be discussed must be carefully planned and sequenced. This enhances the comparison of results from one group to another and ensures that the group process is effective and stays on track.
- *Keep the group size small.* While there is no magical group size, a range of six to twelve seems appropriate for most focus groups. A group has to be large enough to ensure different points of view but small enough to give every participant time to talk freely and exchange comments. Small groups also allow the facilitator to center attention on the key topics.
- *Ensure a representative sample of the target population.* Groups must be stratified appropriately so that participants represent the target population. The group should be homogeneous in experience, rank, and influence within the organization.
- *Facilitators must have appropriate expertise.* The success of a focus group rests with the facilitator, who must be skilled in the

focus group process. Facilitators must know how to control aggressive members of the group, diffusing input from those who want to dominate the group. Also, facilitators must create an environment in which participants feel comfortable offering comments. Consequently, some organizations use external facilitators.

In summary, the focus group is a relatively inexpensive and quick way to determine the strengths and weaknesses of program implementation. However, for a complete evaluation, focus group information should be combined with data from other instruments.

ON-THE-JOB OBSERVATION

Another useful data collection method is observing participants on the job and recording any changes in behavior and specific actions taken. This technique is particularly useful when knowing how the participants use new skills, knowledge, tasks, procedures, or systems is important. The observer may be a member of the L&D staff, the participants' manager, a member of a peer group, or an external resource, such as a mystery shopper. The most common observer, and probably the most practical, is a member of the program staff.

Guidelines for Effective Observation

Observation is often misused or misapplied to evaluation situations, forcing some to abandon the process. The effectiveness of observation can be improved with several guidelines:

- *Observers must be fully prepared.* Observers must fully understand what information is needed and what skills are used or what actions are expected in the program. They must be knowledgeable about the program and have a chance to practice observation skills.

- *The observations should be systematic.* The observation process must be planned so that it is executed effectively and without surprises. The individuals observed should know in advance about the observation and the reason they are being observed. Ideally, they should be observed invisibly or in an unnoticeable way. The timing of the observations should be part of the plan.

There are right times and wrong times to observe a participant. For example, if a participant is observed when work situations are not normal (for example, in a crisis), the data collected may not be a true reflection of routine behavior.

- *Several steps are necessary to accomplish a successful observation:*
  - Determine what behavior will be observed.
  - Prepare the forms for the observer's use.
  - Select the observers.
  - Prepare a schedule of observations.
  - Prepare observers for proper observation.
  - Inform participants of the planned observation, providing explanations.
  - Conduct the observations.
  - Summarize the observation data.
- *The observers should know how to interpret and report their observations.* Observations involve judgment decisions. The observer must analyze the behaviors displayed and the actions taken by the participants. Observers should know how to summarize behavior and report meaningful results.
- *The observers' influence should be minimized.* Except for "mystery" or "planted" observers and electronic observations, completely removing the overall effect of an observer is impossible. The presence of the observer must be minimized, and to the extent possible, the observer should blend into the work environment. If not, participants will display the behavior they think is appropriate, performing at their best.

SELECT OBSERVERS CAREFULLY. Observers are usually independent of the participants. They are typically members of the L&D staff. An independent observer is usually more skilled at recording behavior, at making interpretations of behavior, and is usually unbiased in these interpretations. Using an independent observer reduces the need for learning and development staff members to prepare observers and relieves the operating department or division of the responsibility. Sometimes, recruiting observers from outside the organization is a better option. On the other hand, the independent observer has the appearance of an outsider, and participants may resent this kind of observer if they know about it. The advantage of this approach is keeping biases from entering the decision-making process.

OBSERVATION METHODS. Five methods of observation are appropriate, depending on the circumstances surrounding the type of information needed. Each method is briefly described below:

- *Behavior checklist and codes.* A behavior checklist is useful for recording the presence, absence, frequency, or duration of a participant's behavior as it occurs. A checklist does not provide information on the quality, intensity, or possible circumstances surrounding the observed behavior. It is useful in helping an observer identify exactly which behaviors should or should not occur. Measuring the duration of a behavior may be more difficult and requires a stopwatch and a place on the form to record time intervals. The number of behaviors listed in the checklist should be small and, if they logically occur in a sequence, listed in that order. A variation of this approach involves coding behaviors on a form. While this method is useful when many behaviors are involved, it is more time-consuming because a code is entered that identifies a specific behavior instead of checking an item.

- *Delayed report method.* With a delayed report method, the observer does not use any forms or written materials during the observation. The information is either recorded after the observation or at particular time intervals during it. The observer attempts to reconstruct what has been witnessed during the observation period. The advantage of this approach is that the observer is less noticeable, and no forms are completed or notes taken during the observation. The observer becomes a part of the situation and less of a distraction. An obvious disadvantage is that the information reported may not be as accurate and reliable as it would be if noted as it occurred. A variation of this approach is the 360-degree feedback process in which surveys are completed on other individuals based on observations within a specific time frame.

- *Video recording.* A video camera records behavior in detail. However, this intrusion may be awkward and cumbersome, and the participants may be unnecessarily nervous or self-conscious while being videotaped. If the camera is concealed, the privacy of the participants may be invaded. Because of this, video recording of on-the-job behavior is not frequently used.

- *Audio monitoring.* Monitoring conversations of participants during implementation is an effective observation technique. This method is particularly helpful in telemarketing jobs. While this approach may stir some controversy, it is an effective way to determine whether skills are applied consistently and effectively. For it to work smoothly, the process must be fully explained and the rules clearly communicated.

- *Computer monitoring.* For employees who work regularly with a keyboard, computer monitoring is an effective way to "observe" participants as they perform job tasks. The computer monitors times, sequence of steps, use of routines, and other activities to determine whether the participant performs the work according to the guidelines of the program. As technology continues to be a significant part of the workplace, computer monitoring holds much promise.

THE USE OF ACTION PLANS AND FOLLOW-UP ASSIGNMENTS

In some cases, follow-up assignments can be used to develop implementation and application data. In a typical follow-up assignment, the participant is asked to meet a goal or complete a particular task or program by a set date. A summary of the results of the completed assignment provides further evidence of the success of the program and implementation of new skills and knowledge gained.

The *action plan* is the most common type of follow-up assignment. With this approach, participants are required to develop action plans as part of the program. Action plans contain the detailed steps necessary to accomplish specific objectives related to the program. The process is one of the most effective ways to enhance support of a program and build the ownership needed for successful application and implementation.

The plan is typically prepared on a printed form, such as the one shown in Exhibit 6.4. The action plan shows what is to be done, by whom, and the date the objectives should be accomplished. The action-plan approach is a straightforward, easy-to-use method for

Name_____ Project Leader Signature_____ Follw-Up Date_____

Objective_____ Evaluation Period_____ to_____

Improvement Measure_____ Current Performance_____ Target Performance_____

SPECIFIC STEPS: *I will do this:*	Date	END RESULT: *So that:*
1.		
2.		
3.		
4.		
5.		
6.		
7.		

Expected Intangible Benefits

Barriers: What Got in the Way?

Enablers: What Helped the Process?

Exhibit 6.4. Form for an Action Plan.

determining how participants will change their behavior on the job and achieve success with the program implementation. The approach produces data, answering questions such as:

- What on-the-job improvements have been realized since the program was implemented?
- Are the improvements linked to the program?
- What may have prevented participants from accomplishing specific action items?

Collectively, these data can be used to assess the success of the program implementation. With this information, decisions can be made regarding modification.

Developing the Action Plan

The development of the action plan requires two major tasks: (1) determining the areas for action and (2) writing the action items. Both tasks should be completed during the program and, at the same time, be related to on-the-job, program-related activities. A list of areas for action can be developed with the help of the facilitator. The list may include an area needing improvement or an opportunity for increased performance. Examples of typical questions that should be answered before determining the areas for action are listed below:

- Is it related to the program?
- How much time will this action take?
- Is this expected?
- Are the skills for accomplishing this action item available?
- Who has the authority to implement the actions?
- Will this action have an effect on other individuals?
- Are there any organizational constraints for accomplishing this action item?

Usually, writing specific action items is more difficult than identifying the action areas. The most important characteristic of an action item is that it is written so that everyone involved will know when it is accomplished. One way to help achieve this goal is to use specific action verbs and set deadlines for the completion of each action item. Some examples of action items are:

- Analyze the causes of absenteeism by [date].
- Identify and secure a new customer account by [date].
- Handle every piece of paper only once to improve my personal time management by [date].
- Probe my employees directly about a particular problem by [date].

If appropriate, each action item should indicate other individuals or resources needed for its completion. Planned behavior changes should be observable. They should be obvious to the participant and others when the change takes place. Action plans, as used in this context, do not require the prior approval or input from the participant's manager, although, as in any case, manager support may be helpful.

Successful Use of Action Plans

The action-plan process can be an integral part of implementation and is not necessarily considered an add-on or optional activity. To gain maximum effectiveness from action plans to collect data for evaluation, the following steps should be implemented:

- *Communicate the action plan requirement early.* One of the most negative reactions to action plans is the surprise in its introduction. When participants realize they must develop detailed action plans, they often resist. Communicating in advance that the process is an integral part of implementation will often minimize resistance. When participants understand the benefits before they attend the first meeting, they take the process more seriously and usually perform extra steps to ensure its success.
- *Describe the action planning process at the beginning of the program.* At the beginning of the session, action plan requirements are discussed, including an outline of its purpose, why it is necessary, and the basic requirements during and after the program. Some facilitators furnish a separate notepad for participants to collect ideas and useful techniques for their action plans.

- *Teach the action planning process.* A prerequisite for action planning success is understanding how action plans work and how they are developed. A portion of the program time is allocated to teaching participants how to develop plans. In this session, the requirements are outlined, special forms and procedures are discussed, and a positive example is distributed and reviewed. Sometimes, an entire half-day module is allocated to this process so that participants understand and use it. Any available support tools—such as key measures, charts, graphs, suggested topics, and sample calculations—should be used in this session.

- *Allow time to develop the plan.* When action plans are used to collect data for program evaluation, allowing participants to develop plans during the program is important. Sometimes, having participants work in teams so that they can share ideas as they develop specific plans is helpful. In these sessions, facilitators often monitor individual or team progress to keep the process on track and to answer questions.

- *Have the facilitator approve the action plans.* The action plan must be related to program objectives and, at the same time, represent an important accomplishment for the organization when it is completed. Because participants may stray from the intent and purpose of action planning and not give it the attention needed, the facilitator should sign off on the action plan, ensuring that the plan reflects all the requirements and is appropriate for the program. In some cases, a space is provided for the signature on the action-plan document.

- *Ask participants to isolate the effects of the program.* Although the action plan is initiated because of the program, the actual improvements reported on the action plan may be influenced by other factors. Thus, full credit for the improvement should not be assigned to the action planning process alone. For example, an action plan to reduce product defects could only be partially responsible for the improvement because other factors may affect the defect rate. While effects of the program can be isolated in several ways (described in Chapter Seven), participant estimation is usually more appropriate in the action planning process. Therefore, the participants are asked to estimate the percentage of the improvement directly related to a particular skill learned during the program. This question can be asked on the action plan form or on a follow-up questionnaire.

- *Require that action plans be presented to the team, if possible.* Commitment and ownership of the action plan can best be secured by having the participant describe his or her action plan in front of fellow participants. Presenting the action plan helps ensure that the process is thoroughly developed and will be implemented on the job. If the number of participants is too large, the group can be divided into teams, and one participant can be selected from the team. Under these circumstances, the team will usually select the best action plan for presentation to the group.

- *Explain the follow-up mechanism.* Participants must have a clear understanding of action plan timing, implementation, and follow-up. The method by which data will be collected, analyzed, and reported should be openly discussed. Five options are common:

  - The group is convened to discuss progress on the plans.

  - Participants meet with their immediate managers and discuss the success of the plan. A copy is forwarded to the team.

  - A meeting is held with the evaluator, the participant, and the participant's manager to discuss the plan.

  - Participants send the plan to the evaluator, and it is discussed during a conference call.

  - Participants send the plan directly to the evaluator with no meetings or discussions. This is the most common option.

- *Collect action plans at predetermined follow-up times.* Because an excellent response rate is critical, several steps may be necessary to ensure that action plans are completed and the data are returned to the appropriate individual or group for analysis. Some organizations use follow-up reminders by mail or e-mail. Others call participants to check progress. Still others offer assistance in developing the final plan. These steps may require additional resources, which must be weighed against the importance of having more data. When the action plan process is implemented as outlined in this chapter, the response rates will normally be very high—in the 50 to 80 percent range.

• *Summarize and report the data.* If developed properly, each action plan should contain improvements. Also, each individual has indicated the percentage of improvement directly related to the program, either on the action plan or the questionnaire. The data must be tabulated, summarized, and reported in a way that shows successful application and implementation. Exhibit 6.5 provides a checklist for the success factors for action planning.

☐ Communicate the action plan requirement early.
☐ Describe the action planning process at the beginning of the program.
☐ Teach the action planning process.
☐ Allow time to develop the plan.
☐ Have the program leader approve the action plan.
☐ Require participants to assign a monetary value for each improvement.
☐ Ask participants to isolate the effects of the program (optional).
☐ Ask participants to provide a confidence estimate, when appropriate.
☐ If possible, require action plans to be presented to the group.
☐ Explain the follow-up mechanism.
☐ Collect action plans at the predetermined follow-up time.
☐ Summarize the data.

Exhibit 6.5. Checklist of Success Factors for Action Planning.

Action Plan Advantages and Disadvantages

Although there are many advantages to using action plans, at least two concerns exist:

1. The process relies on direct input from the participant, usually with no assurance of anonymity. As such, the information can sometimes be biased and unreliable.
2. Action plans can be time-consuming for the participant and, if the participant's manager is not involved in the process, the participant may not complete the assignment.

As the material in this section has illustrated, the action plan approach has many inherent advantages. Action plans are:

- Simple and easy to administer
- Easily understood by participants
- Suitable to a wide variety of programs
- Appropriate for all types of data
- Able to measure reaction, learning, behavior changes, and impact
- Usable with or without other evaluation methods

Because of the flexibility and versatility of the process and the conservative adjustments that can be made in analysis, action plans have become important data collection tools for program evaluation.

THE USE OF PERFORMANCE CONTRACTS

The performance contract is essentially a slight variation of the action planning process. Based on the principle of mutual goal setting, a performance contract is a written agreement between a participant and the participant's manager. The participant agrees to improve performance in an area of mutual concern related to the specific learning and development program. The agreement is in the form of a program to be completed or a goal to be accomplished soon after the program's completion. The agreement details what is to be accomplished, at what time, and with what results.

Although the steps can vary according to the specific kind of contract and the organization, a common sequence of events follows:

1. The participant becomes involved in a specific program.
2. The participant and his or her manager mutually agree on a topic for improvement related to the program (What's in it for me?).
3. Specific, measurable goals are set.
4. In the early stages of the program, the contract is discussed and plans are developed to accomplish the goals.
5. After the program is conducted, the participant works on the contract against a specific deadline.
6. The participant reports the results of the effort to his or her manager.
7. The manager and participant document the results and forward a copy to the L&D team, along with appropriate comments.

The process of selecting the area for improvement is similar to the process used in the action planning process. The topic can include one or more of the following areas:

- *Routine performance*—includes specific improvements in routine performance measures, such as production, efficiency, and error rates
- *Problem solving*—focuses on specific problems, such as an unexpected increase in accidents, a decrease in efficiency, or a loss of morale
- *Innovative or creative applications*—includes initiating changes or improvements in work practices, methods, procedures, techniques, and processes
- *Personal development*—involves learning new information or acquiring new skills to increase individual effectiveness

The topic selected should be stated in terms of one or more objectives. The objectives should state what is to be accomplished when the contract is complete. The objectives should be:

- Written
- Understandable by all involved
- Challenging (requiring an unusual effort to achieve)
- Achievable (something that can be accomplished)
- Largely under the control of the participant
- Measurable and dated

The details required to accomplish the contract objectives are developed following the guidelines for action plans presented earlier. Also, the methods for analyzing data and reporting progress are the same as with action plans.

TRANSFER OF LEARNING

One of the important reasons for collecting data at this level is to uncover the barriers to and enablers of the use of skills and knowledge. Although both groups are important, barriers can kill an otherwise successful program. The barriers must be identified and actions must be taken to minimize, remove, or go around the barrier. This problem is serious because barriers exist on every program. When barriers can be removed or minimized, the program has a much better chance of success. Some would define implementation of a successful learning and development program as removing the barriers of success.

While a variety of data collection methods can be used, in each method, some step, process, or effort should be made to identify those barriers. When they are identified, they become important reference points for changes and improvements. Exhibit 6.6 shows the typical barriers that will stifle the success of programs. These are almost universal with any type of program, but others may be specific to the particular setting and the type of program. The important point is to identify them and then use the data in meaningful ways to try to make them less of a problem.

1. My immediate manager does not support the learning.
2. The culture in our work group does not support the learning.
3. No opportunity to use the skills, knowledge, and information from the program.
4. No time to implement the skills.
5. Didn't learn anything that could be applied to the job.
6. Our systems and processes did not support the use of the skills.
7. The resources are not available to implement the skills.
8. Changed job and the skills no longer apply.
9. The program is not appropriate for our work unit.
10. Didn't see a need to implement the program.
11. Could not change old habits.

Exhibit 6.6. Typical Barriers to Successful Implementation.

Along with barriers are the enablers. The enablers are the supporters or enhancers of the transfer of learning. Working with enablers provides an opportunity to make improvements beyond the success that was already achieved. They provide prescriptions for other programs as well and are very powerful. When learning is not actually used successfully on the job, it is a very serious issue.

Perhaps one of the most influential stakeholders in the learning transfer process is the participant's immediate manager. Figure 6.1 shows nine possible stakeholder/time combinations that could be used to enhance the transfer of learning to the job. For example, before the

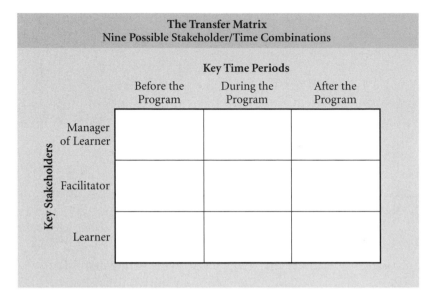

Figure 6.1. Stakeholder/Time Combinations.
Source: M.L. Broad & J.W. Newstrom. (1991). *Transfer of Training:*
Action-Packed Strategies to Ensure High Payoff from Training Investments.
New York: Perseus Books Group. Used with permission.

formal learning program, the manager could meet with the learner to discuss expectations and set specific goals. After the program, the manager could follow up to see whether the expectations and goals have been successfully met. These two blocks, manager before and manager after, are the most powerful blocks to aid the transfer of learning to the job. Unfortunately, managers don't usually see it this way until it has been explained to them in meetings and workshops. They minimize their influence, yet their involvement and actions can make a tremendous difference in the transfer.

DEVELOPING ROI FOR LEVEL 3

In almost every program, participants are expected to change their on-the-job behaviors by applying what they learned in the program. On-the-job application is critical to program success, particularly when the focus is on competencies. Although the use of skills on the job is no guarantee that results will follow, it is an underlying assumption for most programs that, if the knowledge and skills are applied, positive results will occur. A few organizations attempt to take this process a step further and measure the value of on-the-job behavior changes and calculate the ROI. In these situations, estimates are taken from participants, their supervisors, the management group, or experts in the field. The following six steps are used to develop the ROI:

1. Develop the competencies for the target job.
2. Indicate the percentage of job success that is represented by the competencies included in the program.
3. Determine the monetary values of competencies using average salaries and the employee benefits of the participants.
4. Compute the worth of the pre- and post-program skill levels.
5. Subtract the post-program values from the pre-program values.
6. Compare the total added benefits with the program costs.

Perhaps an example will illustrate one technique for measuring the value of on-the-job application. The U.S. government redesigned its introduction to supervision course, a five-day learning solution for newly appointed supervisors. The program focused on eight competencies:

1. Role and responsibilities of the supervisor
2. Communications
3. Planning, assigning, controlling, and evaluating work
4. Ethics
5. Leadership
6. Analyzing performance problems
7. Customer service
8. Managing diversity

The immediate managers of the new supervisors indicated that these eight competencies accounted for 81 percent of first-level supervisors' jobs. For the target group being evaluated, the average annual salary plus benefits for the newly appointed supervisors was $42,202. Thus, multiplying this figure by the amount of job success accounted for by the competencies (81 percent) yielded a dollar value of $34,184 per participant. If a person performed successfully in these eight competencies for one year, the value to the agency would be $34,184. Of course, this assumes that the employees were paid an amount equal to their contribution when they were fully competent.

Using a scale of 0 to 9, managers rated the skills for each of the competencies before the program was conducted. The average level of skills required for job success was determined to be 6.44. The skill rating prior to the job was 4.96, which represented 77 percent of the 6.44 (that is, participants were performing at 77 percent of the level required to be successful in the competencies). After the program, the skill rating was 5.59, representing 87 percent of the level necessary to be successful.

Monetary values were assigned based on the participants' salaries. Performance at the required level was worth $34,184. At a 77 percent proficiency level, the new supervisors were performing at a contribution value of $26,322. After the application of the learning, this value reached 87 percent, representing a contribution value of $29,740. The difference in these values, $3,418, represents the gain per participant attributable to the course. The program cost was $1,638 per participant. Thus, the ROI is:

$$\text{ROI} = \frac{\$3,418 - \$1,368}{\$1,368} = \frac{\$2,050}{\$1,368} \times 100 = 150\%$$

As with other estimates, a word of caution is needed. These results are subjective because the rating systems used are subjective and may not necessarily reflect an accurate assessment of the value of the program. Also, since a program is usually implemented to help the organization achieve its objectives, some managers insist on tangible changes in hard data such as quantity, quality, cost, and time. For them, a Level 3 evaluation is not always a good substitute for Level 4 data, if Level 4 data are available. In this example, an assumption is made that competencies acquired and applied will influence Level 4 business measures.

Although this process is subjective, it has several useful advantages. First, if there are no plans to track the actual impact of the program in terms of specific, measurable business results (Level 4), then this approach represents a credible substitute. In many programs, particularly with skill building for supervisors, identifying tangible changes on the job is difficult. Therefore, alternate approaches to determine the worth of a program or project are needed. Second, this approach results in data that are usually credible with the management group if they understand how they are developed and the assumptions behind the data. An important point regarding the projected ROI for the U.S. government course is that the data on the changes in competence level came from the managers who rated their supervisors. In this specific program, the numbers were large enough to make the process statistically significant.

DATA USE

Data become meaningless if not used properly. As we move up the chain, the data become more valuable in the minds of the sponsors, key executives, and other stakeholders who have a strong interest in the program. While data can be used in dozens of ways, the following are the principal uses for data after it is collected:

REPORT AND REVIEW RESULTS. The most obvious use of the data is to report it to the interested stakeholders to inform them of the program's progress. This data would even go to the participants, who are in some cases providing the data. Figure 6.2 shows how application data might be reported. In this example, six distinct actions need to be taken from this program, which was aimed at minimizing sexual harassment complaints. A target value was set, and two different divisions reported results. The results not only showed the success that was achieved but also areas in which improvement could continue to be needed.

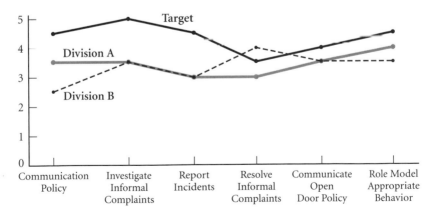

Figure 6.2. Sample Report of Application Data.

ADJUST DESIGN AND IMPLEMENTATION. Sometimes, the data point to problems with the program management and implementation. It may indicate that some aspects of the program are not working well and have to be redesigned. It may indicate that other processes or partial solutions are needed to achieve the desired success. In either case, efforts may have to be taken to adjust the original program plan, which included design, development, and implementation.

IDENTIFY AND REMOVE BARRIERS. As described earlier, one of the most important uses of the data are to drive down the barriers—either remove them, minimize them, or provide a way to go around them.

IDENTIFY AND ENHANCE ENABLERS. Enablers are the opposite of barriers. Enablers are the processes, factors, actions, and elements that make the program a success. These need to be continued and, in some cases, enhanced so that success improves or continues at the same level.

RECOGNIZE SUCCESSFUL INDIVIDUALS. Every program will have individuals who accomplish the goals quite well. They have achieved what they need to and sometimes have exceeded it. Often at this level many success stories can be developed. These become success case studies, detailing how some individual or group has achieved extraordinary performance. Recognition of these groups is powerful and serves as a continuing motivator and perhaps subtle communication for those who have not achieved the same success.

REINFORCE DESIRED ACTIONS. Since the data are collected from individuals who are implementing and applying the program, the presence of questions and other data collection processes serve to reinforce participants for what they should be doing. In a sense, the questionnaire may serve as a reminder of what they should be doing. The interview may signal areas in which they are not doing well. Thus, in essence, data collection alone can drive increased performance.

DEVELOP MONETARY VALUE. As described earlier, the data can be used to estimate the monetary impact using the concept of utility analysis. While this may not be as credible and accurate as developing the ROI from impact data, it nevertheless serves as a useful tool to begin to show the money.

IMPROVE MANAGEMENT SUPPORT. Sometimes, the application and implementation data show a lack of management support or the lack of positive management support. In either case, this data may show how managers need to support and continue to support the program. Also, when success is generated, it may provide management with the type of data that they want to see. Although most are interested in the impact, the money, and the ROI, some want to see things working properly, with positive behavior, things in place, processes being accomplished, and tasks being completed. This becomes satisfying data, possibly more so than reaction and learning.

MARKET FUTURE PROGRAMS. For programs that are replicated in other places, often within the same organization, the application and implementation data show what individuals have achieved, what they have accomplished, and what they have completed. When combined with qualitative comments, this can lead to powerful, persuasive data for the program when it is applied in other locations.

FINAL THOUGHTS

This chapter outlined techniques for measuring application and implementation—a critical issue in determining the success of a program. This essential measure determines not only the success achieved, but areas in which improvement is needed and areas in which the success can be replicated in the future. A variety of techniques are available, ranging from observation to questionnaires to action plans. The method chosen must match the scope of the program. Complicated programs require a comprehensive approach that measures all the issues involved in application and implementation. Simple programs can have a less formal approach and collect data only from a questionnaire.

CHAPTER SEVEN

Measuring and Isolating the Impact of Programs

This chapter focuses on tracking business performance measures and is the last chapter on data collection. Most sponsors regard business impact data as the most important data type because of its connection to business success. For many learning and development programs, a less-than-desired performance in one or more business measures (representing the business need) initiated the program. This chapter covers the specific processes needed to collect these measures. Coverage begins with monitoring the record-keeping systems, moving to action plans, and using questionnaires. These three processes account for most opportunities available for collecting business impact data.

When a significant increase in business performance is noted after a program has been implemented, it is often linked to the program. While the change in performance may be linked to the program, other factors may contribute to the improvement as well. If this issue is not addressed, the link to business impact is not credible. This chapter explores useful techniques for isolating the effects of the program.

WHY MEASURE BUSINESS IMPACT?

Although several obvious reasons exist for measuring business impact, several specific issues support the rationale.

Higher-Level Data

Following the assumption that higher-level data create more value for key stakeholders, the business impact measures offer more valuable data than lower levels. Impact data represent the consequence of the application and implementation of a program. They represent the bottom-line measures that are positively influenced when a program is successful. For some stakeholders, these are the most valuable data.

Breaking the Chain of Impact

The chain of impact can be broken at Level 4, business impact, and this happens in many programs. If the program does not drive business impact data, or at least not enough to create a positive ROI, then the corresponding results may be less than satisfactory. In some cases, success can occur at the previous level but fail at Level 4. Participants may react positively to the program; they learn the skills successfully; and at Level 3, they use the skills on the job. However, when the business impact measure, anticipated to be influenced by the program, does not change, the program does not add value. What could cause this? There are two possibilities. First, the business alignment for the program wasn't completed properly. It was not the right solution. The process outlined in Chapter Two—identifying the need, including the business impact measure—was not completed successfully. It has driven activity and not results.

The second possibility is that other factors drove the business measure in the opposite direction. At first glance, it appears that the program has no value, but in reality, it may have an impact. This issue brings into focus the importance of isolating the effects of a program (covered later in this chapter).

A Business Driver for Many Programs

For most programs, business impact data represent the initial drivers for the program. The problem of deteriorating (or less-than-desired) performance or the opportunity for improvement of a business measure usually leads to a new program. If the business needs defined by business measures are the drivers, then the key measures for evaluating the program are those same business measures. The extent to which measures have changed is the principal determinant of the success of the program.

These are the measures often desired by the sponsor and the ones that the sponsor wants to see changed or improved. They often represent hard, indisputable facts that reflect performance that is critical to the business and operating unit level of the organization.

Show Me the Money Data

Using this level of data, the actual money is developed. Impact data, influenced by the program, can be converted to monetary value to show the monetary contribution of the program. Although this conversion is actually a separate step, it is derived from the business impact data collected in this step. Without credible business impact data linked directly to the program, having a credible monetary value for the program would be difficult, if not impossible. This makes this level of evaluation one of the most critical.

Easy to Measure

One unique feature about business impact data is that they are often easy to measure. Hard and soft measures at this level often reflect key measures that are found in plentiful numbers throughout an organization. It is not unusual for an organization to have hundreds or even thousands of measures reflecting specific business impact items. The challenge is to connect the objectives of the program to the appropriate business measures. This is more easily accomplished at the beginning of the program due to the availability and ease with which many of the data items can be located.

Common Data Types

The irony of this level of data collection is that these data types are the most common. When measuring reaction, learning, or application, the measures have to be created, at least for many programs. However, at the business impact level, the data have been created, except for rare exceptions in which the data may have to be developed. Thus, the good news here is that these are common data items tracked and monitored by someone.

TYPES OF IMPACT MEASURES
Hard Versus Soft Data

To help focus on the desired measures, a distinction is made in two general categories of data: hard data and soft data, described in Chapter Two. Hard data are the primary measurements of improvement, presented through rational, undisputed facts that are easily gathered. They are the most desirable type of data to collect. The ultimate criteria for measuring the effectiveness of management rest on hard data items, such as productivity, profitability, cost control, and quality control. Exhibit 2.6 in Chapter Two provides examples of hard data grouped into categories of output, quality, costs, and time.

Hard data measures are often supplemented with interim assessments of soft data, such as brand awareness, satisfaction, loyalty, and leadership. Although a program designed to enhance competencies or manage change should have an ultimate impact on hard data items, measuring soft data items may be more efficient. Soft data are more difficult to collect and analyze but are used when hard data are unavailable. Soft data are difficult to convert to monetary values; are subjectively based, in many cases; and are less credible as a performance measurement. Exhibit 2.7 in Chapter Two provides a list of typical soft data items grouped into typical categories.

The preference of hard data in programs does not reduce the value of soft data. Soft data are essential for a complete evaluation of a program; success may rest on soft data measurements. For example, in an empowerment program at a chemical plant, three key measures of success were identified: employee stress, job satisfaction, and teamwork.

Most programs use a combination of hard and soft data items in the evaluation. For example, a program to install an operator training program in a manufacturing plant had the following measures of success:

- Reduction of production costs
- Improvement in production schedules
- Reduction in inventory shortages
- Improvement in production capability
- Increased technology leadership

These changes included both hard data (production costs) and soft data (capability, technology leadership). The important point is that both hard and soft data have a place in evaluation. Most programs will use both types of data.

Tangible Versus Intangible

The confusion about the categories of soft data and the often-reduced value placed on soft data were discussed in Chapter Two. This leads to a critical definition in this book. While the terms hard and soft data can be used to discuss impact data, the terms tangible and intangible can also be used. Tangible data represents a category that has been converted to monetary value. Intangibles are defined as data purposely not converted to monetary value (that is, if data cannot be converted to monetary value credibly with a reasonable amount of resources, then it is left as an intangible). This approach has several advantages. First, it avoids the sometimes confusing labels of soft and hard. Second, it avoids the image that being soft equates to little or no value. Third, it brings definition to the situation. In some organizations, a particular data item may be converted to money already and the conversion is credible because it actually becomes tangible. However, in another organization, the same measure has not been converted and cannot be converted with a reasonable amount of resources. Therefore, it is left as intangible. Fourth, it provides a rule that enhances the consistency of the process. This is one of the standards listed in Chapter One. Having this rule ensures that if two people conducted the same evaluation, they would get the same or similar results.

Scorecards

Scorecards, such as those used in sporting events, provide a variety of measures for top executives. In Kaplan and Norton's landmark book, *The Balanced Scorecard,* the concept was brought to the attention of organizations (Kaplan & Norton, 1996). Kaplan and Norton suggested that data can be organized in four categories: process, operational, financial, and growth.

But what exactly is a scorecard? The *American Heritage Dictionary* defines a scorecard from two perspectives:

1. A printed program or card enabling a spectator to identify players and record the progress of a game or competition.

2. A small card used to record one's own performance in sports, such as golf.

Scorecards come in a variety of types, such as Kaplan and Norton's balanced scorecard and the scored set in the President's Management Agenda using the traffic light grading system (green for success, yellow for mixed results, red for unsatisfactory). Regardless of the type, top executives place great emphasis on the concept of scorecards. In some organizations, the scorecard concept has filtered down to various functional business units, and each part of the business has been required to develop scorecards. A growing number of learning and development executives have developed scorecards to reflect their segments of the business.

The scorecard approach is appealing because it provides a quick comparison of key measures and examines the status of the organization. As a management tool, scorecards can be important in shaping and improving or maintaining the performance of the organization through the implementation of preventive programs. Scorecard measures often link to particular learning and development programs. In many situations, a scorecard deficiency measure may have prompted the program in the first place.

Specific Measures Linked to Programs

An important issue that often surfaces when considering ROI applications is the understanding of specific measures that are often driven by specific programs. While there are no standard answers, Exhibit 7.1 represents a summary of some typical payoff measures for specific types of programs. The measures are quite broad for some programs. For example, leadership development may pay off in a variety of measures, such as improved productivity, enhanced sales and revenues, improved quality, cycle-time reduction, direct cost savings, and employee job satisfaction. In other programs, the influenced measures are quite narrow. For example, labor-management cooperation programs typically influence grievances, stoppages, and employee satisfaction. Orientation programs typically influence measures of early turnover (turnover in the first ninety days of employment), initial job performance, and productivity. The measures that are influenced depend on the objectives and the design of the program. The exhibit also illustrates the immense number of measures that can be driven or influenced.

Program	Key Impact Measurements
Absenteeism control/reduction	Absenteeism, customer satisfaction, job satisfaction, stress
Business coaching	Productivity/output, quality, time savings, efficiency, costs, employee satisfaction, customer satisfaction
Career development/ career management	Turnover, promotions, recruiting expenses, job satisfaction
Communications programs	Errors, stress, conflicts, productivity, job satisfaction
Compensation plans	Costs, productivity, quality, job satisfaction
Compliance programs	Penalties/fines, charges, settlements, losses
Diversity	Turnover, absenteeism, complaints, charges, settlements, losses
e-Learning	Cost savings, productivity improvement, quality improvement, cycle times, error reductions, job satisfaction
Executive education	Productivity, sales, quality, time, costs, customer service, turnover, absenteeism, job satisfaction
Labor-management cooperation programs	Work stoppages, grievances, absenteeism, job satisfaction
Leadership development	Productivity/output, quality, efficiency, cost/time savings, employee satisfaction, engagement
Management development	Productivity, sales, quality, time, costs, customer service, turnover, absenteeism, job satisfaction
Orientation, on-boarding (revised)	Early turnover, training time, productivity, performance
Personal productivity/ time management	Time savings, productivity, stress reduction, job satisfaction
Project management	Time savings, quality improvement, budgets
Retention management	Turnover, engagement, job satisfaction
Safety training	Accident frequency rates, accident severity rates, first aid treatments
Sales training	Sales, market share, customer loyalty, new accounts
Self-directed teams	Productivity/output, quality, customer satisfaction, turnover, absenteeism, job satisfaction
Sexual harassment prevention	Complaints, turnover, absenteeism, employee satisfaction
Six Sigma training	Defects, rework, response times, cycle times, costs
Stress management	Medical costs, turnover, absenteeism, job satisfaction
Software support	Productivity, sales, quality, time, costs, customer service, turnover, absenteeism, job satisfaction
Team building	Productivity, sales, quality, time, costs, customer service, turnover, absenteeism, job satisfaction
Supervisor training	Productivity, sales, quality, time, costs, customer service, turnover, absenteeism, job satisfaction
Wellness/fitness programs	Turnover, medical costs, accidents, absenteeism

Exhibit 7.1. Typical Measures for Programs.

A word of caution is needed. Presenting specific measures linked to a typical program may give the impression that these are the only measures influenced. In practice, a particular program can have many outcomes. Exhibit 7.1 shows the most likely measures that arise from the studies that the ROI Institute has reviewed. In the course of a decade, we have been involved in over two thousand studies, and common threads exist among particular programs.

The good news is that most programs are driving business measures. The measures are based on what is being changed in the various business units, divisions, regions, and individual workplaces. These are the measures that matter to senior executives. The difficulty often comes in ensuring that the connection to the program exists. This is accomplished through a variety of techniques to isolate the effects of the program on the particular business measures and will be discussed later.

BUSINESS PERFORMANCE MONITORING

Data are available in every organization to measure business performance. Monitoring performance data enables management to measure performance in terms of output, quality, costs, time, job satisfaction, and customer satisfaction, among other measures. In determining the source of data in the evaluation, the first consideration should be existing databases, reports, and scorecards. In most organizations, performance data suitable for measuring program-related improvement are available. If not, additional record-keeping systems will have to be developed for measurement and analysis. At this point, the question of economics surfaces. Is it economical to develop the record-keeping systems necessary to evaluate a program? If the costs are greater than the expected benefits, developing those systems is pointless.

Identify Appropriate Measures

Existing performance measures should be thoroughly researched to identify those related to the proposed objectives of the program. Often, several performance measures are related to the same item. For example, the efficiency of a production unit can be measured in several ways:

• The number of units produced per hour
• The number of on-schedule production units

- The percentage of equipment used
- The percentage of equipment downtime
- The labor cost per unit of production
- The overtime required per unit of production
- Total unit cost

Each of these, in its own way, measures the effectiveness or efficiency of the production unit. All related measures should be reviewed to determine those most relevant to the program.

Convert Current Measures to Usable Ones

Occasionally, existing performance measures are integrated with other data, and keeping them isolated from unrelated data may be difficult. In this situation, all existing, related measures should be extracted and tabulated again to make them more appropriate for comparison in the evaluation. At times, conversion factors may be necessary. For example, the average number of new sales orders per month may be presented regularly in the performance measures for the sales department. In addition, the sales costs per sales representative are also presented. However, in the evaluation of a program, the average cost per new sale is needed. The average number of new sales orders and the sales cost per sales representative are required to develop the data necessary for comparison.

Developing New Measures

In some cases, data needed to measure the effectiveness of a program are not available, and new data are needed. The evaluator must work with the client organization to develop record-keeping systems, if economically feasible. In one organization, the sales staff's delayed responses to customer requests were an issue. This problem was discovered based on customer feedback. The feedback data prompted a program to reduce the response time. To help ensure the success of the program, several measures were planned, including measuring the actual time to respond to a customer request. Initially this measure was not available. As the program was implemented, new software was used to measure the time.

Several questions regarding this issue were addressed:

• Which department/section will develop the measurement system?
• Who will record and monitor the data?
• Where will it be recorded?
• Will input forms be used?
• Who will report it?

These questions will usually involve other departments or a management decision that extends beyond the scope of evaluators. Often the administration department, operations, or the information technology unit will be instrumental in helping determine whether new measures are needed and, if so, how they will be developed. This action should be a last resort.

THE USE OF ACTION PLANS TO DEVELOP BUSINESS IMPACT DATA

For many projects and programs, business data are readily available. However, at times, data won't be easily accessible to the evaluator. Sometimes, data are maintained at the individual, work unit, or department level and may not be known to anyone outside that area. Tracking down those data sets may be too expensive and time-consuming. When this is the case, other data collection methods may be used to capture data sets and make them available for the evaluator. Three other options are described in this book: the use of action plans, performance contracts, and questionnaires.

Action plans can capture application and implementation data, as discussed in Chapter Six. They can also be a useful tool for capturing business impact data. For business impact data, the action plan is more focused and credible than a questionnaire. The basic design principles involved in developing and administering action plans are the same for business impact data as they are for application and implementation data. However, a few elements unique to business impact are presented in this section. The following steps are recommended when an action plan is developed and implemented to capture business impact data and to convert the data to monetary values.

Set Goals and Targets

As shown in Exhibit 7.2, an action plan can be developed with a direct focus on business impact data. The plan presented in this figure requires participants to develop an overall objective for the plan, which is usually the primary objective of the program. In some cases, a program may have more than one objective, which requires additional action plans. In addition to the objective, the improvement measure and the current levels of performance are identified. This information requires that the participant anticipate the application of skills and set goals for specific performances that can be realized.

The action plan is completed during the program, often with input and assistance from the facilitator. The facilitator actually approves the plan, indicating that it meets the requirements of being **s**pecific, **m**otivating, **a**chievable, **r**ealistic, and **t**ime-based (SMART). The plan can actually be developed in a one- to two-hour timeframe and often begins with action steps related to the program. These action steps are Level 3 activities that detail application and implementation. All these steps build support for, and are linked to, business impact measures.

Define the Unit of Measure

The next important concern is to define the actual unit of measure. In some cases, more than one measure may be used and will subsequently be contained in additional action plans. The unit of measure is necessary to break the process into the simplest steps so that its ultimate value can be determined. The unit may be output data, such as an additional unit manufactured or package delivered, or it can be sales and marketing data, such as additional sales revenue or a 1 percent increase in market share. In terms of quality, the unit can be one reject, one error, or one defect. Time-based units are usually measured in minutes, hours, days, or weeks. Other units are specific to their particular type of data, such as one grievance, one complaint, one absence, or one less person on welfare. The point is to break down impact data into the simplest terms possible.

Place a Monetary Value on Each Improvement

During the program, participants are asked to locate, calculate, or estimate the monetary value for each improvement outlined in their plans. The unit value is determined using a variety of methods such

Name _____ Facilitator Signature _____ Follw-Up Date _____

Objective _____ Evaluation Period _____ to _____

Improvement Measure _____ Current Performance _____ Target Performance _____

Action Steps	Analysis
1. _____	A. What is the unit of measure? _____
2. _____	B. What is the value (cost) of one unit? $ _____
3. _____	C. How did you arrive at this value? _____
4. _____	_____
5. _____	D. How much did the measure change during the evaluation period? (monthly value) _____
6. _____	E. List the other factors that have influenced this change. _____
7. _____	F. What percent of this change was actually caused by this program? _____ %
Intangible Benefits:	G. What level of confidence do you place on the above information? (100% = Certainty and 0% = No Confidence) _____ %

Comments: _____

Exhibit 7.2. Sample Program Action Plan.

as standard values, expert input, external databases, or estimates. The process used in arriving at the value is described in the instructions for the action plan. When the actual improvement occurs, participants will use these values to capture the annual monetary benefits of the plan.

In the worst-case scenario, participants are asked to calculate the value. Using standard values or having participants contact an expert are the best actions. When participant estimates are necessary, participants must show the basis of their calculations, and space for this information should be provided.

Implement the Action Plan

Participants implement the action plan after the program is conducted. The participants follow action plan steps, and the subsequent business impact results are achieved.

Provide Specific Improvements

At the end of the specified follow-up period—usually three months, six months, nine months, or one year—the participants indicate the specific improvements made, usually expressed as a daily, weekly, or monthly amount. This determines the actual amount of change that has been observed, measured, or recorded. Participants must understand the need for accuracy as data are recorded. In most cases, only the changes are recorded, as those amounts are needed to calculate the monetary values of the program. In other cases, before and after data may be recorded, allowing the evaluator to calculate the differences.

Isolate the Effects of the Program

Although the action plan is initiated because of the program, the actual improvements reported on the action plan may be influenced by other factors. Therefore, the program should not be given full credit for all the improvement. For example, an action plan to implement leadership skills could only be given partial credit for a business improvement because other variables might have influenced the impact measures. While several ways are available to isolate the effects of a program, participant estimation is usually most appropriate in the action planning process. Participants are asked to estimate the percentage of the improvement directly related to the program. This question can be asked on the action plan form or in a follow-up questionnaire. Sometimes, preceding this question with a request to identify all the other factors that might have influenced the results is beneficial. This allows the participants to think through the relationships before allocating a portion to this program.

Provide a Confidence Level for Estimates

The process to isolate the amount of the improvement directly related to the program is not precise. Participants are asked to indicate their level of confidence in their estimates. Using a scale of 0 to 100 percent—where 0 percent means no confidence and 100 percent means the estimates represent absolute certainty—participants have a way to express their uncertainty with the estimates.

Collect Action Plans at Specified Time Intervals

An excellent response rate is essential, so several steps may be necessary to ensure that the action plans are completed and returned. Usually, participants will see the importance of the process and will develop their plans during the program. Some organizations use follow-up reminders by mail or e-mail. Others call participants to check progress. Still others offer assistance in developing the final plan. These steps may require additional resources, which must be weighed against the importance of having more precise data. Specific ways to improve response rates were discussed in Chapter Six.

Summarize the Data and Calculate the ROI

If developed properly, each action plan should have annualized monetary values associated with improvements. Also, each individual should have indicated the percentage of the improvement directly related to the program. Finally, participants should have provided a confidence percentage to reflect their uncertainty with the estimates and the subjective nature of some of the data that they provided.

Because this process involves estimates, it may not appear accurate. Several adjustments during the analysis make the process credible and more accurate. These adjustments reflect guiding principles of the ROI methodology. The following adjustments are made:

Step 1   For those participants who do not provide data, the assumption is that they had no improvement to report. This is a very conservative approach.

Step 2   Each value is checked for realism, usability, and feasibility. Extreme values are discarded and omitted from the analysis.

Step 3   Because the improvement is annualized, the assumption is that the program had no improvement after the first year (for short-term programs). Some add value in years two and three. More can be found on this in Chapter Nine.

Step 4   The improvement from Step 3 is then adjusted using the confidence level, multiplying it by the confidence percentage. The confidence level is actually an error percentage suggested by the participants. For example, a participant indicating 80 percent confidence with the process provides a 20 percent error possibility. In a $10,000 estimate with an 80 percent confidence factor, the participant suggests that the value can be in the range of $8,000 to $12,000 (20 percent less to 20 percent more). To be conservative, the lower number is used. Then the confidence factor is multiplied by the amount of improvement.

Step 5   The new values are adjusted by the percentage of the improvement related directly to the program using multiplication. This isolates the effects of the program.

The monetary values determined in these five steps are totaled to arrive at the final program benefit. Since these values are already annualized, the total of these benefits becomes the annual benefits for the program. This value is placed in the numerator of the ROI formula to calculate the ROI.

Advantages of Action Plans

The action-planning process has several inherent advantages as a useful way to collect business impact data. Most of the data are taken directly from participants and often have the credibility needed for the analysis. Also, much of the responsibility for the analysis and evaluation is shifted to the participants as they address three of the most critical parts of the process. In effect, they collect data to show improvements, isolate the effects of the program, and convert data to monetary values. This enables the evaluation to be conducted with limited resources and shifts much of the responsibility to those who apply and implement the program.

USE OF PERFORMANCE CONTRACTS TO MEASURE BUSINESS IMPACT

The performance contract is a variation of the action plan. Based on the principle of mutual goal setting, a performance contract is a written agreement between a participant and the participant's manager. The participant agrees to improve performance in an area of concern related to the program. The agreement is in the form of a goal to be accomplished during the program or after program completion. The agreement details what is to be accomplished, at what time, and with what results.

Although the steps can vary according to the organization and the specific contract, a common sequence of events follows:

1. The employee (participant) becomes involved in the program implementation.

2. The participant and (his or her) immediate manager mutually agree on a measure or measures for improvement related to the program (What's in it for me?).

3. Specific, measurable goals for improvement are set, following the SMART requirements.

4. In the early stages of the program, the contract is discussed, and plans are developed to accomplish the goals.

5. During program implementation, the participant works on the contract against a specific deadline.

6. The participant reports the results of the effort to his or her manager.

7. The manager and participant document the results and forward a copy to the program team along with appropriate comments.

The process of selecting the area for improvement is similar to the process used when preparing an action plan. The topic can cover one or more of the following areas:

- Routine performance related to the program, which includes specific improvements in routine performance measures, such as production, efficiency, and error rates
- Problem solving, which focuses on specific problems related to the program, such as an unexpected increase in accidents, a decrease in efficiency, or a loss of morale
- Innovative or creative applications from the program, which include initiating changes or improvements in work practices, methods, procedures, techniques, and processes
- Personal development connected to the program, which involves learning new information or acquiring new skills to increase effectiveness to influence a personal impact measure

The topic selected should be stated in terms of one or more objectives. The objectives should state what is to be accomplished when the contract is complete. The objectives should be:

- Written
- Understandable by all involved
- Challenging (requiring an unusual effort to achieve)
- Achievable (something that can be accomplished)
- Largely under the control of the participant
- Measurable and dated

The details required to accomplish the contract objectives are developed following the guidelines for action plans presented earlier. Also, the methods for analyzing data and reporting progress are essentially the same as those used to analyze action plan data.

THE USE OF QUESTIONNAIRES
TO COLLECT BUSINESS IMPACT DATA

As described in previous chapters, the questionnaire is one of the most versatile data collection tools and can be appropriate for Level 1, 2, 3, and 4 data. Chapter Six presented a sample questionnaire in which application and implementation data (Level 3) are collected, as well as impact data. Some of the issues discussed in that chapter apply equally in collecting business impact data. Essentially, the design principles and the content issues are the same. However, questionnaires developed for a business impact evaluation will contain additional questions to capture impact data items.

Using questionnaires for impact data collection bring both good news and bad news. The good news is that questionnaires are easy to implement and low-cost. Data analysis is very efficient, and the time to provide the data is often short, making them among the least disruptive data collection methods. However, the bad news is that the data can be distorted, inaccurate, and sometimes missing. The challenge is to take all the steps necessary to ensure that questionnaires are complete, accurate, and clear, and are returned.

Unfortunately, because of the disadvantages, questionnaires represent the weakest method of data collection. Paradoxically, it is the most used method because of its advantages. Of the first one hundred case studies published on the ROI methodology, roughly 50 percent used questionnaires for data collection. They are popular, convenient, low-cost, and fortunately or unfortunately, a way of life. The challenge is to make them better. The philosophy in the use of the ROI methodology is to make the weakest method as credible as possible. Thus, the challenge is to make questionnaires credible and useful by ensuring that they capture all the necessary data, participants provide accurate and complete data, and the return rates are in the 70- to 80-percent range.

The reason that return rates need to be so high is based on Guiding Principle 6 in the ROI methodology—no data, no improvement. If an individual provides no improvement data, the assumption is that the person had no improvement. This is a very conservative principle, but necessary for the credibility of the results. Therefore, using questionnaires will require effort, discipline, and personal attention to ensure proper response rates. It is helpful to remember that this is the least preferred method and is used only when the other methods don't work (that is, business performance data cannot be easily monitored, action plans are not feasible, or performance contracting is not suitable). Three scenarios for questionnaire use are possible.

When You Don't Have a Clue

In the worst-case situation, the evaluator doesn't have a clue which measures have been driven or influenced by the program. For some, this situation may be inconceivable, but in practice it occurs routinely.

Consider the tremendous sums of money poured into executive education, management development, leadership development, and executive coaching. Much of that, if not the vast majority, is implemented without any clue as to how those programs will add value, let alone improve some specific measure that might be connected to the program. When this is the case, the data collection instrument would follow the series of questions shown in Exhibit 7.3. This is much like a fishing expedition, as the evaluator attempts to uncover a particular business measure connected to the program. Still, it could be a useful exercise with some surprising results.

SCENARIO 1. WHEN YOU DON'T HAVE A CLUE

1. How did you use the material from this program?
2. What influence did it have in your work? Team?
3. What specific measure was influenced? Define it.
4. What is the unit value of the measure? (Profit or Cost)
5. What is the basis of this value?
6. How much did the measure change since the program was conducted?
7. What is the frequency of the measure? (Daily, weekly, monthly, etc.)
8. What is the total annual value of the improvement?
9. What other factors could have caused this total improvement?
10. What percent of the total improvement can be attributed to this program?
11. What is your confidence estimate, expressed as a percent, for the above data? 0 percent = no confidence; 100 percent = certainty

---

Exhibit 7.3. Chain of Impact Questions When the Measure Is Unknown.

Question 1 is an attempt to connect the program to the work environment—it's the transition. It is essentially a Level 3 question about application, getting the participants to reflect on what actions they have taken because of the program. Question 2 examines consequences, defining or explaining more specifically the outcomes of their actions, implementation, and behaviors. The influence could be with individual work, the team, or even the organization. Question 3 asks for the specifics, defining the measure. In some cases, if not most, more than one measure may be involved, and these questions can have multiple responses. Question 4 is the actual unit value, which is profit if it is a sales-related output measure or costs if it is a quality or time measure. This is a difficult challenge, but it is doable in some organizations because the unit values are already developed. Question 5 gauges the credibility of the data provided in Question 4. The participant explains how he or she arrived at the unit value. If Question 5 is left blank, the data item is thrown out (but the participants know this from the instructions). In essence, this would be an unsupported claim that is omitted from the analysis (Guiding Principle 8).

Question 6 documents the change, the pre- and post-differences for the specific measure. Question 7 details the specific frequency, such as daily, weekly, or monthly data. The frequency is necessary to calculate the total annual improvement, asked for in Question 8. This is the first-year value of improvement. Most programs will only pay off on the first year of value, although long-term programs will have a longer period. Question 9 requires that participants think through other factors that might have influenced the specific measure that they reported. This is a way of validating the reported change. Initially, the participant may think that the improvement is all directly connected to this program. In reality, other factors are there, and this question provides an opportunity for participants to reflect on the links to other factors. Question 10 then asks the participants to decide, after thinking about other possible factors, what percentage of the improvement came directly from the program, isolating the effects of the program from other influences. Because this is an estimate, it is adjusted for error, asked for in Question 11.

Participants should not be surprised by these questions. They must know that they are coming, and every effort must be taken to get them to respond. Still, many professionals may consider this series of questions a futile exercise—that participants cannot provide responses. Fortunately, the research doesn't support this position. In literally hundreds of studies where this kind of approach is taken, participants can and will provide data connected to the program, assuming of course that a connection to a business measure exists.

The skeptics often consider participants to be unknowing, uncooperative, and irresponsible, validating their point that the data would not be forthcoming. However, participants will provide data for four basic reasons:

1. They are the most credible source, since they are directly involved and understand the full scope of the program and its consequences.

2. It's their work, and they know more about it than anyone. Their performance is being reported and analyzed.

3. This process recognizes their roles as experts. The fact that this question is offered suggests that they are in a position to know, and they appreciate the recognition that they have the expertise to provide the data.

4. They are responsible. For the most part, participants will provide data if they understand why data are needed and how it will be used. Of course, not every participant will warm up to this exercise. It works extremely well for professional, engineering, administrative, management, and technical personnel. Operators, laborers, and entry-level clerical staff may have more difficulty. But in most situations, the participants are responsible and knowledgeable and care about the process. Because of this, the quality and quantity of the data may be surprising.

When the Measure Is a Defined Set

A slightly modified approach to these questions is to assume that the program is influencing a set of measures in a distinct category or group. Exhibit 7.4 shows such an example. Question 1 lists a group of measures that logically could be directly connected to the program. (This is a little easier than the previous scenario, where the set of measures was not known.) This series of questions requires participants to think about specific outcomes but is triggered by potential or possibility. This is even more powerful when the measures are focused on the possible or probable outcomes of the program. The other questions and analysis are similar to what was contained in the previous scenario. This approach has the advantage of being more credible because it connects to a given set of measures.

When the Measure Is Known

Fortunately, with many L&D programs, the actual measure or measures are known. These are the measures tied to the program in the beginning and are often the measures that drive the program. When these are known, the questionnaire can be focused, specific, and credible. Exhibit 7.5 shows a series of questions asked when the measure is known. The important point here is that the person defines the

SCENARIO 2. WHEN THE MEASURE IS IN A DEFINED SET

1. To what extent did this program positively influence the following measures:

	Significant Influence				No Influence	
	5	4	3	2	1	n/a
productivity	○	○	○	○	○	○
sales	○	○	○	○	○	○
quality	○	○	○	○	○	○
cost	○	○	○	○	○	○
efficiency	○	○	○	○	○	○
time savings	○	○	○	○	○	○
employee satisfaction	○	○	○	○	○	○
customer satisfaction	○	○	○	○	○	○
other	○	○	○	○	○	○

2. What other measures were positively influenced by this program?

   _____

3. Of the measures listed above, which *one* is most directly linked to the program? (check only one)

   ☐ productivity   ☐ sales   ☐ quality

   ☐ cost   ☐ efficiency   ☐ time

   ☐ employee satisfaction ☐ customer satisfaction   ☐ other

4. Please define the measure above.

   _____

5. Indicate the specific unit of measurement.

   _____

6. How much did this measure improve since you attended this program?

   _____

7. What is the frequency of the measure?

   ☐ daily   ☐ weekly   ☐ monthly   ☐ quarterly

8. For this measure, what is the monetary value of improvement for one unit of this measure? Although this is difficult, please make every effort to provide the value.

   _____

**Exhibit 7.4. Chain of Impact Questions
When the Measure Is in a Defined Set.**

(Continued)

9. Please state your basis for the estimated value of one unit of improvement you indicated above.

_____

10. What is the total annual value of improvement in the measure you selected above?

_____

11. List the other factors that have caused this total annual improvement.

_____

12. Recognizing that other factors may have caused this improvement, estimate the percent of improvement related directly to this program.   _____%

13. What confidence do you place in the estimates you have provided? (0 is no confidence, 100 is certainty.)   _____%

Exhibit 7.4. Chain of Impact Questions When the Measure Is in a Defined Set, Cont'd.

SCENARIO 3. WHEN THE MEASURE IS KNOWN

1. Please define the measure connected to your program.

2. Define the unit of measure.

3. What is the monetary value of improvement for one unit of this measure?

4. Please state your basis for the value of the unit of improvement you indicated above.

5. How much has this measure improved since the program was conducted?

6. Indicate the frequency base for the measure. Daily, weekly, monthly, quarterly.

7. What is the annual value of improvement in the measure you selected above? Multiply the increase (Question 5) by the frequency (Question 6) times the unit of value (Question 4).

8. List the other factors that could have influenced these results.

9. Recognizing that the other factors could have influenced this annual value of improvement, please estimate the percent of improvement that is attributable (or isolated) to the program. Express as a percentage out of 100 percent.

10. What confidence do you place in the estimates you have provided in the questions above? A 0 percent is no confidence, a 100 percent is certainty.

Exhibit 7.5. Chain of Impact Questions When the Measure Is Known.

measure very precisely, and in some cases it is provided on the questionnaire. The sequencing and outcome of the series of questions are very similar to the two previous exhibits. This scenario is more credible than the previous two, as it focuses on a specific measure that was planned in the beginning and is driving the program.

Response Rates

To ensure an appropriate response, the strategies outlined in Chapter Six apply equally to follow-up questionnaires where business impact data are collected. Questionnaires must be thoroughly explained and, if possible, reviewed prior to achieving the accomplishments outlined in the questionnaire. A list of techniques presented in the previous chapter will not be repeated again.

SELECTING THE APPROPRIATE DATA COLLECTION METHOD FOR EACH LEVEL

This chapter and the previous three presented several data collection methods. Collectively, they offer a wide range of opportunities for collecting data in a variety of situations. Eight specific issues should be considered when deciding which method is appropriate for a situation. These should be considered when selecting data collection methods for other evaluation levels as well.

TYPE OF DATA. Perhaps one of the most important issues to consider when selecting the method is the type of data to be collected. Some methods are more appropriate for business impact. Follow-up surveys, observations, interviews, focus groups, action planning, and performance contracting are best suited for application data, sometimes exclusively. Performance monitoring, action planning, and questionnaires can easily capture business impact data.

PARTICIPANT TIME FOR DATA INPUT. Another important factor when selecting the data collection method is the amount of time participants must spend with data collection and evaluation systems. Time requirements should always be minimized, and the method should be positioned so that it is a value-added activity (that is, the participants understand that this activity is something valuable so they will not resist it). This requirement often means that sampling is used to keep the total participant time to a minimum. Some methods, such as performance monitoring, require no participant time, while others, such as interviews and focus groups, require a significant investment in time.

MANAGER TIME FOR DATA INPUT. The time that a participant's immediate manager must allocate to data collection is another important issue in the method selection. This time requirement should always be minimized. Some methods, such as performance contracting, may require much involvement from the manager before and after program implementation. Other methods, such as questionnaires administered directly to participants, may not require any manager time.

COST OF METHOD. Cost is always a consideration when selecting the method. Some data collection methods are more expensive than others. For example, interviews and observations are very expensive. Surveys, questionnaires, and performance monitoring are usually inexpensive.

DISRUPTION OF NORMAL WORK ACTIVITIES. Another key issue in selecting the appropriate method—and perhaps the one that generates the most concern for managers—is the amount of work disruption the data collection will create. Routine work processes should be disrupted as little as possible. Some data collection techniques, such as performance monitoring, require very little time and distraction. Questionnaires generally do not disrupt the work environment and can often be completed in only a few minutes, or even after normal work hours. On the other extreme, some items, such as focus groups and interviews, may be too disruptive to the work unit.

ACCURACY OF METHOD. The accuracy of the technique is another factor to consider when selecting the method. Some data collection methods are more accurate than others. For example, performance monitoring is usually very accurate, whereas questionnaires can be distorted and unreliable. If actual on-the-job behavior must be captured, observation is clearly one of the most accurate methods. A tradeoff between accuracy and costs of a method has to be examined.

UTILITY OF AN ADDITIONAL METHOD (SOURCE AND TIMEFRAME). Because many different data collection methods exist, using too many methods is tempting. Multiple data collection methods add time and costs to the evaluation and may result in very little additional value. Utility refers to the added value of an additional data collection method. As more than one method is used, this question should always be addressed: Does the value obtained from the additional data warrant the extra time and expense of the method? If the answer is no, the additional method should not be implemented. The same issue must be addressed when considering multiple sources and timeframes.

CULTURAL BIAS FOR DATA COLLECTION METHOD. The culture or philosophy of the organization can dictate which data collection methods are used. For example, some organizations or audiences are accustomed to using questionnaires. They work well within their culture. Some organizations will not use observation because their culture does not support the potential invasion of privacy associated with it.

ISOLATING THE EFFECTS OF THE PROGRAM

In almost every program, multiple influences drive the business measures. With multiple influences, measuring the effect of each influence is imperative, at least to the extent that it is attributed to the program. Without this isolation, program success will be in question. The results will be inappropriate and overstated if it is suggested that all the change in the business impact measure is attributed to the program. When this issue is ignored, the impact study is considered invalid and inconclusive. This places tremendous pressure on evaluators to show the actual value of their programs when compared to other factors. To emphasize the importance of this issue, a few facts need to be discussed.

1. *Other factors are always there.* In almost every situation, multiple factors create business results. The world does not stand still while we implement learning and development programs. Many other functions, processes, or programs attempt to improve the same metrics that are influenced by our programs. A situation in which no other factors enter into the process would be almost impossible.

2. *Without isolation of the program effects, there is no business link— evidence versus proof.* Without taking steps to show the contribution, no business link exists—only evidence that the program could have made a difference. Results have improved, although other factors may have influenced the data. The proof that the

program has made a difference on the business comes from this step in the analysis—isolating the effects of the program.

3. *Other factors and influences have protective owners.* The owners of the function and programs influencing results are convinced that their processes made the difference. Some owners are probably convinced that the results are entirely due to their efforts. They present a compelling case to management, stressing their achievements.

4. *To do it right—this is not easy.* The challenge of isolating the effects of the program on impact data is critical and can be done; but it is not easy for very complex programs, especially when strong-willed owners of other processes are involved. Determination is needed to address this situation every time an impact study is conducted. Fortunately, a variety of approaches are available.

5. *Without it—the study is not valid.* Without addressing this issue, a study is not valid because other factors are almost always in the mix, and the direct connection to learning is often not apparent. In every study, two things should never be done:

   • Taking all the credit for the improvement without tackling the issue.
   • Doing nothing, attempting to ignore the issue.

   Both of these will lower the credibility of the results.

The cause-and-effect relationship between a program and performance can be confusing and difficult to prove, but can be shown with an acceptable degree of accuracy. The challenge is to develop one or more specific techniques to isolate the effects of the program early in the process, usually as part of an evaluation plan conducted before the program begins. Up-front attention ensures that appropriate techniques will be used with minimum costs and time commitments.

Identifying Other Factors: A First Step

As a first step in isolating a program's impact on performance, all key factors that may have contributed to the performance improvement should be identified. This step communicates to interested parties that other factors may have influenced the results, underscoring that the program is not the sole source of improvement. Consequently, the credit for improvement is shared with several possible variables and factors—an approach that is likely to gain the respect of the client.

Several potential sources are available to identify influencing variables. If the learning and development program is implemented on the request of a sponsor, then the sponsor may identify other initiatives or factors that might influence the output variable. Participants are usually aware of other influences that may have caused performance improvement. After all, the impacts of their collective efforts are being monitored and measured. In many situations, they have witnessed previous movements in the performance measures and can pinpoint reasons for changes.

The program implementation team is another source for identifying variables that impact results. Although the needs analysis will sometimes uncover these influencing variables, designers, developers, and facilitators may be able to identify the other factors while implementing the program.

In some situations, the immediate managers of participants may be able to identify variables that influence the business impact measure. This is particularly useful when participants are non-exempt employees (operatives) who may not be fully aware of the other variables that can influence performance.

Subject-matter experts may identify other factors. These are the experts involved in the content of the program. They often analyze the need for the program, help design a specific solution, or provide specifications for implementation. They are knowledgeable about these issues, and their expertise may be helpful in identifying the other factors that could affect the program.

Other process owners may be able to provide input. For most situations, other processes are adding value. Could it be technology, restructuring, job design, new processes, quality initiatives, reengineering, transformation, or change management? These are all likely processes inside an organization, and the owners of these processes will know whether their processes are in place or have been implemented during this same time period.

Finally, in the area in which the program is implemented, middle and top management may be able to identify other influences. Perhaps they have monitored, examined, and analyzed the variables previously. The authority of these individuals often increases the data's credibility.

Taking the time to focus attention on factors and variables that may have influenced performance brings additional accuracy and credibility to the process. It moves beyond presenting results with no mention of other influences—a situation that often destroys credibility. It also provides a foundation for some of the techniques described in this book by identifying the variables that must be isolated to show the effects of a program.

Using Control Groups

The most accurate approach for isolating the impact of a program is the use of control groups in an experimental design process. This approach involves the comparison of an experimental group involved in the program and a control group that is not. The composition of both groups should be as identical as possible and, if feasible, participants for each group should be selected randomly. When this is achieved and both groups are subjected to the same environmental influences, the difference in the performance of the two groups can be attributed to the program.

As illustrated in Figure 7.1, the control group and experimental groups do not necessarily have pre-program measurements. Measurements can be taken during the program and after the program is implemented, and the difference in the performance of the two groups shows the amount of improvement that is directly related to the program.

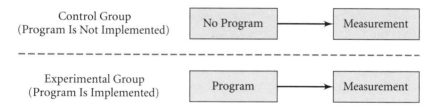

Figure 7.1. Use of Control Groups.

One concern with the use of control groups is that they may create an image of a laboratory setting, which can make some executives and administrators uncomfortable. To avoid this stigma, some organizations conduct a pilot program using participants as the experimental group. A similarly matched, non-participating control group is selected but does not receive any communication about the program. The terms "pilot program" and "comparison group" are a little less threatening than "experimental group" and "control group."

The control group approach does have some inherent problems that may make it difficult to apply in practice. The first major problem is the selection of the groups. From a theoretical perspective, having identical control and experimental groups is next to impossible. Dozens of factors can affect performance, some of them individual, others contextual. To address this problem on a practical basis, it is best to select four to six variables that will have the greatest influence on performance, using the concept of the eighty/twenty rule, or Pareto principle. With the eighty/twenty rule, the factors that might account for 80 percent of the difference and the most important factors are used.

For example, in a sales training program for Dell Computer Corporation, a control group arrangement was used. The program involved regional sales managers, account managers, account executives, account representatives, and sales representatives. The output measures were profit-margin quota attainment, total revenue attainment, profit margin, and various sales volumes. An experimental group was involved in the program and was carefully matched with a control group that was not involved. The equivalent number of participants for the control group was selected at random using the company database. To ensure that the control group and the program group were equivalent, selections were made on three criteria: job positions, job levels, and experience.

Another major problem with control groups is that the process is inappropriate for many situations. For some programs and processes, withholding the program from one group while it is implemented in another may not be appropriate. This is particularly important for critical solutions that are needed immediately. This barrier keeps many control groups from being implemented. Management is not willing to withhold a solution in one area to see how it works in another.

However, in practice, many opportunities arise for a possibility of a natural control group arrangement. If it will take several months for everyone in the organization to be involved in the solution, there may be enough time for a parallel comparison between the initial group and the last group. In these cases, ensuring that the groups are matched as closely as possible is critical so that the first group is similar to the last. These naturally occurring control groups often exist in major enterprise-wide program implementations. The challenge is to address this issue early enough to influence the implementation schedule so that similar groups can be used in the comparison.

Another problem is contamination, which can develop when participants involved in the program group (experimental group) actually communicate with others who are in the control group. Sometimes, the reverse situation occurs when members of the control group model the behavior of the experimental group. In either case, the experiment becomes contaminated as the influence of the program is passed to the control group. This can be minimized by ensuring that control groups and program groups are at different locations, have different shifts, or are on different floors in the same building. When this is not possible, explain to both groups that one group will be involved in the program now and the other will be involved at a later date. Also, appealing to the sense of responsibility of those involved in the program and asking them not to share the information with others might be helpful.

Closely related to the previous problem is the issue of time. The longer a control group and experimental group comparison operates, the more likelihood of other influences affecting the results increases. More variables will enter into the situation, contaminating the results. On the other end of the scale, there must be enough time so that a clear pattern can emerge between the two groups. Therefore, the timing for control group comparisons must strike a delicate balance of waiting long enough for their performance differences to show, but not so long that the results become seriously contaminated.

Another problem occurs when the different groups function under different environmental influences. This is usually the case when groups are at different locations. Sometimes, the selection of the groups can help prevent this problem. Another tactic is to use more groups than necessary and discard those with environmental differences.

Because the use of control groups is an effective approach for isolating impact, it should be considered as a technique when a major ROI impact study is planned. In these situations, isolating the program impact with a high level of accuracy is important, and the primary advantage of the control group process is accuracy.

Using Trend-Line Analysis

Another useful technique for approximating the impact of a program is trend-line analysis. With this approach, a trend line is drawn to project the future, using previous performance as a base. After the program is conducted, actual performance is compared to the trend-line projection. Any improvement of performance over what the trend line predicted can then be reasonably attributed to program implementation. While this is not an exact process, it provides a reasonable estimation of the program's impact.

Figure 7.2 shows an example of a trend-line analysis taken from a shipping department of a book distribution company. The percentage reflects the level of actual shipments compared to scheduled shipments. Data are presented before and after program implementation in July. As shown in the figure, an upward trend on the data began prior to program implementation. Although the program apparently had an effect on shipment productivity, the trend line shows that some improvement would have occurred anyway, based on the trend that had previously been established. Program leaders may have been tempted to measure the improvement by comparing the average six months' shipments prior to the program (87.3 percent) to the average six months after the program (94.4 percent), yielding a 7.1 percent difference. However, a more accurate comparison is the six-month average after the program compared to the trend line (92.3 percent). In this analysis, the difference is 2.1 percent. Using this more conservative measure increases the accuracy and credibility of the process to isolate the impact of the program.

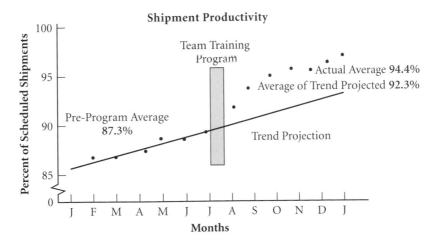

Figure 7.2. Sample Trend-Line Analysis.

To use this technique, two conditions must be met:

1. The trend that has developed prior to the program is expected to continue if the program had not been conducted (that is, would this trend continue on the same path established before the participants attended the program?). The process owner(s) should be able to provide input to reach this conclusion. If the answer is "no," the trend-line analysis will not be used. If the answer is "yes," the second condition is considered.

2. No new variables or influences entered the process during the evaluation period. The key word is "new," realizing that the trend has been established because of the influences already in place, and no additional influences enter the process beyond conducting the program. If the answer is "yes," another method would have to be used. If the answer is "no," the trend-line analysis develops a reasonable estimate of the impact of this program.

Pre-program data must be available before this technique can be used, and the data should have some reasonable degree of stability. If the variance of the data is high, the stability of the trend line becomes an issue. If this is an extremely critical issue and the stability cannot be assessed from a direct plot of the data, more detailed statistical analyses can be used to determine whether the data are stable enough to make the projection. The trend line can be projected directly from historical data using a simple routine that is available with many calculators and software packages, such as Microsoft Excel®.

Forecasting

A more analytical approach to trend-line analysis is the use of forecasting methods that predict a change in performance variables. This approach represents a mathematical interpretation of the trend-line analysis when other variables enter a situation during the evaluation period. With this approach, the output measure targeted by the program is forecast based on the influence of other variables that have changed during the evaluation period. The actual value of the measure is compared to the forecasted value. The difference reflects the contribution of the program.

With the forecasting approach, a major disadvantage occurs when several variables enter the process. The complexity multiplies, and the use of sophisticated statistical packages for multiple variable analyses is necessary. Even then, a good fit of the data to the model may not be possible. Unfortunately, some organizations have not developed mathematical relationships for output variables as a function of one or more inputs, and without them, the forecasting method is difficult to use.

The primary advantage of this process is that it can accurately predict business performance measures without the program, if appropriate data and models are available. The presentation of specific methods is beyond the scope of this book.

Using Estimates

Unfortunately, the most common method of isolating the effects of a program is the use of estimates from individuals. Estimating the amount of improvement connected to a particular program is the least-effective method from an analytical viewpoint and, because it is the weakest method, every step should be taken to make it as credible as possible. The good news is that this can be a very credible process if some precautions are taken, and these are described in this section.

The beginning point in using this method is ensuring that the isolation is performed by the most credible source, and that is often a higher-level manager or an executive removed from the process. The individual who provides this information must be able to understand how the program affects the impact measures. Essentially, there are four categories of input. Often, the most credible are the participants directly involved in the program and the managers of the participants, if they are close to the situation. Customers give credible estimates in unique situations where they are involved. External experts may also be very helpful. These are all described in this section.

PARTICIPANTS' ESTIMATE OF IMPACT. An easily implemented method for isolating the impact of a program is to obtain information directly from participants (users) during program implementation. The effectiveness of this approach rests on the assumption that participants are capable of determining or estimating how much of a performance improvement is related to the program implementation. Because their actions have produced the improvement, participants may have highly accurate input on the issue. They should know how much of the change was caused by implementing the program solution. Although an estimate, this value will usually have considerable credibility with management because they know participants are at the center of the change or improvement. Participant estimation is obtained by asking participants the series of questions:

- What other factors have contributed to this improvement in performance?
- What is the link between these factors and the improvement?
- What percentage of this improvement can be attributed to the implementation of this program?
- What confidence do you have in this estimate, expressed as a percentage? (0 percent = no confidence; 100 percent = complete confidence)
- What other individuals or groups could estimate this percentage to determine the amount attributed to this program?

Table 7.1 illustrates this approach with an example of one participant's estimations. Participants who do not provide information on the questions are excluded from the analysis. Also, erroneous, incomplete, and extreme information should be discarded before analysis. To be conservative, the confidence percentage can be factored into the values. The confidence percentage is a reflection of the error in the estimate. Thus, an 80 percent confidence level equates to a potential error range of plus or minus 20 percent. With this approach, the level of confidence is multiplied by the estimate. In the example, the participant allocates 60 percent of the improvement to the program and is 80 percent confident in the estimate. The confidence percentage is

Factor That Influenced Improvement	% of Improvement Caused by	Confidence Expressed as a %	Adjusted % of Improvement Caused by
Learning program	60%	80%	48%
Process changes	15%	70%	10.5%
Environmental changes	5%	60%	3%
Compensation changes	20%	80%	16%
Other	___%	___%	___%
Total	100%		

Table 7.1. Example of a Participant's Estimation.

multiplied by the estimate to develop a usable value of 48 percent. This adjusted percentage is then multiplied by the actual amount of the improvement (post-program minus pre-program value) to isolate the portion attributed to the program. The adjusted improvement is now ready for conversion to monetary values and, ultimately, use in the return on investment calculation.

Although an estimate, this approach does have considerable accuracy and credibility. Five adjustments are effectively applied to the participant estimate to reflect a conservative approach:

1. Participants who do not provide usable data are assumed to have experienced no improvements.

2. Extreme data and incomplete, unrealistic, and unsupported claims are omitted from the analysis, although they may be included in the "other" benefits category.

3. For short-term programs, it is assumed that no benefits from the program are realized after the first year of full implementation. (For long-term programs, additional years may be used.)

4. The improvement amount is adjusted by the amount directly related to the program, expressed as a percentage.

5. The confidence estimate, expressed as a percentage, is multiplied by the improvement value to reduce the amount of the improvement for the potential error.

When presented to senior management, the result of an impact study is usually perceived to be an understatement of the program's success. The data and the process are considered credible and accurate. As an added enhancement to this method, the next level of management above the participants may be asked to review and approve the estimates from participants.

An example will illustrate the process for participant estimates. A restaurant chain initiated a performance management training program. The program was designed to improve the operating performance of the restaurant chain using a variety of leadership and management skills to establish measurable goals for employees, provide performance feedback, measure progress toward goals, and take action to ensure that goals were met. As part of the program, each store manager developed an action plan for improvement. Managers also learned how to convert measurable improvements into an economic value for the restaurant. Their action plans could focus on any improvement area as long as they considered the performance measure relevant to their goals. Each improvement would have to be converted to either cost savings or restaurant profits. Some of the improvement areas were inventory, food spoilage, cash shortages, employee turnover, absenteeism, and productivity.

As part of the follow-up evaluation, each action plan was thoroughly documented, showing results in quantitative terms, which were converted to monetary values. The annual monetary value for each participant's improvement was calculated from the action plans. The managers were asked to identify the other factors that could have caused part of the improvement. Next, realizing that other factors could have influenced the improvement, managers were asked to estimate the percent of the improvement that resulted directly from the program (the contribution estimate). Restaurant managers are aware of factors that influence costs and profits and usually know how much of an improvement is traceable to the program. Each manager was asked to be conservative and provide a confidence estimate for the above contribution estimate (100 percent = certainty and 0 percent = no confidence). The results are shown in Table 7.2.

Participant	Total Annual Improvement (Dollar Value)	Basis	Contribution Estimate from Manager (Participants)	Confidence Estimate from Store Managers (Participants)	Conservative Value Reported
1	$5,500	Labor savings	60%	80%	$2,640
2	15,000	Turnover	50%	80%	6,000
3	9,300	Absenteeism	65%	80%	4,836
4	2,100	Shortages	90%	90%	1,701
5	0	—	—	—	—
6	29,000	Turnover	40%	75%	8,700
7	2,241	Inventory	70%	95%	1,490
8	3,621	Procedures	100%	80%	2,897
9	21,000	Turnover	75%	80%	12,600
10	1,500	Food spoilage	100%	100%	1,500
11	15,000	Labor savings	80%	85%	10,200
12	6,310	Accidents	70%	100%	4,417
13	14,500	Absenteeism	80%	70%	8,120
14	3,650	Productivity	100%	90%	3,285
Total	$128,722				$68,386

Table 7.2. Estimates of Program Impact from Participants.

Estimation of the program's impact can be calculated using the conservative approach of adjusting for the contribution of the program and adjusting for the error of the contribution estimate. For example, the $5,500 annual value for labor savings is adjusted to consider the program contribution ($5,500 × 60% = $3,300). Next, the value is adjusted for the confidence in this value ($3,300 × 80% = $2,640). The conservative approach yields an overall improvement of $68,386 for this group. Participant 5 did not submit a completed action plan and was discarded from the analysis, although the costs for this participant are still included in the ROI calculation.

Another interesting observation emerges from this type of analysis. When the average of the three largest improvements is compared with the average of the three smallest values, the potential for return on investment could be much larger. If all the participants in the program had focused on high-impact improvements, a substantially higher ROI could have been achieved. This information can be helpful to the management group, whose support is often critical for program success. While an impressive ROI is refreshing, a potentially greater ROI is outstanding.

This example illustrates the power of this methodology when individuals in a particular program focus on different measures. This would be the case for many L&D programs, such as supervisory training, executive development, team building, management development, leadership development, communications, creativity and innovation, problem solving, and negotiations. In those situations, the specific impact measure may not be known at the beginning of the program. However, for other programs, the specific measure or measures are known and are often just a small number. For example, a program designed to improve retention, sales, quality, or safety performance will focus on one or a few measures. This isolation technique is effective in either setting.

Using Focus Groups. The focus group works extremely well for this challenge if the group size is relatively small—in the eight to twelve range. If much larger, the groups should be divided into multiple groups. Focus groups provide the opportunity for members to share information equally, avoiding domination by any one individual. The process taps the input, creativity, and reactions of the entire group.

The meeting should take about one hour (slightly more if multiple factors affect the results or multiple business measures need to be discussed). The facilitator should be neutral to the process (that is, the program leader should not conduct this focus group). Focus group facilitation and input must be objective. The task is to link the results of the program to business performance. The group is presented with the improvement, and they provide input to isolate the effects of the program.

The following steps are recommended to obtain the most credible value for program impact:

1. *Explain the task.* The task of the focus group meeting is outlined. Participants should understand that performance has improved. While many factors could have contributed to the improvement, this group must determine how much of the improvement was related to the program.

2. *Discuss the rules.* Each participant should be encouraged to provide input, limiting his or her comments to two minutes (or less) for any specific issue. Comments are confidential and will not be linked to a specific individual.

4. *Explain the importance of the process.* The participants' role in the process is critical. Because it is their performance that has improved, the participants are in the best position to indicate what has caused this improvement; they are the experts in this determination. Without quality input, the contribution of this program (or any other processes) may never be known.

4. *Select the first measure and show the improvement.* Using actual data, the facilitator should show the level of performance prior to and following program implementation; in essence, the change in business results—the change—is reported.

5. *Identify the different factors that have contributed to the performance.* Using input from experts—others who are knowledgeable about the improvements—the facilitator should identify the factors that have influenced the improvement (for example, the volume of work has changed, a new system has been implemented, or technology has been enhanced). If these are known, they are listed as the factors that may have contributed to the performance improvement.

6. *Ask the group to identify other factors that have contributed to the performance.* In some situations, only the participants know other influencing factors, and those factors should be identified at this time.

7. *Discuss the link.* Taking each factor one at a time, the participants individually describe the link between that factor and the business results. For example, for the program influence, the participants would describe how the program has driven the actual improvement by providing examples, anecdotes, and other supporting evidence. Participants may require some prompting to provide comments. If they cannot provide dialogue regarding this issue, chances are good that the factor had no influence.

8. *Repeat the process for each factor.* Each factor is explored until all the participants have discussed the link between all the factors and the business performance improvement. After these links have been discussed, the participants should have a clear understanding of the cause-and-effect relationship between the various factors and the business improvement.

9. *Allocate the improvement.* Participants are asked to allocate the percent of improvement to each of the factors discussed. Participants are provided a pie chart, which represents a total amount of improvement for the measure in question, and are asked to carve up the pie, allocating the percentages to different improvements, with a total of 100 percent. Some participants may feel uncertain with this process, but should be encouraged to complete this step using their best estimates. Uncertainty will be addressed later in the meeting.

10. *Provide a confidence estimate.* The participants are then asked to review the allocation percentages and, for each one, estimate their level of confidence in their estimates. Using a scale of 0 to 100 percent, participants express their levels of certainty with their estimates in the previous step. A participant may be more comfortable with some factors than others, so the confidence estimates may vary. These confidence estimates will adjust the results.

11. *Ask participants to multiply the two percentages.* For example, if an individual has allocated 35 percent of the improvement to the program and is 80 percent confident, he or she would multiply 35% × 80%, which is 28 percent. In essence, the participant is suggesting that at least 28 percent of the teams' business improvement is linked to the program. The confidence estimate serves as a conservative discount factor, adjusting for the possible error of the estimate. The pie charts with the calculations

are collected without names and the calculations are verified. Another option is to collect pie charts and make the calculations for the participants.

12. *Report results.* If possible, the average of the adjusted values for the group is developed and communicated to them. Also, the summary of all the information should be communicated to the participants as soon as possible. Participants who do not provide information are excluded from the analysis.

This approach provides a credible way to isolate the effects of a program when other methods will not work. It is often regarded as the low-cost solution to the issue because it takes only a few focus groups and a small amount of time to arrive at this conclusion. In most of these settings, the actual conversion to monetary value is not conducted by the group, but is developed in another way. Converting data to monetary values is detailed in Chapter Eight. However, if participants must provide input on the value of the data, it can be approached as another phase of the same focus group meeting. To reach an accepted value, the steps are very similar to the steps for isolation.

Using Questionnaires and Interviews. Sometimes, focus groups are not available or are considered unacceptable for the use of data collection. The participants may not be available for a group meeting or the focus groups may become too expensive. In these situations, collecting similar information via a questionnaire or interview may be beneficial. With this approach, participants must address the same elements as those addressed in the focus group, but with a series of impact questions on a follow-up questionnaire or in an interview. The questionnaire or interview may focus solely on isolating the effects of the program.

MANAGER'S ESTIMATE OF IMPACT. In lieu of, or in addition to, participant estimates, the participants' manager may be asked to provide input as to the program's influence on improved performance. In some settings, the participants' manager may be more familiar with the other influencing factors. Therefore, he or she may be better equipped to provide impact estimates. The recommended questions to ask managers, after describing the improvement, are similar to those asked of the participants. Manager estimates should also be analyzed in the same manner as participant estimates. To be more conservative, actual estimates may be adjusted by the confidence percentage. When participants' estimates have also been collected, the decision of which estimate to use becomes an issue. If some compelling reason makes leaders think that one estimate is more credible than the other, then the more credible estimate should be used. If they are equally credible, the lowest value should be used with an appropriate explanation.

In some cases, upper management may estimate the percent of improvement attributed to a program. After considering additional factors that could contribute to an improvement—such as technology, procedures, and process changes—management applies a subjective factor to represent the portion of the results that should be attributed to the program. While this is subjective, the input is usually accepted by the individuals who provide or approve funding for the program. Sometimes, their comfort level with the processes used is the most important consideration.

CUSTOMER INPUT ON PROGRAM IMPACT. Another helpful approach in some narrowly focused program situations is to solicit input on the impact of programs directly from customers. In these situations, customers are asked why they chose a particular product or service or to explain how their reaction to the product or service has been influenced by individuals or systems involved in the program. This technique often focuses directly on what the program is designed to improve. For example, after implementing a customer service program involving customer response in an electric utility, market research data showed that the percentage of customers who were dissatisfied with response time was reduced by 5 percent when compared to market survey data before the program. Since response time was reduced by the program and no other factor contributed to the reduction, the 5 percent reduction in dissatisfied customers was directly attributed to the program.

Routine customer surveys provide an excellent opportunity to collect input directly from customers concerning their reactions to an assessment of new or improved products, services, processes, or procedures. Pre- and post-data can pinpoint the changes related to an improvement driven by a new program.

When collecting customer input, linking it with the current data collection methods and avoiding the creation of surveys or feedback mechanisms is important. This measurement process should not add to the data collection systems. Customer input could, perhaps, be the most powerful and convincing data if they are complete, accurate, and valid.

INTERNAL OR EXTERNAL EXPERT INPUT. External or internal experts can sometimes estimate the portion of results that can be attributed to a program. When using this technique, experts must be carefully selected based on their knowledge of the process, program, and situation. For example, an expert in quality might be able to provide estimates of how much change in a quality measure can be attributed to a quality training program and how much can be attributed to other factors.

Calculating the Impact of Other Factors

Although not appropriate in all cases, sometimes calculating the impact of factors (other than the program) that influence part of the improvement is possible. In this approach, the program takes credit for improvement that cannot be attributed to other factors.

An example will help explain the approach. In a consumer lending training program for a large bank, a significant increase in consumer loan volume was generated after the program was implemented. Part of the increase in volume was attributed to the program, and the remaining was due to the influence of other factors in place during the same time period. Two other factors were identified: an increase in marketing and sales promotion and falling interest rates, which caused an increase in consumer volume.

With regard to the first factor, as marketing and sales promotion increased, so did consumer loan volume. The amount of this factor was estimated using input from several internal experts in the marketing department. For the second factor, industry sources were used to estimate the relationship between increased consumer loan volume and falling interest rates. These two estimates together accounted for a modest percentage of increased consumer loan volume. The remaining improvement was attributed to the program.

This method is appropriate when the other factors are easily identified and the appropriate mechanisms are in place to calculate their impact on the improvement. In some cases, estimating the impact of other factors is just as difficult as estimating the impact of the program, leaving this approach less advantageous. This process can be very credible if the method used to isolate the impact of other factors is also credible.

USE OF THE TECHNIQUES

With all these techniques available to isolate the impact of a program, selecting the most appropriate techniques for a specific program can be difficult. Some techniques are simple and inexpensive, while others are more time-consuming and costly. When attempting to decide, the following factors should be considered:

- Feasibility of the technique
- Accuracy provided with the technique
- Credibility of the technique with the target audience
- Specific cost to implement the technique
- Amount of disruption in normal work activities as the technique is implemented
- Participant, staff, and management time needed for the particular technique

Multiple techniques or multiple sources for data input should be considered, since two sources are usually better than one. When multiple sources are used, a conservative method is recommended for combining the inputs. The reason is that a conservative approach builds acceptance. The target audience should always be provided with explanations of the process and the subjective factors involved. Multiple sources allow an organization to experiment with different strategies and build confidence with a particular technique. For example, if management is concerned about the accuracy of participants' estimates, a combination of a control group arrangement and participants' estimates could be attempted to verify the accuracy of the estimates.

FINAL THOUGHTS

The good news is that business impact data are readily available and very credible. After describing the types of data that reflect business impact, this chapter provides an overview of several data collection approaches that can be used to capture business data. Many options are available. Some methods are gaining more acceptance for use in impact and ROI analysis. In addition to performance monitoring, follow-up questionnaires, action plans, and performance contracts are used regularly to collect data for an impact analysis. The credibility of data will always be an issue when this level of data is collected and analyzed. Several strategies are offered to enhance the credibility of data analysis.

This chapter also presented a variety of techniques for isolating the effects of a program. The techniques represent the most effective approaches available to address this issue and are used by some of the most progressive organizations. Too often, results are reported and linked with the program without any attempt to isolate the exact portion that can be attributed to it. If learning and development professionals are committed to improving the images of their functions, as well as meeting their responsibilities for obtaining results, this issue must be addressed early in the process for all major programs.

References

Kaplan, R.S., & Norton, D.P. (1996). *The balanced scorecard: Translating strategy into action.* Boston, MA: Harvard Business School Press.

CHAPTER EIGHT

Identifying Benefits and Costs, and Calculating ROI

T o calculate the ROI, two critical steps are necessary: calculating monetary benefits by converting data to monetary values and tabulating the fully loaded costs for programs. While results at lower levels are important, converting the positive outcomes into monetary figures and weighing them against the cost of the program is more valuable from an executive viewpoint. This is the ultimate level in the five-level evaluation framework presented in Chapter One. This chapter explains how learning and development professionals are moving beyond simply tabulating business results to developing monetary values used in calculating ROI. Many methods are available to convert impact data to money and are presented in this chapter.

This chapter also explores the cost of programs, identifying the specific costs that should be captured and some economical ways in which they can be developed. Some costs are hidden and not usually counted. The conservative philosophy presented here is to account for all costs, direct and indirect. Several checklists and guidelines are also included. The monetary values for the benefits are combined with program cost data to calculate the return on investment. This chapter also explores the techniques, processes, and issues involved in calculating the ROI.

WHY CALCULATE MONETARY BENEFITS?

The answer to this question is not always clearly understood. A program could be labeled a success without converting to monetary values, just by using business impact data showing the amount of change directly attributed to the program. For example, a change in quality, cycle time, market share, or customer satisfaction could represent significant improvements linked directly to a new program. For some programs this may be sufficient. However, many sponsors need the actual monetary value and more evaluators take this extra step of converting data to monetary values.

Value Equals Money

For some stakeholders, the most important value is money. As described in Chapter One, there are many different types of value. However, money is becoming one of the most important values, as the economic benefits of programs are desired. This is particularly true for executives, sponsors, clients, administrators, and top leaders. They are concerned about the allocation of funds and want to see the contribution of a program in monetary values. Anything short of this value for these key stakeholders would be unsatisfactory.

Impact Is More Understandable

For some programs, the impact is more understandable when the monetary value is developed. For example, consider the impact of a leadership development program aimed at all the middle managers in an organization. As part of the program, the managers were asked to address at least two measures that matter to them and that have to change or improve for those managers to meet their specific goals. The measures could literally represent dozens, if not hundreds, of different measures.

When the program impact is captured, all these measures have changed, leaving a myriad of improvements, difficult to appreciate without a conversion to monetary value. When the first-year monetary value is developed for each of the measures, the results provide the evaluator and sponsors with a sense of the impact of the program. Without converting to monetary values, understanding the contribution is difficult.

Money Is Necessary for ROI

Monetary value is required to develop ROI. As described in earlier chapters, a monetary value is needed to compare to costs to develop the benefit/cost ratio, the ROI (as a percent), and the payback period. In fact, the monetary benefits become the other half of the equation and are absolutely essential.

Monetary Value Is Needed to Understand Problems

In all businesses, costs are necessary for understanding the magnitude of any problem. Consider, for example, the cost of employee turnover. The traditional records and even those available through an analysis of cost statements will not show the full value or cost of the problem. A variety of estimates and expert input may be needed to supplement cost statements to arrive at a particular value. That's the monetary value needed in a fully loaded format to understand the problem. The good news is that many organizations have developed a number of standard cost items representing issues that are undesired.

For example, Wal-Mart has calculated the cost of having a truck idling one minute at a store waiting to be unloaded. When this is multiplied over the hundreds of deliveries made at a store and spread over five thousand stores, the cost is huge.

Key Steps to Convert Data to Money

Before describing specific techniques to convert both hard and soft data to monetary values, five general steps should be completed for each data item:

1. *Focus on a unit of measure.* First, define a unit of measure. For output data, the unit of measure is the item produced (one item assembled), service provided (one package shipped), or sale completed. Time measures might include the time to complete a program, cycle time, or customer-response time, and the unit is usually expressed in minutes, hours, or days. Quality is a common measure, with a unit being defined as one error, reject, defect, or reworked item. Soft data measures vary, with a unit of improvement representing such things as an absence, a turnover statistic, or a 1-point change in the customer satisfaction index. Exhibit 8.1 provides examples of these units.

UNITS OF MEASURE	
• One Unit Produced	• One Hour of Downtime
• One Student Enrolled	• One Minute of Wait Time
• One Package Delivered	• One Day of Delay
• One Patient Served	• One Hour of Cycle Time
• One Sale Made	• One Hour of Employee Time
• One Loan Approved	• One Hour of Overtime
• One Project Completed	• One Customer Complaint
• One Call Escalation	• One Person Removed from Welfare
• One FTE Employee	• One Less Day of Incarceration (Prison)
• One Reject	• One Rework
• One Error	• One Lost Time Accident
• One Grievance	• One Unplanned Absence
• One Voluntary Turnover	

Exhibit 8.1. Breaking Down the Units of Measure.

2. *Determine the value of each unit.* Now, the challenge. Place a value (V) on the unit identified in the first step. For measures of production, quality, cost, and time, the process is relatively easy. Most organizations maintain records or reports that can pinpoint the cost of one unit of production or one defect. Soft data are more difficult to convert to money. For example, the monetary value of one customer complaint or a 1-point change in an employee attitude is often difficult to determine. The techniques described in this chapter provide an array of approaches for making this conversion. When more than one value is available, usually the most credible or the lowest value is used in the calculation.

3. *Calculate the change in performance data.* Calculate the change in output data after the effects of the program have been isolated from other influences. The change (Δ) is the performance improvement, measured as hard or soft data, that is directly attributed to the program. The value may represent the performance improvement for an individual, a team, a group of participants, or several groups of participants.

4. *Determine an annual amount for the change.* Annualize the change value to develop a total change in the performance data for at least one year (ΔP). Using annual values has become a

standard approach for organizations seeking to capture the benefits of a particular program, although the benefits may not remain constant throughout the entire year. First-year benefits are used, even when the program produces benefits beyond one year if it is a short-term solution. This approach is considered conservative. More will be discussed about this later.

5. *Calculate the annual value of the improvement.* Arrive at the total value of improvement by multiplying the annual performance change (ΔP) by the unit value (V) for the complete group in question. For example, if one group of participants is involved in the program being evaluated, the total value will include total improvement for all participants in the group. This value for annual program benefits is then compared to the costs of the program, usually with the ROI formula presented in this chapter.

An example taken from a labor-management cooperation program at a manufacturing plant describes the five-step process of converting data to monetary values. This program was developed and implemented after the initial needs assessment and analysis revealed that a lack of teamwork was causing an excessive number of labor grievances. The actual number of grievances resolved at Step 2 in the four-step grievance process was selected as an output measure. Exhibit 8.2 shows the steps taken in assigning monetary values to the data, arriving at a total program impact of $546,000.

**SETTING: LABOR-MANAGEMENT COOPERATION
PROGRAM IN A MANUFACTURING PLANT**

Step 1   Define the Unit of Measure.

One grievance reaching Step 2 in the four-step grievance resolution process

Step 2   Determine the Value of Each Unit.

Using internal experts (that is, the labor relations staff), the cost of an average grievance was estimated at $6,500, when time and direct costs were considered. (V = $6,500)

Step 3   Calculate the Change in Performance Data.

Six months after the program was completed, total grievances per month reaching Step 2 declined by ten. Seven of the ten reductions were related to the program ($\Delta = 7$), as determined by first-level supervisors (Isolating the Effects of the Program).

Exhibit 8.2. **Converting Labor Grievance Data to Monetary Values.**

(Continued)

SETTING: LABOR-MANAGEMENT COOPERATION PROGRAM IN A MANUFACTURING PLANT

Step 4   **Determine an Annual Amount for the Change.**

Using the six-month value of seven grievances per month yields an annual improvement of eighty-four. ($\Delta P = 84$)

Step 5   **Calculate the Annual Value of the Improvement.**

Annual Value = ΔP times V

$= 84 \times \$6,500$

$= \$546,000$

Exhibit 8.2. Converting Labor Grievance Data to Monetary Values, Cont'd.

STANDARD MONETARY VALUES

Most hard-data items are converted to monetary values and have standard values. By definition, a standard value is a monetary value on a unit of measurement that is accepted by key stakeholders. These standards have been developed because these are often the measures that matter in the organization. They are important. They reflect problems, and because of that, efforts have been made to convert them to monetary values to show their impact on the operational and financial well-being of the organization. The best way to understand the magnitude of any problem is to put a monetary value on it.

A variety of quality programs spanning the last two decades have focused only on the cost of quality. Organizations have been obsessed with placing a value on mistakes or the payoff of avoiding these mistakes. This is one of the most important outgrowths of quality management systems—the standard cost of items. In addition, a variety of process improvement programs—such as reengineering, reinventing the corporation, transformation, continuous process improvement, and many others—have had a measurement component in which the cost of a particular measure has been developed. Finally, a variety of cost controls, cost containment, and cost management systems have been developed such as activity-based costing. These have forced organizations, departments, and divisions to place costs on activities and, in some cases, relate those costs directly to the revenue or profits of the organization.

Standard values are usually available for the hard data categories of output, quality, and time and Table 8.1 shows how they have been converted to the other hard data category, cost. Output is converted to either profits or cost savings. Output in the form of sales, new customers, market share, and customer loyalty add value through additional profits obtained from additional sales. Outputs where profits are not connected, such as the output of an individual work group, can be converted to savings. For example, if the outputs of a work group can be increased as a result of a particular program with no additional resources needed to drive the output, then the corresponding value is in the cost savings. That is, additional output presented or the cost per unit of output actually goes down, resulting in a cost savings. When quality is improved, the result is either cost savings when quality is a problem or in cost avoidance if the program is preventive—preventing a mistake or a quality issue.

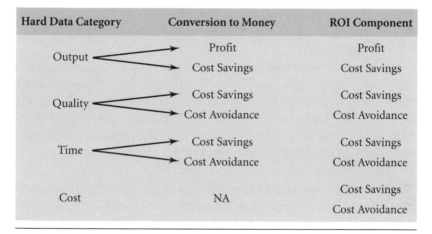

Hard Data Category	Conversion to Money	ROI Component
Output	Profit / Cost Savings	Profit / Cost Savings
Quality	Cost Savings / Cost Avoidance	Cost Savings / Cost Avoidance
Time	Cost Savings / Cost Avoidance	Cost Savings / Cost Avoidance
Cost	NA	Cost Savings / Cost Avoidance

Table 8.1. Converting Hard Data to Money.

Time is converted in the same way. If time is reduced, it is converted to a cost savings. If the time does not increase when normally it should, it represents cost avoidance. Therefore, the ultimate payoff of typical hard data items are profits, cost savings, or cost avoidance. This logic also explains why most ROI studies pay off on cost savings or cost avoidance instead of profits. Those programs directly related to customers and sales are normally converted to profits. Others are converted to cost savings or cost avoidance. The additional details on how these conversions are made are presented next. However, almost all hard data items have been converted to monetary values as standard values.

Converting Output Data to Money

When a program produces a change in output, the value of the increased output can usually be determined from the organization's accounting or operating records. For organizations operating on a profit basis, this value is typically the marginal profit contribution of an additional unit of production or service provided. For example, a team within a major appliance manufacturer was able to boost the production of small refrigerators after a comprehensive work cell redesign program. The unit of improvement was the profit margin of one refrigerator. For organizations that are performance-driven rather than profit-driven, this value is usually reflected in the savings accumulated when an additional unit of output is realized for the same input. For example, in the visa section of a government office, an additional visa application was processed at no additional cost. Thus, an increase in output translated into a cost savings equal to the unit cost of processing a visa application.

The formulas and calculations used to measure this contribution depend on the type of organization and the status of its record-keeping. Most organizations have standard values readily available for performance monitoring and setting goals. Managers often use marginal cost statements and sensitivity analyses to pinpoint values associated with changes in output. If the data are not available, the L&D staff must initiate or coordinate the development of appropriate values.

One of the more important outcomes is productivity, particularly productivity in a competitive organization. Today, most organizations competing in a global economy do an excellent job of monitoring productivity and placing value on it. For example, consider the Snapper, Inc., lawnmower factory in McDonough, Georgia. Ten years ago, it produced forty models of outdoor equipment—now it makes 145. Ten years ago, no robots, lasers, or computer-controlled equipment were available. Now, robots do the welding, lasers cut parts, and computers control the steel stamping processes. The productivity at the factory is three times what it was ten years ago, and the number of people working there is half what it was (Fishman, 2006). At Snapper, each factory worker is measured every hour, every day, every month, and every year. And everyone's performance is posted publicly for everyone to see. Production at the Snapper plant is rescheduled every week according to the pace at which stores sell across the nation. A computer juggles work assignments and balances the various parts of the assembly process. Productivity is not only important, it is measured and valued. Snapper knows the value of improving productivity by an infinitesimal amount because the president knows that the factory must be efficient to compete in a global market with low-cost products. This requires that every factory worker be measured every hour of every day.

The benefit of converting output data to money with this approach is that these calculations are already completed for the most important data items and are reported as standard values. Perhaps no area is more dramatic with the standard values than those in the sales and marketing area. Table 8.2 shows a sampling of measures in the sales and marketing area that are routinely calculated and are considered to be standard values (Farris, Bendle, Pfeifer, & Ribstein, 2006). For example, the first two entries go together. The sales cannot be used in an ROI value until they have been converted to profit. Sales are usually affected by the profit percentage to generate the actual value of the improvement. Other profit margins can be developed for a particular unit, a product line, or even a customer. Retention rates and return rates are routinely developed, as is the lifetime value of a customer. Even these days, the market share and loyalty are developed because they all translate directly into additional sales. For the most part—with the exception of workload and inventories—the value is developed through profits. Even market share and customer loyalty are valued based on sales or additional sales obtained from the customer.

Metric	Definition	Converting Issues
Sales	The sale of the product or service recorded in a variety of different ways: by product, by time period, by customer	This data must be converted to monetary value by applying the profit margin for a particular sales category.
Profit Margin (%)	(Price − Cost)/Cost for the product, customer, time period	The most common way factored to convert sales to data.
Unit Margin	Unit Price Less the Unit Cost	This shows the value of incremental sales.
Channel Margin	Channel profits as a percent of channel selling price	This would be used to show the value of sales through a particular marketing channel.
Retention Rate	The ratio of customers retained to the number of customers at risk of leaving	The value is the money saved to retain a new replacement customer.

Table 8.2. **Examples of Standard Values from Sales and Marketing.**

(Continued)

Metric	Definition	Converting Issues
Churn Rate	Churn rate is the complement of the retention rate. It is the percent of customers leaving compared to the number who are at risk of leaving.	The value is the money saved for acquiring a new customer.
Customer Profit	The difference between the revenues earned from and the cost associated with the customer relationship during the specified period	The monetary value add is the additional profit obtained from customers. It all goes to the bottom line.
Customer Value Lifetime	The present value of the future cash flows attributed to the customer relationship	This is bottom line; as customer value increases, it adds directly to the profits. Also, as a new customer is added, the incremental value is the customer lifetime average.
Cannibalization Rate	The percent of the new product sales taken from existing product lines	This needs to be minimized because it is an adverse effect on existing product with the value add being the loss of profits from the sales loss.
Workload	Hours required to service clients and prospects	The salaries and commissions and benefits from the time the sales staff spends on the workloads
Inventories	The total amount of product or brand available for sale in a particular channel	Since the inventories are valued at the cost of carrying the inventory, space, handling, and the time value of money, insufficient inventories is the cost of expediting the new inventory or lost sales because of the inventory outage.
Market Share	The sales revenue as a percent of total market sales	The actual sales are converted to money through the profit margins. This is a measure of competitiveness.
Loyalty	This includes the length of time the customer stays with the organization, the willingness to pay a premium, and the willingness to search.	The additional profit from the sale or the profit on the premium

Table 8.2. Examples of Standard Values from Sales and Marketing, Cont'd.

Adapted from *Marketing Metrics: 50+ Metrics Every Executive Should Master.* Paul W. Farris, Neil T. Bendle, Phillip E. Pfeifer, & David J. Ribstein. Upper Saddle River, NJ: Wharton School Publishing, 2006.

Calculating the Cost of Quality

Quality and the cost of quality are important issues in most manufacturing and service firms. Because many programs are designed to increase quality, the program team may have to place a value on the improvement of certain quality measures. With some quality measures, the task is easy. For example, if quality is measured with the defect rate, the value of the improvement is the cost to repair or replace the product. The most obvious cost of poor quality is the scrap or waste generated by mistakes. Defective products, spoiled raw materials, and discarded paperwork are all the result of poor quality. Scrap and waste translate directly into a monetary value. In a production environment, for example, the cost of a defective product is the total cost incurred up to the point at which the mistake is identified, minus the salvage value. In the service environment, a defective service is the cost incurred up to the point that the deficiency is identified, plus the cost to correct the problem, plus the cost to make the customer happy, plus the loss of customer loyalty.

Employee mistakes and errors can be expensive. The most costly rework occurs when a product or service is delivered to a customer and must be returned for correction. The cost of rework includes both labor and direct costs. In some organizations, rework costs can be as much as 35 percent of operating expenses.

In one example, a program focused on customer service provided by dispatchers in an oil company. The dispatchers processed orders and scheduled deliveries of fuel to service stations. A measure of quality that was considered excessive was the number of pullouts experienced. A pullout occurs when a delivery truck cannot fill an order for fuel at a service station. The truck must then return to the terminal for an adjustment to the order. This is essentially a rework item. The average cost of a pullout was developed by tabulating the cost from a sampling of actual pullouts. The elements in the tabulation included driver time, the cost of the truck while adjusting the load, the cost of terminal use, and extra administrative expenses. This value was developed and became the accepted standard following completion of the program. Organizations have made great progress in developing standard values for the cost of quality.

Quality costs can be grouped into six major categories (Campanella, 1999):

1. *Internal failure* represents costs associated with problems detected prior to product shipment or service delivery. Typical costs are reworking and retesting.

2. *Penalty costs* are fines or penalties received as a result of unacceptable quality.

3. *External failure* refers to problems detected after product shipment or service delivery. Typical items are technical support, complaint investigation, remedial upgrades, and fixes.

4. *Appraisal costs* are the expenses involved in determining the condition of a particular product or service. Typical costs are testing and related activities, such as product-quality audits.

5. *Prevention costs* include efforts undertaken to avoid unacceptable product or service quality. These efforts include service quality administration, inspections, process studies, and improvements.

6. *Customer dissatisfaction* is perhaps the costliest element of inadequate quality. In some cases, serious mistakes result in lost business. Customer dissatisfaction is difficult to quantify, and arriving at a monetary value may be impossible using direct methods. The judgment and expertise of sales, marketing, or quality managers are usually the best resources to draw from when measuring the impact of dissatisfaction. More and more quality experts are measuring customer and client dissatisfaction with market surveys (Rust, Zahorik, & Keiningham, 1994). However, other strategies discussed in this chapter may be more appropriate for the task.

As with output data, the good news is that a tremendous number of quality measures have been converted to standard values. Exhibit 8.3 shows a sampling of the quality measures that are typically converted to actual monetary value.

The typical definition of these measures can vary slightly with the organization, and the magnitude and the costs can vary significantly. The most common method for converting cost is to use internal failure, external failure, appraisal, or penalty costs. This exhibit shows the tremendous variety of quality measures that are monitored and represents only a small sampling from a typical organization. Some larger organizations literally track thousands of quality measures as standard values have been developed for many of them (Muir, 2006).

STANDARD QUALITY MEASURES	
Defects	Failure
Rework	Customer Complaints
Variances	Delay
Waste	Missing Data
Processing Errors	Fines
Date Errors	Penalties
Incidents	Inventory Shortages
Accidents	Unplanned Absenteeism
Grievances	Involuntary Employee Turnover
Down Time—Equipment	Risk
Down Time—System	Days Sales Uncollected
Repair Costs	Queues

Exhibit 8.3. Examples of Standard Quality Measures.

Converting Employee Time Using Compensation

Saving employee time is a common objective for learning and development programs. In a team environment, a program may enable the team to complete tasks in less time or with fewer people. A major program could drive a reduction of several hundred employees. On an individual basis, a technology program may be designed to help professional, sales, and managerial employees save time in performing daily tasks. The value of the time saved is an important measure, and determining the monetary value for it is relatively easy.

The most obvious time savings are from reduced labor costs for performing the same amount of work. The monetary savings are found by multiplying the hours saved by the labor cost per hour. For example, after using the time management program in one organization, participants estimated that they saved an average of seventy-four minutes per day, worth $31.25 per day, or $7,500 per year. The time savings were based on the average salary plus benefits for the typical participant.

For most calculations, the average wage, with a percent added for employee benefits, will suffice. However, employee time may be worth more. For example, additional costs in maintaining an employee (office space, furniture, telephones, utilities, computers, secretarial support, and other overhead expenses) could be included in calculating the average labor cost. Thus, the average wage rate may escalate quickly. In a large-scale employee reduction effort, calculating additional employee costs may be more appropriate for showing the value. However, for most programs the conservative approach of using salary plus employee benefits is recommended.

When developing time savings, caution is needed. Savings are only realized when the amount of time saved translates into a cost reduction or a profit contribution. Even if a program produces savings in manager time, a monetary value is not realized unless the manager puts the additional time saved to productive use. Having managers estimate the percentage of time saved that is used on productive work may be helpful, if followed up by a request for examples of how the time was used. If a team-based program sparks a new process that eliminates several hours of work each day, the actual savings will be based on a reduction in staff or overtime pay. Therefore, an important preliminary step in developing time savings is determining whether the expected savings will be genuine. This will only happen if the time saved is put to productive use.

Finding Standard Values

As this section has illustrated, standard values are available for all types of hard data and are available in all types of functions and departments. Essentially, every major department will develop standard values that are tracked and monitored in that area. Exhibit 8.4 shows the typical functions in a major organization where standard values would be tracked. Sometimes, it is a matter of understanding the data set that they monitor, collect, and publish. Thanks to enterprise-wide systems

---

STANDARD VALUES ARE EVERYWHERE

• Finance and Accounting	• Customer Service and Support
• Production	• Procurement
• Operations	• Logistics
• Engineering	• Compliance
• IT	• Research and Development
• Administration	• HR
• Sales and Marketing	

Exhibit 8.4. Locating the Standard Values.

software, these functions, including the standard values in some cases, are integrated and available for access to a variety of people. Access may be an issue, and access may need to be addressed or changed to ensure that the data can be obtained.

Some evaluators, using the ROI methodology, have taken the extra step of collecting the standard values from the various systems and developing a handbook of values. This involves tapping into the databases or departmental files of these functions and others. The result is an interesting list of what things are worth. When this has been compiled previously, it has become a much-sought-after document as others looking at cross-functional processes need the value of the measures as well. This would be an excellent program for wide-scale implementations.

DATA CONVERSION WHEN STANDARD VALUES ARE NOT AVAILABLE

When standard values are not available, several strategies for converting data to monetary values are available. Some are appropriate for a specific type of data or data category, while others may be used with virtually any type of data. The challenge is to select the strategy that best fits the situation. These strategies are presented next, beginning with the most credible approach.

Using Historical Costs from Records

Sometimes, historical records contain the value of a measure and reflect the cost (or value) of a unit of improvement. This strategy relies on identifying the appropriate records and tabulating the actual cost components for the item in question. For example, a large construction firm initiated a training program to improve safety. The program improved several safety-related performance measures, ranging from government fines to total workers' compensation costs. By examining the company's records using one year of data, the average cost for each safety measure was developed. This involved the direct costs of medical payments, insurance payments, insurance premiums, investigation services, and lost time payments to employees, as well as payments for legal expenses, fines, and other direct services. Also, the amount of time used to investigate, resolve, and correct any of the issues had to be included. This time involved not only the health and safety staff, but other staff members as well. In addition, the cost of lost productivity, the disruption of services, morale, and dissatisfaction are also estimated to obtain a fully loaded cost. Corresponding costs for each item are then developed.

This quick example shows the difficulty in working to keep systems and databases to find a value for a particular data item. This raises several concerns about using records and reports.

Sorting through databases, cost statements, financial records, and a variety of activity reports takes a tremendous amount of time, time that may not be available for the program. Keeping this part of the process in perspective is helpful. This is only one step in the ROI methodology (converting data to monetary value) and only one measure among others that may need to be converted to monetary value. Resources need to be conserved.

In some cases, data are not available to show all the costs for a particular item. While some direct costs are associated with a measure, often the same numbers of indirect or invisible costs, or costs that cannot be obtained easily, are associated with the program. Calculating the cost of an involuntary turnover is one example.

Figure 8.1 shows the fully loaded costs of turnover and can be compared to the Iceberg Principle (Alrichs, 2000). The visible part of the iceberg is the *green money*—these are the costs that are in the records, reports, and cost statements. Although capturing them all would be difficult, still more difficult and often unavailable are the *blue money* items. These are the invisible costs—the part of the iceberg that cannot be seen from a surface observation. Often labeled hidden or indirect, they can be significant and make converting data to monetary values not only a time-consuming process but one that will involve estimates and expert input.

In some cases, the effort just to secure data from databases becomes difficult. With the proliferation of data warehousing and data capturing systems, combined with existing legacy systems that may not talk to each other, finding the values for a particular cost item becomes a sometimes insurmountable task.

Compounding the problem of time and availability is access. Sometimes, monetary values may be needed from a system or record set that is under someone else's control. In a typical program implementation, the evaluator may not have full access to cost data. Cost data are more sensitive than other types of data and are often protected for many reasons, including the competitive advantage. Therefore, easy access becomes difficult and, sometimes, is even prohibited unless an absolute need to know exists.

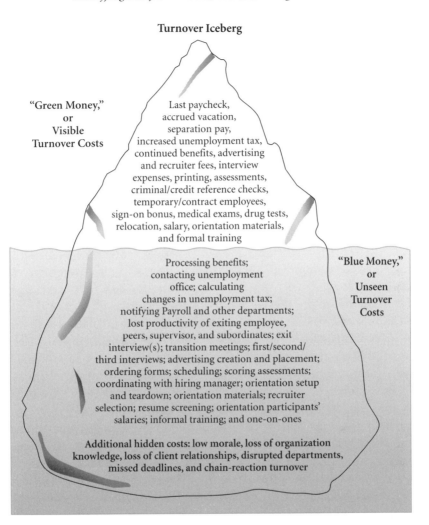

Figure 8.1. Fully Loaded Turnover Costs.

Finally, an acceptable level of accuracy is needed in this analysis. While a measure calculated in the current records may give the impression that it is based on accurate data, this may be an illusion. When data are calculated, estimations are involved, access to certain systems is denied, and different assumptions are necessary (which can be compounded by different definitions of systems, data, and measures). Because of these limitations, the calculated values may be suspect unless care is taken to ensure that they are accurate.

Calculating the monetary value of data using records should be done with caution and only when these two conditions exist:

1. The sponsor approves spending additional time, effort, and money to develop a monetary value from the current records and reports.

2. The measure is simple and available in a few records.

Otherwise, moving to another method is preferred. Other methods may be more accurate and certainly less time-consuming than this particular approach.

Using Input from Experts to Convert Soft Data

When faced with converting soft data items for which historical cost data are not available, using input from experts on the process might be an option. Internal experts provide the cost (or value) of one unit of improvement. Individuals with knowledge of the situation and the respect of management must be willing to provide estimates—as well as the assumptions made in arriving at the estimates. Most experts have their own methodology for developing these values. So when requesting their input, explaining the full scope of what is needed, providing as many specifics as possible, is critical.

Internally, experts are not difficult to find. Sometimes, it is the obvious department, where the data originated or the department was involved in collecting the data. For example, the quality department generates quality measures, the payroll department generates payroll measures, the IT department generates IT data, the sales department generates sales data, and so forth.

In some cases, the expert(s) is the individual or individuals who send the report. The report is sent either electronically or entered into a database, and the origins are usually known. If it is sent on a routine basis, the person sending the report may be the expert, or at least can lead program leaders to the expert. Sometimes, an individual's job title can indicate whether he or she is a possible expert. For example, in an insurance firm, interest arose in determining the value or the cost of a customer appeal. In that company, when a claim was turned down, the customer could appeal the process. A program was implemented to lower the number of customer appeals and the payoff of the program had to be developed based on the reduction of appeals. To find the value, the program leader contacted the individuals with the job title of customer appeals coordinator and in a focus group developed the data directly from them.

When it is not so obvious in the directory, asking may be helpful—asking a few questions may lead to the person who knows. Internally, for almost every data item generated, someone is considered an expert about that data.

Externally, the experts—consultants, professionals, or suppliers in a particular area—can be found in some obvious places. For example, the costs of accidents could be estimated by the workers' compensation carrier or the cost of a grievance could be estimated by the labor attorney providing legal services to defend the company in grievance transactions.

The credibility of the expert is the critical issue when using this method. Foremost among credibility measures is the individual's experience with the process or the measure. This individual must be knowledgeable of the processes for this measure and, ideally, work with it routinely. Also, this person must be unbiased. Experts have to be neutral in terms of the measure's value. They should not have a personal or professional interest in this value. This can be very subtle. For example, a labor relations internal expert (the individual who coordinates grievances for the company) may exaggerate the cost of a grievance to show the impact of his or her particular job. However, since they work with this, they may have the most knowledge, and the bias may have to be filtered in some way. In a case like this, going to an external expert who is not connected with the issue may be more appropriate. Part of the expertise may be based on the credentials of the person: Does he have a degree in this area? Does she hold certification in a related area? This type of information can confirm the person's expertise.

When internal experts have a strong bias regarding the measure or are not available, external experts are sought. External experts must be selected based on their experience with the unit of measure. Fortunately, many experts are available who work directly with important measures, such as employee attitudes, customer satisfaction, turnover, absenteeism, and grievances. They are often willing to provide estimates of the cost (or value) of these intangibles. Because the accuracy and credibility of the estimates are directly related to the expert's reputation, his or her reputation is critical.

In addition, the credentials of external experts—publications, degrees, and other honors or awards—are important for validating and supporting their expertise. For people who are tapped often, their track records of estimating are important. If the value they estimate has been validated in more detailed studies and found to be consistent, this track record could be the most credible confirmation of their expertise to provide this data.

Using Values from External Databases

For some soft data, using cost (or value) estimates based on the work and research of others may be appropriate. This technique taps external databases that contain studies and research programs focusing on the cost of data items. Fortunately, many databases include cost studies of many data items related to programs, and most are accessible through the Internet. Data are available on the cost of turnover, absenteeism, grievances, accidents, and even customer satisfaction. The difficulty is in finding a database with studies or research appropriate to the current program. Ideally, the data should come from a similar setting in the same industry, but that is not always possible. Sometimes, data on all industries or organizations are sufficient, perhaps with some adjustments to suit the program at hand.

For some, the web holds the most promise for finding monetary values for data not readily available from standard values and experts. Tremendous progress has been made—and continues to be made—in web searches to develop monetary values. Here are a few guidelines. General web directories and portals may be very helpful. Although they have quite a bit in common with web search engines, general web directories such as Yahoo, Open Directory, and Look Smart also differ greatly. Even though the databases may include less than 1 percent of what search engine databases cover, general web directories still serve unique research purposes and in many cases may be the best starting point (Hock, 2004).

A specialized directory is more appropriate for accessing immediate expertise in web resources on a specific topic. These sites bring together well-organized collections of Internet resources on specific topics and provide an important starting point.

The search engines hold more promise for searches because of their vast coverage. General web search engines such as Altavista, AllTheWeb, and Google stand in contrast to a web directory in three primary ways:

1. They are much larger, containing over a billion instead of a few million records.

2. Virtually no human selectivity is involved in determining which web pages are included in the search engine's database.

3. They are designed for searching (responding to a user's specific query), rather than browsing and, therefore, provide much more substantial searching capabilities than directories.

Groups, mailing lists, and other interactive forums create a class of Internet resources that too few researchers take advantage of—useful for a broad range of applications, including finding the value of data. These tools can be gold mines.

A range of news resources are also available on the Internet, including news services, news wires, newspapers, news consolidation services, and more. Because some studies around particular values are newsworthy, these may be excellent sources for capturing the values of data. Overall, web searches are an important tool for the evaluator when it comes to collecting the data.

A typical concern of web searches is the quality of the content. Some think that the Internet has low-quality content, although in reality, it is no different from other sources. Right alongside high-quality publications often available on newsstands are those with low-quality content. Here are a few guidelines:

- *Consider the source.* From what organization does the content originate? Look for the organization to be identified both on the web page itself and at the URL. Is the content identified as coming from known sources, such as a news organization, the government, an academic journal, a professional association, or a major investment firm? The URL will identify the owner, and the owner may be revealing in terms of the quality.

- *Consider the motivation.* What is the purpose of this site— academic, consumer protection, sales, entertainment, or political? The motivation can be helpful in assessing the degree of objectivity.

- *Look for the quality of the writing.* If the content contains spelling and grammatical errors, then this can mean content quality problems as well.

- *Look at the quality of the source documentation.* First, remember that even in academic circles, the number of footnotes is not a true measure of the quality of the work. On the other hand, if facts are cited, does the page identify the origin of the facts?

Check out some of the cited sources to see if the facts were actually quoted.

- *Are the site and its content as current as they should be?* If the site is reporting on current events, the need for currency and the answer to the question of currency will be apparent.

- *Verify the facts used in the data conversion using multiple sources, or choose the most authoritative source.* Unfortunately, many facts given on web pages are simply wrong from carelessness, exaggeration, guessing, or for other reasons. Often they are wrong because the person creating the page content did not check the facts.

These are helpful ways to help focus only on the quality content, which is critical when determining the monetary value of a particular measure.

When searching for monetary values, critical thinking should be applied to the information found and the claims that are made. The web has some special and unique attributes and using it to research calls for a certain set of critical thinking questions. Exhibit 8.5 has a few questions that provide a quick reference list for the serious searcher to get to the right information with the right quality and in the right time (Berkman, 2004).

ASKING THE RIGHT QUESTIONS

Before going to the web for business research, ask yourself:

- Why am I choosing the web to perform this research?
- For example, if it's because the web is fast, why is that good?
- If it's because it's free, why is free information best? How much would I pay for good information?
- Is a search engine the best tool to find what I'm looking for on the web?
- Where else might I find the same type of information?
- Would a library or a fee-based database contain the data?

When you find a source of interest on the web, ask yourself:

- Who put this information on the web? Why?
- If it's free, why did the creator make it that way?
- Who gains from having this information on the web?

Exhibit 8.5. Using the Web Appropriately.

When evaluating the authority of the publisher/creator of the information, ask yourself:

- What are the qualifications of this person or organization?
- Why should I trust him or her/it?
- Why are these opinions being offered here?

If a search engine doesn't return the information you're looking for, ask yourself:

- Did I use all the appropriate keywords and phrases?
- Did I follow the search engine's instructions?
- Could the search engine have failed to index the site that includes the information?
- Could the information be online, but as part of the "invisible web" that's inaccessible to search engines?
- Could it mean that the information isn't on the web?
- If so, might it be available from other sources (the library, a journal database, a book or directory, an association, expert, etc.)?
- Could it be that what I'm looking for isn't the kind of information that's easily found on the web? If so, am I better off trying a different type of resource altogether?
- Could it mean that the information simply doesn't exist?

When you find statistical data, ask yourself:

- What/who/where is the original source/creator of the data?
- Is this the most recent version/series of the data?
- Do I have the larger context from which these data were derived?
- Where can I find the methodologies and assumptions used to create these statistics?

On an online news site, ask yourself:

- What makes this a legitimate news-gathering and reporting site?
- What is a legitimate news-gathering and reporting site?
- Can I distinguish editorial from advertising on this site?

Exhibit 8.5. Using the Web Appropriately, Cont'd.

Adapted from *The Skeptical Business Searcher: The Information Advisor's Guide to Evaluating Web Data, Sites, and Sources.* Medford, NJ: Information Today, Inc., 2004.

Linking with Other Measures

When standard values, records, experts, and external studies are not available, a feasible approach might be to find a relationship between the measure in question and some other measure that may be easily converted to a monetary value. This involves identifying existing relationships, if possible, that show a strong correlation between one measure and another with a standard value.

For example, a classical relationship, depicted in Figure 8.2, shows a correlation between increasing job satisfaction and employee turnover. In a program designed to improve job satisfaction, a value is needed for changes in the job satisfaction index. A predetermined relationship showing the correlation between improvements in job satisfaction and reductions in turnover can link the changes directly to turnover. Using standard data or external studies, the cost of turnover can easily be developed, as described earlier. Therefore, a change in job satisfaction is converted to a monetary value or, at least, an approximate value. It is not always exact because of the potential for error and other factors, but the estimate is sufficient for converting the data to monetary values.

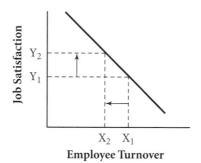

Figure 8.2. Relationship Between Job
Satisfaction and Voluntary Employee Turnover.

Sometimes, finding a correlation between a customer satisfaction measure and another measure that can easily be converted to a monetary value is possible. Usually, a significant correlation exists between customer satisfaction and revenue. Many organizations are able to show a connection between these two measures. By connecting these two variables, estimating the actual value of customer satisfaction is possible by linking it to other measures. Furthermore, a correlation often exists between customer loyalty—which may be defined in terms of customer retention or defection—and the actual profit per customer.

In some situations, a chain of relationships may establish a connection between two or more variables. In this approach, a measure that may be difficult to convert to a monetary value is linked to other measures that, in turn, are linked to measures upon which a value can be placed. Ultimately, these measures are traced to a monetary value often based on profits. A model used by Sears, one of the world's largest retail chains, connects job attitudes (collected directly from the employees) to customer service, which is directly related to revenue growth (Ulrich, 1998).

A 5-point improvement in employee attitudes will drive a 1.3-point improvement in customer satisfaction. This, in turn, drives a 0.5 percent increase in revenue growth. Thus, if employee attitudes at a local store improved by 5 points and previous revenue growth were 5 percent, the new revenue growth would be 5.5 percent.

These links between measures, often called *the service-profit chain*, create a promising way to place monetary values on hard-to-quantify measures. This research practice is significant, and the opportunity for customized work is tremendous.

Using Estimates from Participants

In some cases, participants in the program should estimate the value of improvement. This technique is appropriate when participants are capable of providing estimates of the cost (or value) of the unit of measure improved with the program. When using this approach, participants should be provided with clear instructions, along with examples of the type of information needed. The advantage of this approach is that the individuals who are closest to the improvement are often capable of providing the most reliable estimates of its value.

Using Estimates from the Management Team

Sometimes, participants in a program may be incapable of placing a value on the improvement. Their work may be so far removed from the value of the process that they cannot reliably provide estimates. In these cases, the team leaders, supervisors, or managers of participants may be capable of providing estimates. Therefore, they may be asked to provide a value for a unit of improvement linked to the program.

In other situations, managers are asked to review and approve participants' estimates and confirm, adjust, or discard the values. For example, a program involving customer service representatives was designed to reduce customer complaints. While the program resulted in a reduction of complaints, the value of a single customer complaint was still needed to determine the value of the improvement. Although customer service representatives had knowledge of some issues surrounding customer complaints, they could not gauge the full impact, so their managers were asked to provide a value. These managers had a broader perspective of the full impact of a customer complaint.

In some cases, senior management provides estimates of the value of data. With this approach, senior managers interested in the program are asked to place a value on the improvement based on their perception of its worth. This approach is used when it is difficult to calculate the value or when other sources of estimation are unavailable or unreliable.

Using Staff Estimates

The final strategy for converting data to monetary values is using internal staff estimates. Using all the available information and experience, the staff members most familiar with the situation provide estimates of the value. For example, a program for an international oil company was designed to reduce dispatcher absenteeism and improve other performance problems. Unable to identify a value using other strategies, the training and development staff estimated the cost of an absence to be $200. This value was then used in calculating the savings for the reduction in absenteeism that followed the training. Although the L&D staff may be capable of providing accurate estimates, this approach is sometimes perceived as being biased. It should therefore be used only when other approaches are unavailable or inappropriate.

TECHNIQUE SELECTION
AND FINALIZING THE VALUES

With so many techniques available, the challenge is selecting one or more strategies appropriate for the situation and available resources. Developing a table or list of values or techniques appropriate for the situation may be helpful. The guidelines that follow may help determine the proper selection and finalize the values.

Use the Technique Appropriate for the Type of Data

Some strategies are designed specifically for hard data, while others are more appropriate for soft data. The type of data often dictates the strategy. Standard values are developed for most hard data items. Company records and cost statements are used with hard data. Soft data are often involved in external databases, linking with other measures, and using estimates. Experts are used to convert both types of data to monetary values.

Move from Most Accurate to Least Accurate

Table 8.3 shows the techniques presented in order of accuracy, beginning with the most accurate. Working down the list, each technique should be considered for its feasibility in the situation. The technique with the most accuracy is always recommended if it is feasible for the situation.

Accuracy	Technique Using	Comment
Most Accurate	Standard Values	80 percent of measures that matter have standard values, monetary values that are accepted by stakeholders.
	Company Records and Cost Statements	Use only if complete and fully loaded. Unfortunately, it takes much time to complete.
	Experts	Most have a comprehensive knowledge of the issue and can be unbiased and neutral.
	External Databases of Other Studies	The Internet has opened many opportunities. The studies must have similar settings.
	Linking with Other Measures	More relationships are being developed.
Least Accurate	Estimates	Use most credible source.

Table 8.3. Accuracy of the Techniques to Convert to Money.

Consider the Resources

Sometimes, the availability of a particular source of data will drive the selection. For example, experts may be readily available. Some standard values are easy to find; others are more difficult. In other situations, the convenience of a technique may be an important selection factor. The Internet is making external database searches more convenient.

As with other processes, keeping the time invested in this phase to a minimum is important, so that the total effort for the ROI study does not become excessive. Some techniques can be implemented in much less time than others. Too much time on this step may dampen otherwise enthusiastic attitudes about the use of the methodology.

When Estimates Are Sought, Use the Source with the Broadest Perspective on the Issue

According to Guiding Principle 3, the most credible data source must be used. The individual providing estimates must be knowledgeable of the processes and the issues surrounding the value of the data. For example, consider estimating the cost of a grievance in a manufacturing plant. Although a supervisor may have insight into what has caused a particular grievance, he or she may be limited in terms of a broad perspective. A high-level manager may be able to understand the total impact of the grievances and how that impact will affect other areas. Thus, a high-level manager would be a more credible source because of the broader perspective.

Use Multiple Techniques When Feasible

Sometimes, having more than one technique for obtaining values for the data is beneficial. When multiple sources are feasible, they should be used to serve as comparisons or to provide additional perspectives. The data must be integrated using a convenient decision rule, such as the lowest value. A conservative approach of using the lowest value is recommended as Guiding Principle 4, but only the sources have equal or similar credibility.

Converting data to monetary value does have its challenges. As the particular method is selected and used, several adjustments or issues need to be considered to make it the most credible and applicable value with the least amount of resources.

Apply the Credibility Test

The techniques presented in this chapter assume that each data item collected and linked to a program can be converted to a monetary value. Although estimates can be developed using one or more strategies, the process of converting data to monetary values may lose credibility with the target audience, which may question its use in analysis. Highly subjective data, such as changes in employee attitudes or a reduction in the number of employee conflicts, are difficult to convert. The key question in making this determination is: "Could these results be presented to senior management with confidence?" If the process does not meet this credibility test, the data should not be converted to monetary values but listed as intangibles. Other data, particularly hard data items, would normally be used in the ROI calculation, leaving the highly subjective data expressed in intangible terms.

This issue of credibility when combined with resources is illustrated quite clearly in Figure 8.3. This is a logical way to either convert data to a monetary value or leave it as an intangible and it addresses both the minimum resources. Essentially, if no standard value exists, many other ways are available to capture or convert the data to monetary value. However, there is a question of resources: Can it be done with minimum resources? Some of the techniques mentioned in this chapter—such as searching records, maybe even searching the Internet—cannot be used with minimum resources. However, an estimate obtained from a group or a few individuals would use minimum resources. Then we move to the next challenge, credibility. Our standard credibility test is simple—if an executive who is interested in the program will buy into the monetary value for the measure in two minutes, then it is credible enough to be included in the analysis—if not, then move it to the intangibles. Incidentally, the intangibles are very important and are covered in much more detail in the next chapter.

Review the Client's Needs

The accuracy of data and the credibility of the conversion process are important concerns. Program managers sometimes avoid converting data because of these issues. They are more comfortable reporting that a program reduced youth unemployment from 26 to 18 percent,

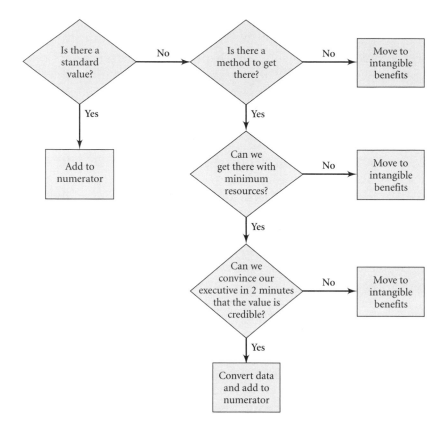

Figure 8.3. Data Conversion Four-Part Test.

without attempting to place a value on the improvement. They may assume that the sponsor will place a value on the reduction. Unfortunately, the target audience for the program may know little about the cost of unemployment and will usually underestimate the actual value of the improvement. Consequently, some attempt should be made to include this conversion in the ROI analysis.

Is This Another Project?

Because the efforts involved in developing a credible monetary value may be extensive and yet desired by the sponsor, an appropriate response to this question is: Yes, it can be done; no, it cannot be done using minimum resources; and yes, it will be another program.

Essentially, bringing up the issue of converting data to monetary value in terms of the resources required is appropriate. Although it is part of the planning for a study, the resources required can be discussed. If the sponsor is interested in converting data to money when it hasn't been done before, then this realistically should be considered a separate program. This keeps it from bogging down the ROI study and places the proper emphasis and resources on the process to do a credible job on the conversion.

Consider a Potential Management Adjustment

In organizations in which soft data are used and values are derived with imprecise methods, senior managers and administrators are sometimes offered the opportunity to review and approve the data. Because of the subjective nature of this process, management may factor (reduce) the data so that the final results are more credible. In one example, senior managers at Litton Industries adjusted the value for the benefits derived from implementing self-directed teams (Graham, Bishop, & Birdsong, 1994).

Consider the Short-Term/Long-Term Issue

When data are converted to monetary values, usually one year of data are included in the analysis—this is Guiding Principle 9, which states that for short-term solutions, only the first-year benefits are used. For some programs, they would be considered long-term. The issue of whether it is short-term or long-term is defined in the context of the time it takes to complete or implement the program. If one individual participating in the program and working through the process takes months to complete it, then it is probably not short-term. Some programs literally take years to implement with even one particular group. In general, it is appropriate to consider a program short-term when the time is a month or less, with one individual learning what needs to be done to make the program successful. When the lag between implementing the program and the subsequent consequences is relatively short, a short-term solution is appropriate. However, when it is long-term, no set time is used, but the time value should be set before the program evaluation. Input should be secured from all stakeholders, including the sponsor, champion, implementer, designer, and evaluator. After some discussion, the estimates of the time factor should be very conservative and should perhaps be reviewed by finance and accounting. When it is a long-term solution, the concept of forecasting will need to be used to estimate multiple years of value.

No sponsor will wait several years to see how a program turns out. Some assumptions have to be made and forecasting must be used.

Consider an Adjustment for the Time Value of Money

Since a program investment is made in one time period and the return is realized at a later time, some organizations adjust program benefits to reflect the time value of money using discounted cash-flow techniques. The actual monetary benefits of the program are adjusted for this time period. The amount of adjustment, however, is usually small when compared with the typical benefits of programs.

Although this may not be an issue for every program, it should be considered on each program, and a standard discount rate should be used. Consider an example of how this is calculated. Assume that a program cost $100,000, and a two-year period will be used before the full value of the investment will be recovered. In other words this is a long-term solution spanning two years. Using a discount rate of 6 percent, the amount of cost for the program for the first year would be $100,000 × 106 percent = $106,000. For the second year it is $106,000 × 106 percent or $112,360. Thus, the program cost has been adjusted for a two-year value with a 6 percent discount rate. This assumes that the program sponsor could have invested the money in some other program and obtained at least a 6 percent return on that investment, hence, another cost is added.

WHY MONITOR COSTS?

Monitoring L&D program costs is an essential step in developing the ROI calculation because it represents the denominator in the ROI formula. It is just as important to capture costs as it is to capture benefits. In practice, however, costs are often more easily captured than benefits.

Of course, one of the most important reasons for monitoring costs is creating budgets for programs. The initial cost of some programs is usually calculated during the proposal for the program. This cost is usually based on those from previous programs, a history that is generated throughout a process of monitoring costs. The only way to have a clear understanding of costs so that they can be used in future programs and budgets is to track them using different categories.

Costs should be monitored in an ongoing effort to control expenditures and keep the program within budget as well. Monitoring cost activities not only reveals the status of expenditures, but also gives visibility to expenditures and influences the team to spend wisely. And of course, monitoring costs in an ongoing fashion is much easier, more accurate, and more efficient than trying to reconstruct events to capture costs retrospectively. Developing accurate costs by different categories builds a database for understanding and predicting costs in the future.

WHY MEASURE ROI?

As discussed earlier, ROI is becoming a critical measure demanded by many stakeholders, including clients and senior executives. It is the ultimate level of evaluation showing the actual payoff of the program, expressed as a percentage and based on the same formula as the evaluation for other types of investment. Because of its perceived value and familiarity to senior management, it is now becoming a common requirement for programs. When ROI is required or needed, it must be calculated. Otherwise, it may be optional unless some compelling reason exists to take the evaluation to this level.

The most compelling reason to calculate ROI is inherent in the advantages of the ROI methodology described in Chapter One. Exhibit 8.6 shows the importance of this process. Many benefits have been achieved in the roughly three thousand organizations that use this methodology. These benefits are captured in follow-up benchmarking and in surveys with these groups. As you can see, the payoffs are not just calculating the ROI but radically changing the way in which the stakeholders perceive the value of the program and also bringing respect and a change of image to those who implement programs.

- Align programs to business needs
- Show contributions of selected programs
- Earn respect of senior management/administrators
- Build staff morale
- Justify/defend budgets
- Improve support for programs
- Enhance design and implementation processes
- Identify inefficient projects or programs that need to be redesigned or eliminated
- Identify successful projects or programs that can be implemented in other areas

Exhibit 8.6. Payoff of the ROI Methodology.

FUNDAMENTAL COST ISSUES

The first step in monitoring costs is to define and discuss several issues relating to a cost-control system. The key issues are presented here.

Monitor Costs, Even If They Are Not Needed

For some programs, the pressure of needing to show the costs in detail or in categories is not necessary. However, because of the reasons listed above and explained in this chapter, beginning the discipline of developing these costs is important. In the future, they will be needed in many situations. Also, even if fully loaded costs (direct and indirect) are not needed, monitoring these costs to keep the discipline and the focus of having all the costs involved is recommended. Then the decision can be made later as to how and when to use the costs and whether to push the program evaluation to the ROI level.

Costs Will Not Be Precise

Although the costs need to be realistic, they do not have to be absolutely precise. Some costs, particularly those in the indirect category, will not be known exactly, and estimates will have to be used. In some situations, the estimates have already been developed as activity-based costs or have been put into standard cost systems. If they have not, estimates from credible sources will suffice. Keeping in mind the resources required for this analysis is important. Spending an excessive amount of time trying to pinpoint the precise cost may be a misuse of resources.

Disclose All Costs

Today, there is more pressure than ever before to report all program costs, or what is referred to as fully loaded costs. This takes the cost profile beyond the direct cost of a program and includes the time participants spend being involved in the program, based on their pay, benefits, and other overhead. For years, management has realized that many indirect costs of a program exist. Now they are asking for an accounting of these costs.

Perhaps this point is best illustrated in a situation that recently developed in state government in which the management controls of a large state agency were examined by the state auditor. The agency prefers not to be identified. A portion of the audit focused on internal learning and development costs. Costs tracked for an intervention usually focus on direct or "hard" costs and largely ignore the cost of time spent participating in or supporting the program. The costs of participant time to prepare for and attend these sessions were not tracked. For one program, including such costs raised the total costs dramatically. The agency stated that the total two-year costs for the specific program were about $600,000. This figure included only direct, out-of-pocket costs to the vendor and, as such, was substantially less than the cost of the time spent by the staff preparing for and attending the various meetings and sessions. When accounting for pre-work and attendance, the figure came to $1.39 million. If the statewide average of 45.5 percent for employee benefits is considered, the total indirect cost of staff time to prepare for and attend meetings related to the program was $2 million. Finally, if the agency's direct costs of $600,000 were added to the $2 million total indirect cost just noted, the total becomes more than $2.6 million.

Among other factors that drive actual costs higher in this example are:

- Cost of travel, meals, and lodging for participants involved in the program
- Allocated salaries and benefits of staff providing administrative and logistic support
- Opportunity costs of productivity lost by staff while doing pre-work and attending meetings

Failure to consider all indirect, or "soft," costs may expose the agency to non-compliance with the Fair Labor Standards Act (FLSA), particularly as the program spreads through the rank and file. Since the FLSA requires that such staff be directly compensated for overtime, it is no longer appropriate for the agency to ask employees to complete assignments and pre-work on their own time. Continuing to handle such overtime work this way may encourage false overtime reporting, skew overtime data, and/or increase the amount of uncompensated overtime. Numerous barriers exist for the agency to determine the true costs of a program:

- Cost systems tend to hide administrative, support, internal, and other indirect or "soft" costs.
- Costs generally are monitored at the division level rather than at the level of individual interventions or activities.
- Cost information required by activity-based cost systems is not being generated.

While this case may be an extreme, it vividly demonstrates that the costs of programs are much more than direct expenditures, and program leaders are expected to report fully loaded costs in their programs.

Fully Loaded Costs

When using a conservative approach to calculating ROI, costs should be fully loaded. This is Guiding Principle 10. With this approach, all costs that can be identified and linked to a program are included. The philosophy is simple: For the denominator, "When in doubt, put it in" (that is, if it is questionable whether a cost should be included, including it is recommended, even if the cost guidelines for the organization do not require it). When an ROI is calculated and reported to target audiences, the process should withstand even the closest scrutiny in terms of its credibility. The only way to meet this test is to ensure that all costs are included. Of course, from a realistic viewpoint, if the controller or chief financial officer insists on not using certain costs, then leaving them out or reporting them as an alternate scenario is best.

Reporting Costs Without Benefits

Communicating the costs of a program without presenting the benefits is dangerous. Unfortunately, many organizations have fallen into this trap for years. Because costs can easily be collected, they are presented to management in many ingenious ways, such as the cost of the program, cost per day, and cost per participant. While these may be helpful for efficiency comparisons, presenting them without benefits may be troublesome. When most executives review program costs, a logical question comes to mind: What benefit was received from the program? This is a typical management reaction, particularly when costs are perceived to be very high.

For example, in one organization, all the costs associated with a major transformation program were tabulated and reported to the senior management team to let them know the total investment in the program. The total figure exceeded the perceived value of the program, and the executive group's immediate reaction was to request a summary of (monetary and non-monetary) benefits derived from the complete transformation. The conclusion was that few, if any, economic benefits were achieved from the program. Consequently, future programs were drastically reduced. While this may be an extreme example, it shows the danger of presenting only half the equation. Because of this, some organizations have developed a policy of not communicating cost data unless the benefits can be captured and presented along with the costs. Even if the benefits are subjective and intangible, they are included with the cost data. This helps maintain a balance between the two issues.

COST-TRACKING ISSUES

The most important task is to define which costs are included in program costs. This task involves decisions that will be made by the L&D staff and are usually approved by the client. If appropriate, the client's finance and accounting staff may need to approve the list.

Prorated Versus Direct Costs

Usually, all costs related to a program are captured and expensed to that program. However, some costs are prorated over a longer period of time. Equipment purchases, software development and acquisitions, and the construction of facilities are all significant costs with a useful life that may extend beyond the program. Consequently, a portion of these costs should be prorated to the program. Using a conservative approach, the expected life of the program is fixed. Some organizations will consider one year of operation for a simple program. Others may consider three to five years. If a question is raised about the specific time period to be used in the proration formula, the finance and accounting staff should be consulted, or appropriate guidelines should be developed and followed.

Employee Benefits Factor

Employee time is valuable, and when time is required on a program, the costs must be fully loaded, representing total compensation, including employee benefits. This means that the employee benefits factor should be included. This number is usually well known in the organization and is used in other costing formulas. It represents the cost of all employee benefits expressed as a percentage of payroll. In some organizations this value is as high as 50 to 60 percent. In others, it may be as low as 25 to 30 percent. The average in the United States is 38 percent (Annual Employee Benefits Report, 2006).

MAJOR COST CATEGORIES

Table 8.4 shows the recommended cost categories for a fully loaded, conservative approach to estimating costs. Each category is described below.

Cost Item	Prorated	Expensed
1. Initial analysis and assessment		✓
2. Development of solutions		✓
3. Acquisition of solutions		✓
4. Implementation and application		
Salaries/benefits for L&D team time		✓
Salaries/benefits for coordination time		✓
Salaries/benefits for participant time		✓
Program materials		✓
Hardware/software	✓	
Travel/lodging/meals		✓
Use of facilities		✓
Capital expenditures	✓	
5. Maintenance and monitoring		✓
6. Administrative support and overhead	✓	
7. Evaluation and reporting		✓

Table 8.4. Program Cost Categories.

Initial Analysis and Assessment

One of the most underestimated items is the cost of conducting the initial analysis and assessment. In a comprehensive program, this involves data collection, problem solving, assessment, and analysis. In some programs, this cost is near zero because the program is conducted without an appropriate assessment. However, as more program sponsors place increased attention on needs assessment and analysis, this item will become a significant cost in the future. All costs associated with the analysis and assessment should be captured to the fullest extent possible. These costs include time, direct expenses, and internal services and supplies used in the analysis. The total costs are usually allocated over the life of the program.

Development of Solutions

One of the more significant items is the costs of designing and developing the L&D program. These costs include time in both the design and development and the purchase of supplies, technology, and other materials directly related to the solution. As with needs assessment costs, design and development costs are usually fully charged to the program. However, in some situations, the major expenditures may be prorated over several programs, if the solution can be used in other programs.

Acquisition Costs

In lieu of development costs, some L&D leaders purchase solutions from other sources to use directly or in a modified format. The acquisition costs for these solutions include the purchase price, support materials, and licensing agreements. Some programs have both acquisition costs and solution-development costs. Acquisition costs can be prorated if the acquired solutions can be used in other programs.

Application and Implementation Costs

Usually, the largest cost segment in a program is associated with implementation and delivery. Eight major categories are reviewed below:

- Salaries and benefits for L&D team time
- Salaries and benefits for coordinators and organizers
- Participants' salaries and benefits
- Program materials
- Hardware/software
- Travel, lodging, and meals
- Facilities (even in-house meetings)
- Capital expenditures

Maintenance and Monitoring

Maintenance and monitoring involves routine expenses to maintain and operate the program. These represent ongoing expenses that allow the new program solution to continue. These may involve staff members, additional expenses, and may be significant for some programs.

Support and Overhead

Another charge is the cost of support and overhead, the additional costs of the program not directly related to a particular program. The overhead category represents any program cost not considered in the above calculations. Typical items include the cost of administrative/clerical support, telecommunication expenses, office expenses, salaries of client managers, and other fixed costs. This is usually an estimate allocated in some convenient way based on the number of training days, then estimating the overhead and support needed each day. This becomes a standard value to use in calculations.

Evaluation and Reporting

The total evaluation cost should be included in the program costs to complete the fully loaded cost. Evaluation costs include the cost of developing the evaluation strategy, designing instruments, collecting data, analyzing data, preparing a report, and communicating the results. Cost categories include time, materials, purchased instruments, surveys, and any consulting fees.

COST ACCUMULATION AND ESTIMATION

Program costs can be classified in two basic ways. One is with a description of the expenditures, such as labor, materials, supplies, travel, and so forth. These are expense-account classifications, which are standard with most accounting systems. The other way to classify is with categories in the program steps, such as initial analysis and assessment, development, and implementation and application, as illustrated earlier in Exhibit 8.4. An effective system monitors costs by account categories according to the description of those accounts but also includes a method for accumulating costs in the process/functional category. Many systems stop short of this second step. While the first grouping sufficiently gives the total program costs, it does not allow for a useful comparison with other programs to provide information on areas where costs might be excessive by comparison.

BASIC ROI ISSUES

Before presenting the formulas for calculating the ROI, a few basic issues are described and explored. An adequate understanding of these issues is necessary to complete this major step in the ROI process.

Definition

The term *return on investment* is occasionally misused, sometimes intentionally. In this misuse, a very broad definition for ROI is offered to include any benefit from the program. ROI becomes a vague concept in which even subjective data linked to a program are included in the concept. In this book, the return on investment is more precise and is meant to represent an actual value by comparing program costs to benefits. The two most common measures are the benefit/cost ratio (BCR) and the ROI formula. Both are presented, along with other approaches to calculate the return or payback.

For many years, L&D leaders sought to calculate the actual return on investment for programs. If the program is considered an investment, not an expense, then it is appropriate to place it in the same funding process as other investments, such as the investment in equipment and facilities. Although the other investments may be quite different, they are often viewed by executives and administrators in the same way. Developing specific values that reflect the return on the investment is critical for the success of programs.

Annualized Values: A Fundamental Concept

All the formulas presented in this chapter use annualized values so that the first-year impact of the program investment can be calculated. Using annualized values is becoming an accepted practice for developing the ROI in many organizations. This approach is a conservative way to develop the ROI, since many short-term programs have added value in the second or third year. For long-term programs, longer time frames are used. For example, in an ROI analysis of a program involving self-directed teams in Litton Industries, a seven-year timeframe was used. However, for short-term L&D programs that last only a few weeks, first-year values are appropriate.

BCR/ROI CALCULATIONS

When selecting the approach to measure ROI, communicating to the target audience the formula used and the assumptions made in arriving at the decision to use this formula is important. This helps avoid misunderstandings and confusion surrounding how the ROI value was actually developed. Although several approaches are described in this chapter, two stand out as preferred methods: the benefit/cost ratio and the basic ROI formula. These two approaches are described next.

Benefit/Cost Ratio

One of the earliest methods for evaluating programs was the benefit/cost ratio. This method compares the benefits of the program to the costs, using a simple ratio. In formula form, the ratio is:

$$BCR = \frac{Program\ Benefits}{Program\ Costs}$$

In simple terms, the BCR compares the annual economic benefits of the program to the costs of the program. A BCR of 1 means that the benefits equal the costs. A BCR of 2, usually written as 2:1, indicates that for each dollar spent on the program, two dollars are returned in benefits.

The following example illustrates the use of the BCR. A behavior modification program designed for managers and supervisors was implemented at an electric and gas utility. In a follow-up evaluation, action planning and business performance monitoring were used to capture the benefits. The first-year payoff for the program was $1,077,750. The total, fully loaded implementation cost was $215,500. Thus, the ratio was:

$$BCR = \frac{\$1,077,750}{\$215,500} = 5:1$$

For every dollar invested in this program, five dollars in benefits were returned. The principal advantage of using this approach is that it avoids traditional financial measures so confusion arises when comparing program investments with other investments in the company. Investments in plants, equipment, or subsidiaries, for example, are not usually evaluated by the benefit/cost method. Some program leaders prefer not to use the same formula to compare the return on program investments with the return on other investments. In these situations, the ROI for programs stands alone as a unique type of evaluation.

Unfortunately, no standards exist that constitute an acceptable BCR from the client perspective. A standard should be established within the organization, perhaps even for a specific type of program. However, a 1:1 ratio (break-even status) is unacceptable for many programs. In others, a 1.25:1 ratio is required, where the benefits are 1.25 times the cost of the program.

ROI Formula

Perhaps the most appropriate formula for evaluating program investments is net program benefits divided by cost. This is the traditional financial ROI and is directly related to the BCR. The ratio is usually expressed as a percentage when the fractional values are multiplied by one hundred. In formula form, the ROI becomes:

$$\text{ROI } (\%) = \frac{\text{Net Program Benefits}}{\text{Program Costs}} \times 100$$

Net benefits are program benefits minus costs. The ROI value is related to the BCR by a factor of 1. Subtract 1 from the BCR and multiply by 100 to get the ROI percentage. For example, a BCR of 2.45 is the same as an ROI value of 145 percent (1.45 × 100 percent). This formula is essentially the same as the ROI for capital investments. For example, when a firm builds a new plant, the ROI is developed by dividing annual earnings by the investment. The annual earnings are comparable to net benefits (annual benefits minus the cost). The investment is comparable to fully loaded program costs, which represent the investment in the program.

An ROI on a program of 50 percent means that the costs are recovered and an additional 50 percent of the costs are reported as "earnings." A program ROI of 150 percent indicates that the costs have been recovered and an additional 1.5 times the costs are captured as "earnings."

An example illustrates the ROI calculation. Public and private sector groups have been concerned about literacy and have developed a variety of programs to tackle the issue. Magnavox Electronics Systems Company was involved in one literacy program that focused on language and math skills for entry-level electrical and mechanical assemblers. The results of the program were impressive. Productivity and quality alone yielded an annual value of $321,600. The total, fully loaded costs for the program were just $38,233. Thus, the return on investment was:

$$\text{ROI } (\%) = \frac{\$321,600 - \$38,233}{\$38,233} \times 100 = 741\%$$

For each dollar invested, Magnavox received $7.40 in return after the costs of the consulting program had been recovered.

Using the ROI formula essentially places program investments on a level playing field with other investments using the same formula and similar concepts. The ROI calculation is easily understood by key management and financial executives who regularly use ROI with other investments.

Profits can be generated through increased sales or cost savings. In practice, more opportunities for cost savings occur than for profits. Cost savings can be generated when improvement in productivity, quality, efficiency, cycle time, or actual cost reduction occur. When reviewing almost five hundred studies with our involvement, the vast majority of the studies were based on cost savings. Approximately 85 percent of the studies had a payoff based on output, quality, efficiency, time, or cost reduction. The others had a payoff based on sales increases, where the earnings were derived from the profit margin. This situation is important for nonprofits and public sector organizations for which the profit opportunity is often unavailable. Most programs will be connected directly to cost savings; ROIs can still be developed in those settings.

Financial executives have used the ROI approach for centuries. Still, this technique did not become widespread in industry for evaluating operating performance until the early 1960s. Conceptually, ROI has innate appeal because it blends all the major ingredients of profitability in one number; the ROI statistic by itself can be compared with opportunities elsewhere (both inside and outside). Practically, however, ROI is an imperfect measurement that should be used in conjunction with other performance measurements (Horngren, 1982).

It is important for the formula outlined above to be used in organizations. Deviations from, or misuse of, the formula can create confusion, not only among users, but also among finance and accounting staffs. The chief financial officer (CFO) and the finance and accounting staff should become partners in the implementation of the ROI methodology. Without their support, involvement, and commitment, using ROI on a wide-scale basis is difficult. Because of this relationship, the same financial terms must be used as those used and expected by the CFO.

Exhibit 8.7 shows some misuse of financial terms in the literature. Terms such as return on intelligence (or information) abbreviated as ROI do nothing but confuse the CFO, who is thinking that ROI is the actual return on investment described above. Sometimes, return on expectations (ROE), return on anticipation (ROA), or return on client expectations (ROCE) are used, confusing the CFO, who is thinking return on equity, return on assets, and return on capital employed, respectively. Use of these terms in the calculation of a payback of a program will do nothing but confuse others and perhaps cause you to lose the support of the finance and accounting staff. Other terms such as return on people, return on resources, return on training, and return on web are often used, with almost no consistent financial calculations. The bottom line: Don't confuse the CFO. Consider this individual an ally, and use the same terminology, processes, and concepts when applying financial returns for programs.

Term	Misuse	CFO Definition
ROI	Return of Information or Return of Intelligence	Return on Investment
ROE	Return on Expectation	Return on Equity
ROA	Return on Anticipation	Return on Assets
ROCE	Return on Client Expectation	Return on Capital Employed
ROP	Return on People	??
ROR	Return on Resources	??
ROT	Return on Technology	??
ROW	Return on Web	??

Exhibit 8.7. Misuse of Financial Terms.

ROI Targets

Specific expectations for ROI should be developed before an evaluation study is undertaken. While no generally accepted standards exist, four strategies have been used to establish a minimum expected requirement, or hurdle rate, for ROI in a program. The first approach is to set the ROI using the same values used to invest in capital expenditures, such as equipment, facilities, and new companies. For North America, Western Europe, and most of the Asian Pacific area, including Australia and New Zealand, the cost of capital is quite low, and this internal hurdle rate for ROI is usually in the 15 to 20 percent range. Thus, using this strategy, organizations would set the expected ROI at the same value expected from other investments.

A second strategy is to use an ROI minimum that represents a higher standard than the value required for other investments. This target value is above the percentage required for other types of investments. The rationale: The ROI process for programs is still relatively new and often involves subjective input, including estimations. Because of that, a higher standard is required or suggested. For most areas in North America, Western Europe, and the Asia Pacific area, this value is set at 25 percent.

A third strategy is to set the ROI value at a break-even point. A 0 percent ROI represents break-even. This is equivalent to a BCR of 1. The rationale for this approach is an eagerness to recapture the cost of the program only. This is the ROI objective for many public sector organizations. If the funds expended for programs can be captured, value and benefit have come from the program through the intangible measures, which are not converted to monetary values, and the behavior change that is evident in the application and implementation data. Thus, some organizations will use a break-even point, under the philosophy that they are not attempting to make a profit from a particular program.

Finally, a fourth, and sometimes recommended, strategy is to let the client or program sponsor set the minimum acceptable ROI value. In this scenario, the individual who initiates, approves, sponsors, or supports the program establishes the acceptable ROI. Almost every program has a major sponsor, and that person may be willing to offer the acceptable value. This links the expectations or financial return directly to the expectations of the individual sponsoring the program.

ROI Is Not for Every Program

The ROI methodology should not be applied to every program. Creating a valid and credible ROI study takes time and resources. ROI is appropriate for programs that:

- *Are very important to the organization in meeting its operating goals.* These programs are designed to add value. ROI may be helpful to show that value.

- *Are closely linked to the strategic initiatives.* Anything this important needs a high level of accountability.

- *Are very expensive to implement.* An expensive program, expending large amounts of resources, should be subjected to this level of accountability.

- *Are highly visible and sometimes controversial.* These programs often require this level of accountability to satisfy the critics.

- *Have a large target audience.* If a program is designed for all employees, for example, it may be a candidate for ROI.

- *Command the interest of top executives and administrators.* If top executives are interested in knowing the impact, the ROI methodology should be applied.

These are only guidelines and should be considered within the context of the situation and the organization. Other criteria may also be appropriate. These criteria can be used in a scheme to sort out those programs most appropriate for this level of accountability.

It is also helpful to consider the programs for which the ROI methodology is not appropriate. ROI is seldom appropriate for programs that:

- Are very short in duration.
- Are very inexpensive.
- Are legislated or required by regulation and would be difficult to change anything as a result of this evaluation.
- Are required by senior management. It may be that these programs will continue regardless of the findings.
- Serve as basic or required skills for specific jobs. It may be more appropriate to measure only at Levels 1, 2, and 3 to ensure that participants know how to do the job and are doing it properly.

This is not meant to imply that the ROI methodology cannot be implemented for these types of programs. However, when considering the limited resources for measurement and evaluation, careful use of these resources and time will result in evaluating more strategic types of programs.

OTHER ROI MEASURES

In addition to the traditional ROI formula, several other measures can be used under the general heading of return on investment. These measures are designed for evaluating other types of financial measures but sometimes work their way into program evaluations.

Payback Period

The payback period is another common method for evaluating capital expenditures. With this approach, the annual cash proceeds (savings) produced by an investment are equated to the original cash outlay required by the investment to arrive at some multiple of cash proceeds equal to the original investment. Measurement is usually in terms of years and months. For example, if the cost savings generated from a program are constant each year, the payback period is determined by dividing the total original cash investment (development costs, expenses, etc.) by the amount of the expected annual or actual savings. The savings represent the net savings after the program expenses are subtracted.

To illustrate this calculation, assume that an initial program cost is $100,000 with a three-year useful life. The annual net savings from the program is expected to be $40,000. Thus, the payback period becomes:

$$\text{Payback Period} = \frac{\text{Total Investment}}{\text{Annual Savings}} = \frac{\$100,000}{40,000} = 2.5 \text{ Years}$$

The program will "pay back" the original investment in 2.5 years.

The payback period is simple to use but has the limitation of ignoring the time value of money. It has not enjoyed widespread use in evaluating program investments.

Discounted Cash Flow

Discounted cash flow is a method of evaluating investment opportunities in which certain values are assigned to the timing of the proceeds from the investment. The assumption, based on interest rates, is that a dollar earned today is more valuable than a dollar earned a year from now.

There are several ways to use the discounted cash flow concept to evaluate a program investment. The most common approach is the net present value of an investment. This approach compares the savings, year by year, with the outflow of cash required by the investment. The expected savings received each year is discounted by selected interest rates. The outflow of cash is also discounted by the same interest rate. If the present value of the savings should exceed the present value of the outlays, after discounting at a common interest rate, the investment is usually considered acceptable by management. The discounted cash flow method has the advantage of ranking investments, but it becomes difficult to calculate.

FINAL THOUGHTS

With some programs, money is an important value. Evaluators strive to be more aggressive in defining the monetary benefits of a learning and development program. Evaluators are no longer satisfied to simply report the business performance results. Instead, they take additional steps to convert impact data to monetary values and weigh them against the program costs. In doing so, they achieve the ultimate level of evaluation: the return on investment. This chapter presented several strategies used to convert business results to monetary values, offering an array of techniques to fit any situation or program.

Costs are important and should be fully loaded in the ROI calculation. From a practical standpoint, some costs may be optional based on the organization's guidelines and philosophy. However, because of the scrutiny involved in ROI calculations, all costs should be included, even if this goes beyond the requirements of the policy.

After the benefits are collected and converted to monetary values and the program costs are tabulated, the ROI calculation becomes a very easy step. Plugging the values into the appropriate formula is the final step. This chapter presented the two basic approaches for calculating the return; the ROI formula and the benefit/cost ratio. Each has its own advantages and disadvantages. Alternatives to ROI development were briefly discussed.

References

Ahlrichs, N.S. (2000). *Competing for talent.* Palo Alto, CA: Davies-Black.

Annual Employee Benefits Report. (2006, January). *Nation's Business.*

Berkman, R. (2004). *The skeptical business searcher: The information advisor's guide to evaluating web data, sites, and sources.* Medford, NJ: Information Today, Inc.

Campanella, J. (Ed.). (1999). *Principles of quality costs* (3rd ed.). Milwaukee, WI: American Society for Quality.

Farris, P.W., Bendle, N.T., Pfeifer, P.E., & Ribstein, D.J. (2006). *Marketing metrics: 50+ metrics every executive should master.* Upper Saddle River, NJ: Wharton School Publishing.

Fishman, C. (2006). *The Wal-Mart effect: How the world's most powerful company really works—and how it's transforming the American economy.* New York: The Penguin Press.

Graham, M., Bishop, K., & Birdsong, R. (1994). Self-directed work teams. In J.J. Phillips (Ed.), *Action: Measuring return on investment* (Vol. 1). Alexandria, VA: American Society for Training and Development, pp. 105–122.

Hock, R. (2004). *The extreme searcher's internet handbook.* Medford, NJ: CyberAge Books.

Horngren, C.T. (1982). *Cost accounting* (5th ed.). Englewood Cliffs, NJ: Prentice-Hall, 1982.

Muir, A.K. (2006). *Lean Six Sigma statistics: Calculating process efficiencies in transactional projects.* New York: McGraw-Hill.

Rust, R.T., Zahorik, A.J., & Keiningham, T.L. (1994). *Return on quality: Measuring the financial impact of your company's quest for quality.* Chicago, IL: Probus.

Ulrich, D. (Ed.). (1998). *Delivering results.* Boston, MA: Harvard Business School Press.

CHAPTER NINE

Measuring the Hard to Measure and the Hard to Value

Intangible Benefits

Learning and development program results include both *tangible* and *intangible* measures. Intangible measures are the benefits or detriments directly linked to a program that cannot or should not be converted to monetary values. By definition, from the guiding principles of the ROI methodology, an intangible benefit is a measure that is purposely not converted to money (that is, if a conversion cannot be accomplished with minimum resources and with credibility, it is left as an intangible). These measures are often monitored after the program has been completed. Although they are not converted to monetary values, they are still an important part of the evaluation process. The range of intangible measures is almost limitless; however, this chapter describes a few common and desired outcomes of programs. Exhibit 9.1 lists common examples of these measures. Some measures make the list because of the difficulty in measuring them, others because of the difficulty in converting them to money. Others are on the list for both reasons.

Being labeled as intangible does not mean that these items cannot be measured or converted to monetary values. In one study or another, each item has been monitored successfully and monetarily

COMMON INTANGIBLES	
• Reputation/Image	• Corporate social responsibility
• Awards	• Networking
• Workforce stability	• Communication
• Customer service	• Stress
• Employee attitudes	• Team effectiveness
• Capability	• Leadership
• Innovation and creativity	• Intellectual capital

Exhibit 9.1. Common Intangibles.

quantified. However, in typical programs, these variables are considered intangible benefits because of the difficulty in measuring the variable or the difficulty in converting the data to monetary value.

WHY INTANGIBLES ARE IMPORTANT

While the concept of intangibles is not new, they are becoming increasingly important. Intangibles drive funding, intangibles drive the economy, and organizations are built on them. In every direction we look, intangibles are becoming not only increasingly important, but critical to organizations. Here's a recap of why they have become so important.

Intangibles Are the Invisible Advantage

When the success behind well-known organizations is examined, intangibles are there. A highly innovative company continues to develop new and improved products; a company with involved and engaged employees attracts and keeps talent. An organization shares knowledge with employees, giving them a competitive advantage. Still another organization is able to develop strategic partners and alliances. These intangibles often don't appear in cost statements and other record-keeping, but they are there, and they make a huge difference.

For some, they are invisible, yet their presence is known. Trying to measure them, identify them, and react to them may be difficult, but the ability to do this exists. These intangibles are transforming the way organizations work, the way employees are managed, the way products are designed, the way services are sold, and the way customers are treated. The implications are profound, and an organization's strategy must deal with these intangibles.

We Are Entering the Intangible Economy

The intangible economy has evolved from changes that date back to the Stone Age. The Stone Age evolved into the Iron Age and then evolved into the Agricultural Age. In the late 19th century and during the early 20th century, the world moved into the Industrial Age. From the 1950s forward, the world has moved into the Technology and Knowledge Age, and these translate into intangibles. During this time, a natural evolution of the technologies has occurred. During the Industrial Age, companies and individuals invested in tangible assets. In the Technology and Knowledge Age, companies invest in intangible assets, such as brands or systems. The future holds more of the same— as intangibles continue to evolve as an important part of the overall economic system (Boulton, Libert, & Samek, 2000).

More Intangibles Are Converted to Tangibles

The good news to report in this chapter, and building on Chapter Eight, is that more data, previously regarded as intangible, are now converted to monetary values. Because of this, classic intangibles are now accepted as tangible measures, and their value is more easily understood. Consider, for example, customer satisfaction. Just a decade ago, very few organizations had a clue as to the monetary value of customer satisfaction. Now, more firms have taken the extra step to link customer satisfaction directly to revenues, profits, and other measures. Companies are clearly seeing the tremendous value that can be derived from intangibles. As this chapter will illustrate, more data are being accumulated to show the monetary value, moving some intangible measures into the tangible category.

Intangibles Drive Programs

Some learning and development programs are implemented because of the intangibles. For example, the need to have greater collaboration, partnering, communication, teamwork, or customer service will drive programs. In the public sector the need to reduce poverty, to employ disadvantaged citizens, and to save lives often drive programs. From the outset, the intangibles are the important drivers and become the most important measures.

MEASUREMENT AND ANALYSIS OF INTANGIBLES

Although intangibles may not be perceived as being as valuable as tangible measures, intangibles are critical to the overall evaluation process. In some programs, intangibles are more important than monetary measures. Consequently, these measures should be monitored and reported as part of the program evaluation. In practice, every program, regardless of its nature, scope, and content, will produce intangible measures. The challenge is to identify them effectively and report them appropriately.

Measuring the Intangibles

Often, we explore the issue of measuring the difficult to measure. Responses to this exploration usually occur in the form of comments instead of questions. "You can't measure it," is a typical response. We disagree; we think anything can be measured. What the frustrated observer suggests is that it is not something you can count, examine, and see in quantities, such as items produced. In reality, a quantitative value can be assigned or developed for any intangible. If it exists, it can be measured. For example, consider human intelligence, which is a complex and abstract factor with many facets and qualities. Yet, IQ scores are assigned to most people and almost everyone seems to accept those scores. The software-engineering institute of Carnegie-Mellon University assigns software organizations a score of 1 to 5 to represent their maturity in software engineering. This score has enormous implications for the organizations' business development capabilities; yet, the measure is practically unchallenged (Alden, 2006).

Several approaches are available for measuring intangibles. Some typical intangibles can be counted. Unfortunately, many intangibles are based on attitudes and perceptions and must be measured in some way. These can come in three basic varieties. One type is to list the intangible item that exists and have the respondents disagree or agree on a 5-point scale. The mid-point then becomes the neutral. Others define various levels of the intangible. For example, a 5-point scale can easily be developed to describe the degrees of reputation ranging from worst case, with a horrible reputation, to best case, with an excellent reputation. Still other ratings can come through an assessment on a scale of 1 to 10 after reviewing a description of the intangible. Table 9.1 lists three intangible items with a full description, and the respondent is asked to indicate the level of that factor in place (Ulrich & Smallwood, 2003). Scales can be created in many ingenious ways, and when repeated and used and refined and modified, often become standards in the industry.

Intangible Measure	Assessment (1 = Low; 10 = High)
Clarity	
We are precise about the decisions we are making.	
We never begin a meeting without being clear about what decisions we will make by the end of the meeting.	
We don't have reviews without knowing what the decision will be as a result of the review.	
We can dissect big ideas (such as quality or market share) into specific decisions with clear alternatives. We create decision pyramids of the little decisions that will lead to other decisions.	
Accountability	
We know who is responsible for a decision and hold that person (or team) accountable if they do or don't make and execute a decision.	
Consensus does not mean everyone gets an equal vote.	
Somebody (individual or team) must make the decision, but should involve others in it. Ideally, the decision should have the support of those who care about it, and general acceptance on the part of those who don't.	
Timeliness	
We have deadlines to make decisions, and we stick to those deadlines. (It's often useful to set a limit of fourteen days to closure on most decisions.)	
We are decisive and demanding on making decisions, and if a team lags, the manager makes it.	

Table 9.1. Measuring the Intangible.
Adapted from Ulrich and Smallwood, 2003.

Another approach to measuring the intangible is to connect the intangible to a measure that is easier to value, a tangible. As shown in Figure 9.1, most hard-to-value measures are linked to an easy-to-value measure. Although this link can be developed through logical deductions and conclusions, having empirical evidence through a correlation analysis is the best approach. However, a detailed analysis would have to be conducted to ensure that a causal relationship exists. Just because a correlation is apparent does not mean that one caused the other. Additional analysis and supporting data could pinpoint the actual causal effect.

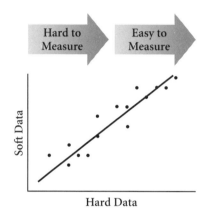

Figure 9.1. The Link Between
Hard-to-Measure and Easy-to-Measure Items.

Through the difficulties of measuring intangibles, remembering that intangibles are often combined with a variety of tangibles to reflect performance is helpful. Also, the intangibles are often associated with non-profit, non-government, or public sector organizations.

Converting to Money

Converting the hard to value to money is challenging to say the least. The examples in this chapter show various attempts to convert hard-to-value measures to monetary values. The interest in the monetary contribution is expanding. The sponsor, who often funds or supports a particular program, is almost always seeking monetary values, among other measures. Many of the stakeholders are interested in the money from programs. Even the participants are asking for the money. "Show me the money" is a familiar request.

The approaches to convert to monetary value were detailed in Chapter Eight. The specific methods used there all represent approaches that may be used to convert the intangibles to monetary value. These will not be repeated here. However, showing the path most commonly used to capture values for the intangibles is helpful. Figure 9.2 shows the typical approach of converting intangibles to monetary value.

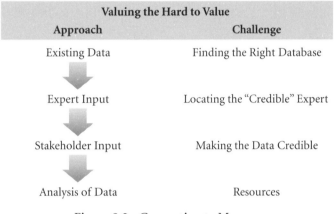

Valuing the Hard to Value	
Approach	**Challenge**
Existing Data	Finding the Right Database
Expert Input	Locating the "Credible" Expert
Stakeholder Input	Making the Data Credible
Analysis of Data	Resources

Figure 9.2. Converting to Money.

The first issue is to locate the data item or to measure it in some way, making sure that it is accurate, reliable, and reflects the concept. Next, an expert may be able to place a monetary value on the item based on experience, knowledge, credentials, and previous track record. Stakeholders may provide their input, although the input should be factored for bias. Some stakeholders are biased in one way or the other—they want the value to be smaller or larger depending on their particular motives. These may have to be adjusted or thrown out altogether based on the biased approaches. Finally, the data are analyzed using the conservative processes described in Chapter Eight, often adjusting for the error in the process. Unfortunately, no specific rule exists for converting each intangible to monetary value. By definition, an intangible is a measure that is not converted to money. If the conversion cannot be accomplished with minimum resources and with credibility, it is left as an intangible.

Identifying Intangibles

Intangible measures can be taken from different sources and at different times in the program life cycle, as depicted in Figure 9.3. They can be uncovered early in the process, during the needs assessment, and planned for collection as part of the overall data collection strategy. For example, an intangible measure, employee satisfaction, is identified and monitored with no plans to convert it to a monetary value. From the beginning, this measure is destined to be a non-monetary, intangible benefit reported along with the ROI results.

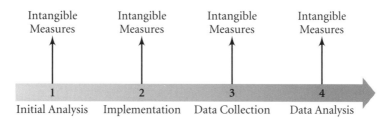

Figure 9.3. Intangible Measures During the Program Life Cycle.

A second opportunity to identify intangible benefits is in the planning process, when the evaluation plan is developed. The planning team can usually identify the intangible measures they expect to be influenced by the program. For example, a managing change program in a large multinational company was planned, and an ROI analysis was desired. The evaluator and other planning members identified potential intangible measures that were perceived to be influenced by the program, including collaboration, communication, and teamwork.

A third opportunity to identify intangible measures presents itself during data collection. Although the measure is not anticipated in the initial program design, it may surface on a questionnaire, in an interview, or during a focus group. Questions are often asked about other improvements linked to a program, and participants usually provide several intangible measures for which no plans are available to assign a value. For example, in the evaluation of a customer service training program, participants were asked what specifically had improved about their work area and relationships with customers as a result of the program. Participants provided more than a dozen intangible measures attributed to the program.

The fourth opportunity to identify intangible measures is during data analysis and reporting, while attempting to convert data to monetary values. If the conversion loses credibility, the measure should be reported as an intangible benefit. For example, in a sales training program, customer satisfaction was identified early in the process as a measure of program success. A conversion to monetary values was attempted, but it lacked accuracy and credibility in the organization. Therefore, customer satisfaction was reported as an intangible benefit.

Analyzing Intangibles

For each intangible measure identified, some evidence of its connection to the program must be shown. However, in many cases, no specific analysis is planned beyond tabulating responses. Early attempts to quantify intangible data sometimes results in aborting the entire process, and no further data analysis is conducted. In some cases, isolating the effects of the program may be undertaken using one or more of the methods outlined in Chapter Seven. This step is necessary when program leaders need to know the specific amount of change in the intangible measure that is linked to the program. In most situations, however, the direct link to this program can be obtained by asking a specific question. For example, in a given list of intangibles, the participant (or other stakeholder) is asked this question: To what extent has this program influenced this measure? A 5-point scale could be used for responses.

Intangible data often reflect improvement. However, neither the precise amount of improvement nor the amount of improvement directly related to a program is usually identified. Since the value of this data is not included in the ROI calculation, intangible measures are not normally used to justify continuing an existing program. A detailed analysis is not necessary. Intangible benefits are often viewed as additional evidence of the program's success and are presented as supportive qualitative data.

CUSTOMER SERVICE

Because of the importance of building and improving customer service, a number of related measures are typically monitored and reported to track the payoff of programs. Several types of customer service programs have a direct influence on these measures.

This metric makes the list because it is perceived as difficult to measure and to convert the data to monetary value. However, in the last two decades, much work has been done in this area, and some of these measures are routinely considered tangible because they are converted to money using one or more of the measures described in Chapter Eight. In that chapter, the technique, linking to other measures, clearly illustrates the most common way in which customer service intangible measures are converted to money. This essentially follows a sequence shown in Figure 9.4, Customer Service Links. The first issue is to create an awareness of a particular product, brand, or service. The next step is to develop attitudes, which define the beliefs, opinions, and intentions about the product, service, or brand, and this leads to usages that describe the purchase habits and loyalty of a customer.

Awareness, Attitudes, and Usage: Typical Questions

Type	Measures	Typical Questions
Awareness	Awareness and Knowledge	Have you heard of Brand X? What brand comes to mind when you think "luxury car"?
Attitudes	Beliefs and Intentions	Is Brand X for me? On a scale of 1 to 5, is Brand X for young people?
Usage	Purchase Habits and Loyalty	Did you use Brand X this week? What brand did you last buy?

Figure 9.4. Customer Service Links.
Adapted from *Marketing Metrics: 50+ Metrics Every Executive Should Master.*
Paul W. Farris, Neil T. Bendle, Phillip E. Pfeifer, and David J. Ribstein.
Upper Saddle River, NJ: Wharton School Publishing, 2006.

This important link is ingrained in most marketing and promotion programs and processes. This has led to a variety of measures that are becoming standard in the industry. Table 9.2 shows customer intangibles and underscores the array of possibilities all aimed at developing awareness, attitudes, and usage. Perhaps the most common is customer satisfaction, which is generally measured on a 1 to 5 scale, although other scales are used. A tremendous amount of research has been accumulated about the value of satisfied customers and the tremendous loss connected with dissatisfied customers. Using elaborate processes of decision tree analysis, probability theories, expected value, and correlations, organizations have developed detailed monetary values showing that movement in sales and profits are connected to a variety of measures, but most importantly to customer satisfaction. Within a given organization, more specific measures can be developed, such as customer response time, sensitivity to costs and pricing issues, and creativity with customer responses. Of particular importance is the timing issue. Providing prompt customer service is a critical issue for most organizations. Therefore, organizations monitor the time taken to respond to specific customer service requests or problems. Although reducing response times is often an objective of a program, the measure is not usually converted to a monetary value. Thus, customer response time is reported as an important intangible measure.

Metric	Definition	Issues	Purpose
Awareness	Percentage of total population that is aware of a brand	Is this prompted or unprompted awareness?	Consideration of who has heard of the brand
Top of Mind	First brand to consider	May be subject to most recent advertising or experience	Saliency of brand
Knowledge	Percentage of population with knowledge of product, recollection of its advertising	Not a formal metric. Is this prompted or unprompted knowledge?	Extent of familiarity with product beyond name recognition

Table 9.2. Customer Service Intangibles.

(Continued)

Metric	Definition	Issues	Purpose
Beliefs	Customers'/ consumers' view of product, generally captured via survey responses, often through ratings on a scale	Customers/ consumers may hold beliefs with varying degrees of conviction	Perception of brand by attribute
Purchase Intentions	Probability of intention to purchase	To estimate probability of purchase, aggregate and analyze ratings of stated intentions (for example, top two boxes)	Measures pre-shopping disposition to purchase
Willingness to Recommend	Generally measured via ratings across a 1 to 5 scale	Nonlinear in impact	Shows strength of loyalty, potential impact on others
Customer Satisfaction	Generally measured on a 1 to 5 scale, in which customers declare their satisfaction with brand in general or specific attributes	Subject to response bias. Captures views of current customers, not lost customers. Satisfaction is a function of expectations.	Indicates likelihood of repurchase. Reports of dissatisfaction show aspects that require improvement to enhance loyalty.
Willingness to Search	Percentage of customers willing to delay purchases, change stores, or reduce quantities to avoid switching brands	Hard to capture	Indicates importance of distribution coverage
Loyalty	Measures include willingness to pay premium, willingness to search, willingness to stay	"Loyalty" itself is not a formal metric, but specific metrics measure aspects of this dynamic. New product entries may alter loyalty levels.	Indication of base future revenue stream

Table 9.2. Customer Service Intangibles, Cont'd.

Adapted from *Marketing Metrics: 50+ Metrics Every Executive Should Master.* Paul W. Farris, Neil T. Bendle, Phillip E. Pfeifer, and David J. Ribstein. Upper Saddle River, NJ: Wharton School Publishing, 2006.

TEAM EFFECTIVENESS

To evaluate the success of teams within an organization, several key measures are monitored. Although the output and quality of the teamwork are often measured as hard data and converted to monetary values, other interpersonal measures may be tracked and reported separately. This made our list because of the difficulty in measuring and the difficulty in converting to money. The good news is that significant progress has been made to evaluate a variety of team effectiveness measures. Standard instruments are available and processes are in place to measure the quality of the team process. Just the volume of the materials, books, and articles focused on teams and how they can work effectively underscores the importance of this intangible.

Cross-functional, high-performance, and virtual teams are important assets for organizations striving to improve performance. Sometimes, team members are surveyed before and after a program to see whether the level of teamwork has increased. The monetary value of increased teamwork is rarely developed as a measure; rather, it is usually reported as an intangible benefit.

Cooperation/Conflict

The success of a team often depends on the cooperative spirit of team members. Some instruments measure the level of cooperation before and after a program, but since converting the findings to monetary values is so difficult, the measure is always reported as an intangible.

In some team environments, the level of conflict is measured. A decrease in conflict may reflect a successful program. In most situations, a monetary value is not placed on such a reduction, and it is reported as an intangible benefit.

Decisiveness/Decision Making

Teams make decisions, and the expedience and quality of the decision-making process often become important issues. Decisiveness is usually measured by how quickly decisions are made. Survey measures may reflect the perception of the team or, in some cases, monitor precisely how quickly decisions are made. The quality of the decisions reflects value as well. Some programs are expected to influence this process, with improvements usually reported as intangible benefits.

Communication

Communication is critical in every team. Several instruments are available to qualify and quantify communication among a team. Positive changes in communication skills or perceptions of skills driven by a program are not usually converted to monetary values but reported as intangible benefits.

The difficulty in turning team effectiveness into monetary value stems from the tremendous variety of team processes, settings, and participants. Essentially, the output of team effectiveness, including teamwork, is measured by the output of the teams, and this can vary significantly. Consider the typical organization in which teams are working throughout every functional area. The measures that are improved are essentially all the measures in the organization. The challenge is to link the team process directly to the measure in question using one or more of the isolation techniques described in Chapter Seven. Then a monetary value is placed on the measure using one or more of the techniques used in Chapter Eight.

INNOVATION AND CREATIVITY

Innovation and creativity are both related to human capital. In this knowledge-based and technology-based economy, they are becoming important factors in organizations' success.

Innovation

For most organizations, innovation is a critical issue. Because innovation comes from employee creativity, it is a human capital issue. Just how important is innovation? Let's put it in perspective. If it were not for the intellectual curiosity of employees—thinking things through, trying out new ideas, and taking wild guesses in all the R&D labs across the country—the United States would have half the economy that it has today. In a recent report on R&D, the American Association for the Advancement for Science estimates that as much as 50 percent of U.S. economic growth during the half century since the Fortune 500 came into existence has been due to advances in technology (Brown, 2004).

After a few years of retrenchment and cost cutting, senior executives across a variety of industries share the conviction that innovation, the ability to define and create new products and services and quickly bring them to market, is an increasingly important source of competitive advantage. Executives are setting aggressive performance goals for their innovation and product-development organizations, targeting 20 to 30 percent improvements in such areas as time to market, development costs, product cost, and customer value (Kandybihn & Kihn, 2004).

But a vast disconnect lies between hope and reality. A recent survey of fifty companies conducted by Booz Allen Hamilton shows that companies are only marginally satisfied that their current innovation organizations are delivering their full potential. Worse, executives say that only half the improvement efforts they launch end up meeting expectations. Several waves of improvements in innovation and product development have already substantially enhanced companies' abilities to deliver differentiated, higher-quality products to markets faster and more efficiently. However, the degree of success achieved has varied greatly among companies and even among units within individual companies. The differences in success stem from the difficulty of managing change in complex processes and organizations associated with innovation and product development.

Some companies have managed to assemble an integrated "innovation chain" that is truly global and allows them to outflank competitors that innovate using knowledge in a single cluster. They have been able to implement a *process* for innovating that transcends local clusters and national boundaries, becoming "meta-national innovators." This strategy of using localized pockets of technology, market intelligence, and capabilities has provided a powerful new source of competitive advantage: more, higher-value innovation at lower costs (Santos, Doz, & Williamson, 2001).

Innovation is both easy and difficult to measure. Measuring the outcomes in areas such as new products, new processes, improved products and processes, copyrights, patents, inventions, and employee suggestions is easy. Many companies track these items. They can be documented to reflect the innovative profile of an organization. Unfortunately, comparing these data with previous data or benchmarking with other organizations is difficult because these measures are typically unique to each organization.

Perhaps the most obvious measure is tracking the patents that are not only used internally but are licensed for others to use through a patent and license exchange. For example, IBM has been granted more patents than any other company in the world—over 25,000 U.S. patents. IBM's licensing of patents and technology generates several billion dollars in profits each year. While IBM and Microsoft® are at the top of the list, most organizations in the new economy monitor trademarks, patents, and copyrights as important measures of the innovative talent of employees.

The development of patents comes from the inventive spirit of employees, and remembering this is helpful. The good news is that employees do not have to be scientists or engineers to be inventive. Even though, at times, invention is thought of only in the context of technology, computing, materials, energy, and so forth, it is transdisciplinary and, therefore, can be extracted from any technological realm and applied to problems in any area (Schwartz, 2004).

Through the years, inventors have been viewed as "nerds," with much of their inventiveness being explained by their particular personality makeup. This is because history is laced with well-known inventors possessing eccentric personalities. The fact is that inventors are usually ordinary people possessing extraordinary imaginations. Many current organizations, regardless of their focus, are placing resources on encouraging employees' creativity, which can lead to significant technological advantages over the competition. To spark this ingenuity, organizations consider innovation a major human capital issue, monitor it appropriately, and take actions to enhance it.

One of the most recognized and respected evaluation processes for innovation is used to develop *Business Week's* list of the most innovative companies (McGregor, 2006). This list of companies that produced the top twenty-five innovations presented in the magazine is both comprehensive and respected. In partnership with Boston Consulting Group, the process involves a senior management survey of innovation that is distributed electronically to executives worldwide early in the year, targeting 1,500 global corporations determined by market capitalization. Executives were instructed to distribute the survey to their top ten executives. The survey is also accessible on several websites. The survey consists of nineteen general questions on innovation and also questions that focus on innovation metrics. For 2006, Apple, Google, 3M, Toyota, and Microsoft rounded out the top five of the list. Although this survey is comprehensive, there is still a lack of progress in measuring the actual monetary value from innovation. Figure 9.5 shows how these respondents measured the success of innovation. This is disappointing, since only 30 percent indicated that they measure the actual ROI on innovation investments.

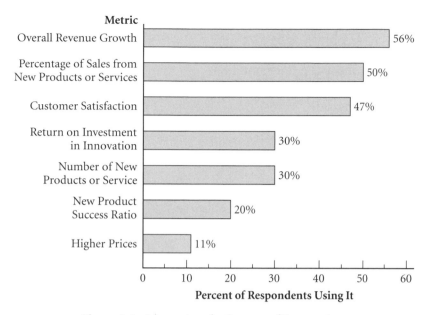

Figure 9.5. Measuring the Success of Innovation.
Adapted from *Business Week*. Boston Consulting Group, 2006.

Creativity

Creativity, often considered the precursor to innovation, refers to the creative experience, actions, and input of organizations. Measuring the creative spirit of employees may prove more difficult. An employee suggestion system, a long-time measure of the creative processes of the organization, flourishes today in many firms and is easily measured. Employees are rewarded for their suggestions if they are approved and implemented. Tracking the suggestion rates and comparing them with other organizations is an important benchmarking item for creative capability. Other measures, such as the number of new ideas, comments, or complaints, can be monitored and measured in some way. Formal feedback systems often contain creative suggestions that can lead to improved processes.

Some organizations measure the creative capabilities of employees using inventories and instruments that are often distributed in meetings and training sessions. In other organizations, statements about employee creativity are included in the annual employee feedback survey. Using scaled ratings, employees either agree or disagree with the statements. Comparing actual scores of groups of employees over time reflects the degree to which employees perceive the improvement of creativity in the workplace. Having consistent and comparable measures is still a challenge. Other organizations may monitor the number, duration, and participation rate for creativity training programs. The last decade has witnessed a proliferation of creativity tools, programs, and activity.

EMPLOYEE ATTITUDES
Employee Satisfaction

An important item monitored by most organizations is employee job satisfaction. Using feedback surveys, executives monitor the degree to which employees are satisfied with their employer, policies, the work environment, supervision and leadership, the work itself, as well as other factors. Sometimes, a composite rating is developed to reflect an overall satisfaction value or an index for the organization, division, department, or region.

While job satisfaction has always been an important issue in employee relations, in recent years it has taken on a new dimension because of the linking of job satisfaction to other measures. A classical relationship with job satisfaction is in the attraction and retention of employees. Firms with excellent job satisfaction ratings often attract potential employees. It becomes a subtle, but important, recruiting tool. "Employers of Choice" and "Best Places to Work," for example, often have high job satisfaction ratings. This relationship between job satisfaction and employee retention has attracted increased emphasis in recent years because turnover and retention are critical issues. The previous chapter presented the classic relationship between on-the-job satisfaction and employee turnover. These relationships are now easily developed using human capital management systems, with modules to calculate the correlation between the turnover rates and the job satisfaction scores for the various job groups, divisions, and departments.

Job satisfaction has taken on new dimensions in connection with customer service. Dozens of applied research programs are beginning to show a high correlation between job satisfaction scores and customer satisfaction scores. Intuitively, this seems obvious. A more satisfied employee is likely to provide more productive, friendly, and appropriate customer service. Likewise, a disgruntled employee will provide poor service. As illustrated in the previous chapter, job attitudes (job satisfaction) relate to customer impression (customer satisfaction), which relates to revenue growth (profits). Therefore, if employee attitudes improve, revenues increase. These links, often referred to as a service-profit-chain, create a promising way to identify important relationships between attitudes and profits in an organization.

Organizational Commitment

In recent years, organizational commitment (OC) measures have complemented or replaced job satisfaction measures. Organizational commitment measures go beyond employee satisfaction to include the extent to which the employees identify with organizational goals, mission, philosophy, value, policies, and practices. The concept of involvement and becoming committed to the organization is a key issue. Organizational commitment more closely correlates with productivity and other performance improvement measures, while job satisfaction usually does not. Organizational commitment is often measured the same way as job satisfaction, using attitude surveys and a 5-point or 7-point scale taken directly from employees. As organizational commitment scores improve (taken on a standard index), a corresponding improvement in productivity should exist.

Employee Engagement

A different twist to the organizational commitment measure is the measure that reflects employee engagement. This involves the measures that indicate the extent to which employees are actively engaged in the organization. Consider the case of the Royal Bank of Scotland Group (RBS). With more than 115,000 employees, RBS considered measuring the effectiveness of its investment in people and its impact on business performance to be a strategic imperative and consequently had been building, validating, and introducing a human capital model that demonstrably links people strategies to performance (Bates, 2003).

RBS moved beyond monitoring employee satisfaction and commitment to measuring whether employees actively improved business results, using an employee engagement model to assess the employees' likelihood of contributing to the bank's profits. This model linked the separate HR information in a consistent way, which was then linked to key business indicators. The outputs enabled the business to understand how to influence the bank's results through its people.

To test and validate the model, RBS' HR Research and Measurement team reviewed all the survey instruments used in HR activities (joiner, leaver, "pulse," employee opinion), along with the HR data available in its HRMS database. The HR team decided to put the employee engagement model into practice in the processing and customer contact centers. In these functions, productivity measures are very important, as these affected customer service. Using the amount of work processed as a throughput measure, they found that productivity increased in tandem with engagement levels. The team was also able to establish a link between increasing engagement and decreasing staff turnover.

Hundreds of organizations now use engagement data, not only reflecting the extent to which employees are engaged and connected with productivity and turnover, but also as selection criteria in the competition for the "Best Places to Work" in *Fortune*, described earlier.

EMPLOYEE CAPABILITY
Experience

While experience is an important measure in any organization, it is particularly important in organizations in which the services are complex, technology is critical, and the job requires a tremendous amount of expertise. Experience can be monitored using experience levels within functions, departments, or jobs. For example, tracking the average length of experience in the sales force, the engineering team, or the IT department may be beneficial. Also, measuring experience by job categories, such as the average years of service for sales representatives, software designers, scientists, or financial analysts, may be helpful. Some organizations measure relevant experience in previous organizations. Recognizing the high mobility in certain professions and fields, experience in other organizations may be just as valuable as experience within the current organization, adding to the depth of understanding of capability.

An experienced workforce has a history, with the expertise to handle a variety of situations. Experienced employees can develop new approaches, new processes, and even new products, based on their experience. On the downside, experienced individuals frequently cost the organization more in terms of salaries, bonuses, and benefits. Also, experienced employees are often in demand and may leave the organization when offered new opportunities with higher pay.

Inexperience rears its ugly head with the employee's inability to perform certain tasks and respond to certain issues. This sometimes leads to frustration on the part of management, internal or external customers, or the employees themselves. On the upside, inexperienced individuals are often more open to new ideas and may be more flexible. Because employees usually join an organization at the entry level, lower salaries are often involved when compared to more experienced employees. Also, if the new hires are not successful in the organization, they can be replaced at less cost.

Some organizations focus on building an environment to capitalize on enhancing work experience. Expertise is developed quickly so that an employee will have five years of experience instead of one year of experience repeated five times. Through rotational assignments, work teams, and a variety of processes, knowledge and skills are transferred from the experienced to the inexperienced and are shared throughout the organization. Experienced employees are placed in roles of training, coaching, and mentoring others across the organization—with the focus on retaining the expertise.

Finally, a rich experience base is often the foundation for the culture and history of the organization. Stories abound throughout organizations about highly experienced people with extraordinary capabilities. Individuals who work for the same organization for forty-five years create cultures and legacies. Many executives are proud of their long-term, highly experienced employees and often profile them in publications and websites, propagating their stories of "how things used to be."

Knowledge

As we have explained in this book, knowledge is a critical issue in the human capital arena. Attempting to measure knowledge overlaps with the measurements of other issues, such as innovation, experience, learning, and competencies. However, listing some of the measures that are being monitored to reflect the value and intensity of knowledge in an organization may be helpful.

The first issue is the level of intensity of knowledge. This could be measured as a percent of revenues spent on research and development or sales from patents pending and awarded and various trademarks. Another approach is to measure the percentage of knowledge workers (those who produce knowledge-based outputs) compared to other employees in the organization. Still another is to understand the amount of money spent on knowledge versus physical assets. The comparison of all expenses in these categories reveals the intensity of knowledge spending at the present time, compared to historical and even future projections.

Second, an important measure gaining some interest is the value added per dollar of employee costs. This was originally developed by Professor Ante Pulic of the University of Graz in Austria. This measure reflects the concentration of knowledge workers in an organization. The calculation is based on totaling all the revenues and subtracting non-employee inputs, which is all purchased expenses, excluding expenses for payroll and benefits. This produces a measure of value added. This measure is then divided by the payroll and benefits costs, which Professor Pulic uses as a proxy for human capital. Thus, the ratio of value added, divided by human capital, reflects how much value added has been created by one monetary unit invested in employees. This is what Pulic refers to as the "value added human capital coefficient" (Stewart, 2001).

Third, the market-to-book ratio divides a company's market value by the book value of its assets (physical, financial, and goodwill). This attempts to explain why the large proportion of the market value is allocated to the intangibles, part of which represents the intellectual capital or knowledge in the organization.

Fourth, a measure that is gaining some interest is called Tobin's q, a statistic invented by Nobel Prize-winning economist James Tobin. It is the ratio of a company's market value to the replacement value of its assets. It is developed by adding depreciation back into book value; as q moves above 1, the market seems to be placing increasing value on a company's intangibles.

These are only four of the measures that reflect the extent of knowledge in an organization. Others are being developed. In the future, additional measures from both the financial community and human capital professionals will be developed and, perhaps, some will become standard.

Learning

Learning is another important ingredient to build the experience base and drive success. Many executives strive to create learning organizations in which many opportunities are available for employees to learn new skills, tasks, and processes necessary to become competitive leaders (Purington, Butler, & Fister, 2004).

Some organizations attempt to measure learning by the investment in formal learning programs and processes, measured by the number of hours involved in learning or the number of programs offered. While the numbers are important as a reflection of the commitment to learning, they do not represent results. Other measures are needed.

Measures of learning are easily developed at the micro level (that is, an individual learning program) but are often difficult and vague at the macro level (that is, all learning programs). A learning measurement at the micro level is a measure of new skills and knowledge in formal learning activities. For example, as employees attend learning programs, a learning measure may be an objective measurement such as testing, simulation, or performance demonstration. Sometimes, informal processes such as self-assessment, team assessment, and facilitator assessment are used. Some organizations measure the amount of learning across programs with informal techniques, using consistent rating scales and integrating data to develop a learning assessment for the entire organization (at the macro level).

In other situations, employees must have a certain body of knowledge in critical jobs, and the challenge is to develop meaningful ways to measure the knowledge. An example from Chapter Five underscores the possibilities. In a large pharmaceutical firm, sales representatives needed to have immediate recall of a vast amount of information on each prescription drug they sold. The sales representative had little time to discuss products with physicians—about three to five minutes. During this time, the representative had to have total recall of all the information about the drug. To ensure that all sales representatives had this instant recall, a knowledge assessment process was implemented. Each sales representative took an exam on each product line every six months using a test with a predetermined cutoff score. If the representative scored poorly, he or she would be allowed to try again after preparing for the next exam. After the second try, the individual was reassigned to a sales support position if the score was unsatisfactory. The important issue in this example is that knowledge is critical to success on the job, and learning is obtained from a variety of sources, not just formal learning programs but through research bulletins, product bulletins, learning-on-demand modules, videos, and a variety of other channels. While this may be an unusual case, it underscores the importance of building knowledge in an organization where knowledge capital is king.

Measures of learning will continue to be a challenge at the macro level as executives continue to explore ways in which a learning organization can be measured in terms of outcomes not inputs.

Competencies

Organizations are interested in developing key competencies in particular areas, such as the core mission, key product lines, and proprietary processes. Core competencies are often identified and implemented in critical job groups. Competencies are measured with self-assessments from the individual employee as well as supervisor assessments. In some cases, other inputs may be necessary to measure competencies. This moves the process beyond simply learning new skills, processes, or knowledge to using the combination of skills, knowledge, and behavior on the job to develop an acceptable level of competence to meet competitive challenges.

In recent years, a quantitative process has been used to place a value on competencies. This concept, usually labeled analysis, shows the value of improving competencies of employees and was discussed in Chapters Three and Six. Ratings are taken to measure the competencies on the job prior to specific HR solutions aimed at increasing those competencies. Post-program ratings are also taken. Improvements in competencies are analyzed and a monetary value is placed on the improvement, based on the salaries of the individuals. For example, if an individual improved his or her competencies by 10 percent and no subsequent compensation adjustment to reflect the improvement has been made, then that employee, theoretically, is worth 10 percent more to the organization. If that employee's salary is $50,000, a value of $5,000 has been added. When these values are compared to the cost of the program, the actual return on investment can be developed. While helpful for understanding the impact of competencies and their potential value, this process has some shortcomings in terms of ignoring what employees actually accomplish while using their competencies. Even with its shortcomings, this process is a tool for placing value on competencies and is used in many organizations (Casio, 2001).

Educational Level

In the knowledge economy, education is critical, and many organizations track educational levels as an important human capital measure. This measure is usually the number of years of formal college and university education, where an average of 4 equates to a bachelor level attainment. In technology and research-based organizations, education is vital for certain job groups. Other organizations may track pre-college educational levels and the percent of employees with a high school diploma or equivalent accomplishment.

Tracking educational levels is important relative to specific goals and desired levels. High levels are not always desired. For example, higher educational levels are necessary in a technology firm, such as Microsoft, but are not required in a retail store chain, such as Wal-Mart. Each company should establish a target and measure the educational level against that target. If the educational level is too high, increased turnover may occur because of perceived over-qualification. The employee may leave when another opportunity becomes available.

Unfortunately, the quality of the credentials to determine a particular level of education has deteriorated. Even the standards for a high school diploma, or the equivalent certificate, are not necessarily the same rigorous standards as a few years ago. At the college level, some credentials are not quite as genuine or rigorous as others, or as they were in the past. The educational landscape is covered with opportunities to obtain degrees and diplomas from unaccredited, unqualified, and inferior sources. Some are even fraudulent. Still another quality issue is the explosive use of distance education to obtain degrees. Some educators argue that quality has deteriorated at the expense of convenience.

Attention

This item on our intangible list may surprise some. However, attention is becoming a very serious problem. It made the list because it is difficult to measure accurately and is also difficult to convert to monetary value. Just how serious is this problem? Trillions of documents circulate in U.S. offices annually. Internet traffic doubles every one hundred days. Approximately two hundred messages flow to managers' desktops daily. This is the attention economy in which one of the scarcest resources isn't ideas or even talent but attention itself (Davenport & Beck, 2001). Many researchers who focus on this topic argue that businesses are headed for disaster unless they can overcome the dangerously high attention deficits that threaten to cripple workplaces. For managers and executives, the problems are two-fold. The first issue is how to get the messages and critical information to employees, consumers, and shareholders, while at the same time allocating their attention to any issues, problems, and ideas in the face of overwhelming options. The challenge is to learn how to manage this critical resource.

One of the important challenges is to discuss how attention is measured. The media industry has been concerned about this from the beginning of the industry. Radio and TV led the way by measuring people listening and watching. Nielsen started the measuring by getting people to keep diaries of what they watched. This was quickly replaced by metering technology that recorded the TV shows that a particular TV set was tuned to. This was updated with a people meter whereby household members pushed a button when they started and stopped a particular TV show. This began to provide demographics for TV watching. Obviously, this is very important, as advertisers are willing to pay based on the number of people who will see the message. Some of the monetary payoff was in knowing that the attention received was huge.

Another way to measure attention is to ask people, asking them to keep a record of how many minutes and hours they spend on a particular task or asking them to recall how much time has been provided. However, the authors of the *Attention Economy* (Davenport & Beck, 2001) created a tool called the Attentionscape to advance the state of self-reported attention measurement. The first step is to create a list of items that occupy your attention, listing everything that has caught your attention in the last twenty-four hours. Next, a test is administered for each item on the list. Exhibit 9.2 shows the attention statements and the individuals could respond ranging from "strongly disagree" to "strongly agree." Next, after the responses have been entered, the Attentionscape program turns out a full-color attention chart.

MEASURING ATTENTION

1. I really concentrated on this, spending quality time on it.
2. I'm excited by this; it is something that makes me happy.
3. I did not feel like I could avoid this; it was necessary or imperative.
4. I might have suffered negative consequences had I not paid attention to this; it was not necessarily positive.
5. This was on my mind, but at a subconscious level; I didn't really have to concentrate on it.
6. I chose to focus on this; it was voluntary.

Exhibit 9.2. Measuring Attention.

Scale: Strongly Agree to Strongly Disagree

This approach provides a basis for understanding current patterns and to see where changes are needed. It can help an individual or an entire organization change its attention habits. Showing where deficits exist can be revealing and lead to action items that can correct the imbalances. For more information on this tool, log onto www.attentionscape.net. This is an area commanding a tremendous amount of research to measure attention more accurately with technology and physiological measurement devices.

LEADERSHIP

Leadership is perhaps the most difficult measure to address. On the surface, it seems easy to measure the outcome because effective leadership leads to effective organizations, but putting a monetary value on the consequences of new leadership behavior is not as easy as it appears. Leadership can (and usually does) make the difference in the success or failure of an organization. Without the appropriate leadership behaviors throughout the organization, resources can be misapplied or wasted, and opportunities can be missed. The news and literature are laced with examples of failed leadership at the top. Instances are everywhere of particular top executives having ineffective leadership styles in the way that they manage the team, employees, shareholders, investors, and the public. Some of these failed leadership stories have been painful and high-profile. At the same time, positive examples exist of how a particular leader, such as Jack Welch, has brought extraordinary success throughout the organization over a sustained period. These leaders often are documented in books, articles, and various lists of admired people and clearly make the difference in their organizations. Obviously, the ultimate measure of leadership is the overall success of the organization. Whenever overall measures of success have been achieved or surpassed, they are always attributed to great leadership—perhaps rightfully so. However, attempting to use that kind of success as the only measure of leadership is a cop-out in terms of human capital accountability. Other measures must be in place to develop system-wide monitoring of the quality of leaders and leadership in the organization.

360-Degree Feedback

Measuring leadership can be achieved in many different ways. Perhaps the most common way is 360-degree feedback. Here, a prescribed set of leadership behaviors desired in the organization is assessed by different sources to provide a composite of the overall leadership capability. The sources often come from the immediate manager of the leader, a colleague in the same area, the employees under the direct influence of the leader, internal or external customers, and a self-assessment. Combined, these assessments form a circle of influence (360 degrees).

The measure is basically an observation of behavior captured in a survey, often reported electronically. This 360-degree feedback has been growing rapidly in the United States, Europe, and Asia as an important way to capture overall leadership behavior change. Since behavior change usually has consequences measured as business impact, leadership improvement should be linked to the business in some way. Leadership development programs aimed at improving leadership behavior and driving business improvement often have high payoff with ROI values in the range of 500 percent to 1,000 percent (Phillips & Schmidt, 2004). This is primarily because of the multiplicative effect as leaders are developed and a change of behavior influences important measures in the leader's team. The ROI methodology, which was used to develop these studies, was described in a previous chapter.

Leadership Inventories

Another way to measure leadership is to require the management team to participate in a variety of leadership inventories, assessing predetermined leadership competency statements. The inventories reflect the extent to which a particular leadership style, approach, or even success is in place. These inventories, while popular in the 1970s and 1980s, are often being replaced by the 360-degree feedback process described earlier.

Leadership Perception

Quality of leadership can also be captured from the perspective of employees. In some organizations employees rate the quality of leadership using several dimensions. Top executives are the typical focal point for this evaluation, along with the employees' immediate managers. The measure is usually taken along with the annual feedback survey in the form of direct statements about the leader; the respondent agrees or disagrees using a 5-point scale. This survey attempts to measure the extent to which the followers in a particular situation perceive the quality, success, and appropriateness of leadership behavior as it is practiced.

The outcomes of leadership development are clearly documented in many case studies involving ROI analysis. Of the literally thousands of studies conducted annually, leadership development ROI studies are at the top of the list, not because conducting them is easier, but because of the uncertainty and the unknown aspects of investing in leadership development. Most leadership development will have to pay off in a particular leader's area. Leadership development produces new skills that are applied on the job and produces improvements in the leader's particular work unit. These can vary significantly. The good news is that almost the only way that a general leadership development program involving executives and leaders from a variety of areas can be evaluated is with money, that is, when particular measures are improved. Looking at those measures individually makes little sense; looking at the monetary value as a whole is more worthwhile. The measures are converted to monetary values using one of the methods discussed in Chapter Eight. The monetary values of the improvements from the first year are combined, giving the total value. This ultimately uses an ROI calculation. Several examples of this approach were included in earlier chapters.

JOB CREATION AND ACQUISITION
Productivity Versus Job Growth

One of the more interesting human capital measures is job creation, one of the criteria *Fortune* magazine uses to select organizations for its "Great Place to Work" list. From an employee perspective, job creation offers future opportunities and challenges, possibly preventing an unwanted turnover statistic. From a public policy perspective, job creation and growth are essential. From the image and corporate citizen perspective, job growth suggests community development. However, job growth for the sake of job growth can breed inefficiencies and bureaucracies.

Wall Street often rewards employers when they are more productive and can trim jobs. Just the announcement that jobs are slashed often sends stock prices up. Wall Street is interested in earnings and profits, and minimizing the number of employees can often increase profits, at least in the short term. For example, consider the announcement of layoffs at Nortel Networks, a manufacturer of telecommunications equipment. When Nortel announced 3,500 job cuts, about 10 percent of its workforce, to reduce costs and boost productivity, investors welcomed the news with a 4 percent increase in share price on the same day (Heinzl, 2004).

Importance of Job Creation and Growth

There is a difference between job creation and growth, both of which are simple human capital measures. *Job creation* is the development of new jobs in the organization; *job growth* is the net gain in jobs, recognizing that some jobs are eliminated, automated, or outsourced. From the perspective of employment stability, employment opportunities, and attracting employees to an organization, job growth is very important. Creating new jobs, particularly those with higher skills and higher pay, is an excellent employee relations and human capital strategy. However, as indicated above, job growth must have a companion focus on productivity. Profitable job growth is the key.

Job growth is also important from the aspect of being a good corporate citizen and a champion in the communities. This is one of the selling points for Wal-Mart as they describe their job growth and the effect of the payroll in the community. Job growth increases the tax base; all politicians love employers who add to the number of jobs, particularly those in the higher skill category. The prospect of new jobs often attracts the attention of community and economic development specialists, offering employers incentives for locating to, or expanding in, a particular area. These new jobs add value to the community, but only if they pay well and produce great corporate citizens.

Probably the most notable reward for job growth comes from the incentives of building new plants. For example, a phenomenon has emerged in the United States whereby local community governments provide exorbitant incentives for automobile manufacturing companies to locate plants in their communities. The most notable example is the situation in Alabama. The state now claims four major plants (Mercedes, Toyota, Honda, and Hyundai) employing 33,800 directly and another 96,200 indirectly. For the most part, the industry was lured to Alabama by a variety of incentives (Maynard, 2003).

Job growth can actually reduce employee turnover. Growth often reduces uncertainty, offers new opportunities, and provides advancement opportunities for the existing workforce. These are often the issues that help attract and retain employees. Because of this, operational stability, which has an impact on operational profits, can be enhanced with job growth.

In recent years, much emphasis has been placed on career management. These programs are designed to help individuals grow and develop in the organization as new jobs are added, enhancing both job satisfaction and engagement—two important measures in the human capital area.

Outsourcing is the reverse of job creation, and a subject that has become an important issue in recent years, both politically and economically. It was explored in detail in Chapter One. Outsourcing has played an essential role in most of today's successful businesses. At the organizational level, outsourcing represents a basic structure of businesses, away from the model designed for the Industrial Age to one more appropriate for today's Knowledge Age. Dozens of studies show that outsourcing can reduce costs, improve productivity, allow more focus on core parts of the organization, improve the quality of processes, products, and services, and free up capital for investment in other parts of the business (Corbett, 2004).

A trend has evolved in the United States in which jobs are outsourced to lower-paying subcontractors. Theoretically, this reduces the expense an organization incurs to get a particular job done. This has created a problem for some organizations in which the employees of subcontractors demand the same wages and benefits as the previous job holders. Some subcontractor employee groups have organized and attempted to negotiate contracts to obtain the same compensation levels. If the same level is provided, the primary rationale for outsourcing is negated.

Another politically sensitive issue is the outsourcing of jobs outside the United States, often referred to as off-shoring. While off-shoring takes place in a variety of countries, the focus is currently on India. Highly skilled technical jobs, particularly in the software industry, are being outsourced to other countries, particularly India, because a job can be completed there for as much as one-third the rates in the United States. Some firms are targets of criticism because of their outsourcing practices and are often ridiculed in the press, criticized on websites, and profiled on the nightly news. Some economists believe that off-shoring is only the market system adjusting to a global economy. Others see outsourcing as a drain on national productivity. Regardless of the position, this is an important issue that must be considered in its entirety.

In summary, job creation and growth are important human capital measures, but only if job growth comes with the proper efficiency, profitability, and value add for the community.

Recruitment Sourcing and Effectiveness

Recruitment sourcing is an important measure directly related to the quality and quantity of candidates and, ultimately, to the success of employees and their stability and longevity. Monitoring recruitment sources enables HR to track candidates to the original person, place, ad, or website. Sometimes, the recruiting channel, such as job fairs, ads, websites, or recruiter, is important. Some recruiting sources are more effective than others and tracking the sources and connecting them to subsequent outcomes is important. The recruiting source or channel can be connected to the hire ratio, which is the percentage of candidates actually employed through the channel. For example, some recruiting sources attract people who are always seeking new jobs. While this may be a way to get bodies in the door, it may not be a good source for a long-term employee. For example, Cisco Systems prefers not to hire employees who are actively looking for a job and have a desire to be employed there.

When tracking a source, reflection on the effectiveness of the sources is important. Using the hire ratio, the percentage of candidates flowing through a source divided by those being hired, the organization can measure how well the source provides appropriate, qualified candidates. Perhaps a more important measure is to compare the turnover in the first year (or months) of employment by recruiting source. In some industries where turnover is high, this period may be the first ninety days of employment. The turnover/recruiting source relationship reflects the stability of the recruiting source. A source that generates a high termination rate may not be the appropriate source to use in the future. Conversely, a source that generates long-term, stable employees becomes a preferred channel. The quality of the new candidates from a specific recruiting source is another consideration. Quality is usually a subjective measure taken directly from the candidate's immediate manager. Surveys administered thirty to sixty days after employment will usually pinpoint quality issues.

All the efforts on recruiting sources and the effectiveness of recruiting must be developed within the context of the organization's affirmative action plans and appropriate compliance initiatives and regulations.

Recruitment Efficiency

Another recruitment measure is to analyze the efficiency of the process, usually expressed as the time taken to fill the job, beginning from the point at which the request for a new employee is submitted and ending when the candidate is actually on the job. The average time to recruit, or the average time to fill jobs, is an important issue. Some intermediate time measures, such as time to offer and time to complete the selection processes, may occur. In organizations in which job growth is necessary or there is high turnover, time to recruit is an important consideration. The faster the response the better, as long as quality is there. Thus, recruitment efficiency would have to be mitigated by the quality and stability of the individual selected through the process.

STRESS

Stress is a familiar term with many individuals, particularly with professional employees. Stress makes our list of intangibles because it is sometimes difficult to measure and difficult to place a monetary value on. The thing about stress is that it is everywhere, and to a certain extent it is invisible. Medicines don't necessarily affect it. Either directly or indirectly, we all feel its effects. But it is not new; it has been in existence since the beginning of man—even traced to prehistoric days. Life was very rough and people killed one another often, sometimes for little reason, and they endured routine suffering. Stress has been around for so many years that it is actually part of our systems. From an evolutionary standpoint, it appears that we may be intended to feel unhappy regarding our circumstances. In our bodies, cortisol, a hormone that is triggered by stress, is prevalent. From a natural position, stress is beneficial and nature has engineered us to feel stress (Easterbrook, 2003).

Some researchers have come to the conclusion that stress is inevitable and a part of life and is not necessarily bad. Studies in organizations have attempted to examine the relationship between stress and productivity. These programs typically show that some stress improves productivity, as individuals feel the pressure to perform and the competitive spirit to perform. The stress of working constantly, maintaining focus, and producing as much as possible effectively raises productivity. As stress becomes excessive, productivity can suffer because stress may have some harmful, lingering side-effects that make individuals less productive.

Some suggest that stress protects people because stressed out individuals are wary of circumstances and plan obsessively to avoid problems and dangers, whereas stress-free, "happy-go-lucky" people may not notice that they are walking into a trap. The current levels of stress we experience as professionals cannot be blamed on the Electronics Age, with cell phones, laptops, and BlackBerries. The stress in the Western world has been rampant for many years, with some logical explanations as to why stress may be at a higher level today than in previous years. One of those is that Westerners sleep less than their forefathers did. Years ago, before electricity, people went to bed right after sundown and got up at daybreak. Today, that is not the case, and people stay up later and sleep less. Also, the population has become much more overweight, and with obesity comes more stress. For others, an excessive intake of sugar, a lack of exercise, and watching TV before going to bed can also increase stress levels. Unfortunately, although reducing sugar intake, watching less TV, and exercising would help reduce stress, most people are not willing to change behaviors to do that. Instead, they take medications to help them cope with stress. Fewer people, especially in the United States, take vacations. People have less time to relax, recharge, and reflect. Therefore, they experience more stress. As lifestyles become better, people have more free time, and free time allows them to worry more over problems that may be secondary or even imaginary. Therefore, while things get better, the level of bad feelings remains unaffected, and thus creates stress.

Also, the freedom of choice sometimes provides additional stress, particularly for women. Years ago, most women married, had children, and stayed home to care for their children. Today, women are often faced with the challenge of maintaining a career and a family, or with choosing to put their careers on hold to raise their children. Making these decisions and living with them has added stress to many women's lives.

Stress is a problem that can potentially pose health risks, but it can be treated with medication; however, when medications are used, instead of changing lifestyles, they can, because of their cost, cause conditions to deteriorate. Thus, from an intangible perspective of public policy, programs are aimed at ways to reduce stress in people to help them live healthier and happier lives. In the employment arena, employers are concerned about the stress level of the employees. Some have instituted work-life balance programs to help employees juggle their many roles and bring balance into their work and personal lives.

Wellness and fitness centers are in place sometimes to reduce stress levels and give employees a place to relax, exercise, and ultimately lower stress. Still others establish specific programs aimed at teaching employees how to recognize their stress levels and do something about them.

One interesting study was conducted by the electric utility industry. This industry was experiencing tremendous changes, reducing the number of employees, having employees do multiple tasks, and trying to cope with a major change. When analyzing needs, an initial assessment revealed the following:

1. High levels of stress, caused by deregulation, restructuring, and job changes, existed in work groups.

2. Stress had led to a deterioration of several performance measures, including medical costs, short-term disability, withdrawal, and job satisfaction.

3. Employees were not often fully aware of stress factors and the effects stress had on them and their work.

4. Employees had inadequate skills for coping with stress and adjusting to, managing, and eliminating high-stress situations.

As a result of this diagnosis, the company embarked on a program that involved several components, as shown in Exhibit 9.3.

Departments or work groups of ten or more people who are committed to improving the satisfaction and effectiveness of their teams will benefit by this more comprehensive approach to stress. The process uses the StressMap® tool as the starting point.

WHAT GROUP MEMBERS WILL LEARN
- How to identify sources of stress and their personal response to them.
- That *individuals* have the ability to make a difference in their lives.
- How to take the first steps to enhance personal health and overall performance.
- How to access resources internally and externally, to help teach personal goals.

WHAT THE GROUP/MANAGER WILL LEARN
- Group profile of sources of stress and response patterns.
- Additional information about sources of both work distress and work satisfaction will be obtained through focus groups.

Exhibit 9.3. Stress Management Program for Intact Work Teams.

(Continued)

- New stress reduction skills specific to the needs of the group.
- Development of recommendations for the next steps to improve work satisfaction and productivity

HIGHLIGHTS

- Through completion of a comprehensive self-assessment tool called StressMap®, individuals will be able to immediately score themselves on twenty-one stress scales dealing with work and home life.
- A three-to-four hour StressMap® debriefing session designed to help individuals better interpret their scores. Total of one day.

PRE-COURSE REQUIREMENTS

- Management commitment to the process. Employees to complete the StressMap® tool and submit a confidential copy.

LENGTH AND FORMAT

- Lead time of three to four weeks minimum for preparation and communication.
- Consultant on-site 1½ days.
- Initial follow-up one to two weeks later on-site or by phone to senior management.

Exhibit 9.3. Stress Management Program for Intact Work Teams, Cont'd.

At the heart of this program was the completion of a comprehensive self-assessment tool called StressMap®. Individuals were able to score themselves on twenty-one stress scales dealing with work and home life as well as learn about their preferred coping style and think about patterns that impact their ability to manage stress. In essence, this program prepared employees to cope with stress and deal with it. After this program was tried as a pilot program, impressive results were realized. The program had an impact on medical costs, absenteeism, and employee turnover. Initially, program leaders thought that safety and health costs would decrease, but little change in the number and costs of accidents occurred. However, several intangibles did emerge, including:

- Employee satisfaction
- Teamwork
- Improved relationships with family and friends
- Time savings

• Improved image in the community

• Fewer conflicts

This study was taken all the way to the ROI level using the methodology described in this book. In the pilot program, monetary gains were generated through three payoff measures representing $423,957. The fully loaded cost of the program was $100,848, resulting in a 320 percent ROI. This is one of many studies conducted to show the impact of stress management programs in organizations (Phillips, Stone, & Phillips, 2001).

In summary, excessive stress levels can be measured in the body in the hormone that is triggered by stress. Excessive stress causes several medical conditions that can be observed and monitored. Measuring stress on a stress meter is not possible at the present time. Questionnaires and surveys can show the stress factors and the causes of stress, enabling individuals to understand what may be creating a sense of stress and what they can do about it.

NETWORKING

The concept of networking, particularly social networks, has been a topic for study for many years. Networking makes our list of intangibles because so many programs seem to enhance or facilitate networking, and networking is difficult to measure and often very difficult to convert to monetary value. Inside an organization, social networks are the way in which much of the work gets done. When any person views an organizational chart, the first thing that comes to mind is: Who are the real players? and How do they work together? The lines on the organizational chart, while showing connections between boxes, do not really capture the way in which things are accomplished. From one organization to another, networking is an important way in which ideas are shared and information is exchanged. Recently, the book *The Tipping Point* brought to the forefront the importance of networking (Gladwell, 2001). Through many stories and examples, Gladwell shows how social networks dramatically influence the adoption of ideas and the development of trends in our society.

While networking occurs naturally, for some organizations, it is enhanced through planned activities. Programs are implemented to foster networking within the organization and with other organizations.

Some events in the meetings and events industry are designed to be networking events.

Is there a value in networks? Is there a value in something that seems to be invisible? When many managers, executives, and other professional employees are so busy meeting goals, deadlines, quotas, standards, and their key performance indicators, do they have time for informal networking on their long lists? Only if there is value in the networking.

Several studies have highlighted the value of networking. One study showed that there was a clear connection between networking and performance. This study showed that teams that were allowed to network seamlessly were higher performers than those that were not allowed to network (Cross & Parker, 2004). Another study conducted with Accenture's Institute for Strategic Change showed that the power of networks was an important lever for improving organizational performance. In this study, technology use and individual expertise did not distinguish the high performers from the low performers. What distinguished high performance were larger and more diversified personal networks than those of the average or low performers (Cross, Davenport, & Cantrell, 2003).

Still other research underscores the importance of social networks for learning and innovation. When the concept of sharing information and sharing knowledge is considered, it is assumed that this would occur primarily through the Internet, websites, and search engines. However, in reality, they are often underused because more people turn to colleagues for information. One such study showed that engineers and scientists were roughly five times more likely to turn to a person for information than to an impersonal source, such as a database or a file cabinet (Linden, Ball, Waldir, & Haley, 2002). But these studies beg the question: Can you actually convert networking to monetary value?

Since networking is so difficult, the impact and outcomes are often unique to the individual. The payoff of a particular networking activity is based on what outcome or consequence comes from that mutual relationship. In a study of a large Canadian bank in which an extensive executive development program was implemented, specific effort was placed on converting networking into money. One of the objectives for this extensive leadership development program was to bring leaders throughout the world together in a variety of assignments and programs. The program lasted eighteen months. To track the individual payoff of networking, one-on-one interviews were conducted for all twenty-two participants. Everyone indicated the benefits of networking, but a few offered specific benefits. For example, two participants teamed to develop a web-based product for small business. The value generated was that their product replaced the need to obtain a similar product from an outside contractor and resulted in significant savings. Still another participant obtained new customers in another country as a result of networking. The profit of the new customer was a direct payoff for networking. Still other stories surfaced and, when totaled, the amount of the networking helped push the study to a positive ROI. Without the networking, it would have been negative (Phillips & Phillips, 2007). This study underscores the individuality and payoff of networking.

It is virtually impossible to track certain measures and attribute a net amount of improvement to networking, although it may be possible in certain unique situations. While meaningful measures of networking may be just keeping records of how the network is evolving, a social network analysis survey may be developed whereby individual networking is tracked. This collects information about the individual, the area, and what specifically is being gained from the networking. Obviously, this is a cumbersome process and is now being replaced by technology.

One organization, Ntag, has developed networking badges for each participant at a networking event. The badges are designed to communicate with each other. When one person is talking to another directly, it is documented on the records of both individuals. It records not only who the conversation is with but for how long it is conducted. It can also automatically generate follow-up information to track the outcome of that particular networking event. This is an excellent example of how technology is helping to measure a hard to measure item.

In summary, networking is a powerful process. On the one hand it seems to be invisible, yet it is an important factor in generating ideas, developing new techniques, and improving organizations.

FINAL THOUGHTS

Get the picture? Intangible measures are crucial to reflecting the success of a program. While they may not carry the weight of measures expressed in monetary terms, they are nevertheless an important part of the overall evaluation. Intangible measures should be identified, explored, examined, and monitored for changes linked to programs. Collectively, they add a unique dimension to the evaluation report since most, if not all, programs involve intangible variables. Although some of the most common intangible measures are explored in this chapter, the coverage is not complete. The range of intangible measures is practically limitless.

References

Alden, J. (2006, May/June). Measuring the unmeasurable. *Performance Improvement*, p. 7.

Bates, S. (2003). Linking people measures to strategy. *Research report R-1342-03-RR*. New York: The Conference Board.

Boulton, R.E.S., Libert, B.D., & Samek, S.M. (2000). *Cracking the value code*. New York: HarperBusiness.

Brown, S.F. (2004, September 20). Scientific Americans. *Fortune*, p. 175.

Casio, W. (2000). *Costing human resources* (4th ed.). Cincinnati, OH: Southwestern Publishing.

Corbett, M.F. (2004). *The outsourcing revolution: Why it makes sense and how to do it right*. Chicago, IL: Dearborn Trade Publishing.

Cross, R., Davenport, T., & Cantrell, S. (2003). *Rising above the crowd: How high performance knowledge workers differentiate themselves*. Accenture Institute for Strategic Change Working Paper.

Cross, R., & Parker, A. (2004). *The hidden power of social networks*. Boston, MA: Harvard Business School Press.

Davenport, T.H., & Beck, J.C. (2001). *The attention economy*. Boston, MA: Harvard Business School Press.

Easterbrook, G. (2003). *The progress paradox*. New York: Random House.

Gladwell, M. (2001). *The tipping point*. Boston, MA: Little, Brown.

Heinzl, M. (2004, August 20). Nortel Network announces job cuts. *The Wall Street Journal*.

Linden, A., Ball, R., Waldir, A., & Haley, K. (2002). *Gartner's survey on managing information*. Number: COM-15–0971. Stamford, CT: Gartner, Inc.

Purington, C., Butler, C., & Fister, S. (2004). *Built to learn: The inside story of how Rockwell Collins became a true learning organization*. New York: AMACOM.

Maynard, M. (2003). *The end of Detroit*. New York: Currency Doubleday.

Kandybihn, A. & Kihn, M. (2004). Raising your return on innovation investment. *Strategy + Business*, (35).

McGregor, J. (2006, April 24). The world's most innovative companies. *BusinessWeek,* p. 63.

Phillips, J.J., & Schmidt, L. (2004). *The leadership scorecard.* Woburn, MA: Butterworth-Heinemann.

Phillips, J.J., & Phillips, P.P. (2007). *The human resources scorecard: Improving human performance* (2nd ed.). Woburn, MA: Butterworth-Heinemann.

Santos, J., Doz, Y., & Williamson, P. (2004, Summer). Is your innovation process global? *MIT Sloan Management Review,* p. 31.

Schwartz, E.I. (2004). *Juice: The creative fuel that drives world-class inventors.* Boston, MA: Harvard Business School Press.

Stewart, T. (2001). *The wealth of knowledge: Intellectual capital in the 21st century organization.* New York: Currency.

Ulrich, D., & Smallwood, N. (2003). *Why the bottom line isn't.* Hoboken, NJ: John Wiley & Sons.

CHAPTER TEN

Reporting Results

With results in hand, what's next? Should the results be used to improve the program, change the program design, show the contribution, justify new programs, gain additional support, or build goodwill? How should the data be presented? The worst course of action is to do nothing. Communicating results is as important as achieving results. Achieving results without communicating them is like planting seeds and failing to fertilize and cultivate the seedlings—the yield simply won't be as great. This chapter provides useful information to help present evaluation data to the various audiences using both oral and written reporting methods.

WHY THE CONCERN ABOUT COMMUNICATING RESULTS?

Communicating results is critical to the accountability of learning and development. While communicating achieved results to stakeholders after the program is fully implemented is important, early communication is also important. Continuous communication ensures that information is flowing so that adjustments can be made, and that all stakeholders are aware of the success and issues surrounding the success of the program.

As Mark Twain once said, "Collecting data is like collecting garbage—pretty soon we will have to do something with it." Evaluation data mean nothing unless the findings are communicated promptly to the appropriate audiences so that they will be aware of the results and can take action if necessary. Here are a few important reasons why communication is necessary.

Communication Is Necessary to Make Improvements

Because information is collected at different points during the learning cycle, the communication or feedback to involved groups is the only way they can take action and make adjustments if needed. Thus, the quality and timeliness of communication become critical issues for making necessary adjustments or improvements. After the skills are used, communication is necessary to ensure that the target audience fully understands the results achieved and how the results could either be enhanced in future programs or in the current program, if it is still operational. Communication is the key to making these important adjustments at all phases.

Communication Is Necessary to Explain Contributions

The contribution of the learning and development program, based on the seven types of measures, is confusing at best. The different target audiences will need a thorough explanation of the results. A communication strategy—including techniques, media, and the overall process—will determine the extent to which they understand the contribution. Communicating results, particularly with business impact and ROI, can appear complicated, even with the most sophisticated target audiences. Communication must be planned and implemented with the goal of ensuring that audiences understand the full contribution.

Communication Is a Politically Sensitive Issue

Communication is one of those issues that can cause major problems. Because the results of a program may be closely linked to political issues within an organization, communication can upset some individuals and, at the same time, please others. If certain individuals do not receive the information or it is delivered inconsistently from one group to another, problems can quickly surface. Not only is understanding the information an issue, but issues of fairness, quality, and political correctness make the task more difficult.

Different Audiences Need Different Information

Because so many potential target audiences need to receive communication on the success of a program, the communication must be tailored directly to their needs. A varied audience will command varied needs. Planning and extra effort are necessary to ensure that the audience receives all the information it needs, in the proper format, and at the proper time. A single report for all audiences is inappropriate. The scope, size, medium, and even the actual information will vary significantly from one group to another, making the target audience the key to determining the appropriate method of communication.

Collectively, these reasons make communication a critical issue, although it is often overlooked or under-valued in programs. This chapter builds on this important issue and shows a variety of techniques for accomplishing all types of communication for various target audiences.

PRINCIPLES OF COMMUNICATING RESULTS

The skills required to communicate results effectively are almost as delicate and sophisticated as those needed to obtain results. The style is as important as the substance. Regardless of the message, audience, or medium, a few general principles apply and are explored next.

Communication Must Be Timely

Usually, learning and development program results should be communicated as soon as they are known. From a practical standpoint, delaying the communication until a convenient time is sometimes best, such as the publication of the next newsletter or the next general management meeting. Several questions are relevant. Is the audience ready for the results in view of other issues that may have developed? Is the audience expecting results? When is the best time to have the maximum impact on the audience? Do circumstances dictate a change in the timing of the communication?

Communication Should Be Targeted to Specific Audiences

As stated earlier, communication is usually more effective if it is designed for a specific group. The message should be specifically tailored to the interests, needs, and expectations of the target audience. The results of a program should reflect outcomes at all levels, including the seven types of data developed in this book. Some of the data are developed during the learning and development program and communicated early. Other data are collected after application and implementation and communicated in a follow-up study. The results, in their broadest sense, may involve early feedback in qualitative terms all the way to ROI values in varying quantitative terms.

Media Should Be Carefully Selected

Certain media may be more effective for a particular group than others. Face-to-face meetings may be better than special bulletins. A memo distributed exclusively to top executives may be more effective than the company newsletter. The proper method of communication can help improve the effectiveness of the process.

Communication Should Be Unbiased and Modest

For communication to be effective, separating fact from fiction and accurate statements from opinions is important. Some audiences may accept communication with skepticism, anticipating biased opinions. Boastful statements sometimes turn off recipients, and most of the content is lost. Observable, credible facts carry far more weight than extreme or sensational claims. Although such claims may capture an audience's attention, they often detract from the importance of the results.

Communication Must Be Consistent

The timing and content of the communication should be consistent with past practices. A special communication at an unusual time may provoke suspicion. Also, if a particular group, such as top management, regularly receives communication on outcomes, it should continue receiving communication even if the results are not positive. If unfavorable results are omitted, the impression that only positive results are reported may be given.

Testimonials Are More Effective Coming from Respected Individuals

Opinions are strongly influenced by others, particularly those who are respected and trusted. Testimonials about program results, when solicited from individuals respected by others within the organization, can influence the effectiveness of the message. This respect may be related to leadership ability, position, special skills, or knowledge. A testimonial from an individual who commands little respect and is regarded as a sub-standard performer can have a negative impact.

The Audience's Opinion of the Program Will Influence the Communication Strategy

Opinions are difficult to change, and a negative opinion about a particular program may not change with the mere presentation of facts. However, the presentation of facts alone may strengthen the opinions held by those who already support the program. Presentation of results helps reinforce their position and provides a defense in discussions with others. An L&D team with a high level of credibility and respect may have a relatively easy time communicating results. Low credibility can create problems when trying to be persuasive.

These general principles are important to the overall success of the communication effort. They should serve as a checklist for the L&D team when disseminating results.

THE PROCESS FOR COMMUNICATING RESULTS

The process of communicating results must be systematic, timely, well-planned, and represent seven components that should occur in the sequence shown in Figure 10.1. The first step is one of the most important and consists of an analysis of the need to communicate results from a program. Possibly, a lack of support for the program was identified, and perhaps the need for making changes to or continuing to fund the program was uncovered. Restoring confidence or building credibility for the program is necessary. Regardless of the triggering events, an important first step is to outline the specific reasons for communicating the results.

The second step focuses on a plan for communication. Planning includes numerous agenda items to be addressed in all communica-

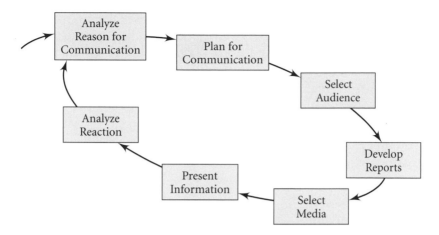

Figure 10.1. A Communications Model for Results.

tions about the program. Planning covers the actual communication, detailing the specific types of data to be communicated, when, and to which groups.

The third step involves selecting the target audiences for communication. Audiences range from top management to past participants, all of whom have their own special communication needs. All groups should be considered in the communication strategy. An artfully crafted, targeted communication may be necessary to win the approval of a specific group.

The fourth step involves developing a report, written material to explain program results. This can include a wide variety of possibilities, from a brief summary of the results to a detailed research report on the evaluation effort. Usually, a complete report is developed. Then selected parts or summaries from the report are used for different media.

Selecting the medium is the fifth step. Some groups respond more favorably to certain methods of communication. A variety of approaches, both oral and written, are available to the program leaders.

The content, detailed information, is presented in the sixth step. The communication is delivered with the utmost care, confidence, and professionalism.

The last step, but not the least significant, is analyzing reactions to the communication. Positive reactions, negative reactions, and a lack of comments are all indicators of how well the information was received and understood. An informal analysis may be appropriate for many situations. For an extensive and more involved communication effort, a formal and structured feedback process may be necessary. Reactions could cause an adjustment to the communication of the same program results to other audiences or provide input for adjustments with future evaluation communications. The various steps in the model are discussed further in the next few sections of this chapter.

THE NEED FOR COMMUNICATION

Because there may be other reasons for communicating results, a list should be tailored to the organization and adjusted as necessary. The reasons for communicating results depend on the specific program, the setting, and the unique needs. Some of the most common are:

- Securing approval for the program and allocating resources of time and money
- Gaining support for the program and its objectives
- Securing agreement on the issues, solutions, and resources
- Building credibility for the learning and development team
- Reinforcing the content and processes used in the program
- Driving action for the improvement of the program
- Preparing participants to provide data for the program evaluation
- Enhancing results throughout the program and the quality of future feedback
- Showing the complete results of the program
- Underscoring the importance of measuring results
- Explaining techniques used to measure results
- Motivating prospective participants to be involved in the program
- Demonstrating accountability for expenditures
- Marketing future programs

Because there may be other reasons for communicating results, the list should be tailored to each organization.

PLANNING THE COMMUNICATIONS

Any successful activity must be carefully planned to produce the maximum results. This is a critical part of communicating the results of the program. Communications planning is important to ensure that each audience receives the proper information at the right time and that appropriate actions are taken. Several issues are important when planning the communication of results:

- What will be communicated?
- When will the data be communicated?
- How will the information be communicated?
- Where will the information be communicated?
- Who will communicate the information?
- Who is the target audience?
- What are the specific actions required or desired?

When an evaluation plan is approved, the communication plan is usually developed, detailing how specific information is developed and communicated to various groups and the expected actions. In addition, this plan details the timeframes for communication and the appropriate groups to receive the information. The evaluator, key managers, and stakeholders need to agree on the extent of detail in the plan. To communicate appropriately with target audiences, three specific documents should be produced. The first report is a detailed impact study showing the approach, assumptions, methodology, and results using all seven data categories. In addition, barriers and enablers are included in the study, along with conclusions and recommendations. The second report should be an eight-page executive summary of the key points, including a one-page overview of the methodology. The third report is a brief, five-page summary of the process and results. These documents should be presented to the different groups according to the list below:

AUDIENCE	DOCUMENT
Participants	Brief summary
Managers of participants	Brief summary

Senior executives	Complete study, executive summary
Learning and development staff	Complete study
Learning and Development Council	Complete study, executive summary
Prospective participants	Brief summary

If this is the first ROI study conducted within an organization, face-to-face meetings should be conducted with the executives. The purpose is to ensure that executives understand the methodology, the conservative assumptions, and each level of data. The barriers, enablers, conclusions, and recommendations are an important part of the meeting. In the future, after two or three studies have been conducted, this group will receive only a one-page summary of key data items. A similar meeting should be conducted with the learning and development council. The council members are advisors to the learning and development department who are usually middle and upper-level executives and managers. Finally, a face-to-face meeting should be held with the learning and development staff in which the complete impact study is described and used as a learning tool.

THE AUDIENCE FOR COMMUNICATIONS

When approaching a particular audience, the following questions should be asked about each potential group:

- Are they interested in the program?
- Do they really want to receive the information?
- Has a commitment to include them in the communications been made?
- Is the timing right for this audience?
- Are they familiar with the program?
- How do they prefer to have results communicated?
- Do they know the evaluator? The learning and development team?
- Are they likely to find the results threatening?
- Which medium will be most convincing to this group?

For each target audience, three actions are needed. To the greatest extent possible, the evaluator or program owner should know and understand the target audience. Also, the evaluator should find out what information is needed and why. Each group will have its own desired amount of information. Some want detailed information, while others want brief information. Rely on the input from others to determine the audience needs. Finally, the learning and development team should try to understand audience bias. Each will have a particular bias or opinion. Some will quickly support the results, whereas others may not support them, and others will be neutral. The team should be empathetic and try to understand differing views. With this understanding, communications can be tailored to each group. This is especially critical when the potential exists for the audience to react negatively to the results.

Basis for Selecting the Audience

The potential target audiences to receive information on program results are varied in terms of job levels and responsibilities. Determining which groups will receive a particular piece of communication deserves careful thought, as problems can arise when one group receives inappropriate information or when another is omitted altogether. A sound basis for proper audience selection is to analyze the reason for the communication, as discussed earlier. Exhibit 10.1 shows common target audiences and the basis for selecting each audience. Several of these stand out as critical. Perhaps the most important audience is the client. This group (or individual) initiates the study, reviews data, and weighs the final assessment of the effectiveness of the program. Another important target audience is the top management group. This group is responsible for allocating resources for the program and needs information to help justify expenditures and gauge the effectiveness of the efforts.

Participants need feedback on the overall success of the effort. Some individuals may not have been as successful as others in achieving the desired results. Communicating the results adds additional pressure to effectively apply the skills and knowledge and improve results in the future. For those achieving excellent results, the communication will serve as reinforcement. Communicating results to participants is often overlooked, with the assumption that, since the study is complete, they do not need to be informed of its success.

Reason for Communication	Primary Target Audiences
• To Secure Approval for the Results	• Client, Top Executives
• To Gain Support for the Program	• Immediate Managers, Team Leaders
• To Secure Agreement with the Issues	• Participants, L&D Team
• To Build Credibility for the L&D Team	• Top Executives
• To Enhance Reinforcement of the Program	• Immediate Managers
• To Drive Action for Improvement	• L&D Team
• To Prepare Participants for the Program	• Immediate Managers, Participants
• To Enhance Results and Quality of Future Feedback	• Participants
• To Show the Complete Results of the Program	• Stakeholders
• To Underscore the Importance of Measuring Results	• Client, L&D Team
• To Explain Techniques Used to Measure Results	• Client, L&D Team
• To Create Desire for a Participant to Be Involved	• Prospective Participants
• To Demonstrate Accountability for Expenditures	• All Employees, Shareholders
• To Market L&D Programs	• Prospective Clients, Executives

Exhibit 10.1. Common Target Audiences.

Communicating with the participants' immediate managers is essential. In many cases, they must encourage participants to apply skills and knowledge from the program. Also, they support and reinforce the objectives of the program. An appropriate return on investment improves the commitment to programs and provides credibility for the learning and development team.

The learning and development team must receive information about results. Whether for a small evaluation or for larger evaluation studies for which a complete team is involved, those who design, develop, facilitate, and implement the program must be provided information on the program's effectiveness. Evaluation information is necessary so adjustments can be made if the program is not as effective as it should have been.

INFORMATION DEVELOPMENT: THE IMPACT STUDY

The type of formal evaluation report depends on the extent of detailed information presented to the various target audiences. Brief summaries of results with appropriate charts may be sufficient for some communication efforts. In other situations, particularly with significant programs requiring extensive funding, the amount of detail in the evaluation report is more crucial. A complete and comprehensive impact study report will usually be necessary. This report can then be used as the basis of more streamlined information for specific audiences and various media. The report may contain the sections detailed in Exhibit 10.2.

General Information
- Background
- Objectives of Study

Methodology for Impact Study
- Levels of Evaluation
- ROI Process
- Collecting Data
- Isolating the Effects of the Program
- Converting Data to Monetary Values

Data Analysis Issues

Results: General Information
- Response Profile
- Success with Objectives

Results: Reaction and Perceived Value
- Data Sources
- Data Summary
- Key Issues

Results: Learning and Confidence
- Data Sources
- Data Summary
- Key Issues

Exhibit 10.2. Format of an Impact Study Report.

(Continued)

Results: Application and Implementation
- Data Sources
- Data Summary
- Key Issues

Results: Impact and Consequences
- General Comments
- Linkage with Business Measures
- Key Issues
- Barriers
- Enablers

Cost of Program

Results: ROI and Its Meaning

Results: Intangible Measures

Conclusions and Recommendations
- Conclusions
- Recommendations

Exhibits

Exhibit 10.2. Format of an Impact Study Report, Cont'd.

While this report is an effective, professional way to present ROI data, several cautions need to be followed. Since this document reports the success of a program involving a group of employees (or participants outside the organization), complete credit for the success must go to the participants and their immediate leaders. Their performance generated the success. Another important caution is to avoid boasting about results. Although the ROI methodology is credible, it still has some subjective issues. Huge claims of success can quickly turn off an audience and interfere with the delivery of the desired message.

The methodology should be clearly explained, along with assumptions made in the analysis. The reader should easily see how the values were developed and how the specific steps were followed to make the process more conservative, credible, and accurate. Detailed statistical analyses should be placed in an appendix.

COMMUNICATION MEDIA SELECTION

Many options are available to communicate program results. In addition to the impact study report, the most frequently used media are meetings, interim and progress reports, the organization's publications, and case studies. Table 10.1 shows the variety of options.

Detailed Reports	Brief Reports	Electronic Reporting	Mass Publications
Impact study	Executive summary	Website	Announcements
Case study (internal)	Slide overview	E-mail	Bulletins
Case study (external)	One-page summary	Blogs	Newsletters
Major articles	Brochure	Video	Brief articles

Table 10.1. A Variety of Options for Communicating Results.

Meetings

If used properly, meetings are fertile opportunities for communicating program results. All organizations have a variety of meetings, and some may provide the proper context for program results. Throughout the chain of command, staff meetings are held to review progress, discuss current problems, and distribute information. These meetings can be an excellent forum for discussing the results achieved in a program when it relates to the group's activities. Results can be sent to executives for use in staff meetings, or a member of the L&D team can attend the meeting to make the presentation.

Regular meetings with management groups are quite common. Typically, items are discussed that will possibly help their work units. A discussion of a learning and development program and the subsequent results can be integrated into the regular meeting format. A few organizations have initiated periodic meetings for all key stakeholders, in which the program leader or evaluator reviews progress and discusses next steps. A few highlights of the program results can be helpful to build interest, commitment, and support for the program going forward.

Interim and Progress Reports

Although usually limited to large evaluation programs, a highly visible way to communicate results is through interim and routine memos and reports. Published or disseminated by e-mail on a periodic basis, they are designated to inform management about the status of the study, to communicate the interim results achieved, and to activate needed changes and improvements.

A more subtle reason for the interim report is to gain additional support and commitment from the management group and to keep the study going. This report is produced by the evaluator and distributed to a select group of stakeholders in the organization. The format and scope may vary considerably and may include a schedule of planned steps/activities, a brief summary of reaction and learning evaluations, initial results achieved from participants, and various spotlights to recognize team members or participants. Other topics may be appropriate. When produced in a professional manner, the interim report can improve management support and commitment.

Routine Communication Tools

To reach a wide audience, the evaluator can use internal, routine publications. Whether a newsletter, magazine, newspaper, or electronic file, these types of media usually reach all employees or stakeholders. The information can be quite effective if communicated appropriately. The scope should be limited to general interest articles, announcements, and interviews.

Results communicated through these types of media must be significant enough to arouse general interest. For example, a story with the headline, "Safety training helps produce one million hours without a lost-time accident," will catch the attention of many people because they may have participated in the program and can appreciate the significance of the results. Reports on the accomplishments of a group of participants may not create interest unless the audience relates to the accomplishments.

For many programs, results are achieved weeks or even months after the program is completed. Participants need reinforcement from many sources. If results are communicated to a general audience, additional pressure may exist to continue the program or similar ones in the future.

Stories about participants involved in the program and the results they achieve create a favorable image. Employees are made aware that the organization is investing time and money to improve performance and prepare for the future. This type of story provides information that employees otherwise may not have known and sometimes creates a desire to participate if given the opportunity.

General audience communication can bring recognition to program participants, particularly those who excel in some aspect of the program application and implementation. When participants deliver unusual performance, public recognition can enhance their self-esteem and their desire to continue their excellent performance. Many human interest stories can come from the use of learning and development programs. A rigorous program with difficult requirements can provide the basis for an interesting story on participants who made the extra effort to implement what they learned.

E-Mail and Electronic Media

Internal and external web pages on the Internet, company-wide intranets, and e-mail are excellent vehicles for releasing results, promoting ideas, and informing employees and other target groups about results. E-mail, in particular, provides a virtually instantaneous means with which to communicate and solicit responses from large numbers of people. For major program evaluation, some organizations create blogs to present results and secure reaction, feedback, and suggestions.

Program Brochures and Pamphlets

A brochure might be appropriate for programs conducted on a continuing basis, where participants have produced excellent results. Also, a brochure may be appropriate when the audience is large and continuously changing. The brochure should be attractive and present a complete description of the program, with a major section devoted to results obtained with previous participants, if available. Measurable results and reactions from participants, or even direct quotes from individuals, could add spice to an otherwise dull brochure.

Case Studies

Case studies represent an effective way to communicate the results of a program. A typical case study describes the situation, provides appropriate background information (including the events that led to the program), presents the techniques and strategies used to develop the study, and highlights the key issues in the program implementation. Case studies tell an interesting story of how the program was implemented and the evaluation was developed, including the problems and concerns identified along the way.

Case studies have value for both internal use and external use. As shown in Exhibit 10.3, the internal use is to build understanding and capability and support internally. Case studies are impressive to hand to a potential client and somewhat convincing for others who are seeking data about the success of learning and development programs. Also, externally, case studies can be used to bring exposure and recognition to the learning and development team and help the organization brand its overall learning function and, in some cases, the organization. A variety of publication outlets are available for case studies—not only in the learning and development print space, but in general publications as well.

INTERNAL USE	EXTERNAL PUBLICATION
Communicate results	Provide recognition to participants
Teach others	Improve image of function
Build a history	Enhance brand of department
Serve as a template	Enhance image of organization
Make an impression	

Exhibit 10.3. Internal and External Use of Case Studies.

PRESENTING INFORMATION
Routine Feedback on Program Progress

One of the most important reasons for collecting reaction and learning data is to provide feedback so that adjustments or changes can be made throughout the life of a learning and development program. For most programs, reaction and learning data are routinely collected and quickly communicated to a variety of groups. Sometimes, application and impact data are routinely communicated using a feedback action plan designed to provide information to several audiences using a variety of media. Some of these feedback sessions result in identifying specific actions that need to be taken. This process becomes comprehensive and has to be managed in a very proactive way.

The following steps are recommended for providing feedback and managing the feedback process. Many of the steps and issues follow the recommendations of Peter Block in his successful consulting book, *Flawless Consulting* (Block, 2000).

- *Communicate quickly.* Whether good news or bad news, it is important to let individuals involved in the program have the information as soon as possible. The recommended time for providing feedback is usually a matter of days and certainly no longer than a week or two after the results are known.

- *Simplify the data.* Condense the data into a very understandable, concise presentation. This is not the situation for detailed explanations and analysis.

- *Examine the role of the learning and development team and the client in the feedback situation.* Sometimes, the learning and development leader is the judge, jury, prosecutor, defendant, or witness. On the other hand, sometimes the client is the judge, jury, prosecutor, defendant, or witness. Examining the respective roles in terms of reactions to the data and the actions that need to be taken is important.

- *Use negative data in a constructive way.* Some of the data will show that things are not going so well, and the fault may rest with the L&D leader or the client. In either case, the story basically changes from "Let's look at the success we've made" to "Now we know which areas to change."

- *Use positive data in a cautious way.* Positive data can be misleading, and if they are communicated too enthusiastically, they may create expectations beyond what may materialize later. Positive data should be presented in a cautious way—almost in a discounting mode.

- *Choose the language of the meeting and communication carefully.* The language used should be descriptive, focused, specific, short, and simple. Language that is too judgmental, macro, stereotypical, lengthy, or complex should be avoided.

- *Ask the client for reactions to the data.* After all, the client is the number one customer, and the client's reaction is critical because it is most important that the client be pleased with the program.

- *Ask the client for recommendations.* The client may have some good recommendations of what needs to be changed to keep a program on track or put it back on track if it derails.

- *Use support and confrontation carefully.* These two issues are not mutually exclusive. At times, support and confrontation are needed for the same group. The client may need support and yet be confronted for lack of improvement or sponsorship. The L&D team may be confronted on the problem areas that are developed, but may need support as well.

- *React and act on the data.* The different alternatives and possibilities should be weighed carefully to arrive at the adjustments and changes that will be necessary.

- *Secure agreement from all key stakeholders.* This is essential to ensure that everyone is willing to make adjustments and changes that may be necessary.

- *Keep the feedback process short.* Letting the process become bogged down in long, drawn-out meetings or lengthy documents is a bad idea. If this occurs, stakeholders will avoid the process instead of being willing participants.

Following these steps will help move the program forward and provide important feedback, often ensuring that adjustments are supported and made.

The Presentation of Results to Senior Management

Perhaps one of the most challenging and stressful communications is presenting an impact study to the senior management team, which also serves as the client for the evaluation study. The challenge is convincing this highly skeptical and critical group that outstanding results have been achieved (assuming they have) in a very reasonable timeframe, addressing the salient points, and making sure the managers understand the process. Two particular issues can create challenges. First, if the results are very impressive, making the managers believe the data may be difficult. On the other extreme, if the data are negative, ensuring that managers don't overreact to the negative results and look for someone to blame will be a challenge. Several guidelines can help make sure this process is planned and executed properly.

Plan a face-to-face meeting with senior team members for the first one or two major impact studies. If they are unfamiliar with the ROI methodology, a face-to-face meeting is necessary to make sure they understand the process. The good news is that they will probably attend the meeting because they have not seen ROI data developed for this type of program. The bad news is that it takes a lot of time, usually one hour for this presentation. After a group has had a face-to-face meeting with a couple of presentations, an executive summary may suffice. At this point, they understand the process, so a shortened version may be appropriate. After the target audience is familiar with the process, a brief version may be necessary, which will involve a one- to two-page summary with charts and graphs showing the six types of measures.

When making the initial presentation, the results should not be distributed beforehand or even during the session but saved until the end of the session. This will allow enough time to present the process and react to it before the target audience sees the ROI calculation. Present the ROI methodology step-by-step, showing how the data were collected, when they were collected, who provided the data, how the effect of the program was isolated from other influences, and how data were converted to monetary values. The various assumptions, adjustments, and conservative approaches should be presented along with the total cost of the program, so that the target audience will begin to buy into the process of developing the ROI.

When the data are actually presented, the results are presented one level at a time, starting with Level 1, moving through Level 5, and ending with the intangibles. This allows the audience to see the reaction, learning, application and implementation, business impact, and ROI. After some discussion on the meaning of the ROI, the intangible measures should be presented. Allocate time for each level as appropriate for the audience. This helps overcome the potentially emotional reactions to a very positive or negative ROI.

Show the consequences of additional accuracy if it is an issue. The tradeoff for more accuracy and validity often means more expense. Address this issue whenever necessary, agreeing to add more data if required. Collect concerns, reactions, and issues for the process and make adjustments accordingly for the next presentation.

Collectively, these steps will help prepare for and present one of the most critical meetings in the ROI process. Figure 10.2 shows this approach to this important meeting with the sponsor. Improving communications with this group requires developing an overall strategy and a defined purpose.

Purpose of the Meeting	Meeting Ground Rules
• Create awareness and understanding of impact • Build support for the ROI methodology • Communicate results of study • Drive improvement from results • Cultivate effective use of the ROI methodology	• Do not distribute the impact study until the end of the meeting • Be precise and to the point • Avoid jargon and unfamiliar terms • Spend less time on the lower levels of evaluation data • Present the data with a strategy in mind

Presentation Sequence

1. Describe the program and explain why it is being evaluated
2. Present the methodology process
3. Present the input and indicators
4. Present the reaction and learning data
5. Present the application data
6. List the barriers and enablers to success
7. Address the business impact
8. Show the costs
9. Present the ROI
10. Show the intangibles
11. Review the credibility of the data
12. Summarize the conclusions
13. Present the recommendations

Figure 10.2. Presenting the Impact Study to Executive Sponsors.

Streamlining the Communication

Obviously, executives and management groups will not come to a face-to-face meeting for repeated evaluation studies, nor will they read a complete impact study. Therefore, an executive summary should be used. This represents about a six- to ten-page summary of the entire report. Still, the process can be further streamlined by considering a one-page summary, as shown in Exhibit 10.4. This summary, representing an impact study on a leadership program for first-level managers, shows the key data collected. This is the ultimate in efficient communication, but is effective only when the managers understand the different types of data. The audiences must be educated on the

Program Title:	The Leadership Challenge
Target Audience:	First-Level Managers (2000)
Duration:	Four days

RESULTS					
Level 1: Reaction	Level 2: Learning	Level 3: Application	Level 4: Impact	Level 5: ROI	Intangible Benefits
Exceeded 4.0 rating except on one measure (3.9 for provided me with new information)	48 percent improvement in skills or knowledge	43 percent of time spent on tasks requiring skills or knowledge	Improvements in sales, quality, productivity, costs, and efficiency. Total improvement: $329,201	105 percent	Job satisfaction Improved teamwork Improved communication

Technique to Isolate Effects of Program:	Participant estimates
Techniques to Convert Data to Monetary Value:	Standard values with external experts and participant estimates
Fully Loaded Program Costs:	$160,754

Exhibit 10.4. Sample One-Page ROI Impact Study.

methodology so they can understand the streamlined communications. You can use this streamlined communication on a progressive basis, gradually moving managers to this more streamlined method.

Building Scorecards

Ultimately, the management team will need a scorecard showing the impact of L&D overall. This would show evaluation data that bridges all the L&D programs and utilizes all the different types of data outlined in this book. The concept of building a broader scorecard called the macro scorecard is explained in Figure 10.3. Essentially, when any program is evaluated at Level 0 or Level 1, for example, this represents a scorecard of performance for that program. As the evaluation data are collected at higher levels including Levels 2, 3, and 4, each program essentially has a scorecard of performance. These are micro-level scorecards. The challenge is to take selective data sets out of the micro scorecard and use them in the overall macro-level scorecard. For example, the typical Level 1 evaluation form may contain twelve to fifteen items. This is entirely too much data to include on the overall macro scorecard.

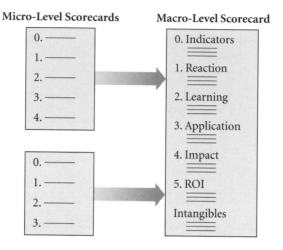

Figure 10.3. Micro-Level to Macro-Level Scorecard.

An example of a macro scorecard representing a large banking organization is shown in Exhibit 10.5. In this example, over forty measures are collected, representing key data points collected in the evaluation of learning and development programs across the organization. These data sets represent very powerful data, particularly as the data are reported at the higher levels.

0. INDICATORS

1. Number of employees involved

2. Total hours of involvement

3. Hours per employee

4. Training investment as a percent of payroll

5. Cost per participant

I. REACTION AND PLANNED ACTION

1. Percent of programs evaluated at this level

2. Ratings on seven items versus target

3. Percent with action plans

4. Percent with ROI forecast

Exhibit 10.5. Sample Scorecard Report.

II. LEARNING

1. Percent of programs evaluated at this level

2. Types of measurements

3. Self-assessment ratings on three items versus targets

4. Pre/post—average differences

III. APPLICATION

1. Percent of programs evaluated at this level

2. Ratings on three items versus targets

3. Percent of action plans complete

4. Barriers (list of top ten)

5. Enablers (list of top ten)

6. Management support profile

IV. BUSINESS IMPACT

1. Percentage of programs evaluated at this level

2. Linkage with measures (list of top ten)

3. Types of measurement techniques

4. Types of methods to isolate the effects of programs

5. Investment perception

V. ROI

1. Percent of programs evaluated at this level

2. ROI summary for each study

3. Methods of converting data to monetary values

4. Fully loaded cost per participant

INTANGIBLES

1. List of intangibles (top ten)

2. How intangibles were captured

AWARDS

1. ASTD

2. Corporate University awards

3. *CLO* magazine

4. *Training* magazine

Exhibit 10.5. Sample Scorecard Report, Cont'd.

REACTIONS TO COMMUNICATION

The best indicator of how effectively the results of a program have been communicated is the level of commitment and support from the managers, executives, and sponsors. The allocation of requested resources and strong commitment from top management are tangible evidence of management's positive perception of the L&D results. In addition to this macro-level reaction, a few techniques can measure the effectiveness of the communication efforts.

Whenever results are communicated, the reaction of the target audiences can be monitored. These reactions may include non-verbal gestures, oral remarks, written comments, or indirect actions that reveal how the communication was received. Usually, when results are presented in a meeting, the presenter will have some indication of how the results were received by the group. The interest and attitudes of the audience can usually be quickly evaluated. Comments about the results—formal or informal—should also be noted and tabulated.

Learning and development team meetings are an excellent arena for discussing the reaction to communicating results. Comments can come from many sources, depending on the particular target audiences. When major program results are communicated, a feedback questionnaire may be used for an entire audience or a sample of the audience. The purpose of this questionnaire is to determine the extent to which the audience understood and/or believed the information presented. This is practical only when the effectiveness of the communication has a significant impact on future actions of the L&D staff.

USING EVALUATION DATA

One of the most important reasons for collecting evaluation data and communicating them to different audiences is to make improvements. After all, the principle premise for evaluation is to improve processes—not necessarily to evaluate the performance of a particular group. With process improvement in mind, Table 10.2 shows some of the typical uses of evaluation data as they relate to the different levels. Many of the uses focus on making the programs better for the future. Others are involved in improving support through reinforcement and commitment for learning and development programs.

Use of Evaluation Data	Appropriate Level of Data				
	1	2	3	4	5
Adjust Program Design	✓	✓			
Improve Program Delivery	✓	✓			
Influence Application and Impact			✓	✓	
Enhance Reinforcement for Learning			✓		
Improve Management Support for Learning			✓	✓	
Improve Stakeholder Satisfaction			✓	✓	✓
Recognize and Reward Participants		✓	✓	✓	
Justify or Enhance Budget				✓	✓
Develop Norms and Standards	✓	✓	✓		
Reduce Costs		✓	✓	✓	✓
Market L&D Programs	✓		✓	✓	✓
Expand Implementation to Other Areas				✓	✓

Table 10.2. Using Evaluation Data.

Someone or some group must be charged with the responsibility of ensuring that these appropriate actions are taken. Sufficient effort is rarely focused on this area. Therefore, there is a lack of follow-through. If these ultimate changes or improvements are not made, much of the value of the evaluation is lost. For many programs, particularly those of a comprehensive nature, the original project plan for the evaluation study includes all the steps throughout the process—communicating results, tracking the improvements that must be made, and making adjustments and changes to the program. This ensures that the appropriate use of data does not get left out or that the resources are not applied to it. This is a final piece of the puzzle.

FINAL THOUGHTS

The final step in the evaluation of learning and development programs, communication of results, is a crucial step in the overall evaluation process. If this step is not taken seriously, the full impact of the results will not be realized and the study may be a waste of time. The chapter began with general principles and steps for communicating results, which can serve as a guide for any significant communication effort.

The various target audiences were discussed and, because of its importance, emphasis was placed on the executive group. A suggested format for a detailed evaluation report was also provided. Much of the chapter included a presentation of the most commonly used media for communicating results, including meetings, client publications, and electronic media. A final issue regarding the ROI methodology will be discussed in the next chapter: implementing a comprehensive measurement system.

Reference

Block, P. (2000). *Flawless consulting* (2nd ed.) San Francisco, CA: Pfeiffer.

CHAPTER ELEVEN

Implementing and Sustaining a Comprehensive Evaluation System

⟋⟋⟍ E ven the best-designed process, model, or technique is virtually worthless unless it is effectively and efficiently integrated within the organization. Often, resistance to the additional evaluation arises. Some of this resistance is based on fear, misunderstanding, and lack of knowledge. Some is real, based on actual barriers and obstacles. Although the process presented in this book is a step-by-step, methodical, and simplistic procedure, it can fail if it is not integrated properly, fully accepted, and supported by those who must make it work within the organization. This chapter focuses on some of the key issues needed to overcome resistance to implementing a comprehensive evaluation process in an organization.

WHY THE CONCERN ABOUT IMPLEMENTING AND SUSTAINING EVALUATION?

With any new process or change, there is resistance. Resistance may be especially great when implementing a process as complex as ROI. To implement a comprehensive evaluation process and sustain it as an important accountability tool, the resistance must be minimized or removed. Successful implementation essentially equates to overcoming resistance. The four key reasons why a detailed plan should be in place to overcome resistance are explained below.

Resistance Is Always Present

Resistance to change is a constant. Sometimes, good reasons for resistance are present, but it often exists for the wrong reasons. The important point is to sort out both kinds of resistance and try to dispel the myths. When legitimate barriers are the basis for resistance, minimizing or removing them altogether is the challenge.

Implementation Is Key

As with any process, effective implementation is the key to its success. This occurs when the new technique, tool, or process is integrated into the routine framework. Without effective implementation, even the best process will fail. A process that is never removed from the shelf will never be understood, supported, or improved. Clear-cut steps must be in place for designing a comprehensive implementation process that will overcome resistance.

Consistency Is Needed

As this process is implemented, consistency is an important consideration. With consistency comes accuracy and reliability. To ensure that consistency is achieved, a clearly defined process is needed with procedures to use each time an evaluation is conducted. Proper implementation will ensure that this occurs.

Efficiency Is Necessary

Cost control and efficiency will always be issues in any major undertaking, and evaluation is no exception. During implementation, tasks must be completed efficiently and effectively. Doing this will help ensure that the process costs are kept to a minimum, time is used appropriately, and the process remains affordable.

IMPLEMENTING THE PROCESS: OVERCOMING RESISTANCE

Resistance appears in many ways, as comments, remarks, actions, or behaviors. Exhibit 11.1 shows some comments that indicate open resistance to the increased evaluation. Each of these represents an issue that needs to be resolved or addressed in some way. A few of the comments are based on realistic barriers, while others are based on myths that must be dispelled. Sometimes, resistance to the process reflects underlying concerns. The individuals involved may have a fear of losing control of their processes, and others may feel that they are vulnerable to actions that may be taken if the process is not successful. Still others may be concerned about any process that brings change or requires additional learning efforts.

OPEN RESISTANCE

- It costs too much.
- It takes too much time.
- Who is asking for this?
- This is not in my job duties.
- I did not have input on this.
- I do not understand this.
- What happens when the results are negative?
- How can we be consistent with this?
- This looks too subjective.
- Our managers will not support this.
- ROI is too narrowly focused.
- This is not practical.

Exhibit 11.1. Typical Objections to the Use of the ROI Methodology.

Program team members may resist evaluation and ROI and openly make comments similar to those listed in the exhibit. Heavy persuasion and evidence of tangible benefits may be needed to convince learning and development team members that this is a process that must be used and is in their best interest to make successful. Although most clients would like to see the results of the learning and development program, they may have concerns about the information they must provide and about whether their performance is being judged along with the evaluation of the program. In reality, they may express some of the same fears listed in the exhibit.

The challenge is to implement evaluation systematically and consistently so that it becomes normal business behavior and a routine and standard process designed into programs. The implementation necessary to overcome resistance covers a variety of areas. Figure 11.1 shows actions outlined in this chapter, presented as building blocks to overcoming resistance. They are all necessary to establish the proper framework to dispel myths and remove or minimize barriers. The remainder of this chapter presents specific strategies and techniques around each of the ten building blocks identified in Figure 11.1. They apply equally to the learning and development staff and to the client organization, and no attempt is made to separate the two in this presentation. In some situations, a particular strategy would work best with the learning and development team. In reality, all may be appropriate for both groups in certain cases.

Figure 11.1. Building Blocks for Overcoming Resistance.

ASSESSING THE CLIMATE

As a first step toward implementation, some organizations assess the current climate for achieving results. One way to do this is to use a survey to determine current perspectives of the management team and other stakeholders in regard to results of learning and development programs. The Appendix shows an example of a survey designed for this purpose. Another way is to conduct interviews with key stakeholders to determine their willingness to implement additional measurements and evaluation. With an awareness of the current status, the learning and development leaders can plan for significant changes and pinpoint particular issues that need support as more evaluation.

DEVELOPING ROLES AND RESPONSIBILITIES

Defining and detailing specific roles and responsibilities for different groups and individuals addresses many of the resistance factors and helps pave a smooth path for implementing additional evaluation.

Identifying a Champion

As an early step in the process, one or more individual(s) should be designated as the internal leader or champion for evaluation. As in most change efforts, someone must take responsibility for ensuring that evaluation is implemented successfully. This leader serves as a champion and is usually the one who understands measurement and evaluation best and sees vast potential for its contribution. More importantly, this leader is willing to teach others and will work to sustain sponsorship.

Developing the Evaluation Leader

The evaluation leader is usually a member of the learning and development team who has the responsibility for evaluation. This person holds a full-time position in larger learning and development teams or a part-time position in smaller teams. In a few situations, client organizations may also have an evaluation leader who pursues evaluation from the client's perspective. The typical job title for a full-time evaluation leader is manager of measurement and evaluation. Some organizations assign this responsibility to a team and empower it to lead the evaluation effort.

In preparation for this assignment, individuals usually have special training that builds specific skills and knowledge. The role of the evaluation leader is quite broad and serves a variety of specialized duties. In some organizations, the implementation leader can take on many roles, ranging from problem solver to communicator to cheerleader.

Leading the evaluation process is a difficult and challenging assignment that requires special skill building. Fortunately, programs are available that teach these skills. For example, one such program is designed to certify individuals who are assuming a leadership role in the implementation of the ROI evaluation (www.roiinstitute.net). This certification is built around ten specific skill sets linked to successful evaluation implementation, focusing on critical areas of data collection, isolating the effects of the program, converting data to money, presenting evaluation data, and building capability. This process is quite comprehensive but may be necessary to build the appropriate skills for taking on this challenging assignment.

Establishing a Task Force

Making evaluation work may require the use of a task force. A task force is usually a group of individuals from different parts of the learning and development team or client team who are willing to develop a comprehensive measurement and evaluation process and implement it in the organization. The selection of the task force may involve volunteers, or participation may be mandatory, depending on specific job responsibilities. The task force should represent the necessary cross section for accomplishing stated goals. Task forces have the additional advantage of bringing more people into the process and developing more ownership and support for the evaluation. The task force must be large enough to cover the key areas, but not so large that it becomes cumbersome and difficult to function. Six to twelve members is a good size.

Assigning Responsibilities

Determining specific responsibilities is a critical issue because confusion can arise when individuals are unclear about their specific assignments in the evaluation process. Responsibilities apply to two areas. The first is the measurement and evaluation responsibility of the entire learning and development team. Everyone involved in learning and development must have some responsibility for measurement and evaluation. These responsibilities include providing input on the design of instruments, planning specific evaluations, analyzing data, and interpreting the results. Typical responsibilities include:

- Ensuring that the initial analysis for the program includes specific business impact measures;

- Developing specific application objectives and business impact objectives for the program;
- Keeping participants focused on application and impact objectives;
- Communicating rationale and reasons for evaluation;
- Assisting in follow-up activities to capture application and business impact data; and
- Providing technical assistance for data collection, data analysis, and reporting.

While having each member of the learning and development team involved in all these activities may not be appropriate, each individual should have at least one or more responsibilities as part of his or her routine job duties. This assignment of responsibility keeps evaluation from being disjointed and separated during programs. More importantly, it brings accountability to those directly involved in measurement and evaluation.

Another issue involves technical support. Depending on the size of the learning and development team, establishing a group of technical experts to provide assistance with evaluation may be helpful. When this group is established, the learning and development team must understand that the experts are not there to relieve them of evaluation responsibilities only to supplement with technical expertise. These technical experts are typically the individuals who have participated in the certification process to build special skills. When this type of support is developed, responsibilities involve six key areas:

1. Designing data collection instruments;
2. Providing assistance for developing an evaluation strategy;
3. Analyzing data, including specialized statistical analyses;
4. Interpreting results and making specific recommendations;
5. Developing an evaluation report or case study to communicate overall results; and
6. Providing technical support in all phases of the measurement and evaluation.

The assignment of responsibilities for evaluation is also an issue that needs attention throughout the evaluation process. Although the learning and development team must have specific responsibilities during an evaluation, requiring others to be in support functions to help with data collection is not unusual. These responsibilities are defined when a particular evaluation strategy plan is developed and approved.

ESTABLISHING GOALS AND PLANS

Establishing goals, targets, and objectives is critical to the implementation, particularly when several programs are planned. This includes detailed planning documents for the overall process as well as individual evaluation studies. Several key issues relating to goals and plans are covered here.

Setting Evaluation Targets

Establishing specific targets for evaluation levels is an important way to make progress with measurement and evaluation. As discussed throughout this book, not all programs should be evaluated to the ROI level. Knowing in advance to which level a program will be evaluated helps in planning which measures will be needed and how detailed evaluation must be at each level. Exhibit 11.2 shows an example of the targets for evaluation at each level. Target-setting should be completed early in the process with the full support of the learning and development team. Also, if practical and feasible, the targets should have the approval of key managers—particularly the senior management team.

LEVEL	TARGET
Level 1, Reaction and Planned Action	100 percent
Level 2, Learning and Confidence	80 percent
Level 3, Application and Implementation	30 percent
Level 4, Business Impact and Consequences	10 percent
Level 5, ROI	5 percent

Exhibit 11.2. Evaluation Targets in a Large Organization with Many Programs.

Developing a Timetable for Implementation

An important part of implementing additional measurement and evaluation is establishing timetables for the complete implementation. This document becomes a master plan for the completion of the different elements presented earlier. Beginning with forming a team and concluding with meeting the targets previously described, this schedule is a program plan for transitioning from the present situation to the desired future situation. The items on the schedule include developing specific ROI studies, building staff skills, developing policy, and teaching managers the process. Figure 11.2 shows an example of this plan. The more detailed the document, the more useful it becomes. The program plan is a living, long-range document that should be reviewed frequently and adjusted as necessary. More importantly, it should always be familiar to those who are working with evaluation.

	J	F	M	A	M	J	J	A	S	O	N	D	J	F	M	A	M	J
Team Formed	█																	
Responsibilities Defined	█																	
Policy Developed		█	█															
Targets Set		█																
Workshops Developed			█	█	█	█												
ROI Study (A)						█	█	█										
ROI Study (B)								█	█	█	█							
ROI Study (C)										█	█	█	█					
L&D Teams Trained							█	█										
Managers Trained																█	█	
Support Tools Developed				█	█													
Guidelines Developed		█	█	█	█													

Figure 11.2. Implementation Plan for a Large Organization.

REVISING OR DEVELOPING POLICIES AND GUIDELINES

Another part of planning is revising or developing the organization's policy concerning measurement and evaluation. The policy statement contains information developed specifically for the measurement and evaluation process. It is developed with input from the learning and development team and key managers or stakeholders. Sometimes, policy issues are addressed during internal workshops designed to build skills for measurement and evaluation. The policy statement addresses critical issues that will influence the effectiveness of the measurement and evaluation process. Typical issues include: adopting the five-level framework presented in this book, requiring Level 3 and 4 objectives for some programs, and defining responsibilities for the learning and development team.

Policy statements are important because they provide guidance and direction for the staff and others who work closely with evaluation. These individuals keep the process clearly focused and enable the group to establish goals for evaluation. Policy statements also provide an opportunity to communicate basic requirements and fundamental issues regarding performance and accountability. More than anything else, they serve as learning tools to teach others, especially when they are developed in a collaborative and collective way. If policy statements are developed in isolation and do not enjoy ownership from the staff and management, they will not be effective or useful.

Guidelines for measurement and evaluation are important for showing how to use the tools and techniques, guide the design process, provide consistency in the ROI process, ensure that appropriate methods are used, and place the proper emphasis on each of the areas. The guidelines are more technical than policy statements and often contain detailed procedures showing how the process is undertaken and developed. They often include specific forms, instruments, and tools necessary to facilitate the process.

PREPARING THE TEAM

Team members may resist additional measurement and evaluation. They often see evaluation as an unnecessary intrusion into their responsibilities, absorbing precious time and stifling their freedom to be creative. The cartoon character Pogo perhaps characterized it best when he said, "We have met the enemy, and he is us." Several issues must be addressed when preparing the program team for ROI implementation.

Involving the Team

For each key issue or major decision involving measurement and evaluation, the team should be involved in the process. As policy statements are prepared and evaluation guidelines developed, team input is essential. Resistance is minimized if the team helped design and develop it. Using meetings, brainstorming sessions, and task forces, the team should be involved in every phase of developing the framework and supporting documents for measurement and evaluation.

Using Measurement and Evaluation as a Learning Tool

One reason the learning and development team may resist measurement and evaluation is that the effectiveness of programs will be fully exposed, putting the team's reputations on the line. They may have a fear of failure. To overcome this, measurement and evaluation should be clearly positioned as a tool for learning and not a tool for evaluating learning and development team performance, at least during its early years of implementation. Team members will not be interested in developing a process that will reflect unfavorably on their performance.

Evaluators can learn as much from failures as from successes. If a program is not working, finding out quickly is best so that the issues are understood first-hand, not from others. If a program is ineffective and not producing the desired results, the failure will eventually be known to clients and/or the management group, if they are not aware of it already. A lack of results will cause managers to become less supportive of the program or other programs in the future. If the weaknesses of programs are identified and adjustments are made quickly, not only will more effective programs be developed, but the credibility and respect for measurement and evaluation will be enhanced.

Teaching the L&D Team

The L&D team and evaluators usually have inadequate skills in measurement and evaluation and will need to develop some expertise. Measurement and evaluation are not always a formal part of their job preparation. Consequently, the evaluators must learn the comprehensive measurement and evaluation, including the ROI methodology and its systematic steps. In addition, the evaluator must know how to develop an evaluation plan, collect and analyze data from the evaluation, and interpret results from data analysis. The evaluators must have special training as described earlier. For the remainder of the learning and development team, a one- to two-day workshop is needed to build adequate skills and knowledge for understanding the process, appreciating what the process can do for the learning and development success and the client organization, seeing the necessity for it, and participating in a successful implementation.

INITIATING EVALUATION STUDIES

The first tangible evidence of using a comprehensive measurement and evaluation process may be the initiation of the first program for which an impact ROI or study is planned. Several key issues are involved in identifying the programs and keeping them on track.

Selecting the Initial Program

Selecting a program for impact/ROI analysis is an important and critical issue. Only specific types of programs should be selected for comprehensive, detailed analysis. Typical criteria for identifying programs for analysis are those that involve large groups of participants; are expected to have a long life cycle; when completed, are linked to major operational problems/opportunities; are important to strategic objectives; are expensive; are time-consuming; have high visibility; and have management's interest in evaluation. Using these or similar criteria, the learning and development team must select appropriate programs to consider for an impact/ROI evaluation. Ideally, sponsors should agree with or approve the criteria.

Developing the Planning Documents

Perhaps the two most useful documents are the data collection plan and the ROI analysis plan. The data collection plan shows what data will be collected, the methods used, the sources, the timing, and responsibilities. The ROI analysis plan shows how specific analyses will be conducted, including isolating the effects of the program and converting data to monetary values. Each evaluator should know how to develop these plans. These documents were discussed in detail in Chapter Two.

Reporting Progress

As the programs are developed and implementation is under way, status meetings should be conducted to report progress and discuss critical issues with appropriate team members. This keeps the learning and development team focused on the critical issues, generates the best ideas for addressing particular problems and barriers, and builds a knowledge base for better evaluations of other programs. Sometimes, this group is facilitated by an external consultant, perhaps an expert in the ROI process. In other cases, the evaluator may facilitate the group.

In essence, these meetings serve three major purposes: reporting progress, learning, and planning.

Establishing Discussion Groups

Because a comprehensive measurement and evaluation may be considered difficult to understand and apply, establishing discussion groups to teach the process may be helpful. These groups could supplement formal workshops and other learning activities and are often very flexible in their format. Groups are usually facilitated by an external ROI consultant or by the evaluation leader. In each session, a new topic is presented and discussed thoroughly. Concerns and issues about the topic are discussed, including how they apply to the organization. The process can be adjusted for different topics as the needs of the group drive the issues. Ideally, participants in group discussions should have an opportunity to apply, explore, or research the topics between sessions. Assignments such as reviewing a case study or reading an article are also appropriate between sessions to further the development of knowledge and skills associated with the process.

PREPARING THE SPONSORS AND MANAGEMENT TEAM

Perhaps no group is more important to the success of measurement and evaluation than the management team that must allocate resources for the learning and development and support measurement and evaluation implementation. In addition, the management team often provides input and assistance for the measurement and evaluation. Specific actions for preparing and training the management team should be carefully planned and executed.

One effective approach for preparing executives and managers for more measurement and evaluation is to conduct a briefing on ROI. Varying in duration from one hour to half a day, this practical briefing provides critical information and changes perceptions needed to enhance support for ROI use. Because managers and executives have a keen interest in ROI, they will usually come. Managers leave the briefing with an improved perception of the use of ROI, the potential impact of programs, and a clearer understanding of their roles for implementing the ROI methodology. More importantly, they often develop a renewed commitment to react to and use the data collected by the ROI methodology.

A critical issue that must be addressed before using ROI and additional measurement and evaluation is the relationship between the learning and development team and key managers. A productive partnership is needed and requires each party to understand the concerns, problems, and opportunities of the other. Developing this type of relationship is a long-term process that must be deliberately planned and initiated by key learning and development team members. Sometimes, the decision to commit resources and support learning and development is based on the effectiveness of this relationship.

REMOVING OBSTACLES

As additional measurement and evaluation is implemented, there will be obstacles to progress. Many of the concerns discussed in this chapter may be valid, while others may be based on unrealistic fears or misunderstandings.

Dispelling Myths

As part of the implementation, attempts should be made to dispel the myths and remove or minimize the barriers or obstacles. Much of the controversy regarding measurement, evaluation, and ROI stems from misunderstandings about what the process can and cannot do and how it can or should be implemented in an organization. After years of experience with comprehensive measurement and evaluation and ROI and observing reactions during hundreds of evaluation studies and workshops, many misunderstanding regarding measurement and evaluation and ROI have been recognized. These misunderstandings are listed below as myths about the ROI methodology:

- Measurement and evaluation is too complex for most users.
- Measurement and evaluation is too expensive, consuming too many critical resources.
- If senior management does not require ROI, there is no need to pursue it.
- ROI is a passing fad.
- ROI is only one type of data.
- ROI is not future-oriented; it only reflects past performance.
- ROI is rarely used by organizations.
- Measurement and evaluation cannot be easily replicated.

- Measurement and evaluation is not credible. It is too subjective.
- ROI is not possible for soft programs.
- Isolating the influence of other factors is not always possible.
- ROI is appropriate only for large organizations.
- No standards exist for measurement and evaluation.

For more information on these myths, see www.roiinstitute.net.

Delivering Bad News

Perhaps one of the most difficult obstacles is addressing inadequate, insufficient, or disappointing news. This is an issue for most program leaders and other stakeholders involved in programs—how to address a bad-news situation. Exhibit 11.3 shows the specific steps and issues that are important to consider when addressing bad news. As you can see from the exhibit, the time to think about bad news is early in the process, never losing sight of the value of bad news. In essence, bad news means that things can change and need to change and that things can get better. The team and others have to be convinced that good news can be found in a bad-news situation.

- Never fail to recognize the power to learn and improve with a negative study.
- Look for red flags along the way.
- Lower outcome expectations with key stakeholders along the way.
- Look for data everywhere.
- Never alter the standards.
- Remain objective throughout the process.
- Prepare the team for the bad news.
- Consider different scenarios.
- Find out what went wrong.
- Adjust the story line to "Now we have data that show how to make this program more successful." In an odd sort of way, this becomes a positive spin on less-than-positive data.
- Drive improvement.

Exhibit 11.3. How to Address Bad News.

MONITORING PROGRESS

A final part of the implementation of a comprehensive measurement and evaluation process is monitoring the overall progress made and communicating that progress. Although it is an often-overlooked part of the process, an effective implementation plan can help keep the measurement and evaluation on target and let others know what the process is accomplishing for learning and development and for the client.

The initial schedule for implementation provides a variety of key events or milestones. Routine progress reports should be developed to communicate the status and progress of these events or milestones. Reports are usually developed at six-month intervals but may be more frequent for short-term programs. Two target audiences, the program team and senior managers, are critical for progress reporting. All team members should be kept informed of the progress, and senior managers need to know the extent to which measurement and evaluation is being implemented and how it is working within the organization.

FINAL THOUGHTS

Even the best model or process will die if it is not used and sustained. This chapter explored the implementation of a comprehensive measurement and evaluation process and the ways to sustain its use. If not approached in a systematic, logical, and planned way, measurement and evaluation will not become an integral part of the learning and development cycle and, therefore, the accountability will suffer. This chapter presented the different elements that must be considered and issues that must be addressed to ensure that measurement and evaluation implementation is smooth and uneventful. This is the most effective way to overcome resistance to additional measurement and evaluation. The result provides a complete integration of measurement and evaluation as a mainstream activity.

Appendix

How Results-Based Are Your Workplace Learning and Performance Programs? An Assessment for the L&D Staff

The success of workplace learning and performance (WLP), human resource development (HRD), organization development (OD), and education and training depends on the extent to which various programs, courses, and solutions focus on results. If the programs are achieving results and helping the organization meet its goals, the function is considered to be a contributing part of the organization—adding value from several perspectives. Consequently, the support for WLP and the evaluation of WLP can be enhanced. The following instrument provides an assessment of the extent to which WLP programs are achieving results.

The instrument can be used in the following ways:

- To identify gaps where improvements are needed in the measurement and evaluation of WLP

- To provide a discussion tool for the status and success of WLP programs

- To serve as a periodic assessment of progress being made to increase the effectiveness of WLP programs, particularly with the WLP staff

- To compare one group in an organization to another or, perhaps, one organization to another

The target audience for this instrument is anyone involved directly in WLP. It is particularly useful for those who have a direct or indirect influence on measurement and evaluation, whether full-time or part-time. These individuals are in a position to change much of the practice and policy of measurement and evaluation.

Terminology: The term "program" refers to learning courses, projects, solutions, or initiatives. CEO refers to the top executive or administrator in the entity being assessed. WLP is used instead of HRD, training, learning, development, OD, and education.

Instructions: This instrument should be completed without discussion. Please provide a candid response. The results should be tabulated and discussed with colleagues, where appropriate.
Select the most correct response for each item below.

1. WLP efforts consist of:
   a. usually one-time, seminar-type approaches.
   b. a full array of courses and programs to meet individual needs and desires.
   c. a variety of programs implemented to improve the organization.

2. Most new WLP programs are initiated:
   a. when a program appears to be successful in another organization.
   b. by request of top management.
   c. after a needs analysis has indicated that the program is needed.

3. When determining the timing of formal learning programs and the specific target audiences, we:
   a. have lengthy, non-specific courses for large audiences.
   b. offer routine programs to specific job groups.
   c. deliver learning just before skills are needed, and only to those people who need it.

4. In an economic downturn, the WLP function will:

   a. be the first to have its staff reduced.

   b. be retained at the same staffing level.

   c. suffer no staff reductions and possibly increase.

5. Budgeting for WLP is based on:

   a. last year's budget.

   b. whatever the top WLP leader can "sell."

   c. a zero-based system, justifying it on a program-by-program basis.

6. WLP programs are funded through:

   a. the WLP department budget.

   b. the overall administrative budget.

   c. operating and sales budgets.

7. The principal group that must justify WLP expenditures is:

   a. the WLP department.

   b. various staff areas, including human resources.

   c. key managers.

8. Over the last two years, the WLP budget, as a percent of operating expenses, has:

   a. decreased.

   b. remained stable.

   c. increased.

9. Business alignment (that is, aligning WLP programs directly to a business need) is accomplished:

   a. rarely, if ever.

   b. occasionally, when it is obvious (for example, customer service training).

   c. repeatedly through a formal process of analysis and alignment.

10. The concern for the method of evaluation in the design and implementation of an WLP program occurs:

    a. after the program is completed.

    b. when the program is developed, before it is conducted.

    c. before the program is developed, when it is conceived.

11. WLP programs, without some formal method of evaluation, are implemented:

    a. regularly.

    b. seldom.

    c. never.

12. Reaction data are collected during a WLP program:

    a. frequently, when the facilitator requests it.

    b. *only* when new programs are implemented or major changes are made in the program.

    c. one hundred percent of the time.

13. Reaction data focus on:

    a. how the participants enjoyed the program.

    b. measures such as learning environment, facilitator, and recommended changes.

    c. issues such as relevance, importance, and intent to use knowledge and skills, as well as the above measures.

14. When collected, reaction data are:

    a. filed away, but rarely used.

    b. used occasionally, when requested.

    c. routinely used to make changes and report success.

15. Reaction data, with specific planned actions, are:

    a. never collected.

    b. collected occasionally.

    c. collected with almost all WLP programs.

16. Reaction data across programs are combined and integrated in an overall report:

    a. never.

    b. only when requested.

    c. routinely, using technology and consistent questions.

17. Learning measurements are taken during WLP programs:

    a. infrequently—only when required.

    b. occasionally, with certain types of programs.

    c. frequently—40 to 60 percent of the time using a variety of learning measurement processes.

18. Learning measurements consist of:

    a. informal self-assessments only.

    b. formal objective tests only.

    c. a combination of formal and informal measurement.

19. Formal tests are checked for both reliability and validity:

    a. never.

    b. when requested by the legal department.

    c. when the test scores have a consequence on employees in performance situations.

20. Learning measures are integrated and combined across programs:

    a. never.

    b. when requested, for similar programs only.

    c. routinely, using consistent instruments and questions.

21. Follow-up evaluation for application and behavior change are collected:

    a. almost never.

    b. occasionally—less than 10 percent of the time.

    c. at least 20 to 30 percent of the time.

22. Follow-up data collection for application and behavior change use:

    a. surveys and questionnaires only.

    b. surveys, questionnaires, and interviews only.

    c. a variety of methods from a variety of sources.

23. When an employee completes a WLP program and returns to the job, his or her supervisor usually:

    a. makes no reference to the program.

    b. asks questions about the program and encourages the use of the material.

    c. requires use of the program material and gives rewards when used successfully.

24. When an employee attends an external program, upon return, he or she is required to:

    a. do nothing.

    b. submit a report summarizing the program.

    c. evaluate the program, outline plans for implementing the material covered, and estimate the value of the program.

25. During follow-up evaluation, the barriers and enablers to application are captured:

   a. never.

   b. occasionally for particular types of programs.

   c. routinely to analyze reasons for success and failure.

26. Follow-up application data are used to make changes and drive improvements:

   a. never.

   b. occasionally, to satisfy the needs of the WLP staff only.

   c. regularly and communicated to several audiences.

27. Impact studies showing the contribution of programs are conducted:

   a. never.

   b. only one or two times.

   c. routinely on major, important programs.

28. When impact studies are conducted to show the contribution of learning, some method to isolate the effects of learning on the impact data is:

   a. not utilized.

   b. occasionally used when control groups can be used.

   c. always addressed in these types of studies.

29. The actual monetary value of the impact of learning is developed:

   a. never.

   b. only with special measures, such as sales.

   c. routinely to show the monetary contribution.

30. Intangible data linked to workplace learning and performance are:

   a. never considered or collected.

   b. occasionally considered and collected.

   c. always considered, collected, and linked to the programs.

31. Intangible data are converted to monetary value:

   a. never.

   b. occasionally, when required.

   c. always, if it can be accomplished credibly with minimum resources.

32. The return on investment in WLP is measured:
    a. never.
    b. primarily by observations by management and reactions from participants.
    c. by ROI calculations based on measures such as increased productivity, cost savings, or improved quality.

33. ROI studies of major programs are developed:
    a. never.
    b. occasionally, when required by executives.
    c. routinely, for key programs.

34. Data from impact and ROI studies are used to:
    a. justify the existence of a program only.
    b. satisfy the needs of the WLP staff only.
    c. show the contribution, build support, and drive important changes.

35. When conducting impact and ROI studies, our approach is to:
    a. do everything we can to maximize (perhaps exaggerate) the data.
    b. use a logical analysis and place a value on the conclusion.
    c. use conservative adjustments and standards to understate the results.

36. The results of WLP programs are communicated:
    a. when requested, to those who have a need to know.
    b. occasionally, to members of management only.
    c. routinely, to a variety of selected target audiences.

37. For key studies involving impact and ROI, face-to-face meetings with senior executives as a communication tool are conducted:
    a. never.
    b. only at the request of the top executive.
    c. when there's a new executive audience or the first introduction of this level of analysis.

38. Evaluation data for application, impact, and ROI studies are routinely communicated:
    a. never.
    b. through an executive summary.
    c. through a variety of methods, including streamlined communication such as a one-page summary.

39. In the collection, analysis, and communication of evaluation data, technology is used:

    a. never.

    b. for Level 1 and 2 evaluation only.

    c. routinely, to integrate and communicate data in a scorecard.

40. The role of participants in learning and development is a:

    a. requirement to attend and participate in learning activities.

    b. requirement to attend, participate, and apply skills and knowledge.

    c. requirement to participate, apply new skills to achieve results, and provide data to the WLP staff.

41. The WLP staff involvement in evaluation consists of:

    a. no specific responsibilities in evaluation, with no formal training in evaluation methods.

    b. part of the staff having responsibilities for evaluation, with some formal training.

    c. all members of the staff having some responsibilities in evaluation; all staff members have been trained in evaluation.

44. The manager responsible for WLP interfaces with the CEO:

    a. never, WLP is a delegated responsibility.

    b. occasionally, when the CEO requests it.

    c. frequently, to keep the CEO informed and involved.

43. The top executive's involvement in the implementation of WLP programs is:

    a. limited to sending invitations, extending congratulations, awarding certificates, etc.

    b. monitoring progress, opening/closing speeches, presentation on the outlook of the organization, etc.

    c. participation in a major program to see what's involved, conducting a segment in a major program, requiring key executives to be involved, etc.

44. On the organization chart, the WLP manager:

    a. is more than two levels removed from the top executive.

    b. is two levels below the top executive.

    c. reports directly to the top executive.

45. Key management involvement in implementing WLP programs is:

    a. very minor; only WLP specialists conduct programs.

    b. limited to a few specialists conducting programs in their area of expertise.

    c. significant; on the average, over half of the programs are conducted by managers outside the WLP function.

46. New programs are developed:

    a. internally, using a staff of designers and specialists.

    b. by vendors. We usually purchase programs and courses to meet our needs.

    c. in the most economical and practical way to meet deadlines and cost objectives, using internal staff and vendors.

47. Costs for WLP are accumulated:

    a. on a total aggregate basis only.

    b. on a program-by-program basis.

    c. by specific process components such as development and delivery, in addition to a specific program.

48. To ensure that learning is transferred into performance on the job, we:

    a. encourage participants to apply what they have learned and report results.

    b. ask managers to support and reinforce learning and report results.

    c. utilize a variety of learning transfer strategies appropriate for each situation, including the above.

49. Most managers view the WLP function as:

    a. a questionable function that wastes too much time of employees.

    b. a necessary function that probably cannot be eliminated.

    c. an important resource that can be used to improve the organization.

50. With the present WLP staff and attitude toward results, the WLP contribution to the organization can:

    a. never be assessed.

    b. be assessed but probably with excessive cost.

    c. be assessed (or is being assessed) with little to moderate cost.

HOW RESULTS-BASED ARE
YOUR WLP PROGRAMS?
Analysis of Test Scores

Score the test as follows. Allow:

1 point for each (a) response.

3 points for each (b) response.

5 points for each (c) response.

The total should be between 50 and 250 points.

The score can reveal much about workplace learning and performance in an organization and, in particular, the attitude toward evaluation and measurement. A perfect score of 250 is probably unachievable. It represents utopia and is an ultimate goal of many WLP functions. Conversely, a score of 50 reveals a dysfunctional organization with inappropriate methods to implement workplace learning and performance programs. The scores can be analyzed by examining four ranges.

SCORE RANGE	ANALYSIS OF SCORE
200 to 250	This organization represents the best of workplace learning and performance in action. Little or no improvement is needed. WLP programs are effective, efficient, and results-based. Management support is great. WLP functions with this rating are leaders in this important field and setting examples for others. The implementation of WLP is extremely effective in this organization.
150 to 199	This organization is probably better than average for WLP functions. There is some room for improvement, but present efforts appear to be headed in the right direction. There is some success with achieving results and evaluating programs. The approach appears to be appropriate, but additional emphasis is needed to position WLP to contribute more in the future. Management support is moderate.
100 to 149	Improvement is needed in this organization. The attitude toward, and approach of, WLP is less than desirable. Present methods and processes are ineffective. Management support is very weak. Emphasis needs to be

placed on securing appropriate management support to change the philosophy and approach to WLP.

50 to 99   In this organization there is little or no concern for achieving results with learning programs. The WLP function is dysfunctional and ineffective and needs improvement if it is to survive. Urgent attention is needed from top management to change the approach of the implementation of workplace learning.

─w─ Glossary

Analyst   These individuals collect the data to determine whether the program is needed. They are also involved in analyzing various parts of the program. Analysts are usually more important in the beginning, but may provide helpful data throughout the program.

Barriers   Factors that impede the implementation of the program.

Bystanders   The bystanders are the individuals who observe, sometimes at a distance, the program. They are not actively involved as stakeholders, but are concerned about the outcomes, including the money. These bystanders are important, because they can become cheerleaders or critics of the program.

CEO/Managing Director/Agency Executive   This person is the top executive in an organization. The top executive could be a plant manager, division manager, regional executive, administrator, or agency head. The CEO is the top administrator or executive in the operating entity where the program is implemented.

Chain of Impact   The process, level-by-level, that must be followed to develop impact and ROI.

Enablers   Factors that support or enhance the implementation of the program.

Evaluator   This individual evaluates the program. This person is responsible for measurement and evaluation, following all the processes outlined in this book. If this is a member of the program team, extreme measures must be taken to ensure this person remains objective. It may also be a person who is completely independent of the program. This individual performs these duties full- or part-time.

Finance and Accounting Staff   These individuals are concerned about the cost and impact of the program from a financial perspective. They provide valuable support. Their approval of processes, assumptions, and methodologies is important. Sometimes, they are involved in the program evaluation; at other times they review the results. During major programs, this could include the organization's finance director or chief financial officer.

Hard Data   Data items that can by converted to monetary values.

Immediate Managers   The individuals who are one level above the participant(s) involved in the program. For some programs, this person is the team leader for other employees. Often they are middle managers, but most important, these people have supervisory authority over the participants in the program.

Intangible Measures   Measures that are purposefully not converted to monetary values because they cannot be easily converted with a reasonable amount of resources.

Learning Transfer   The transfer of skills and knowledge learned during the program to the workplace.

The Organization   The organization is the entity within which the particular program or process is evaluated. Organizations may be companies (either privately held or publicly held); government organizations at the local, state, federal, and international levels; nonprofits; or non-government organizations. They may also include educational institutions, associations, networks, and other loosely organized bodies of individuals.

Participants   The individuals who are directly involved in the program. The term "employee," "associate," "user," or "stakeholder" may represent these individuals. For most programs, the term "participant" appropriately reflects this group.

Program Manager   The individual(s) responsible for the project, program, initiative, or process. This is the individual who manages the program and is interested in showing the value of the program before it is implemented, during its implementation, and after it is implemented.

Program Team   The individuals involved in the program, helping to analyze and implement it. These are individual team members who may be full- or part-time on this particular program. On larger-scale programs, these individuals are often assigned full-time, on a temporary basis, or, sometimes, on a permanent basis. On small programs, these may be part-time duties.

ROI (Return on Investment)   The net benefits (benefits minus costs) divided by the costs of the program.

Reliable Test   A test that is stable or consistent over time.

Soft Data   Data items that cannot be easily converted to monetary values.

Sponsor/Clients   The individual(s) who fund, initiate, request, or support a particular project or program. Sometimes referred to as the sponsor, it is the key group—usually at the senior management level—who cares about the program's success and is in a position to discontinue or expand the program.

Stakeholder   A stakeholder is defined as any individual or group interested in or involved in the program. Stakeholders may include the functional manager where the program is located, the participants, the organizer, the program leader, facilitators, and key clients, among others.

Tangible Measures   Measures that are easily converted to monetary values.

Valid Test   A test that measures what it is designed to measure.

—⁓— Index

⟶ About the Authors

Jack J. Phillips, Ph.D., is a world-renowned expert on accountability, measurement, and evaluation. He provides consulting services for Fortune 500 companies and major global organizations. The author or editor of more than fifty books, Dr. Phillips conducts workshops and makes conference presentations throughout the world.

His expertise in measurement and evaluation is based on more than twenty-seven years' of corporate experience in the aerospace, textile, metals, construction materials, and banking industries. Dr. Phillips has served as training and development manager at two Fortune 500 firms, as senior human resource officer at two firms, as president of a regional bank, and as management professor at a major state university.

This background led Dr. Phillips to develop the ROI methodology, a revolutionary process that provides bottom-line figures and accountability for all types of learning, performance improvement, human resource, technology, and public policy programs.

Dr. Phillips regularly consults with clients in manufacturing, service, and government organizations in forty-four countries in North and South America, Europe, Africa, Australia, and Asia.

Books most recently authored by Phillips include *Show Me the Money* (Berrett-Koehler, 2007); *Building a Successful Consulting Practice* (McGraw-Hill, 2006); *Investing in Your Company's Human Capital: Strategies to Avoid Spending Too Much or Too Little* (Amacom, 2005); *Proving the Value of HR: How and Why to Measure ROI* (SHRM, 2005); *The Leadership Scorecard* (Elsevier Butterworth-Heinemann, 2004); *Managing Employee Retention* (Elsevier Butterworth-Heinemann, 2003); *Return on Investment in Training and Performance Improvement Projects* (2nd ed.) (Elsevier Butterworth-Heinemann, 2003); *The Project Management Scorecard* (Elsevier Butterworth-Heinemann, 2002); *How to Measure Training Results* (McGraw-Hill, 2002); *The Human Resources Scorecard: Measuring the Return on Investment* (Elsevier Butterworth-Heinemann, 2001); *The Consultant's Scorecard*

(McGraw-Hill, 2000); and *Performance Analysis and Consulting* (ASTD, 2000). Dr. Phillips served as series editor for ASTD's In Action casebook series, an ambitious publishing project featuring thirty titles. He currently serves as series editor for Elsevier Butterworth-Heinemann's Improving Human Performance series, and for Pfeiffer's new series on Measurement and Evaluation.

Dr. Phillips has received several awards for his books and work. The Society for Human Resource Management presented him an award for one of his books and honored a Phillips ROI study with its highest award for creativity. The American Society for Training and Development gave him its highest award, Distinguished Contribution to Workplace Learning and Development. *Meeting News* named Dr. Phillips one of the twenty-five most influential people in the Meetings and Events industry, based on his work on ROI for the industry.

Dr. Phillips has undergraduate degrees in electrical engineering, physics, and mathematics; a master's degree in decision sciences from Georgia State University; and a Ph.D. in human resource management from the University of Alabama.

Dr. Jack Phillips has served on the boards of several private businesses—including two NASDAQ companies—and several nonprofits and associations, including the American Society for Training and Development. He is chairman of the ROI Institute, Inc., and can be reached at (205) 678–8101 or by e-mail at jack@roiinstitute.net.

Patricia Pulliam Phillips, Ph.D., is president of the ROI Institute, Inc., the leading source of ROI competency building, implementation support, networking, and research. She is also chair and CEO of The Chelsea Group, Inc., an international consulting organization supporting organizations and their efforts to build accountability into their training, human resources, and performance improvement programs, with a primary focus on building accountability in public sector organizations. She helps organizations implement the ROI methodology in countries around the world—including South Africa, Singapore, Japan, New Zealand, Australia, Italy, Turkey, France, Germany, Canada, and the United States.

After a thirteen-year career in the electrical utility industry, Dr. Patti Phillips took advantage of the opportunity to pursue a career in a growing consulting business, where she was introduced to training, human resources, and performance improvement from a new perspective—a perspective that directly reflected her values of accountability, ROI evaluation. Since 1997, she has embraced the ROI methodology by committing herself to ongoing research and practice. To this end, Dr. Phillips has implemented ROI in private sector and public sector organizations. She has conducted ROI impact studies on programs such as leadership development, sales, new-hire orientation, human performance improvement, K–12 educator development, educators' National Board Certification mentoring, and faculty fellowship. Dr. Phillips is currently expanding her interest in public sector accountability through application of the ROI methodology in community- and faith-based initiatives, including Citizen Corps, AmeriCorps, and the Compassion Capital Fund.

Dr. Phillips teaches others to implement the ROI methodology through the ROI certification process, as a facilitator for ASTD's ROI and Measuring and Evaluating Learning workshops and as adjunct professor for graduate-level evaluation courses. She speaks on the topic of ROI at conferences such as ASTD's International Conference and Exposition and ISPI's International Conference.

Dr. Phillips' academic accomplishments include a Ph.D. in international development and a master's degree in public and private management. She is certified in ROI evaluation and has earned the designation of Certified Performance Technologist. She has authored a number of publications on the subject of accountability and ROI, including *Show Me the Money* (Berrett-Koehler, 2007); *Return on Investment Basics* (ASTD, 2005); *Proving the Value of HR: How and Why to Measure ROI* (SHRM, 2005); *Make Evaluation Work* (ASTD, 2004); *The Bottom Line on ROI* (Center for Effective Performance, 2002), which won the 2003 ISPI Award of Excellence; *ROI at Work* (ASTD, 2005); the ASTD in Action casebooks *Measuring Return on Investment* Vol. III (2001), *Measuring ROI in the Public Sector* (2002), and *Retaining Your Best Employees* (2002); the ASTD Info-line series, including *Planning and Using Evaluation Data* (2003), *Mastering ROI* (1998), and *Managing Evaluation Shortcuts* (2001); and *The Human Resources Scorecard: Measuring Return on Investment* (Butterworth-Heinemann, 2001). Dr. Phillips' work is published in a variety of journals. She can be reached at patti@roiinstitute.net.

Pfeiffer Publications Guide

This guide is designed to familiarize you with the various types of Pfeiffer publications. The formats section describes the various types of products that we publish; the methodologies section describes the many different ways that content might be provided within a product. We also provide a list of the topic areas in which we publish.

FORMATS

In addition to its extensive book-publishing program, Pfeiffer offers content in an array of formats, from fieldbooks for the practitioner to complete, ready-to-use training packages that support group learning.

FIELDBOOK Designed to provide information and guidance to practitioners in the midst of action. Most fieldbooks are companions to another, sometimes earlier, work, from which its ideas are derived; the fieldbook makes practical what was theoretical in the original text. Fieldbooks can certainly be read from cover to cover. More likely, though, you'll find yourself bouncing around following a particular theme, or dipping in as the mood, and the situation, dictate.

HANDBOOK A contributed volume of work on a single topic, comprising an eclectic mix of ideas, case studies, and best practices sourced by practitioners and experts in the field.

An editor or team of editors usually is appointed to seek out contributors and to evaluate content for relevance to the topic. Think of a handbook not as a ready-to-eat meal, but as a cookbook of ingredients that enables you to create the most fitting experience for the occasion.

RESOURCE Materials designed to support group learning. They come in many forms: a complete, ready-to-use exercise (such as a game); a comprehensive resource on one topic (such as conflict management) containing a variety of methods and approaches; or a collection of like-minded activities (such as icebreakers) on multiple subjects and situations.

TRAINING PACKAGE An entire, ready-to-use learning program that focuses on a particular topic or skill. All packages comprise a guide for the facilitator/trainer and a workbook for the participants. Some packages are supported with additional media—such as video—or learning aids, instruments, or other devices to help participants understand concepts or practice and develop skills.

- *Facilitator/trainer's guide* Contains an introduction to the program, advice on how to organize and facilitate the learning event, and step-by-step instructor notes. The guide also contains copies of presentation materials—handouts, presentations, and overhead designs, for example—used in the program.
- *Participant's workbook* Contains exercises and reading materials that support the learning goal and serves as a valuable reference and support guide for participants in the weeks and months that follow the learning event. Typically, each participant will require his or her own workbook.

ELECTRONIC CD-ROMs and Web-based products transform static Pfeiffer content into dynamic, interactive experiences. Designed to take advantage of the searchability, automation, and ease-of-use that technology provides, our e-products bring convenience and immediate accessibility to your workspace.

METHODOLOGIES

CASE STUDY A presentation, in narrative form, of an actual event that has occurred inside an organization. Case studies are not prescriptive, nor are they used to prove a point; they are designed to develop critical analysis and decision-making skills. A case study has a specific time frame, specifies a sequence of events, is narrative in structure, and contains a plot structure—an issue (what should be/have been done?). Use case studies when the goal is to enable participants to apply previously learned theories to the circumstances in the case, decide what is pertinent, identify the real issues, decide what should have been done, and develop a plan of action.

ENERGIZER A short activity that develops readiness for the next session or learning event. Energizers are most commonly used after a break or lunch to stimulate or refocus the group. Many involve some form of physical activity, so they are a useful way to counter post-lunch lethargy. Other uses include transitioning from one topic to another, where "mental" distancing is important.

EXPERIENTIAL LEARNING ACTIVITY (ELA) A facilitator-led intervention that moves participants through the learning cycle from experience to application (also known as a Structured Experience). ELAs are carefully thought-out designs in which there is a definite learning purpose and intended outcome. Each step—everything that participants do during the activity—facilitates the accomplishment of the stated goal. Each ELA includes complete instructions for facilitating the intervention and a clear statement of goals, suggested group size and timing, materials required, an explanation of the process, and, where appropriate, possible variations to the activity. (For more detail on Experiential Learning Activities, see the Introduction to the *Reference Guide to Handbooks and Annuals*, 1999 edition, Pfeiffer, San Francisco.)

GAME A group activity that has the purpose of fostering team spirit and togetherness in addition to the achievement of a pre-stated goal. Usually contrived—undertaking a desert expedition, for example—this type of learning method offers an engaging means for participants to demonstrate and practice business and interpersonal skills. Games are effective for team building and personal development mainly because the goal is subordinate to the process—the means through which participants reach decisions, collaborate, communicate, and generate trust and understanding. Games often engage teams in "friendly" competition.

ICEBREAKER A (usually) short activity designed to help participants overcome initial anxiety in a training session and/or to acquaint the participants with one another. An icebreaker can be a fun activity or can be tied to specific topics or training goals. While a useful tool in itself, the icebreaker comes into its own in situations where tension or resistance exists within a group.

INSTRUMENT A device used to assess, appraise, evaluate, describe, classify, and summarize various aspects of human behavior. The term used to describe an instrument depends primarily on its format and purpose. These terms include survey, questionnaire, inventory, diagnostic, survey, and poll. Some uses of instruments include providing instrumental feedback to group members, studying here-and-now processes or functioning within a group, manipulating group composition, and evaluating outcomes of training and other interventions.

Instruments are popular in the training and HR field because, in general, more growth can occur if an individual is provided with a method for focusing specifically on his or her own behavior. Instruments also are used to obtain information that will serve as a basis for change and to assist in workforce planning efforts.

Paper-and-pencil tests still dominate the instrument landscape with a typical package comprising a facilitator's guide, which offers advice on administering the instrument and interpreting the collected data, and an initial set of instruments. Additional instruments are available separately. Pfeiffer, though, is investing heavily in e-instruments. Electronic instrumentation provides effortless distribution and, for larger groups particularly, offers advantages over paper-and-pencil tests in the time it takes to analyze data and provide feedback.

LECTURETTE A short talk that provides an explanation of a principle, model, or process that is pertinent to the participants' current learning needs. A lecturette is intended to establish a common language bond between the trainer and the participants by providing a mutual frame of reference. Use a lecturette as an introduction to a group activity or event, as an interjection during an event, or as a handout.

MODEL A graphic depiction of a system or process and the relationship among its elements. Models provide a frame of reference and something more tangible, and more easily remembered, than a verbal explanation. They also give participants something to "go on," enabling them to track their own progress as they experience the dynamics, processes, and relationships being depicted in the model.

ROLE PLAY A technique in which people assume a role in a situation/scenario: a customer service rep in an angry-customer exchange, for example. The way in which the role is approached is then discussed and feedback is offered. The role play is often repeated using a different approach and/or incorporating changes made based on feedback received. In other words, role playing is a spontaneous interaction involving realistic behavior under artificial (and safe) conditions.

SIMULATION A methodology for understanding the interrelationships among components of a system or process. Simulations differ from games in that they test or use a model that depicts or mirrors some aspect of reality in form, if not necessarily in content. Learning occurs by studying the effects of change on one or more factors of the model. Simulations are commonly used to test hypotheses about what happens in a system—often referred to as "what if?" analysis—or to examine best-case/worst-case scenarios.

THEORY A presentation of an idea from a conjectural perspective. Theories are useful because they encourage us to examine behavior and phenomena through a different lens.

TOPICS

The twin goals of providing effective and practical solutions for workforce training and organization development and meeting the educational needs of training and human resource professionals shape Pfeiffer's publishing program. Core topics include the following:

Leadership & Management
Communication & Presentation
Coaching & Mentoring
Training & Development
e-Learning
Teams & Collaboration
OD & Strategic Planning
Human Resources
Consulting